D1635959

Standing on the Premises of God

Standing on the Premises of God

The Christian Right's Fight to Redefine America's Public Schools

Fritz Detwiler

WAGGONER LIBRARY
TREVECCA NAZARENE UNIVERSITY

NEW YORK UNIVERSITY PRESS

New York and London

NEW YORK UNIVERSITY PRESS
New York and London

© 1999 by New York University
All rights reserved

Library of Congress Cataloging-in-Publication Data
Detwiler, Fritz, 1947–
Standing on the premises of God : the Christian Right's fight to
redefine America's public schools / Fritz Detwiler.
p.   cm.
Includes bibliographical references and index.
ISBN 0-8147-1914-7 (alk. paper)
I. Title. 1. Religion in the public schools—United States.
2. Christian Right (Organization). 3. Religious fundamentalism—
United States. 4. Church and education—United States.
LC111 .D45 1999
379.2'8'0973—dc21   99-006790
                          CIP

New York University Press books are printed on acid-free paper,
and their binding materials are chosen for strength and durability.

Manufactured in the United States of America

10 9 8 7 6 5 4 3 2 1

To Vera
Who taught me the importance of public education

To Phyllis
Who taught me to understand public education

To Nalani, Corissa, and Ainsley
Whose future depends on public education

Contents

Acknowledgments

As a young teenager, I remember attending youth fellowship at our church each Sunday evening. One of the highlights of those weekly gatherings was singing the "old gospel hymns" of Methodism. "Standing on the Promises of God" was one of my favorites. Its martial tempo and counterpoint refrain brings to my mind the aggressive, soul-winning spirit of nineteenth-century evangelical Protestantism. Its theme of personal perfection reflected the Methodist holiness tradition of its author, Russell Kelso Carter. "Standing on the Promises" continues to be popular in Methodist and holiness circles.

Carter's hymn serves as a point of departure for this work. The book's title intentionally plays on the text of Carter's song, changing it only to suggest the most important contrast that exists between the holiness Methodism of my youth and the sociopolitical themes of the Christian Right. Whereas Carter's hymn emphasizes personal dedication to Christ as savior and the confidence for holy living that develops, the Christian Right stresses the application of God's revelation to the social and political dimensions of American culture.

Changing "promises" to "premises" highlights the theological source from which the Christian Right draws its transformative mission. In that theological arena, "premises" itself takes on a dual meaning. One of its definitions is grounding ideas or assumptions. From the perspective of the Christian Right, these presuppositions, as they call them, fall into two clearly distinct categories—a Bible-centered worldview and a human-centered orientation, with the former defined as good and the latter designated as the enemy of true Christianity. "Premises" also refers to place, territory, or location. Again, from the perspective of the Christian Right, public education belongs to the divinely ordained and structured family, not to the state. Therefore, properly envisioned within that theological orientation, public schools stand on the premises of God. This book demonstrates the dual meaning of "premises" by constructing a religiously framed model of the Christian Right as a social movement and by applying that model to an analysis of the movement's criticism of contemporary public education.

Such a work would not have been possible without the help of a great many people. First among these are two professors in graduate school to whom I owe an immeasurable debt for having the faith and patience to invest in me their knowledge and understanding of American religion. C. Conrad Cherry introduced me to the pivotal role theology plays in defining the categories and tensions of the American religious landscape; Paul Harrison helped me discover the significance of the social, ethical, and ritual dimensions of religion.

I would also like to thank John Bahner and Steve Thompson of the Institute for the Development of Educational Activities for their insight and courage in addressing the issue of Christian Right criticism of public education. Before many others in the educational community were willing to even acknowledge the problems facing local schools, IDEA held national conferences on the subject and dedicated part of its summer Fellows Program to the controversy. Jerry Warren and Julie Peterson of the Comprehensive Health Education Foundation also deserve recognition for their ongoing commitment to understanding and exploring the deeper dimensions of the controversies.

Many other people have helped me work through various aspects of the project. Students in my seminar on the Christian Right at Adrian College forced me to become clearer on the precise points of difference between the Christian Right and the various constituencies that supply the movement with its core supporters. Kelly West, in particular, provided thoughtful questions and helpful interpretations of primary source materials. Her efforts in organizing my constantly expanding materials on the subject gave me the freedom to know that a particular reference would be at hand when needed. Other colleagues at Adrian College willingly donated their time to reading parts of the manuscript and offering helpful suggestions: Dr. Roger Fechner added perspective on the intellectual foundations of the Enlightenment and the Scottish Common Sense Philosophy; Dr. Michael McGrath explored with me the intellectual connections in the Christian Right; Dr. Jerry Stewardson clarified theological points in the larger Christian tradition; Dr. George Somers provided an anthropological lens for the chapter on religion; and Ms. Agnus Caldwell pointed me to the most current research on social movements. President Stanley Caine and Dean James Borland enabled me to complete the project through their generous support of my sabbatical leave.

Several others deserve mention as well for their contributions to my grasp of the larger issues related to education. Bonnie Dana, Assistant District Administrator of the Unified School District of Antigo, Wisconsin, generously shared her research on Outcome-Based Education with me. Charles Park, Professor Emeritus of Education at the University of Wisconsin, Whitewater, supplied me with a studied historical perspective on Christian Right involvement in educational issues. Chaplain Mark Eckel, Lenawee Christian School, Adrian, Michigan, enriched and corrected my grasp of Francis Schaeffer and Abraham Kuyper through countless hours of conversation. And Dr. Melissa Pflüg contributed to my interpretation of anthropological theories of social change in general and revitalization movements in particular.

My deepest gratitude is reserved for Nancy McClure, who endured and helped me meet countless deadlines, and Dr. Diane Henningfeld, whose numerous suggestions and diligent reading of the manuscript greatly improved the text. I also reserve sincere appreciation for Jennifer Hammer at New York University Press, whose faith in the project never wavered.

Finally, to my wife and children I extend heartfelt gratitude for the support and freedom they provided me in order to complete this project.

Introduction

In 1997, a conservative California Republican gubernatorial candidate named Al Checci called for mandatory competency testing for teachers every five years. Citing the "appalling" fact that only 310 teachers had been fired or dismissed in the state in 1995, Checci remarked, "Only a handful of the 250,000 teachers in the entire state of California lost their jobs for incompetence. Common sense tells us that this is patently ridiculous." At the same time Checci was trying to make a political issue of teacher incompetence in California, South Carolina activist Ray Moore was warning parents on the other side of the continent about the dangers of the public schools. Promoting a program named Exodus 2000, Moore called on Christian parents to negate the corrupting influences of the public schools by withdrawing their children.[1]

Twenty years ago, teachers were among America's most respected professionals and the nation's public school system was the envy of the world. By the late 1990s, however, they no longer enjoy the same degree of respect from the public. Teachers are accused of widespread incompetence. Schools are blamed for destroying the moral fabric of our society. What has happened to public education in those twenty years to provoke so much dissatisfaction? Why have once-marginalized voices come to occupy a central place in the formation of public discourse about education? How did Pat Robertson, James Dobson, and Phyllis Schlafly emerge as more trustworthy spokespersons about public education, in the view of millions of Americans, than the nation's secretary of education?

The combined factors for this reversal of the general public's perception of education are complex. One of the most important ingredients is the growth in social and political influence that conservative Christians have enjoyed during the last two decades. Led by a loose-knit network of Christian Right organizations, religious conservatives have raised their voices in protest against a public education system that they believe no longer represents their interest or values. The education establishment, which once relegated religious conservatives to the margins of the culture, has been forced by Christian Right activism and political sophistication to recognize them as important players in public discussions about the present condition and future direction of America's schools.

The problem many educators face in entering into serious dialogue with their critics is that they typically do not understand these conservatives enough to grasp the nature of their charges or to respond effectively to them. The conservatives operate from religious presuppositions not shared by most educators or even large segments of the society; consequently, educators often do not even comprehend the reasons why conservatives are dissatisfied with the public schools. This book speaks directly to that cognitive vacuum. It explains how and why the present crisis developed from the standpoint of the Christian Right.

My focus is on the Christian Right as a religiously grounded social movement. I define the movement as a loose network of conservative Christian activists guided by certain presuppositions, which center on the nature of reality or truth, the role of the public schools in protecting and advancing that truth, the reasons for the collapse of public education, and the theological justification for using political tactics to achieve a complete transformation of contemporary American culture. More precisely, I focus on the critique the Christian Right advances against public education based on the incongruity the movement's leaders perceive between their truth presuppositions (that is, the way they envision the world), and those that they believe presently guide public education. My purpose is to show that the critiques and the strategies employed by the Christian Right to achieve their goals are reasonable and justified within the context of their worldview. In other words, I will argue that the Christian Right worldview legitimates Al Checci's comments on teacher incompetence and Ray Moore's warnings regarding the dangers of the public schools.

Our task does not end there, however. If the Christian Right is religiously grounded and motivated, then logic demands that we interpret the Christian Right using religious categories. There are two underlying reasons for employing this approach. It gives legitimacy to religious standpoints and is therefore consistent with the movement's basic criticism of public education. This means that for purposes of analysis we will assume what Clifford Geertz calls "the native's point of view" and grant the potential legitimacy of religiously grounded criticism of public education. Adopting such an approach also provides a legitimate basis from which to apply the interpretive categories of the academic discipline of religious studies. If the Christian Right is a religious movement, then such analytical categories as symbolism, mythos, and ritual performance are appropriate tools of investigation.

The methodological approach applied here is not limited to religion, however. The Christian Right is also a social movement, that is, "a collectivity acting with some degree of organization and continuity outside of institutional channels for the purpose of promoting or resisting change in the group, society, or world order of which it is a part."[2] Because it is a social movement, the critical perspectives of sociology and anthropology provide important insight for assessing the future prospects of the movement. Sociological classifications allow us to regard the Christian Right as a value-oriented movement that seeks cultural revitalization. In this sense, it resembles a revitalization movement in which participants reinvest the world with meaning and significance.[3] "Value-oriented" with regard to the Christian Right means that it seeks general rather than specific change within the society.[4] Calling it a revitalization movement suggests that the Christian Right seeks general change in the culture by means of a return to ethical principles that have their origins in the mythos, symbolism, and ritual practices of the group.[5] In this respect, I will focus on the ideational dimension of the movement. Thus, the approach used here begins by granting the legitimacy of religious perspectives in relation to public education. It goes on, however, to use the theories and methods of religious studies, sociology, and anthropology to analyze the way in which the Christian Right raises these issues and the way in which the movement is progressing toward the goal of cultural transformation.

Through my years of involvement with the educational establishment on issues related to the Christian Right, I have found such an approach necessary. The fact is that many of the critics' complaints about the quality of public education are justified. An unsettling number of high school graduates are functionally illiterate in a number of areas critical to their future employment and the strength of our democratic system. But although many Americans agree with the Christian Right on the seriousness of the problem, fewer citizens accept either the movement's analysis of the causes of the problem or the Christian Right's proposed solutions. Nevertheless, because of this widespread perception of the failures of public education, educators opposed to Christian Right alternatives cannot refuse to acknowledge the reality of the problems simply because they are brought up by religious activists. Further, Christian Right complaints about educators who disregard religiously grounded criticism are often well founded. Many educators reflect the larger culture's general lack of understanding of religion, religious people, and religious worldviews. For such Americans, this book provides a necessary foundation for understanding religion. This approach also shows educators and the general public that the challenges to public education voiced by the Christian Right are neither irrational nor insubstantial once we grant the movement's foundational presuppositions about the nature of things. The real crux of the conflict is not found in this or that specific criticism. Rather, educators concerned about Christian Right involvement in public education will discover that the heart of the matter goes back to the sufficiency and acceptability of the movement's grounding presuppositions. Any serious discussion between movement activists and public educators must focus on the matters of fundamental importance on which both sides agree and disagree. Finally, the following chapters provide educators and the general public with a full understanding of the extent and nature of the changes the Christian Right seeks in contemporary education. The text considers the reasons why Christian Right leaders focus on public education and what methods they employ in restructuring American education to meet their theologically grounded cultural vision.

One vital factor in understanding the impact of the Christian Right in the arena of public education is the way in which the movement's cultural vision finds expression in localized protests and controversies. These local skirmishes tend not to be unrelated. What often appears to many educators as a spontaneous educational controversy arising among concerned parents in the community may very well be an extension of a social movement of national scope. Despite the loose structure of the Christian Right network, a great deal of coordination exists among the various organizations. The informality of these relationships belies the degree of agreement the groups share with respect to a set of presuppositions about the march of history and the proper structure of American society. Those presuppositions provide the basis for Christian Right critiques.

Thus, in order to evaluate what is probably the most significant social movement in the United States today, we must be conversant with the basic presuppositions that give the movement its identity, purpose, and coherence. Only then can we comprehend the scope and the depth of the Christian Right. These fundamental ideas also define the goals and strategies of the movement. They provide its motivation and inform its vision of a culturally transformed society. Finally, we must recognize that the main focus of the Christian Right as a social movement is a complete cultural transformation and a restructured social order that is redemptive to the nation and its people. As such, the movement functions as a religiously grounded revitalization movement whose interests overflow the boundaries of American politics. The Christian Right, then, is best understood as a reformative social movement that intends to bring every aspect of the culture into conformity with its divinely revealed beliefs, values, and structures.[6] What needs to be explored is whether the religious foundations of the movement are adequate to the task of cultural transformation that the Christian Right has defined as its overarching goal.

Throughout this work the reader will find that, in some cases, I am in agreement with Christian Right presuppositions and analysis and at other points I have significant differences. To the degree that the method of analysis is consistent with the presuppositions of the Christian Right, I attempt to present educational issues from the movement's point of view. I do not refute Christian Right criticism of public education or provide a cookbook response to movement activists. To the degree that this method differs from the presuppositions of the Christian Right, it provides an interpretive bridge between the reader and the Christian Right.

Truth

Our journey into the world of the Christian Right begins at the most important entry point to the movement, its guiding concept of the nature of truth. Before we enter that world, however, we need to orient ourselves to the epistemological landscape that describes *truth* outside the Christian Right boundaries in the larger society. In the regions outside the movement, we discover two distinct cognitive terrains that differ from each other as much as they differ from the Christian Right concept of truth. To our left, we recognize the rugged and unsettled environment of postmodernism and poststructuralism. As we survey the horizon, we see the landscape populated with many younger academics and members of generations X, Y, and Z. From their standpoint, shared concepts of truth do exist, but they deny that such concepts have any relationship to truth itself. Postmodernists further argue that perceptions of shared concepts of truth, when deconstructed, turn out to be faulty. They contend that all ideas are primarily reflections of the class, gender, and racial status of those who hold them. Truth, therefore, is self-referencing. Even though all of us may use the same vocabulary, postmodernists argue that the contextual baggage each of us uses to frame our understanding of a particular term is not the same contextual framework that others employ. No universally shared meaning ultimately exists. Truth statements are biased assertions of individuals; they need to be deconstructed, not in order to get at the "real meaning" of the truth statement, but to identify the biases that frame the use of the word by the speaker and the reader.

Christian Right leaders seem to locate nearly all contemporary educational theorists in the postmodern camp. They believe that the reforms advocated by the educational elite are grounded on postmodern presuppositions and that these are then transmitted into the public schools through teacher training schools and faculty development programs. The lenses through which Christian Right theorists assess curricular and pedagogical innovations focus only on this part of the terrain of contemporary education. What they see leads them to identify in postmodernism and poststructuralism the inherent moral relativism of the position and the degree to which it takes us down the road to intellectual chaos. They view with equal alarm what others see as the strength of this new perspective, its permitting diverse voices to be heard without privileging one over the other. The Christian Right concludes that the integration of postmodern viewpoints into America's schools has led to a *dumbing down* of public education. Diversity of viewpoints has been achieved, in the assessment of movement leaders, at the cost of a declining emphasis on traditional academic standards and the accepted canons of historical and literary merit.

Outside the boundary of the Christian Right and to our right, an entirely different landscape unfolds before us. It is the more ordered but somewhat hazy terrain of modernism. Its settled dells give comfort to most mainstream Americans. Modernists tend to believe that though objective truth does exist, human expressions of that truth are conditional and fragmentary. Truth, therefore, is always in the process of being discovered or reinterpreted as new evidence and improved analytical tools become available. Modernists place great faith in the power of reason to discover that truth, either through the empirical method or through rational discourse and analysis. Along with classical liberals, modernists hold in high regard the values of reasonability, civility, individual rights, tolerance, and respect for diverse opinions. Most Americans believe that these codes of moral and social conduct provide the structure through which public disputes should be resolved. The town hall symbolically stands at the center of the modernist community. When disagreements arise, modernists invite all parties to sit at their tables and conduct themselves according to the accepted mores of the modernist camp. Because they believe that ultimate truth does exist, they are reluctant to conclude that some disputes cannot be resolved because the positions taken by the discussants are incompatible. They are eager to open the gate between the Christian Right and their environment, but the gate usually swings only one way—toward their camp. Modernists typically refer to those who stay on the other side of the gate as intransigent, uncompromising, and extreme in their viewpoints, failing to realize that they are no more open in their viewpoints than their critics. What they do not understand is that from the Christian Right perspective, participation in such discussions requires religious participants to abdicate their basic values.

Having mapped out the general contours of cognitive reality outside the boundaries of the Christian Right worldview, we now proceed inside the gate. As we enter, we see that not everyone on this side of the gate lives under the same cultural canopy. We do note, however, that each of the differentiated communities shares to a significant degree a concept of the nature of truth that we will classify as biblical Christianity.[7] Biblical Christians assert that truth can be known with absolute certainty, that truth does not change from one historical era to another, that it is received by humans from divine sources in propositional statements, and that the divine sources reveal the criteria against which all other truth claims must be assessed. In applying these principles, biblical Christians have often been willing, however unintentionally, to adopt modernist solutions to resolve incongruities between biblical interpretation and scientific discovery. The most significant example of this tendency occurs in the shifting interpretations creationists have given to biblical passages as new and conclusive geological evidence emerges from the modernists' scientific camp.[8]

As we enter the biblical Christian circle, we discover that the landscape is quite orderly and very well groomed. One explanation for this order is the degree to which biblical Christians emphasize reason and rational structure. Whereas modernists' notions of order are limited by their fragmentary and conditional conception of truth, no such lack of clarity and precision exists inside the gate. To many modernists, however, the clarity and precision inside the territory of biblical Christians seem to fade into a maze that lacks order. For such modernists, the confusion exists in their minds because they view clarity and precision through different lenses. Biblical Christians see the structure of reality and the content of truth through the eyes of divine revelation. Everything is oriented to this revealed reality and truth. Once the foundational principles are established, all other knowledge falls into place. Though not completely consistent in its application, the rational structure of the biblical Christian world appears coherent to the people on their side of the fence.

Since each of these definitions of truth starts from a different set of presuppositions regarding the source, authority, and form of truth, pedagogical and curricular discussions within public education are quite complex. Teachers, mainstream parents, students, and biblical Christian parents may have quite different understandings of truth that require diverse forms of transmission and assessment. Because these presuppositions are seldom identified by the individuals involved in the discussions, participants can easily end up talking past each other. Further, since there is no agreement about what form of truth ought to provide the foundation for public education, the various parties may expect very different outcomes from the educational process.

Public Education

Not only does the landscape take on a very different character on the two sides of the fence; the schools that dot the terrain in the various regions look very different as well. They are constructed in very different ways and found in very different locations in relation to the larger community. Most Americans see the public schools in terms of what we can call the "mainstream school web." In this view, responsibility for the public schools rests with a combination of four groups: government (both federal and state), the community (including the citizenry, religious leaders, and local business and industry), parents, and the staff of professional teachers and administrators (including professional organizations and unions). Each sphere recognizes the legitimacy of the other spheres. Conflicts that emerge within this web tend to be over which sphere exercises the most influence at a given time or over the purposes for which they exercise their power. School boards are ultimately responsible for negotiating the operation of the schools within this web. It is their duty to mediate among the various interests in order to produce a quality educational experience for the district's children.

With the increased involvement of the federal and state governments in public education funding and policy formation in recent years, many mainstream citizens agree with the Christian Right complaints that the web is out of balance and that parents are now at a significant disadvantage. Some mainstream Americans also agree with Christian Right activists that the relative position of parents has been weakened by the growing influence of the teachers' unions. For these reasons, Christian Right calls for an increased role for parents and more local control of the schools often fall upon sympathetic ears outside its own constituencies. What differentiates most citizens, even those who want more local control of the schools, from the Christian Right, is that most Americans accept the relative balance among competing interests that the mainstream web provides.

Biblical Christians tend to operate with a different perception of the lines of authority and responsibility in public education. The "Christian Right school web" reflects the basic presuppositions that these activists bring to public discourse about education. From their perspective, public schools are an extension of the divinely ordained institution of the family. Overall responsibility for their operation rests with Christian parents. All other interest groups must accede to the authority of the parents. Christian parents have an obligation, given to them by God, to monitor the schools and make sure that they are run in a manner consistent with biblical principles. When the schools deviate from that mandate, parents have the duty to seek to return the schools to their proper foundation by exerting influence on teachers and administrators or by running for the school board if such a step is necessary. If schools fail to respond properly to such pressure, parents face the option of removing their children from the public schools. Should parents choose this course of action, they will need to further choose between home schooling and Christian schools; and since both of those alternatives place a financial burden on Christian parents, the Christian Right now directs its efforts toward restructuring public education so that more options exist for Christian parents. For example, the movement works to form charter schools consistent with the values and principles of the parents and seeks alternative methods of school funding in order to reduce the financial burden on parents of home schooling their children or sending them to Christian schools.

Many present-day educational controversies involving the Christian Right have as their ultimate purpose creating educational opportunities for Christian children that do not conflict with biblical principles. Since the ultimate purpose of even the public schools is to "educate children in the fear of the Lord" (according to biblical Christians), Christian parents cannot simply abandon the public schools. Even if they remove their children, they have the divine responsibility to bring the public schools into harmony with God's intended purpose for them.

Given the fundamental conceptual differences between the mainstream and Christian Right school webs, controversies over public education take on a deeper significance. The problem from the perspective of Christian Right activists is not that this or that specific book or instructional method is objectionable to them. It is that the entire basis upon which the public schools operate is flawed. From their side of the fence, it appears that the schools have moved so far away from their proper function and structure that immediate action is necessary. When educators and administrators display real or perceived hostility toward Christian parents seeking to return the schools to their proper foundation, the suspicions of the Christian parents are merely confirmed.

As indicated in our discussion of the nature of truth, even when school authorities and mainstream community members take Christian Right objections seriously, the disputes cannot be settled simply by "getting the two parties together." This is not to suggest that a strategy of open rational discourse will not work with many religiously conservative parents. Many biblical Christians remain strongly committed to public education and do not seek to transform the schools into Christian enclaves. Bridgebuilders, an evangelical organization based in southern California, for example, achieves very positive results in bringing such parents together with school administrators to discuss and resolve concerns using methods appropriate to a democratic society.[9] Core Christian Right activists, however, do not find such mediation strategies acceptable. Given their uncompromising commitment to absolute truth, their interest lies in transforming, not compromising with, the public school establishment. All of the current debates and controversies about education involving the Christian Right are connected to this goal of transformation and can be fully understood only within the context of the Christian Right worldview.

The Christian Right

The social origins of the contemporary Christian Right are well grounded in colonial American history. Leaders such as David Barton of Wallbuilders and Rus Walton of the Plymouth Rock Foundation speak fondly of the Calvinist Puritan roots of America. They view as true Christian heroes the English Puritans who risked their lives in the effort to establish a holy commonwealth in the wilderness of the New World. Their purpose was to demonstrate to the morally and spiritually corrupt church and government of England that a perfected Christian community was possible. In order to accomplish this end, Puritans covenanted with each other and with God to live their lives in accord with God's divinely revealed truth. John Winthrop's manifesto, "A Model of Christian Charity," sets forth the theopolitical nature of their sojourn into the wilderness.[10] It called them to an awareness of the divine test that lay before them. Their worthiness for the holy experiment upon which they were about to embark would be determined by the results of their efforts. If they truly were among those God had elected to represent His will on earth, their endeavors would be rewarded by God. Such results would be a clear indication of their worthiness for the covenant relationship for which God had chosen them. In order to protect their experiment, the Puritans established a political system that limited public offices to church members. Magistrates were expected to conduct the civil affairs of the community according to the divine principles that God revealed to them in the Scriptures and that the Puritan clergy interpreted for them.

The Puritans experienced only moderate success, but the idea of a divinely ordained society that subscribed to biblical principles long survived them. So did the notion that the destiny of the people depends on whether citizens are worthy to carry forth their divinely appointed task of building a Christian nation. From the Christian Right perspective, we as a nation have failed to fulfill the divine purpose God intended for us. And though the final judgment of God has not yet descended upon us, we are well on the road to realizing what Winthrop called the "price of the breach" we have created.

Although the Christian Right traces its roots back to the Calvinist Puritans, the roots of the contemporary social movement are more immediately grounded in the religiously unsettled decades of the first quarter of the twentieth century. The movement initially grew out of dissatisfaction Christian fundamentalists experienced with the larger culture as it increasingly adopted modernist perspectives. Through the next half century, the precursor of the contemporary Christian Right remained strongest in the South among white, mainly fundamentalist, evangelical Protestants.[11] Although a number of Christian Right–type organizations developed during that period, they had few successes even in the South and had virtually no impact outside that region.[12] Movement leaders and their organizations lacked political and technological sophistication. As a result, their protests rarely affected the public schools outside an occasional book protest or parental complaint. That changed during the late 1970s and early 1980s with the emergence of the "New" Christian Right. In these years, conservative Republicans mobilized the Christian Right through a campaign designed to politicize white evangelicals. This was part of the Reagan presidential campaign's "Southern strategy." As a result of the combined efforts of conservative Republican strategists and the new core of Christian Right leaders, a more politically and technologically sophisticated social movement developed. The movement broadened its base of leadership and appeal far beyond Fundamentalism to include a number of other religiously conservative traditions. The most important new constituencies were pentecostals/charismatics, holiness Christians, confessional or Reformed Christians, and other "born-again" evangelicals.[13] It is from these groups that the Christian Right presently draws its core constituency. One further indication of the expansion of the Christian Right beyond its fundamentalist roots is the fact that a number of Roman Catholics, and a much smaller number of Eastern Orthodox Christians and Orthodox Jews, are part of the movement's leadership.

Scholarly Perspectives on the Christian Right

With the increasing influence of the Christian Right during the 1980s, scholars began to pay considerable attention to the movement, social scientists taking the lead. A number of important works by theologians and religious studies scholars also appeared. Most of them fall into one or another of four categories: the social histories of the Christian Right emphasizing recent developments within the movement,[14] political analyses focusing on voting patterns and the connection between the Christian Right and the Republican Party,[15] sociological treatises addressing the "culture war"[16] between the movement and the larger society,[17] and theological comparisons of Fundamentalism and orthodox Christianity.[18] Together these approaches identify some important distinctive features of the movement.

Studies by political scientists suggest that during the past two decades the growth of the Christian Right has been closely associated with an increasing social conservatism among religious Americans. Though it is difficult to tell whether the Christian Right created that shift or simply took advantage of it, a close connection developed between the Christian

Right and politically conservative Americans. Both found a home within the Republican Party during the Reagan years and beyond. As suggested above, the connection was not accidental. Formal Christian Right links with the GOP became stronger in the late 1970s in anticipation of the 1980 presidential election. To increase their chances of regaining the White House, conservative Republicans designed the Southern Strategy to appeal to traditionally conservative white evangelicals who tended to vote Democratic. The Republican leadership devised the strategy using sophisticated voter analysis that focused on the attitudes and issues of southern white voters. Data indicated to the Republicans that they could win the presidency in 1980 by concentrating their efforts on the new white and conservative popular majority. Republican strategist Kevin Phillips concluded that his party did not need the support of African Americans to gain the Oval Office. This meant that Republicans were free to make appeals directed solely to white conservatives without having to worry about the reactions of African Americans.[19]

One of the keys to the success of the Southern Strategy turned on the issue of whether Republicans could capture the existing white evangelical vote and, at the same time, expand their base of support among previously apolitical white southern evangelicals. To facilitate this strategy, Republicans courted leading southern evangelical preachers and televangelists and helped them develop several new religiously oriented political organizations. The four most important expressions of this new alliance were Robert Billing's National Christian Action Coalition, Robert Grant's Christian Voice, Jerry Falwell's Moral Majority, and Ed McAteer's Religious Roundtable.[20] All were created with the help of Republicans to influence the 1980 elections, and all were fairly short-lived: the operations of all four groups peaked by the mid-1980s. Eventually, other more politically and technologically sophisticated Christian Right groups took their place. What was particularly important about Reagan's Southern Strategy was its conscious blending of Republican politics with the mythos and symbols of southern conservative white evangelical Protestantism. From its very beginning, the Christian Right has been closely aligned with the Republican Party.[21]

Political analysis of the voting patterns of southern white evangelicals shows that the Southern Strategy continued to be a major source of political strength for the Republican Party in the late 1990s. However, beyond their utility in demonstrating the growing connection between conservative Christian voters and the Republican Party, these studies are of limited value here. The voting-pattern analyses tend to use very general categories of religious voters, and therefore we cannot draw sophisticated conclusions about the degree to which the various evangelical subgroups have moved into the Christian Right camp. Most studies classify religious voters as evangelicals, mainstream Protestants, Catholics, or Jews. Some studies further subdivide evangelicals along racial lines or add categories for Mormons and other nonevangelical sectarian groups.

The problem with these classifications is that they fail to appreciate the breadth of subgroups to which the category "evangelicals" extends and the importance of such distinctions in analyzing the potential of the Christian Right as a social movement. For example, no contrasts are drawn among holiness Christians, pentecostals, fundamentalists, and "born-again" evangelicals even though each of these groups has its own distinct identity and gives nuanced interpretations to the same religious symbols. Within evangelical circles, these distinctions are very important in terms of the way they express religious commitment and the believer's particular orientation to the larger world. Thus, we are left wondering whether fundamentalists, holiness Christians, pentecostals, and born-again Christians cluster around particular issues more or less than other voters.[22]

A further limitation of such categorizations of the movement is that they provide little insight into identifying exactly where the threshold between Christian Right evangelicals and non–Christian Right evangelicals lies on a cluster of political and social issues. We are left with a broad description of the Christian Right that presumes a fair degree of theological and religious homogeneity within the movement. Given the almost exclusively fundamentalist character of the early phases of the Christian Right, this presumption is historically justified. However, the contemporary Christian Right is a much more complex religious movement drawing from a number of theological traditions. In fact, though elements of fundamentalist theology continue to inform the movement, the theological center of the contemporary Christian Right is not nearly so close to Fundamentalism as it was in the past.

The Christian Right that emerged in the 1980s as a religiously grounded social movement has close historical ties to earlier forms of the Christian Right, but its contemporary expression is much more highly organized and politically sophisticated and has much greater appeal to a larger constituency. The newly constituted movement continues to evolve politically by constructing vast grassroots networks of state and local chapters that can be called upon for action on specific issues. It also continues to develop its appeal to the larger society as a social movement by honing its mythos and symbols into rhetorical forms that appeal to increasingly wider segments of the American mainstream. Framed mostly within rhetorical structures that define issues in moral terms, the Christian Right offers Americans alternative explanations and solutions for presently deteriorating social conditions.[23] What distinguishes the contemporary Christian Right from its earlier forms is its shift from a norm-based to a value-based social movement. In other words, the Christian Right no longer defines itself in terms of particular causes or specific issues. As a value-based movement, it seeks to transform the entire culture by gaining control of the social institutions that define and transmit that culture. In short, despite the tendency of social scientists to focus on the political dimension of the Christian Right, the Christian Right is not a political movement. It is a religiously grounded revitalization movement.

Though valuable in drawing critical distinctions between the Christian Right and mainstream orthodox Christianity, existing theological analyses of the movement are not particularly helpful in developing our understanding of its religious character. Their worth is not insubstantial, however. To those unfamiliar with the basic doctrines and practices of orthodox Protestantism, the Christian Right can appear to fall within the historic mainstream of the faith, as many of its leaders claim. But in fact, many of the most characteristic theological emphases of the movement are inconsistent with the mainstream of Reformation Protestantism, let alone the larger Christian tradition. Indeed, the core tenets of leaders like Pat Robertson, James Dobson, and Jerry Falwell are much more characteristic of the new developments that arose within American Protestantism in the nineteenth and early twentieth centuries in response to the rise of modernism. More specifically, the nuances Christian Right sources give to such ideas as *authority, creation, Jesus Christ,* and *the Church* suggest that the movement is dependent both on its fundamentalist heritage and on concurrent developments within the Calvinist side of that heritage.[24] While taking from Fundamentalism the ideas of biblical inerrancy and complete confidence in the propositional truth of the Scriptures, the contemporary Christian Right also integrates into its worldview the very conservative confessional theological teachings of J. Gresham Machen and Cornelius Van Til, who presented their attacks on modernism in the first third of the twentieth century at Princeton Theological Seminary and at Westminster Theological Seminary in Philadelphia.

The movement's new center revolves around two intellectuals, Francis Schaeffer and Rousas John Rushdoony. Both studied under Machen and

Van Til at Westminster. Schaeffer provides the movement with a Reformed theology of culture. Rushdoony is the clearest voice within the movement advocating a political theology, and it is equally indebted to the Reformed tradition. The fact that Schaeffer and Rushdoony are not well known outside of conservative evangelical circles in no way diminishes their importance inside the movement.

The impact of Schaeffer and Rushdoony is particularly relevant to the emergence of the Christian Right as an identifiable social movement that transcends its fundamentalist roots. Schaeffer's theology of culture frames the present cultural crisis within a historical battle between the forces of biblical Christianity and secular humanism. That language is now the lingua franca of the movement. In fact, Robert Conover, executive director of the Christian Defense League, stated on national television that his organization, along with other politically active conservative Christian groups, intends to transform the public discourse on political and social issues into the dualistic framework of biblical Christianity versus secular humanism.[25] Rushdoony's influence has been just as substantial if even less clearly noted than Schaeffer's impact. His political theology articulates the movement's common understanding of the divine structure and purpose of society. Many Christian Right leaders tend to shy away from being closely identified with Rushdoony, but his articulation of the envisioned social and political world of the Christian Right and his emphasis on cultural transformation are reflected in the mission statements of all the leading Christian Right organizations. Contemporary Christian Right leaders frame their understanding of the present condition of American society and their proposed solutions within the structure of Schaeffer's and Rushdoony's thought. To be specific, if the Christian Right is to defeat secular humanism in the culture war, the nation must be reconstructed in order to extend God's sovereign will to all dimensions of the culture.

Worldview: Points of Convergence and Divergence

The theoretical perspective that guides this study of the Christian Right and public education is congruent with the movement's guiding worldview at several points and in conflict with it at other critical points. At the most basic level, I take religion just as seriously as the Christian Right does. My model proceeds from the phenomenological presupposition that religion begins with the apprehension of sacred power.[26] The Christian Right worldview begins from a similar point. It is far more specific than mine, however, in limiting the identity of the sacred power to conservative Christian concepts of God and restricting legitimate human apprehension of it to biblical revelation. Beyond this rather important distinction, I agree with the Christian Right that this power is real and that it is of a type that sets it apart from other experiences. Religious claims transcend other claims and seek legitimacy beyond the normal realm of human experiences.

The main point of divergence between Christian Right presuppositions and those that guide this study lies in the way humans apprehend sacred power. For the Christian Right, this apprehension is direct, it reveals precise truth with absolute certainty, and it is conditioned neither by historical change nor human reception. From my perspective, the apprehension of the sacred is just as direct as for the Christian Right, but human conceptualizations, interpretations, and expressions are neither absolute nor unconditioned. Religious truth claims, to my mind, gain a sense of objectivity and certainty from a complex process in which humans create that perception. This *objectification of the subjective* results, as Peter Berger and Thomas Luckmann describe it, from a continuous process of construction in which the social group legitimates particular formulations and rejects others.[27] What appears to the religious believer as absolute truth is actually a human construction that reflects the historical and cultural context in which the claims arise. This explains why historical theologians can show that Christian Right representations of "orthodox Christian tradition" differ markedly on important points from the theological expressions of earlier periods of Christian history. Christian Right representations of the tradition reflect a historical conditioning grounded in their social, political, and cultural experiences.

A secondary point of contrast begins with a conviction, shared with the Christian Right, that its motives and methods are primarily grounded in religion and that its goal is cultural transformation. This study, however, is underpinned by traditional scholarly methods derived both from cultural and theological studies and from suggestions made by Walter Capps for investigating the religious dimension of the Christian Right as a social movement.[28] The recent work on revitalization movements, particularly as defined by anthropologist Melissa Pflüg, that grounds such phenomena in indigenous religious categories also informs this work.[29] A final important assumption here is that revitalization movements begin to emerge at crisis points in which religious believers can no longer tolerate the incongruity of the situation.[30]

Using these points of departure, my model for analyzing Christian Right criticism of public education resembles an hourglass. At the base, situational incongruity rises to the point where the existing worldview and ritual processes of the group can no longer adequately sustain the group against the forces that threaten its envisioned world. As the group coalesces into a social movement, it filters its strategies and tactics through the "conversional" methods of conservative Christianity. These are the myths, symbols, and rituals that sustain the movement. This is the neck of the hourglass in that it both focuses the group and filters its agenda as a social movement. At the top of the hourglass stands a fully revitalized culture based on biblical principles. The task of this study is to assess the capacity of the religious resources the Christian Right brings to its efforts at social transformation. Our basic question is whether these religious resources are powerful enough to accomplish the movement's ends.

As we move toward an explanation of the Christian Right worldview that sustains and defines the movement, we will view it from as close to the "native's point of view" as possible. However, I caution the reader that explaining the Christian Right worldview perspective is not the same as "going native." This representation of the Christian Right viewpoint does not equate with the way in which movement activists view the world. My purpose is hermeneutical insofar as it intends to bridge the gap between the Christian Right and mainstream Americans in terms of the movement's analysis of contemporary public education.

Public Education: Points of Convergence and Divergence

In assessing Christian Right criticism of public education, I support its leadership's concerted efforts to bring public discourse to the level of grounding presuppositions. In this regard, the Christian Right is extremely serious about ideas and the rational relationship among them. An exploration of the critic's arguments, strategies, and goals regarding public education reveals its earnestness, the depth at which it addresses the issues, and the coherence of the leaders' positions on public education. My approach stands in tension with theirs because it finds the presuppositions upon which they base their analysis of and prescription for public education much too narrow for a pluralistic society and in conflict with the democratic values of the society and its public school system.

Perhaps my point of greatest agreement with Christian Right analyses of public education is the claim that religion played a much more explicit role in defining and directing public education in the past than it does today. The religious impulse was certainly central in the first efforts at public education in the New England classical schools. It continued in the founding of the common schools and was maintained through the decades of massive immigration of southern and eastern European Roman Catholics and Jews. Throughout this era, the religious impulse in American education identified almost completely with various forms of Protestant Christianity.

Christian Right claims that present-day public schools are hostile to religion or that they have completely purged religious influences from the curriculum seem off target, however. Religion in the schools may not be as explicit as it once was, but that does not necessarily mean that contemporary public schools do not embody and express the values of religiously mainstream America. Many teachers and administrators in the public schools are people of faith, to use Ralph Reed's term. They simply do not experience the same degree of incongruity between their religious faith and public instruction as the Christian Right does.

One key factor for my argument on this point focuses on the particular form of religious belief embraced by many public educators and parents of public school children. Christian Right arguments presume that all Americans can be divided into two religious categories, what might be called *pure religionists* and *pure secularists.* Pure religionists reject the legitimacy of any secular forms of knowledge or any pedagogical practices that are not explicitly consistent with their religious beliefs. Pure secularists reject the legitimacy of any religious forms of knowledge or any pedagogical practices that hint of religion. My sense of contemporary America suggests that most teachers, administrators, and parents fall into a middle position better described as *modified religionists.*

A modified religionist understanding of religion leads to the acceptance of a basic congruity between religious and more secularized expressions of truth. The differences modified religionists do identify between their religious and secularized lives are differences in emphasis. They do not view them as contradictions. Further, they see little or no conflict between their religiously informed moral values and the basic democratic principles of compassion, tolerance, respect, and civility that ideally ground our public lives. To their minds, these are just as much religious values as they are social or political ones. They also find common cause with many people of other faiths on this point. They recognize the presence of these same values in Christianity, Judaism, Islam, Buddhism, and other great faiths of the world. Since these values are highly promoted in the public schools, they see no basic conflict between religion and the schools. Therefore, many Americans simply do not accept Christian Right claims that the public schools have fallen victim to a secular humanist conspiracy.

Although there is evidence that the religious impulse is still present in American public education, Christian Right observations about the gradual purgation of explicitly religious perspectives and content from public school materials and curricula that has occurred over the past thirty years is legitimate.[31] Religious content is unnecessarily excluded from courses in the social sciences, the humanities, and the arts. This is particularly significant in the study of American culture, where religion has been such a powerful force in our culture's construction. As significant as this abrogation of religious content is, the purgation of religion also occurs at a much more substantive level as well. Not only do America's schools tend to exclude religious content, they also appear to be even more strongly committed to excluding explicitly religious perspectives from public education.[32] Public school students are rarely exposed to religious interpretations of content, and they are not asked to look at materials from a religious point of view. This exclusion of religious perspectives from public school curricula may be necessary in our highly pluralistic culture; however, it can rob students of an understanding of and tolerance for explicitly religious points of view. It is also offensive to conservative Christians to have their points of view systematically excluded from the schools. Nonetheless, the alternative seems to require the inclusion of so many religious perspectives as to bring instruction to a halt.

Beyond the difficult issue of the inclusion of religion in public school curricula, much Christian Right criticism regarding the gradually decreasing role parents and local school boards play in determining the distinctiveness of their schools seems well placed. The decline began in the 1950s and 1960s when progressive educators convinced the American people that federal government intervention was necessary to address a whole range of social issues. From health care to poverty, from special education to discrimination, the schools became the focus of intense efforts by the government to remediate social problems and to reduce the disparity in the quality of public education nationwide. At about the same time, the federal government encouraged schools to enhance their math and science offerings to help support American foreign policy. Beyond the continued presence of a zealous anticommunist emphasis in civics, history, and other subjects, schools accelerated math and science education to make the United States more competitive with Soviet advances in the space program. Gradually, governmental interests came to drive curricular content.

Another important factor contributing to the decline in local control of schools was the increased emphasis placed by the educational establishment on the professionalization of the teaching profession. Max Weber long ago drew the connection between the increased rationalization of the society and the growth of bureaucracy. Along with that growth came increased specialization and professionalization. These were legitimated by an increased reliance on technical expertise. The result in public education was that teachers and the educational establishment became the experts. Schools often excluded parents from the decision-making process because the parents did not have the proper credentials in child development, educational theory, and instructional methods. Eventually, increased professionalization and its accompanying reliance on technical expertise led to the formation of vast educational bureaucracies of experts at the state and federal level. Through regulation and state and federally funded programs, the responsibility of local communities for school policy and curricular content declined just as the costs of increased standards of education were passed on to the same local communities in the form of higher taxes.

The final factor that led to the loss of local responsibility for schools relates closely to the growing professionalization of education. Curricular and pedagogical design became more "scientific." The redefinition of instruction in terms of behavioral psychology, developmental psychology, and social group interaction produced an entire subculture of educational consultants, who, often without adequately testing and substantively discussing the acceptability of the presuppositions that guided these new approaches to education, marketed packaged programs of instruction designed to address specific problems in the educational delivery process. Schools that adopted these innovations faced two problems. Only the most progressive districts stopped to analyze the degree to which this or that new program would fit into the larger program of instruction. Furthermore, many teachers and school administrators adopted particular programs merely because a single teacher or a group of teachers attended a conference, became enthusiastic about the program, and brought it back to begin implementation. This lack of systematic assessment of programs created a tendency for fadism in the schools, one curricular or pedagogical approach quickly replacing another. Researchers conclude that the average life span of a given program is about three years.[33] Parents thus conclude that the schools are in chaos as their children move through one instructional fad to the next. Educators have been slow to recognize this problem. Parents seldom understand the purpose of the innovations and become confused by them. This confusion creates in parents the sense that they are becoming further removed from their children's education and that the educational system is out of control.

The cumulative effect of these gradual changes in public education has been a growing lack of confidence in the schools on the part of the general public. The Christian Right has been quick to fan the flames of this growing discontent. In some cases, movement leaders have even manufactured crises in order to increase public dissatisfaction with public schools.[34] The overall purpose of these controversies is not to improve the quality of public education. At the micro level it is to serve the ideological ends of the privatization of American education and the extension of federal and state funding of education to religious and parochial schools. At the macro level it is designed to bring a key social institution into further conformity with biblical principles.

Overview

This book is designed for a wide audience that includes scholars in the social sciences and religious studies, professionals in the field of public education, and general readers who have an interest in the Christian Right. Because some familiarity with religion is essential if one is to understand a religiously grounded interpretation of the Christian Right, an extended discussion of religion is provided. It includes a working definition, which roots religion in four types of apprehension of the sacred; an exploration of worldviews and the social processes of their maintenance and legitimation; and an inquiry into the nature of myths, rituals, and symbols and the functional role they play in the lives of religious people. I use the categories pure religionist, modified religionist, and pure secularist to describe the religious character of Americans. From a different angle, they can be characterized according to the different ideas they have about the relationship between religion and the civic order. These positions are termed the *redeeming right,* the *moderate middle,* and the *liberal left,* with the redeeming right most insistent on providing the society with a sectarian religious foundation and the liberal left most insistent on keeping personal religious belief separate from the public sphere.

Peter Berger's concept of the sacred canopy and Jonathan Z. Smith's notion of situational incongruity are helpful in analyzing the difficulties that the Christian Right has encountered in attempting to implement its reforms. The problem is that the present structure and content of American public education is incongruous with the sacred canopy under which the Christian Right lives. The points of incongruity establish the foundation from which the movement derives its specific criticism of public education. Three of the movement's most active leaders in the area of educational reform and some of their specific objections to public education curricula and pedagogy provide a focus for the discussion:, the Christian Coalition's Pat Robertson, Focus on the Family's James Dobson, and Robert Simonds, president of the National Association of Christian Educators/Citizens for Excellence in Education frame their complaints within the larger structure of their worldviews. Robertson and Dobson are arguably the two most important national leaders within the Christian Right. They also represent two different religious traditions within the movement; Robertson is most closely linked with pentecostalism, whereas Dobson's background is within the holiness tradition. Simonds had a wide influence in developing grassroots activists in the early 1990s and attempted to find "common ground" with the educational establishment in the mid-1990s. His publications are a major source of coherent information, reasoned arguments, and effective political organizing strategies for concerned parents at the local level.

The Christian Right can be understood only by starting with the theologically informed assumptions and the core principles of the biblical Christian worldview. A subset of conservative Protestantism, biblical Christians are most likely to adopt a pure religionist standpoint toward the larger culture. It is possible to trace the particular formulation of their assumptions and principles to the conservative Calvinist theological defense of the Christian faith against modernism articulated at Princeton Theological Seminary before the 1930s and, later, at Westminster Theological Seminary in Philadelphia. The presuppositions include beliefs about the nature of truth, the authority upon which it rests, the way truth is known by humans, the degree to which humans know it, and implications of these truth claims for personal and cultural revitalization. Key passages from Christian Right documents show how movement theoreticians incorporated these presuppositions into their social goal of cultural transformation. One also needs to see that in addition to the important points at which biblical Christians, with their presuppositions, overlap with the Christian Right, there are important distinctions that exist between them. Looking closely at these undergirding presuppositions, it is enlightening to note points at which they seem to fail to meet their own standards.

Theological innovations, based on biblical Christianity as a starting point, provide the ideological basis for the Christian Right as a social movement. In particular, the writings of Francis Schaeffer and Rousas John Rushdoony give rise to a distinctly Christian Right theology. Both thinkers stand in the larger tradition of nineteenth-century Dutch Calvinist thought. Schaeffer's theology of culture not only frames much of the criticism that Christian Right activists express against the curricular dimensions of American public schools but also verbalizes the mythos of the Christian Right. From Rushdoony the Christian Right gains a political theology that informs the remaining objections that movement activists have to the curricular, pedagogical, and structural components of our nation's schools. In addition, Rushdoony's political theology articulates the symbolic web that defines the Christian Right's ideal conception of society. Combined, these two sources supply the Christian Right's unifying identity. The emergence of this theological framework constitutes the single most important religious factor in the recent development of the Christian Right as an effective social movement. It has permitted the leaders of Christian Right organizations to articulate a common purpose, agenda, and strategy for the movement that well serve Christian Right ends.

How does the Christian Right function as a social movement to achieve its goal of cultural transformation? Research indicates that religiously charged social movements use conflict generation to generate a movement culture. The existence and propagation of such movement cultures depend, in large part, on the degree to which they can adapt the mythos and symbolic webs of target subcultures and of the larger culture to achieve their ends. This provides the ideational dimension of the movement. In terms of the structural or institutional component of the Christian Right, the movement may be divided into three tiers, following the lead of Peter Berger and Thomas Luckmann. At the top level, the cultural elite formulate the overarching canopy under which the movement rests as it devises the strategic model through which it attempts to achieve cultural transformation. At the middle level, the knowledge workers operate the organizations that communicate with the movement's grass roots. They have multiple functions. They must transmit to the local activists the symbolic web and mythos that frames specific issues and controversies; they must generate in their constituents a sense of conflict, through which they strengthen the movement in both numbers and commitment; and they must create in the minds of their present and possible future constituents a perception of effectiveness. At the third level, the foot soldiers of the movement generate the controversies using the organizational and informational structures provided by the knowledge workers.

It is important to know who these activists are, that is, what their religious characteristics are. Six clusters of people of faith provide the movement with its core membership. These are fundamentalists, holiness Christians, pentecostals/charismatics, born-again evangelicals, Roman Catholics, and confessional Christians in the Reformed tradition.

The strategic model the Christian Right reflects in attempting to achieve its transformational goals within the arena of public education is presuppositionalism. The presuppositional approach proceeds incrementally, first by gaining a hearing, then by defining the issues, and finally by reforming the society to conform to biblical principles. In the first stage of this model, members of the Christian Right seek recognition as legitimate participants in public discourse on American education. I refer to this step as inclusion or, using Ralph Reed's poignant phrase, seeking a "place at the table." At the second stage, the movement seeks to gain control of the debate by injecting its curricula and pedagogy into the schools. Because the Christian Right tries to exclude its competition at this level, I refer to the second stage as exclusion; in Robert Simonds's words, it is "seeking safe passage through the schools for Christian children." At the final stage, the Christian Right attempts to gain control, first over the education of their children and then over the education of all children in public and private schools, through a total transformation of the existing structure of public education.

The religious tools that the Christian Right utilizes selectively against objectionable public school curricula and pedagogy are its mythos, its symbolic web, and its ritual process of cultural transmission. When history courses and standards, multicultural and bilingual education, and Bible-as-history courses are the issues, the movement's mythos and its transmission come to the fore. The symbolic web of the Christian Right is the more noticeable tool in controversies over sex education, diversity training, drug and alcohol counseling, school meals programs, school-to-work programs, and creationism. When it comes to Christian Right objections to methods of pedagogy, those tend to be expressed in terms of the movement's use of ritual processes to effect cultural transformation.

The four case studies exemplify the tactics of the Christian Right and permit application of the theoretical analysis of the movement. The protests in a 1991 controversy in Adrian and Blissfield, Michigan, school districts illustrate how the Christian Right uses the mythos of secular humanism to attack educational reform processes. The next two cases are related in time and form. They are the Vista, California, and Lake County, Florida, conflicts, which spanned about six years beginning in 1990. The Vista case illustrates the stealth tactics of the movement, and the Lake County case exemplifies the mythos of American national and cultural superiority. Both cases also show what happens when grassroots Christian Right activists take control of local school districts. The final case, highlighting the 1998 Colorado ballot initiative for public funding of religious schools, represents the legislative-judicial dimension of the Christian Right strategy. It also shows how the movement adapts its rhetoric to appeal to the democratic and classic liberal values of mainstream America.

To what extent are the religious components of the Christian Right able to sustain it as a social movement? In particular, how effective is the presuppositional strategy in achieving the goals of the movement? Answers to these questions may be suggested by evaluating the strengths and weakness of the Christian Right's mythos, symbolic web, and ritual processes in terms of their potential effectiveness both among the constituents who form the movement's grassroots core and in the society's general citizenry.

1

Religion

Several years ago, residents living near a grain elevator in Fostoria, Ohio, claimed to see an apparition of Jesus on one of the storage silos. The silo quickly became a pilgrimage site for Christians living in the area. As more and more pilgrims, skeptics, and curious onlookers regularly gathered, enterprising locals set up shop and hawked t-shirts, bumper stickers, and other such wares. True believers claimed to receive healing and other powers from the apparition. After a few months, a crisis developed between the true believers and a presumably unconvinced fisherman who tired of having to go through all the traffic congestion on the way from his house to his favorite fishing hole. He resolved the crisis by throwing paint balloons on the silo, attempting to mar the sight and end the congestion. Now seeing their silo splattered with blotches of unsightly paint, the elevator owners decided to paint the entire silo. Only a few true believers protested the company's decision and the silo was painted. Miraculously, even after the silo received a new coat of paint, the true believers testified to the persistence of the apparition.

When I viewed the silo in the middle of the summer prior to its desecration, I had some difficulty recognizing the apparition. After schooling by others, I finally could see what might be taken for a crude and very incomplete outline of a male with facial hair clothed in a gown. Since I did not experience the healing or other power that others claimed they had experienced, I wondered how the pilgrims knew it was Jesus. Why, for example, could it not have been the Buddha, the angel Gabriel, Lord Krishna, or Master Kung Fu-zu? The reason was obvious: the soybean storage silo was in Fostoria, Ohio, where it was being viewed by Christians. In subsequent months, I continued to ponder the conclusion I had reached. Could there have been something about the apparition that would have led Buddhists, Muslims, Hindus, and Confucians also to recognize it as Jesus? To answer that question, we need to know something of Christianity and its doctrines surrounding the person of Jesus Christ. We also need to understand something about the nature of religion and the apprehension of sacred power.

The Essence of Religion

In *Religion in Essence and Manifestation,* Gerardus van der Leeuw argues that religion has its origins in the apprehension by humans of a particular kind of power. Scholars of religion refer to these moments as *hierophanies* or appearances or manifestations of the sacred to humans.[1] Van der Leeuw uses the Latin term *numen,* glossed as "sacred power," to refer to this power in its pure and complete nature. Western religions tend to associate this sacred dimension with God and God's creation. Religions like Christianity refer to hierophanies as God's self-disclosure or revelation. Other religions tend to describe the phenomenon in less personalistic terms. For Hindus it is *Brahman,* for Chinese religions the *Dao,* and for the Lakota of North America, *wakan.* In all of these traditions, religious people testify to the existence of a sacred dimension and associate it with a particular kind of power.

As humans apprehend this power, we recognize it by the attributes we confront in the encounter. In many traditions, human accounts of such an encounter, even taken collectively, do not exhaust or fully represent the power that expresses itself to humans. In Islam, the Qur'an suggests in Sura 13 that even Gabriel's recitation of the ninety-nine names of Allah does not fully represent God. Judaism illustrates this human limitation in the reluctance of Jews to speak the name of Yahweh. In Madhyamika Buddhism, Nagarjuna conceptualizes it as *sunya* or the emptiness of all teachings and doctrines of Buddhism. Daoists address the problem in the opening lines of the *Dao De Jing:*

> The Dao that can be told of
> Is not the Absolute Dao;
> The Names that can be given
> Are not the absolute names.[2]

These examples illustrate the second characteristic of religion. As apprehended by humans, sacred power is mysterious. It is beyond the human capacity to fully comprehend.

Although humans cannot completely grasp the essence of sacred power, we can identify it when it presents itself to us. Sacred power has a particular nature that is identified more by qualitative than quantitative dimensions. This exclusive quality separates it from all other types of power. Christianity traditionally uses the term *supernatural* to describe this uniqueness. Other traditions see less distinction between the organic and the inorganic, the material and the immaterial dimensions of reality. For them, sacred power is merely sacred, or set apart. Sacred objects, places, times, and people have this quality. Profane objects, places, times, and people do not.[3] This is the third characteristic of the sacred: it can be known by humans.

Another attribute of sacred power is that it exhibits both transcendent and immanent qualities. Its transcendence confronts us in two ways. Religious persons know that it exists outside of them, independent of their emotional, mental, and volitional capacities.[4] From a substantive standpoint, this means that sacred power is not a human creation, nor can it be reduced to human psychological or emotional needs. Religious persons also know that from a functional standpoint, the sacred power draws them out of themselves toward *otherness*. Otherness can take the form of a personal relationship with Jesus Christ, a burning bush not otherwise consumed, or a mystical experience of oneness with the sacred. It can also be found in human relationships. Mahayana Buddhism expresses this in *compassion*. Confucianism calls it *ren,* a disposition of humanity toward another person. Christians recognize it in terms of the *imago dei* (the image of God) in all persons. In each of these example, the sacred presence draws us out of ourselves and into relation with the other realities with which we share the cosmos.

The immanent dimension of sacred power affects humans at the most intensely personal level. It comes to and confronts us in the immediate situation in which we stand, for example, in the light from heaven that confronted Paul in the midst of his anger against Christians. The enlightenment of Buddha came to him directly after he seemingly had exhausted all roads to the sacred center. The recitations of the angel Gabriel to Muhammad in the caves outside Mecca occurred in the most private of moments. Sacred power thus penetrates to the very deepest recesses of human existence. It encounters us at the most basic level of our primal fears, hopes, expectations, and desires; it speaks to the most significant questions of human existence at the most personal and yet the most cosmic levels. This suggests that transcendence and immanence do not exist as two opposite forces but rather are the ends of a continuum that stretches from the broadest reaches of human existence to its most intimate depths.

Sacred power has the further quality that it drives us into action. The force of its power redirects and transforms us so that our life is brought into greater conformity with the nature of the power that appears to us. In Western religions, this quality is denoted by the term *holy*. In these traditions (Judaism, Christianity, and Islam), sacred power is presumed to be beneficial to humanity's ultimate interests and to be beneficent towards humans. Simply stated, God is good and so is the creation that comes from God. This leaves Jews, Christians, and Muslims with the problem of theodicy. If God and the creation are good, from where does evil come? Many Christians find the solution to the difficulty by attributing the destructive aspects of sacred power to the realm of evil. In most cases, this means Satan and his minions.[5] Christians who choose this alternative sometimes tend to completely externalize evil. They believe that humans are inherently good; therefore, the evil that flows from them must be the consequence of evil forces at work within them in opposition to God's will and plan for the creation.

This tendency to ascribe inherent goodness and beneficence to sacred power is not shared by all religious traditions. In Hinduism, for example, devotees of the goddess Kali worship her despite the fact that her power is intensely destructive to human well-being. Kali's power is traditionally associated with bloodletting and death. Her devotees do not themselves necessarily take on Kali's destructive qualities in their actions. Rather, they revere Kali out of a deep respect for her power and out of a recognition that such power is part of the nature of existence itself. In other traditions, such as the Ojibwa belief system, sacred power is associated more with potentiality or potency than with moral goodness or evil. The moral dimension of sacred power arises when humans appropriate power for particular good or evil purposes. Another idea about the moral nature of sacred power comes from the ancient Greek religions. According to Greek mythology, Zeus and other divine beings care little about human welfare. They simply use their power for their own ends. That humans often get caught in the actions of the gods is of little concern to the divine beings. Humans are merely expected to deal with fate as they encounter it. This amorality of the gods led ancient Greek philosophers, who celebrated the power of human reason, to reject the Greek gods and seek more rational explanations for the human situation. Their writings provided the foundation for Western philosophy and science. For some religious people throughout Western history, the development of Western philosophy and science, therefore, has been linked to a rejection of religion and divine ex-

planations for things. Among biblical Christians who derive their historical understanding from Francis Schaeffer's theology of culture, Western
philosophy and science, stripped of their religious dimensions, constitute
the source of the man-centered worldview that stands in opposition to the
Christian worldview. By relying on reason and empirical analysis alone,
this human-centered worldview works in opposition to religion and is its
chief enemy. Proponents of such a viewpoint, according to Schaeffer, are
secular humanists.

All of these characteristics of religion are consistent with the explicitly
religious presupposition of Christian Right leaders. In language consistent
with our discussion of sacred power, they believe that God exists; God
alone is God; God is immanent through the creation, Jesus Christ, the
Holy Spirit, and the verbally inspired Bible; God is the transcendent sovereign over all creation; and God is directly involved at the most intimate
levels in our lives. Though opposed to the secular humanist worldview,
most biblical Christians and the leadership of the Christian Right are not
opposed to science or reason itself. Quite the opposite. Movement leaders
believe that their agenda for public education is highly supportive of both
science and reason. Their criticism focuses on the exclusion of Christian
presuppositions guiding the application of reason and the study of science.
When viewed from biblical Christian presuppositions, science and reason
are appropriate and important parts of the public school curriculum.

The Manifestation of Religion

Our discussion of the essence of religion suggests something of what the
religious people who viewed the soybean-tank Jesus might have encountered. It still leaves unanswered the question of why they saw Jesus rather
than Moses, the Buddha, or the angel Gabriel. The answer to this question
lies in the way humans respond to the sacred presence. Not all humans
react in the same way to the presence of sacred power. Some respond affectively. They define the sacred presence emotionally in terms of feelings.
Others react cognitively. They try to mentally grasp and explain what has
happened to them. Still others respond volitionally. They find their lives
redirected, and they seek to bring their lives into conformity with what
they have encountered. In reality, human reactions to the sacred typically
involve all three responses as well as a fourth one, a cultural response. Individuals receive encounters with sacred presence within the particular

cultural framework that orients them to the world. This is why the pilgrims to the soybean silo saw Jesus. Their cultural framework, including their particular religious orientation, identified the apparition within the set of affective, cognitive, and volitional responses that are characteristic of their cultural context.

Returning to our analysis of the Christian Right, each of the first three types of responses closely corresponds to a particular religious constituency from which the movement draws its core membership. Pentecostals/charismatics emphasize more the affective response in marking the presence of the Holy Spirit. Fundamentalists privilege the cognitive with their emphasis on correct doctrine and belief as verbally inspired through the holy Scriptures. Holiness Christians tend to measure the presence of God in their lives through their volitional emphasis on living the moral or holy life.[6] To be sure, these are relative, not absolute, distinctions in emphasis.

What distinguishes adherents of the traditions that associate with the Christian Right from those that do not is the particular cultural framework from which they draw their orientation to contemporary American society. From a religious point of view, Christian Right constituents contextualize their perspectives through filtering lenses consistent with Francis Schaeffer's theology of culture and Rousas John Rushdoony's political theology. In order for the movement to increase its level of support within these religious communities, it must convince the adherents to modify their current orientations by putting on Christian Right filtering lenses. The fact that the movement has constructed its perspective through the participation of Christian Right leaders from each of these various religious communities bodes well for its potential success. The leaders, at least, are convinced that there is complete coherence between their perspectives and the religious outlooks of their potential converts.

The Affective Response to the Sacred

The classic description of the affective response to the sacred is found in Rudolph Otto's famous phrase *"mysterium tremendum et fascinans,"* which, in translation from the Latin, suggests that we perceive sacred power as a mysterious presence that both attracts and repulses us. Van der Leeuw describes the reaction as "amazement . . . and in extreme cases fear."[7] We are attracted by a sense of empowerment that we want to experience repeatedly. We are repulsed when we realize how overwhelming its power is and how impotent and inadequate we feel in its presence. Even when the sacred presence comes to us as a still small voice rather than an experience of overwhelming potency, we feel both attraction and repulsion.

Not all people who apprehend the sacred power experience its force to the same degree. In some ritual traditions, the sacred presence confronts religious initiates in a much more restrained way than religious specialists who have cultivated deeply powerful involvement with it. An illustration of this point comes to us from the peyote hunt of the Central American Huichol culture. Near the end of the pilgrimage to the sacred site, all of the Huichol initiates are led into a valley, where they hunt and ingest peyote. For the Huichol, peyote provides both the vehicle of transcendence and the manifestation of sacred power in their lives. The resulting experience of the sacred presence for the new initiates is far less overwhelming than it is for their spiritual guide. One Huichol spiritual guide named Ramón has spent years as a liminal person straddling the threshold between the sacred and profane dimensions. Because of his greater experience in these matters, he is far more capable of experiencing and bearing the power in its full potency than are those who are led into its presence for their first experience.[8] Within the Christian tradition, this same phenomenon is illustrated by the contrast between Jesus' experience of divine presence on the cross and the catechant experiencing communion for the first time.

A distinctive characteristic of the affective response is the tendency of people to experience the sacred in a particularly intense way. Alan Watts describes this as a "concentration in the present."[9] Apprehending sacredness alters our sense of time and space because we become totally immersed in what we are experiencing. Such intensity of experience relates both to the nature of the power apprehended and the particular type of human response to it. Zen Buddhists who experience *satori* refer to this intensification of the present as paying attention. In evangelical Christian circles, the same intensification occurs as a born-again experience. Although it has become somewhat formalistic in some evangelical circles, many Christians who have been born again can remember and identify the exact context in which the experience occurred and have a strong sense that it was an overwhelming experience that shook them to the core of their being.

The Cognitive Response to the Sacred

Pilgrims to the silo responding cognitively seek first to comprehend their encounter. The cognitive response aims at integrating the presence of the apparition with what we know and understand about the truth of things. We do this by filtering it through the reality structures or worldview familiar to us. The main reason the pilgrims saw Jesus rather than Buddha was that the overwhelming majority were Christians rather than Buddhists. Filtering occurs at two different levels. At the cultural level, the dominant worldview and symbol systems provide the overall context. But the cultural context must always be legitimated at the level of individual experience. Thus, the cognitive response begins within the particular set of experiences from which individuals construct their perspectives on the world. For demographic and cultural reasons, the apparition on the soybean tank in Fostoria, Ohio, could not have been any other figure than Jesus (or perhaps, in a more Catholic community, Mary) if it was apprehended as a sacred presence. The majority could not have seen the Buddha, the angel Gabriel, or the Zulu prophet Isaiah Shembe. Indeed, anyone claiming that it was any other sacred presence than Jesus would have been put on the defensive by the gathered pilgrims.

I draw my theoretical understanding of this cognitive response process from *The Social Construction of Reality,* by Peter Berger and Thomas Luckmann. As they describe it, the process begins in the subjective consciousness of the individual. When we first encounter the otherness of the sacred presence, it seems unfamiliar to us. We try to make sense out of the experience by connecting it to what is familiar to us where and when we can. These conceptualizations often lack precision and clarity because of the ambiguous and unique character of sacred power and our unfamiliarity with it. Being limited to our experiences, our cognitive maps are never quite adequate. So we seek to legitimate our conceptualizations by sharing them with others. When our ideas are not accepted, we modify them or try to convince others of their validity. In rare cases, the strength of an individual's experience may eventually convince others to change their views. When enough people make such modifications, the cultural context shifts, even if ever so slightly. After we make the necessary changes and people are in agreement, we tend to believe that our descriptions of reality have the status of objective truth. In the example of the pilgrims, what they saw *was* Jesus. This objectification of the subjective[10] means that socially accepted interpretations of reality begin from the subjective experience of the individual's encounter with otherness.

In our daily routine, we are seldom aware that such a process of constructing reality continually operates. We accept these conceptual constructions as objectively true. In some cases, people literally stake their lives on such conceptualizations, defending truth to their death or the death of others. Our interpretations of the sacred appearance become integrated into our cognitive map or frames of reference in many ways. Most commonly they are expressed individually as symbols or collectively in stories, legends, folk tales, and other literary forms. At a more complex level, they may be expressed as mythology, religious truths, symbolic events, or philosophic principles. Their expression in these more complex forms often necessitates the involvement of intellectuals, who weave the various elements into an existing worldview. In turn, organizational activists present them to ordinary people in the form of a coherent story that seems to make sense and appears to be practical in its application.

The most comprehensive explanations of reality, in terms of both depth and breadth, comprise worldviews. A worldview is the way a person in a given society "sees [himself or herself] in relation to all else. . . . It is, in short, a [person's] idea of the universe."[11] Because worldviews are so inclusive of every dimension of a person's life, people rarely recognized them as constructions. Thus, as long as they function well, worldviews tend to lead people to merely accept what they perceive to be reality as being grounded in the nature of things. Even with their superior depth and breadth, however, worldviews are not inherently religious. They are religious only to the degree that they testify to the existence of sacred power, to a sacred dimension to reality, or to a sacred reality separate from personal human interests. Worldviews are secular when their authority stems from sources not deemed by their adherents to be sacred. When religious and secular authorities disagree about reality constructs, it is usually over the issue of which particular forms of expression are believed to be more real. Many secularists tend to give much greater weight to scientific and philosophic reality systems. Others define reality more in terms of affective or moral terms. Secularists typically see religious and mythological systems as inferior forms of knowledge resting on superstition or primitive knowledge; they judge their own systems to be more authoritative. For rational secularists, the authority rests in scientific objectivity and empiricism. For affective or moral secularists, the basis for such claims is the immediacy of subjective experience. In contrast, religionists insist that their reality systems not only are just as practical and sensible as secular systems, but that they are even more authoritative because they operate from an understanding of reality that is more inclusive and more penetrating than secular systems.

Worldviews are most typically expressed by religious people through mythology. Within the academic discipline of religious studies, *mythology* refers quite simply to sacred stories that have as their main themes the most significant questions of human existence, our ultimate concerns. Included are questions regarding the nature and origin of the cosmos; human nature, identity, and place; and human destiny.[12] In many Eastern religious traditions, the line between myth and history is almost impossible to draw with any assurance. For example, in some modern languages of India, the word *itihasa* denotes what Westerners would call history; the word *purana* denotes myth. The problem is that these words often occur in the compound *itihasapurana,* meaning history/myth, thus confusing the distinction between the two.[13] In Western religious traditions, the lines of demarcation between myth and history appear, at first glance, to be clearer. In our common Western application of the words, whereas "myths deal with God or gods and 'events' which may not literally have happened, history deals with past facts and so reports what actually did happen."[14] In practice, however, the distinction does not hold. Is what is taught in history or social studies classes history, fact, myth, or fiction? The question ultimately turns not on whether a particular event did or did not happen but on the presuppositions that determine the basis upon which we decide whether it did or did not occur. For example, events are included or excluded from history books because of their relevance to the dominant cultural (or national) myth. Current multicultural controversies surrounding the teaching of history clearly illustrate the soft distinction between history and myth. In the postmodern era, each cultural minority seeks to advance the legitimacy of its mythos by expanding and remolding the accepted cultural history. The ultimate educational validation comes when our history becomes part of the larger mythos.

With respect to the present controversies over public education, the battle is not just over competing secularist versus religious worldviews. It also involves the tendency of those on each side of the debate to reify their own particular conceptual framework by linking it to ideological interests. Ideologies, according to Berger and Luckmann, arise when a segment of the population corrupts and devolves religious and secular world-views into a defense of the narrow self-interests of their particular group.[15] Ideologies prevent dialogue on the issues because they are closed systems. As such, their cognitive frameworks typically lose the characteristics of ambiguity and incongruity normally associated with worldview con-structs. They also function to drive out the transcendent (religious or sec-ular) dimensions of most worldview constructs in which apprehension of the other as transcendent occurs.

Even when the opposing party identifies ideological elements in the conversation, the proponents are likely to argue that their reasons and mo-tives are misunderstood. For educators, this means that their defense of certain values and presuppositions about the nature of education leads them to believe that what they advocate truly is in the best interest of children and the society. Christian Right activists accused of defending their class, gender, or racial interest argue that their stance merely reflects the divine order of the larger sacred reality. In both cases, their advocacy represents a noble effort to live in closer harmony with what they hold to be the ultimate order of things.

As surprising as many educators may find this statement, in many cases Christian Right activists are more prepared than professionals within the educational establishment to discuss controversial issues at the deepest level of grounding presuppositions. This is largely due to the methodolog-ical and strategic principles that guide Christian Right criticism of public education. Their presuppositional approach intentionally pushes contro-versies in that direction, and most movement activists beyond the grass-roots level are very explicit and intentional about the presuppositions that orient their challenges. Educational professionals, though, particularly at the district level, are often unaware of the nature of the presuppositions that guide their educational philosophy and pedagogy. That unawareness arises primarily from the way teachers are trained and the overwhelming day-to-day pressures they face. In this regard, public educators are similar to the majority of Americans. The presuppositions that inform their lives are simply accepted as the way things are. In most cases this acceptance is absolutely necessary for people to function in their everyday lives. For many people it is only when they are confronted by alternative construc-tions that they recognize that there are a number of ways of conceptualiz-ing reality, each of which is taken by its adherents to be both practical and sensible.

The Volitional Response

The volitional dimension refers to the intentional acts we perform as a response to our apprehension of sacred power. In the example of the Fostoria pilgrims, it relates both to the way in which their encounter with an apparition of Jesus changes the moral character of their lives and the ritual actions they perform in order to bring themselves again into the presence of the sacred power. Thus, the volitional response contains both a moral and a ritual component.

The moral side of the volitional response concerns the way in which religious persons order their lives in relation to what they perceive to be the ultimate structure and nature of existence. We express this notion in terms of our attempts to reorient our lives so that they are "in a 'right' relationship with the sacred cosmos."[16] The reorientation can be either world-confirming or world-transforming. If the religious person views the larger culture as more or less in harmony with the sacred order of things, the moral dimension tends to reinforce existing relations and hierarchies among persons. If the religious person views the larger culture as corrupt or in sharp contrast to the sacred order, the moral dimension tends to seek to transform the existing social order to bring it into greater conformity with the sacred order.

The moral dimension has both a functional and a substantive quality. Functionally, it provides us with a sense of security "against the nightmare threats of chaos."[17] It opens to us the ultimate order of things and shows us that existence is not random or without meaning. Substantively, the moral dimension leads us to conclude that there is a way to live that is intrinsically right and good beyond whatever practical benefits it may accord us.[18] This tendency is reflected in Immanuel Kant's notion of moral obligation or duty. In contrast to utilitarians such as John Stuart Mill, who measured the moral worth of an act in terms of its beneficial consequences, Kant argued that consequences are irrelevant in determining the moral worth of an action. For Kant, the right action is that which moves from a sense of obligation or duty to the universal moral order. A deed is moral simply because it is the right thing to do.

Kant's approach leaves us with the problem of identifying the right thing. Within Western culture, three contrasting means for identifying moral values predominate.[19] For pure secularists, moral values are determined primarily through the use of human reason or emotion alone. Modified religionists combine human reason and emotion with divine revelation. They hold that although the ultimate order of things is divinely created and partially revealed in Scripture, the human ability to grasp that order and the values contained in it comes through the application of human reason or the disposition of the conscience. Pure religionists favor an approach that identifies Scriptures as the sole defining source and measure of moral values. Human reason may be used to understand the relationship between those values or the meaning of the values, but the ultimate criteria by which the legitimacy and meaning of values is determined is divine revelation. Put simply, pure religionists such as biblical Christians believe moral values are right and good because they come from God.

Religious and secular Americans may find a great deal of overlap among the moral values they acknowledge as important, but religious persons tend to assert the superiority of moral values because of their divine origin and define them primarily in relation to their divine source. By rooting such values in ultimate rather than human sources, religious people tend to believe that the values to which they subscribe transcend mere human self-interest. The term *higher law* is often used by Christians to identify appeals to ultimate sources. Higher law seeks to legitimate moral actions in terms of God's will even if those actions seemingly violate ordinary standards of human well-being and comfort.

The higher-law tradition, of course, has a long history in American culture. It was one of the bases of colonial protest against British occupation. It provided legitimacy for the causes of both sides in the Civil War. In the middle decades of the twentieth century, it was used to justify opposition to segregation and to promote women's rights. Higher law also provides the moral foundation for biblical Christians working for contemporary cultural transformation. Christian Right leaders, for example, frequently cite Samuel Rutherford's *Lex Rex* to justify their opposition to the moral values of the larger culture. In his seventeenth-century treatise, the Scottish moral philosopher Rutherford argued that even the king is subject to God's law. Contemporary movement leaders use Rutherford's arguments in criticizing democratic processes and democratically elected leaders. Rousas John Rushdoony exemplified this appeal to higher law in a conversation with Bill Moyers that was part of a PBS documentary on Christians in politics. When Moyers questioned Rushdoony about his rejection of democracy, Rushdoony responded that he opposes it not because he wants to but because democracy is contrary to God's law.[20] Though not all Christian Right leaders share Rushdoony's conclusion that democracy is completely contrary to God's law, the movement's major voices all assert that America's political and legislative processes are subject to moral sanction when they are not in complete harmony with God's law.

In contrast to the moral dimension, which focuses on the issue of moral conformity to ultimate realities, the ritual dimension of the volitional response has to do with the means by which humans bring themselves into the presence of those ultimate realities. This includes both the identification of appropriate processes and the creation of the necessary environments for humans to recapture or return to the sacred presence. Ritual belongs in the volitional dimension because ritual action involves intentional acts on the part of humans.[21] Humans construct ritual environments in order to create contexts in which they can experience the fusion of the everyday world of social existence and the world of sacred reality.[22] In this sense, rituals function as vehicles of transcendence. Religious persons employ them in order to transcend their ordinary experiences and apprehend sacred presence. Beyond their functional purpose, rituals also contain a substantive element. Humans are transformed by sacred power in the ritual process. A reciprocal situation is created, in which "life affected by power turns toward power and seeks participation with it."[23] In ritual environments infused with sacred presence, humans seeking an experience of power are seized by that power and the seizure transforms the participant's entire orientation to the world. Clifford Geertz observes that in the Balinese ritual process, participants become entranced and claim to cross a threshold into another order of existence.[24] When the Balinese return to the everyday world, they see this world as a partial fulfillment of a "wider reality which corrects and completes it."[25] By having experienced the way things are through ritualized perfection, participants are now able to see perfection even in the "ordinary, uncontrolled, course of things."[26] Further, the transformative power and reorientation of the ritual process leads them to seek to transform the everyday world so that it more fully corresponds to sacred reality.

Typically, such transformative ritual processes involve three stages: separation, liminality, and reincorporation.[27] In the separation phase, ritual participants begin to move from their ordinary everyday existence toward the sacred existence they hope to encounter. As they complete the separation, they enter into a liminal phase, in which their orientation shifts to the sacred center. Here they encounter the sacred presence. The experience also binds the participants together and to the sacred dimension through their collective reorientation to the sacred center. In one of the forms of this liminal experience, which Victor Turner calls *normative communitas,* the sacred presence transforms the participants to the point where their orientation to the world changes. As they return from the ritual experience in the third stage and reenter their normal social existence, participants find that the norms and moral values through which they normally express themselves in social existence have been given a new quality and significance. The ritual actors are now empowered with the fellow-feelings they have experienced in the liminal stage. Rather than just being markers for their social behaviors, their normative and moral actions proceed from an ennobled feeling of commitment to the humanity of others and to the ultimate source of sacred power.[28] The ritual process of separation, liminality, and reincorporation serves as a vehicle of transcendence in the sense that it empowers participants by relating them to the sacred dimension and to the purpose of existence and by causing them to discover the humanity of others during the liminal stage. Participants emerge from the ritual process with feelings of loyalty to each other, a willingness to sacrifice for the larger reality they have experienced, and a sense of connectedness to the sacred presence that empowered them.[29]

In our illustration of the soybean-tank Jesus, ritual actions were emerging as the pilgrims continually returned to the sacred site. Those unaffected by the presence of sacred power merely hawked their wares or became part of the crowd that gathered to satisfy their curiosity. The pilgrims, however, often prayed together and waited for God's power to come into their lives. In the process, a certain camaraderie developed among the participants; and their testimonies of the power they experienced in that sacred place provided motivation for other seekers to come to the site. The location served as a kind of magic circle pivot, as Arnold van Gennepp describes it. It provided the occasion for sacredness to come into play in a particular situation among a specific group of persons.[30] If van Gennepp and others who follow his lead are correct, then ritual becomes a powerful tool that transforms otherwise profane space and activities into magic circle pivots. What determines whether a particular situation becomes a focusing lens through which participants experience sacred existence is the orientation and environment the ritual leaders and participants structure into the context.[31]

Such ritual processes of sacred transformation are absolutely essential to religiously based social movements. Through ritual processes and environments, potential constituents can be brought into the social movement, endowed with a sense of normative communitas, and reoriented to the world in a way that is directed toward the transformation of the culture. In this sense, Christian Right efforts to transform the orientation and environment of the public schools into one more consistent with their worldview presuppositions must be understood in the context of ritual performance and the creation of sacred space. Educational leaders have long recognized public schools as agents of social transformation. Educators also understand the way curriculum and, more importantly, pedagogy ideally function ritually to effect the transformation. Christian Right activists agree with educators on these points. But their actions are directed toward a transformation of students that will bring future generations into their sacred center by enabling them to see the way things are even in the midst of the "ordinary, uncontrolled, course of things." The Christian Right focus on public education, then, involves the attempt to control the nature of the socialization process characteristic of American public education.

The Cultural Response

The cultural response to the sacred presence represents the cumulative expression of the affective, cognitive, and volitional responses to the sacred presence. It rests on a different order than the previously discussed responses. Here individual reorientation assumes the form of a social movement. From the religious perspective, the cultural dimension centers on the human impulse to transform ordinary social existence into conformity with sacred existence. Apprehensions of the sacred presence at the individual level do not always lead to involvement in a social movement. For example, the cultural impulse did not develop among the pilgrims in Fostoria, Ohio. Though the apparition of Jesus may have empowered the lives of some individuals affectively, cognitively, and volitionally, it did not result in a social movement geared to reconstructing social and cultural life within Fostoria in ways consistent with sacred existence.

The cultural response operates at the level of collective habitual patterns of behavior, the entire range of products of human action, whose meaning is contained in symbols and whose structure is given coherence through symbolic webs of significance.[32] The cultural response, therefore, operates at the level at which humans attempt to redefine the symbolic webs of significance that give coherence to human action. The degree of conflict this might create within the larger culture depends on the way a given group views the presently constituted webs. The more incongruity people perceive between the existing culture and the sacred dimension of life, the more conflict they might experience with it. As a religiously grounded revitalization movement, the Christian Right has chosen to express the conflict they see in terms of efforts to reconstruct the entire culture in ways that are more congruent with their vision of things.

Because of the nature of religion, religious persons are likely to see greater conflicts than nonreligious persons at the cultural level. Religious persons stand in relation to culture in a sacred way. They see the depth dimension of culture. Religion opens for them the "ultimate, infinite, unconditional" dimension of every aspect of life,[33] a dimension that is hidden or closed to nonreligious persons. When the webs of significance upon which the culture rests are woven around nonreligious presuppositions, this depth dimension of culture disappears—at least from public life. Most typically, the depth dimension is expressed by religious persons symbolically. In this sense, religious symbols are touch points between the mundane world and the world of sacred existence. Such symbols may be concrete (e.g., the Christian cross) or abstract (e.g., the concept of the Virgin Birth).

Symbols are more powerful instruments of communication than rational discourse or formal statements of religious belief, partly because they penetrate our experience at a number of different levels—the cognitive, the affective, the volitional, and the physical. Symbols also eclipse literal understandings because of their power to produce multiple meanings on multiple levels. They emit to us many levels of meaning and lead us in a number of directions as we explore their full complexity. Symbols are both multivalent and multivocal: they potentially speak to us at many different levels and with many different voices.

The multivalent character of symbols leads us toward deeper and more complex clusters of meanings, values, and significations. For example, the cross for Christians is a much more powerful representation of Christianity than any set of doctrines articulated by various ecclesiastical authorities. The reality it presents to Christians involves a whole complex of events surrounding the life, death, and resurrection of Jesus Christ that engage adherents at a number of different levels. But even more significantly, the cross opens to Christians the divine order of creation itself and the Creator who brought it into existence. As the Christian cross points to a particular event, it opens Christians to reality at its deepest and broadest levels. Though these deeper and more complex understandings of reality may be hidden from us at the conscious level, symbols still operate in framing our relation to the world we encounter. Symbols, then, are opaque, and that is what gives them their depth.[34] Secular symbols do not have the same breadth or depth, according to religious people, because they do not open us to significations beyond the human, rational, or material dimensions of existence. Because of their greater depth and breadth, religious symbols provide a structure and orientation to life that is prior to all other stances in life.

The multivocal dimension of symbols sometimes creates confusion in our minds, since symbols express different meanings in different cultural contexts. For example, the swastika appears as a symbol in the cultures of the Diné (Navaho), the Hindus, and Hitler's Third Reich. Yet the meanings of the swastika are quite different. For the Diné, it relates to the healing power of Whirling Logs within the Blessing Way ceremony. For Hindus, it symbolizes the wheel of *samsara,* or rebirth, which links them to their karmic past and future. For Nazis, the swastika symbolizes the lightning-like power that the Nazis used to bring their vision of Aryan culture into existence. Because symbols are multivocal, we can never assume that a person in a different cultural or religious context shares the meaning we attribute to a particular symbol. This presents a particular difficulty for public school educators when confronted by religiously motivated challenges. Even though a symbol familiar to the general public might be used by a Christian Right challenger (e.g., parents' rights), the cluster of meanings, values, and significations represented in it may be quite different to the Christian Right activist and the non–Christian Right parent.

Humans typically are not always aware of the webs of symbolic significations that guide their behavior. Indeed, for most of our lives, we operate as if these behaviors and perceptions of truth are normal. Taking our significations as common-sense knowledge,[35] we presume that the connections between elements of this common-sense knowledge are given in reality. We assume that what we take to be true is, in fact, true because it is so closely connected to other truths that we also take as fact. We tend to be so convinced of the truth of our understanding that we frequently consign anyone whose orientation runs counter to common sense as we see it to the categories of irrationality, madness, and extremism. This tendency partially explains why so many of the combatants in the educational theater of the contemporary culture war in America simply assume that their opponents are blind, irrational, or dishonest. When, for example, the educational establishment describes Christian Right critics as irrational extremists, it does so, in large part, because the significations given to events by educators reflect their webs of meaning. Their webs are so different from those operating in the Christian Right that the actions of the movement protesters appear to be irrational or extremist. The same is true in reverse to some degree. However, because of the nature of the strategy employed by the Christian Right, movement activists tend to have a better understanding of the logic system of the educators than the educators have of the Christian Right web.

To illustrate this point, we might consider the issue of prayer in the public schools. Many mainstream educators operate from a set of symbolic meanings that consign religion to the private or individual sphere out of respect for the pluralistic values they hold. From this perspective, organized prayer symbolically represents a negation of both the private nature of religion and the plural character of religious America. For mainstream educators who are also religious persons, exclusion of prayer from the public schools constitutes neither a rejection of the significance of prayer nor a denial of the value of religion in a person's life. It is simply counterproductive to weaving the social webs of significance from which the larger culture is constructed. For Christian Right activists operating out of a different symbolic web, exclusion of prayer from the public schools constitutes a rejection of the value of prayer and hostility toward religion in general. From their perspective, prayer is neither inherently individual nor inherently private. It is a ritual process that relates people to the ultimate nature of existence and the sacred order that defines proper human behavior. The presence of prayer in the schools legitimates that dimension of existence and moves students who are exposed to prayer into an environment in which God's presence may be made manifest to them. Prayer, for the Christian Right, operates at the level of a deep symbol that opens to us the entire web of significance that defines our orientation to the world. For this reason, participants on the two sides of the issue are seldom able to reach accommodation with each other even at the level of understanding the significance of the symbol.

In Western religions, the most powerful of these deep symbols are god-terms, terms that speak to the foundation upon which reality exists. The deep symbols, as Edward Farley calls them, contain within them the essential meanings and values that shape all aspects of the individual's awareness of social reality.[36] Deep symbols present to a culture the criteria by which it understands itself, by which it orients itself to both the present and the future, and according to which it assesses the adequacy of everything we experience. Like other symbols, deep symbols arise within a particular historical context in relation to a given community. They proceed, as Clifford Geertz says, along particular cultural pathways.[37]

Highly integrated cultures find a strong degree of coherence between what is taken to be of ultimate significance and the degree to which that ultimate significance is expressed symbolically in every cultural product. In such highly integrated cultures, deep symbols and the webs of significance into which they are woven are clearly identifiable. During the medieval period of Roman Catholic Europe, for example, everything cultural took its meaning and significance from the church, which symbolized God's presence in the world. In architecture, poetry, and philosophy, the triangle relating humanity, God, and the church dominated culture. In less integrated cultures, little or no coherence may exist among the various cultural products because they are not bound together as a mutual expression of a core set of deep symbols with shared meaning, value, and significance. That is, various institutions within a given culture may operate at cross purposes to each other because they do not share a common orientation that goes beyond the relative self-interest of the institution. This appears to be the condition of contemporary American culture and, from the perspective of biblical Christians, is one of the major causes of what they perceive to be the cultural decay of our society.

Religious America

Christian Right attempts to transform American culture proceed from a set of assumptions about the religious character of our nation's people that are not shared by the mainstream culture. The most important of these assumptions is expressed in a dualistic understanding of American society that divides Americans into "Christian" and "secular humanist" camps. The deep symbols of "Christian" and "secular humanist" have specific meaning to the Christian Right. This framework equates Christian with biblical Christians and associates secular humanism with atheists and all other religionists, including Christians who do not share the worldview presuppositions of biblical Christianity. According to movement theorists, secularists are in control of American culture. The present ascendency of the secularists is the consequence of a long secular humanist conspiracy in America that dates back to the Enlightenment. Since the time of John Dewey, secularists have used the public schools as a means of ideological indoctrination in order to transform school children into secularists. Although such a dualistic interpretation of the religious character of the American people fits well into the Christian Right symbolic web, from the mainstream point of view it is highly reductionistic and fails to account for the complexity of American religion.

According to the way Americans identify their own religious orientation, the majority of Americans are Christian and only a small percentage of the general population are secularists. Surveys of the religious commitments of Americans have consistently shown that the vast majority of Americans consider themselves to be religious persons, exhibit religious behavior, and profess religious beliefs. For example, over 90 percent of Americans believe in God, a statistic that has not changed significantly in fifty years.[38] About 40 percent attend religious services on a regular basis, a figure that is about the same as it was in the late 1930s.[39] Nearly 85 percent of Americans identify themselves as Christians, and of those, Protestants outnumber Roman Catholics by a bit more than a two-to-one ratio. With only about 7 percent claiming "no religious affiliation" as late as 1997, it is hard to believe Christian Right claims that America is a secular nation.[40]

Perhaps the most distinctive feature of American religion is its increasing diversity. *The Encyclopedia of American Religion* lists more than seventeen hundred religious organizations in America, classified, according to similarities in historical development and theology, into twenty identifiable religious traditions or families. The majority of these families are broadly Christian; they include the Western (Roman Catholic and Anglican) and Eastern (Orthodox) liturgical groups, Lutherans, Reformed groups, pietists/Methodists, holiness groups, pentecostals, free church denominations, Baptists, independent fundamentalists, liberals, Latter-day Saints, and Christian Scientists. The Christian families comprise nearly nine hundred denominational groups. Since the *Encyclopedia* does not mention individual congregations independent of larger denominations, we may conclude that within the United States there are more than one thousand different expressions of Christianity. The non-Christian families include Middle Eastern religions (e.g., Judaism, Islam, Zoroastrianism, and Bahai), the Ancient Wisdom Family (e.g., Rosicrucianism, Occult Orders, Theosophy, and I AM Groups), the Magick Family (e.g., Ritual Magick, witchcraft and neopaganism, voodoo, and Satanism), the Eastern Family (e.g., Hinduism, Jainism, Sikhism, and various forms of Buddhism), and the spiritualist, psychic, and New Age family.[41] Given this diversity, it is unreasonable to suggest that any one group or cluster of groups could claim to speak for all people of faith within the United States.

In addition to the diversity of religious traditions existing in present-day America, diversity also exists within many of these groups with respect to theology and cultural attitudes. Theologically, the diversity ranges from those who insist on absolute adherence to beliefs and practices literally and rigidly interpreted to those who allow for a greater range of beliefs and some flexibility in ritual practices. Culturally, the diversity ranges from those who insist on protecting themselves from the moderating forces of the larger culture to those who see little difficulty in adhering to their religious traditions and functioning comfortably in the larger society. Two interpretive models, one theological, the other cultural, can help us understand the way this diversity functions in our society. Both identify three points on a continuum stretching from the more modernist worldviews to more traditional ones. The categories are Christian in context since the largest majority of religious persons within the United States and within the Christian Right are Christians. These labels are not exclusive to Christianity, however. They apply equally to other religious traditions such as Judaism and Islam in America.

Theological Distinctions

The theological model places the "liberal left" on one end of the continuum, the "redeeming right" on the opposite end,[42] and the "moderate middle" in between.[43] Keeping in mind that these are theological/cultural categories rather than political ones, there is no necessary connection between theological/cultural orientation and political ideology, even though there may be strong correlations. The strongest correlations quite naturally tend to occur nearer the poles of the continuum. On the aggregate, most religious Americans tend to be both politically and theologically/culturally closer to the moderate-conservative end of the continuum than their secular counterparts.[44]

The liberal left is most accepting of the larger culture and the diversity within it. It tends toward an Arminian or high view of human nature in its emphasis on the ability of humans to overcome or repair their fallen condition. For this reason, liberal leftists tend to hold human reason in high regard and credit its capacity to discover truth independent of revelation.

They emphasize God's mercy and love more than God's justice or sovereignty. The liberal left leans toward a view of Scripture that emphasizes the human dimension and the historical context of the biblical record and sees the Bible more as a valuable record of the past than as a detailed source of absolute truth. In the public arena, the liberal left associates religion with morality and finds common cause with other religious traditions on moral issues with relative ease. Along with this emphasis on morality, liberals tend to emphasize human well-being over personal salvation. They reject any literal reading of the Bible that claims exclusive insight into the divine-human condition. Thus, they are open to various understandings and interpretations of truth. Their source of religious knowledge derives as much from human feeling and human reason as it does from the Scriptures. They tend to de-emphasize special revelation (God's active intervention in human affairs) as compared to general revelation (the knowledge of God that comes through the order of nature). Finally, liberals see little contradiction between religion and contemporary empirical science. They believe that, ultimately, they can know truth through a variety of means. For religious liberals, accommodation to the culture does not necessarily imply that they are secularists. Their religious perspective is such that they can operate comfortably within the larger secularized culture.

At the other end of the spectrum, the redeeming right is far more suspicious of the larger culture and the diversity within it. In fact, its rejection of modernism and modern culture is one of its distinguishing features.[45] The redeeming right tends to hold an Augustinian or low view of human nature, which emphasizes human sinfulness and sees cultural and religious diversity in terms of the moral categories of sin and corruption. Although those on the redeeming right are divided on the means and the degree to which humans can overcome their fallen condition, the redeeming right is in agreement that relief from the condition of sin comes from God and is limited to those who are truly Christian. Believers on the right emphasize God's intervening activity in human affairs through the historical record described in the Bible, miracles such as spiritual healing, the continuing work of the Holy Spirit, and the enduring power of prayer. They understand the Bible to contain the inerrant word of God and thus believe that divine will and divine truth are open with absolute certainty to Christians. This puts them in a position of rejecting the authority of science when it contradicts their reading of the Scriptures; yet, there is a broad range of opinion within the right on the degree to which science and the Scriptures are in conflict. Redeeming right Christians also tend to emphasize personal salvation over the well-being of humanity in this world, although many conservative Christians are involved in social action through volunteer organizations and rescue missions.

The moderate middle stands at the midpoint between these two poles of the theological continuum. Moderates tend toward a serious understanding of the nature of sin and thus acknowledge the existence of evil in the world. Moderates tend to be somewhat suspicious of those who differ from them, but they are supportive of the full participation of all Americans in the culture. Most middlers believe that the human condition is quite redeemable and that humans are capable of doing good through the faculties given to them by God. They take the problem of sin more seriously than most liberals and have some concern for personal salvation. Moderates also are likely to accept the Bible as the inspired word of God but disagree with redeeming right claims that the Bible is literally true and inerrant. They differ from liberals in the weight they give to the biblical record when it contradicts tendencies within the modern culture. Although still able to operate at a level of relative comfort in the larger culture, moderate middlers are more critical of the culture than are liberals. This stance derives from their view of human nature that emphasizes the human inclination to rely too heavily on one's own abilities. At the same time, however, they respect and appreciate the way humans use those resources to produce a relatively comfortable life. Moderates turn to a number of sources for their religious knowledge. Chief among these is the Scriptures. However, they hold that because the Scriptures reflect a specific time and place far removed from twentieth-century America, one's reading of the Scriptures must be modified by human reason, religious tradition, and human experience.

It is difficult to ascertain the exact percentage of American Christians who fit each of these three categories in America, but it is safe to suggest that the liberal left is the smallest of the three. In the past, the moderate middle has been larger than the redeeming right, but there is fairly strong evidence that they may now be about equal in strength.[46] It also appears that education and socioeconomic status constitute a moderating force even within the redeeming right.[47] Conservative Christian college students and seminary-trained clergy tend to hold more moderate positions within the redeeming right on a whole range of theological and moral issues than rank-and-file redeeming right congregants.[48]

Of these three theological categories, the Christian Right draws the majority of its core constituents from the redeeming right, though a large number of people in the moderate middle are sympathetic to many of the concerns and issues raised by movement leaders. Even within the redeeming right, however, the Christian Right's strength is probably no more than about 35 to 40 percent. Efforts to increase support for the movement from the redeeming right create two types of problems for movement leaders. Many redeeming right Christians believe that involvement in the political and social institutions of the larger culture constitutes compromise with Satan and thus are not willing to engage in social action. Other redeeming right Christians are theologically close to the Christian Right but take much more liberal stances toward political and social issues. Movement leaders must therefore convince apolitical redeeming rightists to become active politically in the fight against Satan; at the same time they must convince the more politically and socially liberal redeeming rightists that the present social order is sinful and in danger.

Cultural Distinctions

The second model, the cultural continuum, focuses on the diverse stances religious and nonreligious Americans alike take regarding the degree of congruity or incongruity they see between religious presuppositions and the presuppositions that guide the larger culture. These differ from theological distinctions in that they do not measure theological orthodoxy, focusing instead on the level of comfort Americans feel with religious and secular truth claims. I refer to the two poles and the center position on the cultural continuum as pure religionists, pure secularists, and modified religionists. Much of the rhetoric of the contemporary culture war waged by Christian Right advocates identifies the cocombatants as pure religionists versus pure secularists, but such a dualistic approach ignores the realities of the religious demographics in American culture. From a strictly numerical standpoint, the decisive struggle for control of the culture is between pure religionists and modified religionists. Although framing the battle between people of faith and secularists serves the Christian Right well as a rhetorical foil, the relative absence of any significant number of pure secularists in the culture makes the claim highly suspect.

For our purposes, the term *pure religionists* refers to those people who seek to view the world consistently from the perspective of a set of purely religious presuppositions. For these people, religion is not only very important in their lives, but it also has an almost exclusive hold on their orientation to the world. They accept its exclusive claims and seek to operate from a religious perspective in all aspects of their lives. They condemn secular sources of knowledge because secularists deny the existence of ultimate divine authority. Pure religionists do not necessarily retreat from the world; they may have to work and interact with the larger secularized culture. But they are the group that experiences the greatest incongruity and cognitive dissonance when they do act in the secularized sphere. People in this group tend to be the most distrustful of the public school system and are the most receptive to Christian Right rhetoric about public education. The Christian Right draws its strongest support from this segment of the American public, which fact gives further support to the claim that the Christian Right as a movement must be understood in terms of religious categories and modes of interpretation.

On the other end of the continuum from the pure religionists, we find the pure secularists. They are similar to the pure religionists in that they tend to view the world consistently and exclusively from a single set of presuppositions, but they differ in giving no weight to religious beliefs and practices. Pure secularists seek to exclude religious means of gaining knowledge from their personal and social lives. Given the relative absence of pure religionist influences in the larger culture, they experience little incongruity with the secularized culture in this regard. They maintain comfort in the larger culture by seeking to ostracize religious activities and influences from it; they are fearful of pure religionists' attempts to seek legitimacy in the public arena. By this definition, pure secularists comprise no more than 9 percent of the adult American population and more likely closer to 7 percent.[49] Thus, though they are a convenient target for the Christian Right, their numerical strength is rather small.

In between these two more cognitively unified stances lies a vast middle group that combines elements of religious and secular perspectives. These modified religionists assign significance to religious beliefs and practices at the deepest level of their own being but, at the same time, operate comfortably in nonreligious or secular areas of life. Modified religionists may claim that religion is very important or only somewhat important to them. If it is very important, they tend to restrict its importance to their personal lives and perhaps to their moral conduct in the secularized culture. The importance religion has in their lives typically is balanced by other perspectives that are also important to them. People in this group function with multiple provinces of meaning in their lives.[50] They are able to move in and out of various worldview contexts without being overcome by the possible tensions between them or being overwhelmed by the constant movement. They appear to have reached an accommodation among those provinces that enables them to operate in a secularized world while holding on to their religious commitments. The incongruity they may feel between the religious and secularized dimensions of their lives is not enough to provoke them into an affective, cognitive, volitional, or cultural crisis. Because they operate comfortably in multiple provinces of meaning, they tend to be more tolerant of religious and cultural diversity. Although no precise statistics are available on the number of modified religionists within the culture, extrapolation from the available data suggests that this is by far the largest segment of the American population. Because of their numerical strength, modified religionists hold the key to the future success of the Christian Right. If Christian Right pragmatists are able to bring the movement more to the political and religious center, they may find enough support among the modified religionists to achieve their goals. Because of the exclusive worldview perspective of the core constituency of the Christian Right, however, movement pragmatists run the risk of alienating their base among pure religionists by moderating their appeals to attract modified religionists.

Religion does make a difference in the way in which people perceive, orient themselves to, and operate in the larger culture. The statistical evidence suggests that Americans overwhelmingly describe themselves as religious persons but that there is great diversity in terms of the meaning and significance Americans give to their professed religious commitments. The unique characteristics of religious worldviews and the diversity among religious Americans are both significant factors in comprehending Christian Right efforts to transform American culture as well as their prospects for success. By gaining a greater appreciation for and understanding of the religious character of Christian Right criticisms, educators facing such challenges can gain substantial insight into the exact nature of the controversies. A better understanding of religion in general can also enable them to both affirm the significance of religion and identify the religious constituencies within their community from which they might gain support. In both cases, a deeper understanding of the nature of religion and how it operates in orienting people to their world contributes to a better grasp of the complexity of the culture in which we live.

2

Situational Incongruity

With Ronald Reagan's election as president of the United States in 1980, a newly revitalized Christian Right eagerly awaited the arrival of its long-anticipated golden age. Reagan's inaugural theme, "It's morning again in America," fueled their hope. The motif resonated with the culturally conservative Christian longing for a resurrection of American culture. These redeeming right Christians anticipated a transformation that would return the nation to what they perceived as its Christian foundations and would reverse the moral decay that they had long believed had infected the culture. For nearly a century, this faithful remnant of the nation's Puritan forebears had endured marginalization from the cultural and political center of the nation. Now the conservative Christians stood at the very gates of political power awaiting the newly elected president's call for the religious revitalization of the culture. But it never became a reality. Although Reagan clearly advanced the Christian Right agenda in his rhetoric and in his mainstreaming of political leaders into politics,[1] by the end of his second term Christian Right leaders concluded that their social agenda would not be accomplished. Their hopes gradually turned to frustration as the redeeming right's social agenda gradually receded to the back burner of Republican politics. The redeemed America envisioned by culturally conservative Christians seemed as far as ever from being realized.

In spite of the Republican failure to aggressively push the Christian Right social agenda, the Reagan administration aggressively continued to court the biblical Christian vote. Tim LaHaye, the head of the California Moral Majority, accepted the 1984 Reagan-Bush reelection committee's invitation to become a liaison between the administration and the large pool of potential conservative evangelical voters.[2] LaHaye's selection was not by accident. He was well known to the southern California conservatives who had promoted Reagan's presidential ambitions. He was one of the founders of the Moral Majority and immediately upon its founding became head of the California chapter. LaHaye had developed a respected reputation as a fundamentalist marriage-and-family counselor, but he was propelled into the national spotlight within the Christian Right through the publication of an immensely popular series of books that identified secular humanism as the cause of America's cultural and moral decline. Beginning with *The Battle for the Mind* (1980), LaHaye detailed the way that the secular humanist worldview had infected American culture, posing the most significant challenge to the God-centered worldview of biblical Christians. Along with two companion volumes, *The Battle for the Family* (1982) and *The Battle for the Public Schools* (1983), LaHaye showed how a secular humanist conspiracy had gained control of the nation's social institutions, the most important of which was the public schools. LaHaye's books provided the explanation biblical Christians sought for legitimating their growing discomfort with America's schools. At the same time, his books sounded the alarm for others who had not yet reached the same degree of discomfort. By the time LaHaye accepted the position of liaison in the Reagan-Bush reelection campaign, he had already become the American most responsible for popularizing the secular humanist conspiracy theory among grassroots religious conservatives.

In a twist of irony, at exactly the time when LaHaye was actively working for the transformation of the culture within the Reagan camp, career professionals in Reagan's Department of Education were developing a strategy for launching the most massive educational reform effort in decades. The reforms were clearly grounded in liberal assumptions about the nature and function of the public schools, the moral and intellectual development of children, and the role of the government in defining national and state educational policy. That reform effort was undertaken in the guise of educational restructuring in the late 1980s; in many cases, it took the form of Outcome-Based Education (OBE). Thanks to LaHaye's work and the critique of conservative Christians such as Gary Bauer, who was assigned to the Department of Education, Christian Right critics immediately identified these reforms as clear and compelling evidence of the conspiracy by secular humanists to take control of the schools in order to indoctrinate Christian children and turn them against their parents' values.

For a number of reasons, Christian Right hopes for a resurrected America began to fade during the last four years of the Reagan presidency. The movement's lukewarm support for George Bush in 1988 indicated that its constituents no longer trusted national political leaders with the Christian Right agenda. They concluded that political power alone would not accomplish their goal of a transformed America. As they shifted their focus to the grassroots level, the leaders knew that they had to convince a substantial number of Americans that their vision for America was the right one. In responding to that challenge with respect to public education, the movement's leadership needed to accomplish two goals. They had to express their agenda in such a way that it connected to the deep symbols and mythos of both biblical Christians and social conservatives. They also had to convince people that America's schools were in crisis and in need of transformation.

The Sacred Canopy

The biggest problem the Christian Right faced in securing a resurrected America was that most Americans did not share its vision of reality. The difficulties the movement encountered in attempting to overcome this problem are complex and multifaceted. Perhaps the most obvious hurdle was that the general population seemed to be comfortably located within a set of worldview assumptions that stood in stark contrast to the Christian Right at important points. Equally obvious to those within the movement was the challenge of politicizing the substantial number of religiously conservative Americans who shared many religious assumptions with the Christian Right but who remained outside the political arena. The final obstacle the movement faced in accomplishing its goal was probably the most problematic. As Christian Right leaders gained the attention of increasing numbers of Americans, they had to convince them that the movement's description of the current state of the culture was accurate and that their analysis of the causes of and solutions for the present situation was both practical and sensible.

From a theoretical perspective, the difficulty the Christian Right faced relates to the complex nature of what Peter Berger calls "sacred canopies."[3] A sacred canopy, according to Berger, provides believers with a protective shield that shelters them from the chaos of life stripped of any order, meaning, and significance. Under the canopy, adherents deal with the problems of daily life in such a way that they can transcend their immediate situation and locate the problems they face within ultimate structures of reality. In order to be successful, religious canopies must present to the faithful a view of reality that is both practical and sensible. It must be practical to the degree that believers can actually function in the world and satisfy their basic needs. It must also be sensible enough to provide people with confidence that the world that appears to them is relatively consistent with the world they believe really exists. No religion would survive if it lacked either the practicality or the sensibility to allow its followers to exist in relative comfort within the world. Well-constructed canopies permit the people protected by them to pay little or no attention to the deepest questions of existence in the course of their normal lives. Under such canopies, we take the world for granted because it more or less works for us, it makes sense to us, and we have the sense of security that comes from knowing that the world really does exist the way we think it does. In situations of relative calm, most people seldom take notice of the canopy or concern themselves with the precise nature of its construction. We simply function under the canopy, assuming that it is strong enough to protect us from any threats of chaos existing just outside its cover.

As products of human understanding, canopies are fragile. Their fragility derives from two sources. At one level, the incompatibility of the ideas woven into the canopy itself may eventually surface in times of crisis. At another level, the canopy's moorings may gradually weaken when the deeper presuppositions about the nature of the things are no longer sufficient to account for present realities. Well-constructed canopies can withstand enormous pressures from the realities of life. But even the best-constructed canopies are not perfect. There is always the possibility that the inherent flaws of the protective shield may become exposed and weaken the entire structure. Most commonly, this occurs when the incongruity between the world as experienced and the world as perceived becomes so great that it can no longer be accounted for. Crisis occurs when, because of increasing external threats, the shield cannot be extended fast enough or the inconsistencies cannot be reconciled. When events reach this point, the old paradigms no longer hold.

The greatest moments of human history arise in precisely these situations. One of the most important of these events for the current controversies in education can be traced back to the discoveries of Galileo and Copernicus, when the beginnings of the scientific revolution overthrew the existing dominant worldview of Western culture. For the Christian Right, an equally significant event occurred in the Protestant Reformation from the fifteenth through the seventeenth century. During this time, a newly configured religious worldview sought to reestablish its legitimate place at the center of Western civilization. These responses, constructing a new worldview or reconfiguring an existing one, are two of the options open to people threatened by the collapse of their canopy.

In the face of contemporary cultural crises such as that confronting education, some people simply deny the existence of the threats or consign them to the realms of evil or ignorance and dismiss them. Such responses leave the believers in a particularly vulnerable situation as the new realities continue to bombard their weakened canopies. Other people race from one canopy to another, seeking a new solution to the crisis from outside the old system. If they find a new system that seems to have practical and sensible answers to the new realities, the new believers may be unaware of the flaws existing in the new canopy. Either the new believers deem these flaws acceptable or the conditions do not presently exist that will make those weaknesses apparent. In the third option, people remain under the old canopy but modify it so that the new realities are sufficiently integrated. Here a necessary adjustment of the canopy occurs that acknowledges the significance of those events and alters the canopy's basic presuppositions. In all three responses to the collapse of the sacred canopy, the problem religious people face is identical. It is the need to rectify the present situation by bringing religious resources to bear.[4]

In their studies of such crisis situations within a variety of cultures, Clifford Geertz and Jonathan Z. Smith note that rectification typically does not occur by helping people avoid the absurdity, pain, and injustice that arise when the incongruity becomes too great for them. It begins by helping them transcend the immediacy of their present situation in order to search for answers at the deepest and most profound levels of reality. It succeeds when people in crisis situations are able to find a way of life that brings their lives into conformity with reality at its deepest level. It succeeds on a social level when groups are able to transform the society in such a way that the tension between the way they choose to live their lives and the external realities is significantly reduced. This occurs most completely when the newly defined culture integrates all the dimensions of the culture under the new canopy. At this level, religion as expressed through the sacred canopy functions to bring coherence to our lives at all levels of religious apprehension: the emotional, the cognitive, the volitional, and the cultural levels. Such solutions cannot be equated with solving the problem. Rather, the solutions emerge when traditional patterns and categories are redefined under the new canopy and are found to be adequate to the present situation.[5]

Put in the context of this theoretical structure, the problem the Christian Right faces is the need to manage and create enough situational incongruity that the basis of the existing resistance to its efforts begins to crumble. This conclusion supports the theoretical insights of Lewis Coser, David Aberle, and Kenelm Burridge that social movements create meaning and identity out of crisis.[6] In terms of Christian Right outreach to apolitical conservative Christians, this means convincing these Christians that their religious worldview demands that they take an interest in transforming American culture. That task is more difficult with some potential constituencies than with others. Some conservative pietistic evangelicals, for example, tend to believe that participation in the political process necessarily forces them to compromise with corruption in the world. Their faith remains steadfastly oriented toward personal salvation both for themselves and for others. The idea of cultural or social salvation contradicts their exclusive emphasis on the individual character of the Christian life. In similar fashion, premillennial fundamentalists who hold that the end of the world is near believe that no purpose is served by trying to transform a nation so close to its apocalyptic end.

With respect to other Americans who see some degree of comfort in the Christian Right canopy, the task is to modify the canopy so that others will be welcome under it without feeling that they have had to compromise their religious or political convictions. When the target group is political conservatives, this means rounding off the sharp edges of explicitly religious rhetoric. The movement's vanguard has seemingly accomplished this task by employing a great deal of rhetorical sophistication and symbolic manipulation. The harsh religious edge of the Moral Majority has given way to the language of family, tradition, freedom of choice, parents' rights, and, in a continued affirmation of the movement's religious character, Judeo-Christian values. By reframing its agenda within the idioms of classical liberalism and cherished mainstream American values, the Christian Right has been able to find common cause with political conservatives even though the sources of authority to which the two groups point and their ultimate visions for the nation might otherwise be quite incompatible.

In the effort to bring religious conservatives into its camp, the Christian Right has adopted a strategy of extending the canopy of evangelical Protestantism into the political realm. To accomplish that, strategists have reshaped religious symbols to bridge the gap between mainstream Protestant Christianity and the movement's own particular brand of political theology. This is a delicate task. Christian Right leaders must construct the bridge without raising theological suspicions among very diverse groups of American Protestants. To some degree, the religious diversity of the movement's leadership facilitates this transition even while the leadership moves further out of the camp of mainstream evangelical Protestantism and into the camp of a particularly narrow strain of orthodox Calvinism. They have adopted two methods in the attempt to draw mainstream Protestants toward the Christian Right. They have constructed a master narrative, the great American monomyth,[7] and they have exploited a historical tendency within Christianity toward dualism.

The great American monomyth refers to Christian Right efforts to reconstruct American history so that the only positive prominent voice that is permitted to speak is the conservative Christian voice. Perhaps the purest representation of this phenomenon is David Barton and his organization, Wallbuilders. Using a number of media, Barton has led the charge for popularizing the notion that all the great forces leading to the founding of the American nation were Christian. At the Christian Coalition's 1994 Road to Victory Conference, for example, Barton described William Penn's Pennsylvania Constitution as resting on two principles: "Principle number one: Whatever is Christian is legal. Principle number two: Whatever is not Christian is illegal."[8] Although not as widely cited as Barton, Rus Walton of the Plymouth Rock Foundation provided similar resources for the monomythic narrative of the Christian Right. Speaking of the nation's roots, Walton declared, "The American system is the political expression of Christian ideas."[9] The purpose of these arguments is to show evangelical Christians that involvement in the political arena is fully consistent both with the Christian faith and with the responsibility of being an American citizen. In this regard, Walton has gone so far as to call the American constitution "divinely inspired."[10] For reasons that should be obvious, such depictions of the American nation and the privileged role of Christianity in it become problematic when carried outside conservative Christian circles. Within those circles, however, the American monomyth plays an important role in extending the canopy to other Christians.

Closely related to the great American monomyth is the tendency among Christian Right writers to utilize the drift toward dualistic thinking that has long been a part of Christian thought. Although closely related to a heresy within Christian tradition called Manichaeanism, dualism serves the movement well in establishing a locus for the incongruity many conservative Christians feel with contemporary American society. Movement writers express this by reducing all human perspectives to two worldviews: the Christian or God-centered worldview emphasizes the sovereignty of God, divine revelation, and the sinfulness of humanity. The secular or human-centered worldview emphasizes the sovereignty of human reason, human folly, and human pride. Since only two options exist in this scheme, all religious and secular perspectives that differ significantly from the Christian Right's worldview on one or more of these points are categorized as human-centered. The most frequently mentioned expression of the human-centered perspective is secular humanism. This brings us back to Tim LaHaye.

LaHaye and most other leaders within the Christian Right believe that America has fallen victim to the forces of a secular humanist conspiracy. In *The Battle for the Mind,* LaHaye defines secular humanism as "man's attempt to solve his problems independently of God." He attributes the moral decline in America during the last half century to humanism. Humanism, he claims, "has moved our country from a biblically based society to an amoral 'democratic' society."[11] Many Christian Right leaders associate democracy with humanism, thereby contrasting it with God's law, which is not subject to human whim or bias. Again for obvious reasons, proponents play down the antidemocratic dimension of the Christian Right canopy considerably in rhetoric directed to non-Christian audiences.

Movement writers most often associate the distant roots of the present secularist conspiracy with Renaissance humanism or the Enlightenment. Some authors, such as Francis Schaeffer, trace it as far back as the ancient Greeks. Within education, accounts of the conspiracy often begin with Horace Mann and the common-school movement. Although Mann was a religious conservative by faith profession, Christian Right educational historians revile him for his Unitarianism as well as for his efforts to make the religious foundation of the common schools more generic and less sectarian Protestant.[12] They also criticize Mann for bringing government into education, thereby undermining the Christian foundation of the home. As much as they condemn Mann, however, the Christian Right reserves the full force of its criticism for John Dewey and the progressive movement within education.[13] Dewey's association with the formal secular humanist movement in America sufficiently proves his intention, as well the intentions of all subsequent progressive educators, to undermine the Christian faith of America's school children. Having gained entrance to the schools, secular humanists go about stripping the schools of all remaining vestiges of biblical religion in order to have the freedom to fully indoctrinate public school students with secular humanist philosophy.

Although arguments about a secular humanist conspiracy resonate well within conservative Christian circles, they do not play particularly well to larger American audiences. Thus, if Christian Right discomfort with public education is to gain any credibility beyond its own religious constituencies, movement leaders know they have to appropriate a different set of symbols to gain trust among the general population. The Christian Right is well positioned to meet that challenge. Movement ability to transform public education received an important boost in 1983 when the National Commission on Excellence in Education published its report. Entitled *A Nation at Risk,* the document depicted a dramatic decline in the effectiveness of public education. The report and the wide publicity it received from secular and religious conservative voices fueled public dissatisfaction with public education. Whether or not the commission's findings were valid,[14] the report spawned a veritable avalanche of conservative attacks on public education in general and the educational establishment in particular. One important player in advancing the criticism was Robert Simonds. Simonds had gained a minor reputation among southern California Christian Right leaders for his denunciation of public education and the teachers' unions. He served on the National Forum to Implement the National Commission on Excellence in Education Report. His Citizens for Excellence in Education, formed in 1984, took its name from the commission and its work. As the decade progressed, the conservative criticism of the failure of the public schools from leaders like Simonds gradually produced a change in the attitude of the general populace toward America's system of public education.

When *A Nation at Risk* boosted the Christian Right cause against public education, movement strategists were ready to take advantage of the opportunity. During the 1970s, Francis Schaeffer had promulgated his presuppositional strategy in conservative evangelical circles to advance the prolife movement. Christian Right strategists appropriated Schaeffer's conversional methods for their cause and directed it toward the general public. In brief, presuppositionalism as popularized by Francis Schaeffer forced nonbelievers to a point of cognitive crisis by increasing their perception of incongruity between the world they believed existed and the world they experienced. The success the Christian Right achieved in joining this strategy with the burgeoning conservative criticism of public education during the 1980s was remarkable. Even though most Americans continued to rate their own public schools quite highly, not having experienced any public school crisis with their own children, they gradually accepted conservative and Christian Right arguments about the poor condition of American education. By the early 1990s, the Christian Right was able to bring the crisis home to local school districts by linking little-understood educational reforms mandated by state and federal education establishments with public anxieties about New Age religion and, to a lesser degree, Satanism.

Incongruity, Public Education, and the Christian Right

Perhaps the best way to understand the perspective of the Christian Right is to listen as its leaders express the incongruity between their faith stance and America's system of public education. Pat Robertson and James Dobson are essential for the discussion because of their overall importance in the movement. Robert Simonds is included because of his importance in educational controversies specifically. Although Robertson has received much more attention in the literature than Dobson and Simonds, Dobson is more influential within conservative Christian circles than Robertson. Simonds has had the most direct impact on provoking crises in local school districts. These are not the only voices, but they are the most important for framing the context of controversies related to the Christian Right and public education.

Pat Robertson and the Christian Coalition

Pat Robertson's assessment of contemporary public education contains many of the most common themes of the Christian Right. Robertson pictures the schools in a state of decline, and he frames that decline within the context of the American monomyth. According to Robertson, America was conceived as a Christian nation, dedicated in its origins to God. At the time of its founding, the nation was governed by the Bible. The founders' belief in moral righteousness and the righteousness of their cause gave early Americans a sense of an exalted status. During the past two hundred years, the nation has fallen from this high place. The slide from God's grace began when the people turned away from God, thereby tearing apart the protective hedge with which God had surrounded

America. Several signs of America's fall from righteousness include the legalization of abortion, the spread of pornography, the expulsion of religion from the schools, and the persecution of people of faith.[15]

Robertson continues this theme of America's fallen condition in comments related to the rash of shootings that occurred in America's schools in recent years. In commenting about an incident in 1998, Robertson opines that the increased violence and loss of discipline in schools can be traced directly to the removal of the Ten Commandments from the schools. Lacking exposure to those moral rules, America's school children no longer have anything to restrain them from violence and destructive behavior. The longer the Commandments are kept out of the schools, the more good kids will turn bad.[16]

Robertson's *700 Club* news broadcasts often feature horror stories about the present condition of America's schools. One story on the home school movement features Michael Farris, president of the National Center for Home Education, and characterizes the schools as antifamily, antiparent, and anti-Christian. Farris cites as evidence Outcome-Based Education, sex education, condom assemblies, and substandard education.[17] Another story features Pete DuPont, policy chairman for the National Center for Policy Analysis, describing public school curricula as guided by political correctness rather than scholarship. "Forget the Three R's: today's classrooms are based on touchy-feely reforms like 'cooperative learning,' 'invented spelling,' and 'whole math,' where the emphasis is on shaping behavior and attitudes, not aptitude."[18]

The more immediate cause of such behavior might be the absence of biblical religion, but Robertson describes the deeper source of the failure of America's public schools in conspiratorial language.[19] In his many books and on his *700 Club* television program, Robertson often calls attention to the threat secular humanism poses to contemporary America. He also continues to link the nation's political and economic oligarchy to a medieval conspiracy known as the Illuminati, relating its rise in power to biblical prophecy.[20]

Robertson's involvement in educational issues began to receive public attention in the mid-1980s. His 1988 presidential campaign educational plank focused on a phonics literacy campaign for the public schools. Christian Right advocates prefer phonics over whole language because its approach to language is more consistent with biblical literalism and absolute standards of right and wrong.[21] Robertson also criticized teachers. In his secular humanist conspiratorial framework, Robertson viewed teachers as, at best, unsuspecting dupes of a secular humanist elite that controlled the public schools. In the worst cases, he occasionally intimated that teachers were coconspirators. For example, in 1984 Robertson announced on his daily *700 Club* television program:

> The teachers who are teaching your children are not necessarily nice, wonderful servants of the community. They are activists supporting . . . one set of values and a number of the values which they espouse are: affirmative action, ERA, gun control legislation, sex education, illegal teacher's strikes, nuclear freeze, federal funding for abortions, decriminalization of marijuana, etc.[22]

Robertson has compared the educational system of this country to that of Nazi Germany and the Soviet Union. He argues that, like Nazi Germany and the Soviet Union, the American government is stealing the children from their parents and indoctrinating them with "a philosophy that is amoral, anti-Christian and humanistic." The children will end up with a "collectivist philosophy that will ultimately lead toward Marxism, socialism and [a] communistic type of ideology."[23]

Robertson used the creation of the Christian Coalition (CC) in 1989 to shift his political focus from the national to the local level.[24] Coalition executive director Ralph Reed explained the strategy shift: "I honestly believe that in my lifetime we will see a country once again governed by Christians . . . and Christian values. What Christians have got to do is take back this country, one precinct at a time, one neighborhood at a time, and one state at a time."[25] This change in orientation became characteristic of the new leadership in the Christian Right that emerged at about the same time. Beginning with the 1990 San Diego school board elections, Robertson's strategy and that of the Christian Coalition became clear—quietly generate a large voter turnout among their constituency without attracting the attention of their opponents. On the so-called stealth strategy, Reed commented, "That's just good strategy. It's like guerrilla warfare. If you reveal your location, all it does is allow your opponent to improve his artillery bearing. It's better to move quietly, with stealth, under the cover of night."[26]

The strategy worked: voters elected a significant number of conservative Christians, some of them virtually unknown outside their religious circles, to office in San Diego county. There was a firestorm of protest from Coalition opponents who viewed secretive campaigns for public office as a subversion of the democratic process. Once in power at the school board level, the newly elected Christian Right candidates introduced measures to integrate creationism in science curricula, replace sex education with "abstinence-only" programs, and remove educational reforms supported by the national educational bureaucracy. The long-term weakness of the strategy became evident when citizens in San Diego and other "stealth" communities used democratic processes of elections and recall to remove many of the Christian Right school board members from office. It soon became clear to Reed and Robertson that they needed to find a new long-term solution to the crisis in education.

After the election of George Bush to the presidency in 1992, Reed concluded, "This stealth thing is bad for the movement. It isn't the future. It's the past."[27] The game plan developed by the Christian Right strategists, including Robertson and Reed, was, in reality, a revised stealth strategy. Instead of hiding candidates, they trained candidates to hide the movement's agenda. Reed and Robertson were particularly well suited to the task. In his book *Politically Incorrect* and through his public pronouncements, Reed framed the Coalition's agenda in the mainstream language of classical liberalism.[28] Following the advice of the Heritage Foundation, Reed moderated Robertson's rhetoric to appeal to common sense values rather than religious mandates and theological absolutes. Reed's ability to redefine issues in terms of mainstream values can be seen in his treatment of the topic of parents' rights. Almost all Americans would grant the legitimacy of the right of parents to influence the education and religious values of their children; yet, the Christian Right uses this common sense notion to obscure the deep contextual differences that ground Christian Right understandings of that notion. By employing a phrase like *parental rights,* the Christian Right reframed the legitimate concerns of all parents for their children in terms of the symbols of the movement's worldview. This had the advantage of allowing the Christian Right to appear to support mainstream values when they were pursuing another agenda. Left undiscussed in such encounters were the theological and political presuppositions upon which Christian Right efforts were based and to whose ends its activities were directed.

In 1993, Reed and the Coalition exhibited the revised strategy in their efforts to gain control of a number of local school boards in New York City. Though the efforts proved only moderately successful, the campaign demonstrated the ability of the Coalition to work within a broad-based and religiously and ethnically diverse coalition. Meanwhile, Robertson continued his conspiracy-based attacks on contemporary American society and public education in his publications and on his *700 Club* television program. Reed spoke to the external audience in rhetoric that might gain sympathy among those outside the movement while Robertson continued to court the religiously conservative constituency inside the movement in much more explicitly religious language and frameworks.[29]

Reed's efforts to put a moderate spin on Robertson's harshest pronouncements eventually provoked negative responses from other leaders within the Christian Right. In particular, James Dobson, Gary Bauer, and Bay Buchanan all accused Reed of compromising on key moral issues in order to increase his own political power as well as that of Robertson and the Coalition. These denunciations indicated a growing rift within the Christian Right between the politically oriented pragmatists such as Reed and the theologically oriented ideologues such as Dobson and Bauer.[30] By the time Reed left the Christian Coalition in 1997, the organization claimed a following of nearly 2 million members and supporters, although the financial condition of the CC suggested far less firmness. In late 1997, the Coalition laid off a number of staffers, ceased publication of its flagship magazine *The Christian American,* and withdrew its financial support from the Samaritan Project. The Samaritan Project was designed to build bridges between the Coalition and racial and ethnic minorities.[31]

The organization's new leadership team of former Reagan cabinet member Don Hodel as CC president and ex–Washington state congressman Randy Tate as executive director pledged to "link the Reagan revolution with the rising influence of active people of faith."[32] Statements by Randy Tate that the Coalition will return to an emphasis on social issues seem to indicate that the CC is ready to shift away from moderation in order to reclaim its influence within the Christian Right. Tate's background as an activist in opposing gays and lesbians, in supporting school prayer, and for making all abortions illegal gives further support to this observation. The shift was not evident in 1998 in Coalition press releases and position papers on public education. The issues they supported most strongly in 1998 reflected the more moderate language of contemporary conservatism—school vouchers, parental choice, charter schools, free religious expression by students and teachers in schools, school prayer, and opposition to sex education. Meanwhile, Christian Coalition Road to Victory Conferences were still filled with the religiously grounded rhetoric of the Christian Right. Where the future lies for the Christian Coalition is uncertain. But it is clear that the organization has lost some of its status as the preeminent leader of the Christian Right.[33] Its future may be determined by activities of the myriad of state and local chapters, many of which are far less reserved than the national organization in explicitly displaying a much purer Christian Right agenda.

James Dobson and Focus on the Family

If Ralph Reed and the Christian Coalition pioneered the stealth strategy, Focus on the Family's James Dobson raised it to an art form. Dobson is arguably the single most powerful figure within the Christian Right. In a 1989 survey of Protestant denominational clerics, only Billy Graham ranked higher among influential conservative leaders.[34] Howard Phillips, chair of the Conservative Caucus, notes, "Of the people out there working, Dr. Dobson probably has the largest following, budget, and staff."[35] Through his Colorado Springs–based organization Focus on the Family (FoF), Dobson controls a vast media empire with more than fifty forms of communication including magazines, radio programs, videotapes, movies, and summer camps.

Dobson's *Focus on the Family* magazine has a wider circulation than *Parents* magazine. His first parenting book, *Dare to Discipline,* which advocates corporal punishment of children, sold about 1.4 million copies. More than 60 million watched his first privately distributed film. Dobson's following is at least two and one-half times as large as that of the Christian Coalition, and the annual contributions to Dobson and his closely related lobbying and policy formation organization, the Family Research Council, are estimated to be five times those of the Coalition.[36] In 1998, his daily thirty-minute radio program, *Focus on the Family*, was heard on nearly twenty-nine hundred stations in North America and broadcast in seven languages on approximately thirteen hundred facilities in more than seventy countries outside of North America.[37] In 1996, *Time* magazine included him in its semifinal list of the twenty-five most influential people in the nation. In the same year, *Newsweek* magazine listed him among the five most listened-to radio personalities in the nation. Dobson was the only Christian Right voice on that list.[38] Yet, even with this preeminent status, Dobson was virtually unknown outside biblical Christian circles until his 1998 attack on the leadership of the Republican Party. This was no less true of scholars than the media.[39] Almost all recent academic treatments of the Christian Right give far more attention to Robertson and the Christian Coalition than to Dobson and his organizations.

Dobson's relative obscurity is not by accident. He has intentionally stayed "below the radar," reportedly even joking about his anonymity with his associates.[40] Nevertheless, in the twenty-plus years of Focus on the Family's existence, James Dobson has gradually politicized his followers and brought them into the ranks of the Christian Right. Until the mid-1990s, many conservative Christians could continue to feel comfortable with Dobson's family and child-rearing advice without having to identify with his political and social agenda. However, by the end of the decade, he has become far more open and insistent about his larger agenda, and the clear distinction between his role as Christian psychologist and his role as Christian Right leader has almost completely disappeared.

Describing Dobson's tactics as a stealth strategy is not to suggest that he has remained silent or even moderate on social issues. It merely means that he has cultivated a relationship with his followers and avoided building any relationships with the American mainstream. Dobson's pronouncements on the current condition of American culture have never been restrained. In 1990, two years before Pat Buchanan's "Civil War" speech at the Republican National Convention, Dobson and Gary Bauer, his associate at the Family Research Council, used the same uncompromising military language in their *Children at Risk: The Battle for the Hearts and Minds of Our Kids,* a jeremiad against American public education. Echoing La-Haye's theme of a secular humanist conspiracy, *Children at Risk* describes the present situation in terms of a battle between Bible-believing Christians whose culture has been torn from them and secular humanists who have risen to positions of dominance and control in every institution of our society. According to Dobson and Bauer, "Nothing short of a great Civil War of Values rages today throughout North America. Two sides with vastly differing and incompatible worldviews are locked in a bitter conflict that permeates every level of society."[41] The combatants are clearly defined, with biblical Christians on the side of righteousness in defense of the nation's founders and secular humanists, who have stolen the culture from Christians, on the other side. The "struggle now is for the hearts and minds of the people. It is a war over *ideas.*"[42] Later in the book, the authors make clear the exact nature of the attack:

The campaign to isolate children from their parents and to indoctrinate them with humanistic ideas is being waged primarily in the public schools, as I have indicated. I must emphasize, however, that the Judeo-Christian system of values is still very evident in many educational districts. That is what makes for bloody conflict.[43]

Dobson's analysis of the present situation in public education leads him to the conclusion that though many districts valiantly strive to protect the Judeo-Christian ethos in the face of enormous pressure to change, others are part of the humanist conspiracy to isolate children from their parents.[44] In this scenario, teachers become powerless victims of the humanist conspiracy or unsuspecting pawns in the battle. To illustrate the point, Dobson claims in a 1994 letter to FoF supporters that the demise of the public schools is not the fault of most of the teachers—who are dedicated and underappreciated. "They are not the source of the problem. It is their leftist *unions,* the misguided academics, and the intrusion of the federal government that we vigorously oppose."[45] In a more recent article, Dobson echoes his sentiments about teachers and more directly links what they are asked to teach to a secular humanist conspiracy. In an article critical of math and science scores on standardized tests, Dobson writes, "My purpose here, therefore, is not to bash the teaching profession, but to look past the local scene to focus on the broader picture." What does the broader picture show us? First, "Traditional curricula (English, math, science, reading and writing) has been replaced by politically correct ideology and untested revolutionary ideas. Of equal concern to academic issues is the homosexual and lesbian agenda that is being promoted in many schools." Second, "A powerful educational monopoly has gained control of today's schools and is shaping them to fit its liberal, self-serving agenda."[46] He urges public school teachers seeking protection from the conspiracy to quit their present teachers' union and join the Association of American Educators, which "now speak[s] on behalf of teachers who believe in traditional values and the family."[47]

To assist Christian teachers caught in the cross fire, FoF publishes the *Teachers in Focus* magazine, directed toward public school teachers. Its articles often advise Christian teachers on how to survive in the public school either by surreptitiously infusing explicitly Christian materials into their instruction or by undermining the "secular" basis of the curricula they are given to teach. For example, in the October 1998 issue, Francis Beckwith, a popular Christian Right critic of the public schools, gives the following advice to teachers who have religious objections to content and materials they are expected to use in their classrooms. "Take steps to minimize any bias as you teach your material. This may involve modifying classroom activities, changing homework assignments, passing out supplementary readings, presenting alternative viewpoints or making other changes." The purpose here is not to achieve balance or fairness. "Secular thinking is so ingrained in our culture that it's often considered neutral. But it's not. And the more you educate yourself, your peers and your students, the easier it will be to break the bonds of secularism in our schools—and in our society."[48]

To further assist teachers and school administrators who wish to use the schools to promote biblical Christian viewpoints, FoF provides a number of movies and videotapes edited for public school use. The aim of the magazine and the videos is to provide resources to teachers who want to defend Judeo-Christian traditional values "both at home and in our educational institutions." According to a Focus newsletter, the defense of these values in both the private and the public arenas is a "primary reason Focus on the Family exists."[49] Dobson also endorses Eric Buehrer's Gateways to Better Education, an organization that helps teachers transform their classrooms into arenas for Christian instruction. In one such promotion, *Focus on the Family* magazine featured a pamphlet titled *A Gift for Teacher*. The pamphlet implies that public school teachers can use their discussions of Christmas as an opportunity to teach religious dogmas to their students. They are further encouraged to use Christmas carols instead of secular songs in their classroom activities. At least one expert on church-state affairs concludes that the booklet, if interpreted and employed broadly, could lead teachers to violate the law.[50]

Dobson seems to suggest religious beliefs and practice should be part of normal classroom activities. In *Children at Risk,* Dobson and Bauer argue that the best solution to problems related to the sexual revolution would be to lead children into a deep and personal relationship with Jesus Christ. Noting that such a solution is inappropriate within the public schools, Dobson and Bauer nevertheless believe the schools can contribute to solving the problem by teaching "the basics of the Judeo-Christian value system which has permeated our society for hundreds of years. Included in this instruction should be the nature of the family, how it was designed to function."[51] This last phrase, "as it was designed to function" indicates that Dobson's views are fully consistent with the grounding presuppositionalism of the Christian Right. This is true both of the presupposition of the nature of the family and of the biblical principles upon which social institutions are intended to rest. Furthermore, in his efforts to promote school prayer, Dobson argues that there is nothing wrong with requiring students to profess belief in an "unnamed God." Should any non-Christians object, they should be removed from the classroom or protected in some other way. "The Supreme Court decision banning non-specific school prayer (or even silent prayer)," he writes, "is an extreme measure, and I regret it. The tiny minority of children from atheistic homes could easily be protected by the school during prayerful moments."[52]

Beyond the rather cavalier assumption that anyone who might object to school-sponsored and -directed prayer is necessarily an atheist, Dobson ignores the problems that his solution might create for the public schools. These difficulties are discussed by Justice Robert Jackson in the 1948 *McCollum v. Board of Education* Supreme Court decision and reiterated by Justice Anthony Kennedy in the 1988 *Mozert v. Hawkins County Board of Education* case. Jackson noted that if "everything objectionable" to any particular religious group is removed from public schools, "we will leave public education in shreds."[53] In order to protect parents' rights without reducing the public school curricula to "shreds," one California Superior Court judge ruled in *McKamey v. Mt. Diablo Unified School District* (1983) that although parents may withdraw their children from objectionable curricula, they do not have the right to impose their religious objections on the curriculum as a whole. In his ruling, Judge David A. Dolgin held that parents have the right to bar their own children from reading objectionable passages, but parents cannot exercise the same right on behalf of all students.[54]

In sum, Dobson describes the public schools as the arena where the most crucial battle between biblical Christians and secular humanists must be fought. His analysis of almost every educational issue from sex education to reading curricula highlights the danger to our children that the liberal secular "educrats" pose as long as they are in control of the public schools. The solution he proposes does not extend to the promotion of particular religious beliefs or doctrines in the public schools. Rather, he seeks to bring public school pedagogy and instruction into conformity with the biblical Christian worldview. From his writings, we can conclude that he apparently sees no problem with excluding any curricular activity or pedagogy that contradicts or stands in tension with the particular religious doctrine or dogma that the child's parents hold.[55] This is precisely the same solution for public education advocated by Robert Simonds.

Robert Simonds and Citizens for Excellence in Education

During the first half of the 1990s, Robert Simonds, through his organization, the National Association of Christian Educators/Citizens for Excellence in Education (NACE/CEE), was the single most influential Christian Right activist speaking exclusively to educational issues.[56] Like
Robertson's and Dobson's, Simonds's assessment of the present condition
of public education led him back to the dangers of secular humanism. Put
simply, his belief was that the public schools were controlled by a secular
humanist ideology, which was hostile and stood in complete opposition to
Christian values. In the introduction to NACE's 1983 edition of *Communicating a Christian World View in the Classroom,* Simonds wrote:

> There is a great war being waged in America. . . . This is a battle for the
> heart, mind, and even the very soul of every man, women, and especially
> every child in America . . . it is America's Last Great War. . . . The combatants
> are "secular humanism" and "Christianity.". . . . The Christian is the key to
> God's victory over Satan and the atheism of secular humanism. We can
> change our world in this generation! Our job is to evangelize, while time
> remains. Our schools are the battleground.[57]

Unlike Robertson and Dobson, Simonds was not hesitant to call Christians to use the schools for conversion. In fact, while Simonds taught at
Orange Coast Community College, he used his classroom to develop and
promote what he calls Impact Evangelism. In a speech at Calvary Chapel,
San Jose, California, Simonds explained his method:

> I have often been accused of being a little too radical in education and that
> I want to preach Christ to the public schools and you're not supposed to do
> that. You're breaking the law when you do that. I said, "Am I?" I don't break
> the law, I just put a nice overhead like the one up here on a 12 by 12 screen
> with a Scripture. I explain to everybody what it means. Of course I do that.
> And I tell them how Jesus dies for their sins and if they accept Him, He will
> save them. And heaven and hell and all those things. I tell them all about
> that, but it's not big deal.[58]

Demonstrating his attitude toward pluralism and the religious neutrality of
public educational institutions, Simonds continued by saying that inevitably "the little Jewish girl or somebody who is against Christianity or
a Hare Khrisna [*sic*] would object." Roy Grimm, who wrote a dissertation
on Simonds's Impact Evangelism, describes Simonds's response:

Simonds would then encourage the student to file an objection with the college president. The college president would then find some way to minimize the controversy. Simonds would continue to encourage the student to press charges against him in court. Consequently, he faced two trials for "preaching in class" and a third for his sponsorship of a student group which distributed Bibles on campus. He claims to have won all three.[59]

Grimm then quotes Simonds as saying, "And, as a teacher, trials are the most precious thing that can happen to you because you have a total forum in a trial for preaching Christ, and God always vindicates you."[60]

Simonds resigned his position at Orange Coast in 1984 after receiving a series of "calls" to dedicate his full time to forming his two closely related organizations, NACE and CEE. The purpose of NACE seemed to be to provide Christian teachers in the public schools with an alternative professional organization and resources to combat secular humanism. It appears not to be well developed or very active. CEE was geared more toward community activism than teachers. Its goal was to develop strategies and resources for changing the public schools into an environment consistent with biblical principles. In school board battles during the early to middle 1990s, CEE was a major strategic resource. The organization also produced a number of publications designed to help local activists identify and understand the precise way in which secular humanism was being promoted in their local districts.

In his efforts to transform America's public schools, Simonds promoted Community Impact Evangelism (CIE) to help committed conservative Christians turn their local public schools into "Christian World View Perspective" schools.

> Minimally, such a Christian World View in public schooling would serve to (a) replace the putative anti-Christian bias with an attitude of respect for religion in general, the significance of Christianity in American and world history, a recognition, if not celebration of Christian holidays, and moments of silence, if not school prayer; (b) replace the teaching of only evolutionary theory with a dual model regarding human origins: evolution and "Scientific Creationism;" (c) replace moral relativism with the transmission of "traditional American values" and a clear sense of "right and wrong" especially in sex education regarding promiscuity, abortion, and homosexuality; (d) replace student autonomy and self-direction with teacher authority and discipline; (e) replace collectivist internationalism with an affirmation of the free enterprise system and American nationalism.[61]

Simonds claimed that this did not violate church-state separation because it required schools only to bring their curricula and pedagogy into conformity with biblical Christian principles. It did not require them to teach those principles as religious doctrine.

To this end, Simonds announced in 1994 his intention to develop a curricular model based on the Christian World View Perspective for adoption in public schools. The effort would be centered in the National Center for Reconciliation and Reform at the University of Northern Colorado under the direction of Dr. Arnold Burron, professor of education at UNC, and William Spady, the chief promoter of Outcome-Based Education. The center would offer its resources to public school districts to help negotiate the unsettled waters of educational reform.[62] Simonds intended to use the center to promote what he called an "Enhanced Traditional Core Curriculum" or "Enhanced OBE," which would "define clearly what and how history will be taught in our schools. All forms of higher order thinking skills (*real* ones) will be included in the 'enhanced' process of teaching factual, actual American history."[63] At its inception, Simonds convinced the mainstream Association for Supervision and Curriculum Development (ASCD) to endorse the effort. With William Spady's cooperation, ASCD officials met Simonds to launch the project but left responsibility for its implementation in the hands of Simonds. Two years after the announcement, the center had attracted no clients and existed in name only. The failure of the National Center for Reconciliation and Reform left Simonds rather bitter. His attempts to bridge the gap between Christian Right critics of public education and the educational establishment crumbled on two fronts. Public schools did not embrace them, and the efforts at cooperation with the "enemy" cost Simonds as much as a third of his CEE constituency.[64] Because of his efforts at compromise, Simonds "fell from grace" as a leading Christian Right authority in the area of educational reform.

Discouraged by his failure to save public school children "from atheism, homosexuality, the occult, drugs, children having children, abortion, brainwashing and crippling psychology," Simonds tried to revitalize CEE by turning up his rhetoric in opposition to the public schools. In a February 1998 letter to his constituents, Simonds announced that he was changing directions. After fifteen years of trying to gain "safe passage" for Christian children in the public schools, the Lord led Simonds to counsel his followers to abandon public education. Simonds wrote,

CHRISTIANS MUST EXIT THE PUBLIC SCHOOLS as soon as it is feasible and possible. The price in human loss, social depravity and the spiritual slaughter of our young Christian children is no longer acceptable (and certainly never was!). We have tried hard to find common ground and will continue. School leaders have used this for a stalling tactic, rather than an open dialogue for solutions.[65]

Through a project named Rescue 2010, Simonds hopes by 2010 to create the conditions through which students of Christian parents have a real opportunity to abandon the public schools. This is a pressing necessity if Christian parents are to have any chance to "save our Christian children from the philosophy of atheistic humanism and its destructive elimination from heaven, of our church children." The project's ten listed purposes read like a litany of Christian Right complaints about the public schools. The first one, however, sets the tone for those that follow:

First and probably foremost is that many otherwise good teachers and certainly almost all our curriculum bases the instruction unit on a humanist world view, with all its anti-Christian worldly values, which is the current ideology in education. This is done very subtly and constantly undermines and contradicts a child's Biblical, godly belief and value (right vs. wrong) base for thinking. It wears on a child's mind until faith in God and Biblical principles simply breaks down and becomes extinct. Satan has then won! That's happening every day. The Christian plea goes unheard. The children are being lost.[66]

The strategy for accomplishing Rescue 2010's goals also reflects Christian Right tactics with respect to public education. Tax breaks and vouchers are not enough. "We must go back to what worked best for America. The only way to do this is to privatize all public education. Secularists, atheists and homosexuals could have their own schools, but they could not force tax-payers to subsidize their schools. Our system would be thoroughly re-formed and improved."[67]

Until these long-term goals can be accomplished, Simonds asks Christian teachers to hold the line against secular humanism. He pledges his organization to continue his strategies of "seeking 'common ground' on controversial issues; seeking 'safe-passage' of all K–12 children throughout the system unharmed spiritually and morally or academically [un]stunted; organize Christians in every school district to become involved in their local schools, to oversee and insure the above objectives." In addition, Simonds now also promotes efforts to get a Bible curriculum based on the principles of biblical inerrancy and literalism in all thirty thousand high schools (now in three hundred) and to get schools to include Simonds's "Christian/American Culture" course in all the nation's high schools.[68]

From the words and actions of Pat Robertson, James Dobson, and Robert Simonds, we can see that Christian Right leaders view with alarm the present condition of the public schools. Although they cite falling academic standards as indicators of the failure of America's schools, they believe the real danger of the public schools is secular humanism. All three leaders accept the monomythic vision of an idealized Christian past in which the culture "worked better" because the nation's schools promoted biblically based values. From their perspective, the growing incongruity between their values and those of the schools has reached a point where the schools can no longer be trusted by Christian parents to educate their children. Whether or not Christian Right rhetoric has created that incongruity and fanned the flames of criticism because of a larger agenda of cultural hegemony is not important to grassroots activists. The reality is that if President Reagan's dream of "morning again in America" is ever to be realized, the efforts by concerned Christians to raise the shade of secular humanism must begin now.

3

Presuppositional Foundations

In the early 1990s, Christian Right activists began attacking the *Quest* reading program for its alleged promotion of New Age religion and secular humanism. One such critic was Focus on the Family's James Dobson. The criticism came as a surprise to the series editor, since Dobson was a contributor to the original *Quest* textbook back in 1979. When later questioned about the appropriateness of the series by a Focus reader, Dobson wrote that he had mixed reactions to it. He congratulated the editor on two points. The series employed the services of "several prominent Christian psychologists" in devising and developing the *Quest* program. Further, the "writings of reputable Christian authors are to be found among its recommended resource materials." Dobson also wrote, "Many of the morals it teaches (termed 'values,' or 'social skills') are fully compatible with a Christian perspective. And *Quest's* emphasis on the importance of communication between family members and peers deserves commendation."[1]

But in spite of these positive qualities, Dobson did not endorse the series. He based his objections on the fact that *Quest* included writings that, in his judgment, could not be approved by Christian parents. "Along with its good points, the program has what I feel are some serious problems. The authors of *Quest* have attempted in certain instances to incorporate the work of secular humanists into their curriculum, thus introducing elements clearly unacceptable to Christians." Even where *Quest* included values "potentially compatible with Christian mores," the "interpretation and application are completely subject to the individual instructor's personal biases. This meant that, in the hands of an atheistic or anti-Christian teacher, *Quest* could become a vehicle for communicating some distinctly un-Christian values." In other words, Dobson concluded, unless Christian teachers were in control of the discussion of those values, Christian parents could not assume that these writings would be used properly. The conclusion he drew was that the *Quest* program was inappropriate for use in public school classrooms because of the potential danger the series presented for Christian children when teachers used the materials in ways that are not completely compatible with Dobson's interpretation of Christian values.[2]

Dobson's assessment of *Quest* materials serves as a perfect illustration of the difficulties public school curricula present to the Christian Right. From the perspective of leaders like Dobson, in order for Christian parents to find schools acceptable, both the content of textbooks and the pedagogical techniques and assessment criteria used by public school teachers in the operation or their classrooms must be completely compatible with the Christian worldview. Christian Right activists take this position for specific reasons related to their presuppositions about the nature of truth, the sources from which it is derived, and the authority it commands even outside the religious sphere. Other conservative Christians, on the basis of their own presuppositions, depart from the Christian Right on the worldview assumptions that guide their assessments of public education. Various Christian Right theorists and activists give differing degrees of emphasis to the specifics of the worldview presented here, but they share a widespread agreement on these points. In fact, many of these points are characteristic of the larger biblical Christian community from which the Christian Right derives its leadership and core constituency.[3] This means that many of the basic presuppositions that guide the Christian Right find common acceptance among many other Christians outside the movement. Yet the Christian Right remains a subgroup within that community because certain other presuppositions held by movement leaders are not historically consistent with the worldview of many biblical Christians. These presuppositions include the absolutistic emphasis the Christian Right places on biblical authority and on the unconditional and ahistorical nature of truth. The differences also extend to the way various religious traditions within evangelical Protestantism identify the criteria that define a true Christian, what the various traditions see as the appropriate relationship between biblical Christians and the public order, and what should be the character of Christian action in the public sphere.

The worldview presuppositions that follow the theological lines of the larger biblical Christian community are my focus for the current discussion. Sometimes Christian Right thinkers diverge from this tradition, and it is important to note the divergence. For the distinctive components of the Christian Right worldview that separate it from the wider tradition of biblical Christianity, see chapter 4. The Christian Right worldview owes an enormous theological debt to the biblical Christian tradition. Specifically, it proceeds from the heritage of classic intellectual fundamentalism developed more than a half century ago at Princeton Theological Seminary by a line of great thinkers, stalwarts of Calvinism including Charles Hodge, Benjamin Warfield, and J. Gresham Machen. From the 1870s through the 1930s, conservative Christians looked to Princeton to provide them with the ammunition to confront, expose, and defeat liberalism in American Protestantism.

The Princeton theologians portrayed Christian teaching as an unbroken line of thought from Augustine in the fourth century to Calvin in the sixteenth century. They believed that they were the rightful stewards of that tradition and thus claimed the authority to speak for the entirety of Christian orthodoxy. In their treatment of the history of Christian thought, they were little concerned with the historical development of the tradition, nor did they accept the claim that the tradition needed to be contextualized for each generation. They believed that the Reformed tradition provided the basis for all Christian doctrine and tradition. As Higher Criticism brought the veracity of the Scriptures into question in the nineteenth century, Princeton theologians such as Warfield developed the doctrine of biblical inerrancy.[4] Warfield, in particular, insisted that the truth of Scripture rested in its divine authority, not on any human or naturalistic basis. Later, as liberalism began its ascendancy in American religion, Machen wrote *Christianity and Liberalism* to defend the faith against the onslaught. In it, he argued that modernism and biblical Christianity were two totally different religions. From the orthodox Calvinists at Princeton came the intellectual foundations for the twentieth-century biblical Christian worldview.[5] A full discussion of the connection between Princeton and the Christian Right appears in chapter 4; for now, it will suffice to note that the heirs of the Old Princeton Theology nurtured and inspired the two thinkers most responsible for articulating the distinctive components of the Christian Right worldview, Francis Schaeffer and Rousas John Rushdoony.[6]

Although theologians laid the foundations of modern Fundamentalism and biblical Christianity at Princeton, Machen and others at the seminary clearly differentiated themselves from popular Fundamentalism at one important point. By the 1930s, most fundamentalists accepted the principles of dispensationalism, which links the events described in the New Testament book of Revelation with a time line derived from the ninth chapter of the Old Testament book of Daniel. Dispensational thinkers such as John

Nelson Darby believed that this combination revealed to them God's outline of history, beginning with the creation and culminating with the apocalyptic Second Coming of Christ. Dispensationalists argued that they were living in the final times that would usher in Christ's return and the millennial kingdom of God. They were premillennialists, believing that before God established the millennial kingdom, He would destroy evil in a final conflagration known as the battle of Armageddon. The conclusion drawn by premillennialists was that events were in the hands of God and that there was nothing they could do to bring about the kingdom of God on earth except to prepare themselves for eternity. Efforts to transform or save the social order were fruitless. Most fundamentalists, therefore, because of their dispensational views, removed themselves from social involvement and prepared for the Second Coming.

Machen and others at Princeton dismissed premillennial dispensationalism. For them, as for Calvin before them, the task of Christians was to fight the good fight in opposing evil. Human sinfulness dictated that a completely Christian world was an impossibility, but the Calvinists at Princeton believed that they were responsible for assuming control of the social order in order to limit the damage done by evil forces and to protect true Christians from evil's grasp. Through God's saving grace, they could discern from the Scriptures what God demanded of them. Since in their view God's sovereignty extended to all of creation, they believed that their efforts should be directed to extending God's truth and will to all of human society. This, of course, demanded that they become involved in the social order. Thus, while adopting similar assumptions about the nature of truth, the intellectual biblical Christians at Princeton, and later at Westminster Theological Seminary, distanced themselves from popular Fundamentalism. Nevertheless, because they did proceed from a shared set of assumptions about the nature of truth, we can draw a close connection among Fundamentalism, biblical Christianity, and the Christian Right.

The Nature of the Problem

Representatives of biblical Christianity like to picture themselves as the faithful stewards of the historical Christian tradition. According to their claims, their formulations of that tradition extend in an unbroken line from the early church in the first century to the present day. A number of historical theologians challenge that assertion. As Jarislov Pelikan, James

Barr, George Marsden, and others have shown, the particular formulation of the Christian tradition presented by contemporary biblical Christians diverges even from that of the Protestant Reformers in significant ways.[7]

One of the most important departures from the worldview of the Protestant Reformers of the fifteenth and sixteenth centuries is the tendency of contemporary biblical Christians to add modernist assumptions to the Reformers' premodernist perspective. This is particularly ironic since most biblical Christians identify modernism as the most significant heresy among moderate and liberal Christians. Yet, as biblical scholar James Barr notes, contemporary conservative evangelical Christians share with the modernist segment of present-day mainstream culture many of the same epistemological roots in eighteenth-century rationalism and material views of reality.[8] For example, though conservative Christians may hold to a literal interpretation of heaven and hell as geographically specific locations in a three-story universe (a premodern concept), their attempts to establish the truth of the claim often revert to material conceptions of those places (a physical heaven and hell) and rational evidence for their existence (modern epistemological concepts).

The discrepancies between competing premodern and modern frames of reference is of less concern to biblical Christians than to those outside that subculture. What is important to biblical Christians is that the people who accept this worldview are able to reduce the incompatibility to a point where it does not cause the average believer to question the grounding presuppositions. In other words, whether a worldview is internally coherent (although not necessarily consistent) is of greater importance to believers than whether others who do not accept that worldview find inconsistencies in it. If the components seem to fit together without challenging the credibility of people's understanding and their experiences, then the fact that the basic presuppositions may conflict at a deeper level is of little concern to them. Those problems are left to the theologians and biblical scholars to resolve. Even at that level, as Barr notes with respect to issues related to creation, the incongruities between belief and experience disappear as theologians and scholars reinterpret the scriptural source of those beliefs to minimize the discontinuity between the findings of modern science and the literal biblical record.[9]

Such difficulties with logical consistency in matters of religious belief are not restricted to pure Christian religionists, of course. Modified religionists are just as likely not to question the potential or actual contradictions among the presuppositions that guide their worldview. These inconsistencies within the worldviews of modified religionists and pure secularists are the precise points at which the Christian Right attacks its opponents. As we will see, the Christian Right understands that the process of both individual and cultural conversion begins by exposing its competitor's contradictory presuppositions. The more movement leaders can make people aware of these contradictions, the more incongruity people will experience between the world they live in and the world they envision. Because modified religionists in contemporary America feel far more "at home" in their universe than do pure religionists and pure secularists, they are far less likely to recognize any conflicts in their cognitive maps of reality. In turn, this means that modified religionists are much less likely to be aware of the presuppositions that guide their understanding of everyday life and thus much less capable of defending them. They are therefore vulnerable to those who seek to explore or exploit the inconsistencies or unsettling implications of their basic principles. The point is that by being highly intentional and explicit about their worldview presuppositions and by understanding the weaknesses in the presuppositions of others, the Christian Right occupies a position of initial advantage in matters of public debate.

A similar vulnerability exists among most public school educators. From my conversations with classroom teachers and administrators nationwide, I get the sense that they pay little attention to the reality assumptions that ground the materials and methods they use in their schools. There are perhaps good reasons. At the practical level, teachers and administrators simply do not have the time to assess the metaphysical and epistemological implications of the content and pedagogy they adopt. To some degree, this claim is modified by the attention that contemporary educators pay to learning theory and various learning styles identified in the research. Even here, however, they typically take the research at face value without a deeper investigation into the basic assumptions about reality, human nature, and truth that stand behind it. Further, because public school educators operate from a set of presuppositions about the nature of things that the larger culture widely accepts, they experience only minimal cognitive dissonance. They "feel at home in the universe," as William James once described it. Because of this degree of comfort with the world around them, educators typically are far less aware of the metaphysical and epistemological presuppositions that guide their understanding of the nature of truth than are the Christian Right activists who challenge them. Incongruities that do arise in the materials or pedagogy often do not receive serious consideration until educators are challenged on these points. Thus, when asked to explain or defend a particular pedagogical method such as higher order thinking, most educators are not prepared to elucidate the presuppositions that ground their methods and strategies. My experience shows that too often educators do not take such challenges seriously. They tend either to dismiss criticism by attributing irrational motives to their challengers or to use bureaucratic and political maneuvering to stifle the issues.

The problem with such a response is that their challengers, if connected to national organizations, will not accept this reaction. The materials Christian Right activists receive from national groups prepare well-organized critics to undermine the credibility of public school curricula and pedagogy by identifying and demonizing the intellectual traditions from which they claim these educational strategies have been derived. The purpose of such responses is to raise doubt in the minds of parents, the general public, and educators themselves about the validity and acceptability of public education. When educators do not understand the presuppositions that ground their approaches, the public is left with the impression that the critic's charges are both legitimate and accurate. This is precisely the intention of Christian Right strategy toward public education. Its purpose is to provoke in the public a crisis of confidence in which the contradictions inherent in American public education are brought to light and explicitly identified. What Christian Right leaders are counting on is that their own presuppositions about the nature of things will appear to be more solidly grounded in eternal verities than will those of public educators when the latter are made clear to the public. Such a tactical approach demands that public school educators become more intentional and explicit about what they are doing and why. It also demands that they become acutely aware of the worldview presuppositions that ground their critics so that they can understand and effectively respond to the nature of the charges against them. What the present situation calls for, then, is an understanding of the grounding presuppositions that guide the views of education all the participants bring to the discussion. The problem public school educators face is that there is no systematic discussion in the literature of the theological foundation of their critics' presuppositions. Therefore, it is here that we begin by examining the truth claims that drive the Christian Right view of things.

The Way Things Are

The keystone that holds the biblical Christian worldview together is the assumption that the Bible is the ultimate source of truth. It is ultimate in several senses. In the first place, no other source of truth is prior to it, and thus it provides the standard by which all truth claims are judged. Further, its truth applies to every aspect of human life. Finally, it contains the direct revelation of God to humanity unconditioned by human frailty, corruption, or error. This approach to the Scriptures claims to remove the possibility of human error and caprice from the system of human knowledge of truth. Any incongruities that arise under this canopy are not a result of any flaw either in the source of truth or in its human reception. Rather, all discrepancies stem from the forces that control the larger world and seek to undermine biblical truth.

Christian Right activists tend to underplay these characteristics of truth in framing their opposition to public education since they run so counter to the truth assumptions of the cultural mainstream. They nevertheless found expression in a 1998 court case brought against the Lee County, Florida, school board. After an election in which Christian Right candidates won a majority, the board voted to institute a Bible-as-history course. They based the curriculum on materials provided to the school board by the National Council on Bible Curriculum in the Public Schools (NCOBCITPS). NCOBCITPS materials describe such biblical events as the parting of the Red Sea, Moses' reception of the Ten Commandments, and the Resurrection of Christ as historical facts. In what can only be described as a rather inconsistent decision, the court allowed the Old Testament course to stand, even though it represented miraculous events as historical, but disallowed the New Testament course on the grounds that claims about the factual nature of the Resurrection were doctrinal religious claims, not historical facts. Neither the board majority nor the curriculum's supporters were willing to concede that such claims were religious rather than historical.[10] The Lee County case suggests that Christian Right activists are becoming more bold in asserting the ultimate nature of their truth claims.

Documents circulated internally within the Christian Right provide support for the claim that this view of the Bible and its conception of truth drive movement critiques of public education. For example, a Coalition on Revival (COR) publication, *A Manifesto for the Christian Church,* identifies several important assumptions about the Bible and its relationship to the secular world. Developed under the leadership of Jay Grimstead in the 1980s, COR continues to provide an intellectual and strategic foundation for Christian Right efforts at cultural transformation. The COR manifesto states the basic tenets of the movement, and the accompanying "Sphere Documents" provide an analysis of the current cultural situation and a prescription for transforming it in accordance with biblical principles. There is a long list of Christian Right activists who endorse the manifesto. In delineating the basic principles upon which Christian Right efforts rest, the manifesto asserts:

> The Bible is the Final Test of All Truth Claims. We affirm that this God-inspired, inerrant Bible is the only absolute, objective, final test for all truth claims, and the clearest verbal picture of reality that has ever come into the hands of mankind. By it, and it alone, are all philosophies, books, values, actions, and plans to be measured as to the consistency with reality, visible and invisible. Whatever statements or values are in opposition to the statements and values of the Bible err to the degree of their opposition.[11]

This is the epistemological equivalent of James Dobson's comments about the *Quest* materials noted earlier. The biblical Christian claim is not that all other knowledge should be dismissed as false. Any knowledge is appropriate for public schools if it fully conforms to biblical truth.

As it impacts public school instruction, this means that the content of all course materials must be consistent with biblical truth (as interpreted). If it does not, the content lacks legitimacy and must be rejected. The problem, for example, with Darwinian evolution is that its assumptions are contrary to biblical revelation. Even though most public school biology teachers long ago abandoned Darwinian evolution for modified and more sophisticated theories of evolution, the evolutionary perspective they continue to adopt is equally invalid because it derives from Darwinian sources that have already been established as contrary to biblical truth. Because natural evolution denies a divine creator and rejects the idea of a divine creation, it therefore denies God's ultimate authority over the universe. Since divine revelation establishes that authority in the Scriptures, any truth claims based on contrary assumptions are erroneous and must be purged from the schools.

This is not to say that the Christian Right never uses data from secular sources. Materials produced by Christian Right special purpose groups often cite secular authorities to establish the legitimacy of their claims. This is just as true for Christian Coalition position papers as it is for James

Dobson's parenting advice. In such cases, these groups include secular knowledge because it both gives the appearance of a non–religiously grounded stance and provides secular support for biblical truth. For example, a Concerned Women for America (CWA) "News Flash" on sex education and herpes cites Peter Leonne, medical director of the HIV/STD program in Wake County, North Carolina, as an authority on the matter. To the uninformed reader, Leonne's presumed expertise derives from the secular position he occupies, not his theological orientation. CWA further establishes the legitimacy of the claim by noting that it is taken from the *Washington Times,* a presumably secular source. This gives the appearance that CWA claims about the dangers of sex education programs have the support of secular authorities.[12] However, CWA publicizes Leonne's assessment not only to serve its own political purposes but also because it is fully consistent with biblically derived assessments of sex education programs. In the final analysis, the secular authority and expertise Leonne brings to the discussion has nothing to do with the truth of his conclusions.

The second implication of the Bible's ultimate truth is that it is the ultimate authority in every sphere of human existence. This means that the final standard by which public school curricula and pedagogy are judged is scriptural. In the pure religionist view of biblical Christians, the Bible is not just the authority for religious, spiritual, theological, and moral truth. It applies equally as the authoritative source for our knowledge in medicine, laws, government, economics, psychology, and every other sphere of human activity. Again, the COR manifesto makes the point clearly and unequivocally:

> The Bible States Reality for All Areas of Life and Thought. We affirm that the Bible is not only God's statements to us regarding religion, salvation, eternity, and righteousness, but also the final measurement and depository of certain fundamental facts of reality and basic principles that God wants all mankind to know in the spheres of law, government, economics, business, education, arts and communication, medicine, psychology, and science. All theories and practices of these spheres of life are only true, right, and realistic to the degree that they agree with the Bible. The Bible furnishes mankind with the only logical and verbal connection between time and eternity, religion, and science, the visible and invisible worlds.[13]

God is sovereign over all creation and therefore requires humans to structure their public and private lives in accord with the mandates for human existence that God reveals in the Scriptures. Although not all biblical Christians would extend the authority of biblical mandates so widely, Christian Right leaders are clear about the full extent to which they are applicable.

Accompanying the COR manifesto's call to apply biblical truth to all spheres of human society are a series of essays called "Christian World View Documents." Authored by many notable Christian Right activists, the documents detail the precise biblical passages that provide the authority for restructuring various spheres of American social, political, and cultural life.[14] Subtitled "applying Biblical principles to every sphere of life and thought," the seventeen documents cover every field of social activity from law to medicine, from education to the family. Each of the documents is subdivided into three sections. The preface provides an overall definition of the issues and the history of that particular social institution from ancient to contemporary times.

The second section, "Statements of Affirmation and Denial," contains the heart of the Christian Right worldview and social agenda expressed in the sphere documents. Here may be found many statements that support or reject various principles or ideas that govern that specific sphere of society. For example, the "Education Sphere Document" contains statements regarding the nature of education, the nature and the role of the teacher, the role of the student, and methods of instruction. The subsection on the nature of education affirms that "in its most basic meaning, education is the triune God teaching His truth to mankind." It denies "that education is solely mental or physical activity associated with learning the thoughts and experiences of other human beings." Again, "We affirm that truth is what is known to God about Himself and all of His creation, and that it is absolute, eternal, and objective. . . . We deny that truth is solely what is known to one or more individuals or to mankind collectively, and that it is relative, temporal, or subjective." With respect to the nature and role of the teacher, "We affirm that a teacher is a presenter of God's truth and a guide to its discovery by students through the ministry of God's Holy Spirit. . . . We deny that any teacher can without the cooperation of the Holy Spirit, guide others adequately to an understanding of God's truth."[15] Each of the affirmations contains at least one scriptural passage that provides the authoritative basis for the truth claim.

In communications to their own constituencies, Christian Right critics of public education frequently either cite biblical texts to support their analyses and grievances or cite other published works that make those connections. For example, David Barton, of Wallbuilders, writes that when confronted by criticism, people of faith should "examine and ensure that the criticisms were not deserved (cf. 1 Peter 2:16, 19–20; Romans 2:24). If they were unfounded, then be careful not to scorn or mock the source or to return an evil word against them (cf. Romans 12:17; Isa. 28:22)."[16] NACE/CEE's Robert Simonds also makes liberal use of scriptural passages in his President's Letters, as does Tim LaHaye in his books on public education. And, referring to James Dobson's homey style, a *Christianity Today* article described Dobson as merely a marketer of "Scriptural principles and traditional American commonsense."[17]

The logical connection between the biblical passages Christian Right activists cite in order to establish the authority for a particular criticism and the inferences they draw from the text is not always clear to the casual observer. For example, the Coalition on Revival sphere document on education urges public school teachers to use language and illustrations familiar to the students. The document states, "We deny that it is possible for teachers to produce adequate learning in students when they use language and ideas outside the students' daily life and language."[18] The biblical authority for this practice is Ephesians 4:29. In the Revised Standard Version of the Bible, that passage is "Let no evil talk come out of your mouths, but only such as is good for edifying, as fits the occasion, that it may impart grace to those who hear." Other connections between pedagogical methods and Scripture are even less obvious. At the grassroots level, most of these connections go unchallenged by Christian Right activists. They simply accept the connection as valid. At the levels of the intellectual elite and the organizational activists, the connections seem valid because they are read within the context of the overarching theology of culture and political theology that grounds the movement.

In preparing materials for secular public consumption, Christian Right activists often remove biblical and theological references. Focus on the Family materials provide a good illustration of this de-scripturalizing. FoF produces numerous videotapes, movies, and other materials, scripted to avoid constitutional challenges on church-state separation. The message contained in these materials is completely consistent with the materials prepared for more religious settings. Once again, the litmus test is scriptural compatibility, even if the scriptural references are removed. One reason for such "sanitizing" is that those outside the Christian Right do not subscribe to the theological foundations of the movement and therefore might not draw the same inferences from the biblical passages. Rather than confuse the issue by provoking possible battles over the interpretation of Scriptures, Christian Right strategists frame their arguments to the general public within the context of the secular culture. This has the added benefit of seeming to provide secular justifications for their complaints and proposed solutions. By invoking secular authorities, Christian Right leaders seem to be moving within the worldview of the larger culture and therefore appear as another interest group with a particular point of view. Michael Farris, head of the Home School Legal Defense Association, former general counsel to Concerned Women for America, and unsuccessful Christian Coalition–supported candidate for lieutenant governor in Virginia, emphasizes this point. Farris admits that it is just good strategy for Christian Right activists to conceal the biblical roots of their views and frame the issues in terms of "right and wrong."[19] In another example, James Dobson insists on being referred to as "Doctor Dobson" (a reference to his Ph.D. in psychology), but his books and radio programs contain virtually no references to scholarly psychological literature.[20]

The third section of the COR sphere documents contains a "call to action," specifically directing Christians to enter the public sphere and attempt to bring the biblical principles enunciated in the sphere document into public policy and the operation of social and civic institutions. Both general and specific actions are recommended. A "general action" called for in education includes "examining earnestly these affirmations and denials in light of God's Word to see if they are true, and informing us directly of those points in which they believe we have departed from Scripture or logic." A "specific action" invites Christians to first bring their institutions (church schools, missionary activities, etc.) into conformity with these principles.[21]

The COR documents make it clear that these affirmations and denials refer to endeavors in education and other spheres of human activity in the public arena carried out by all persons, not only Christian institutions. Robert Simonds makes this point explicitly in his call to transform public schools into Christian worldview perspective schools. He argues that calling for public schools to become consistent with biblical principles is acceptable for Christian Right activists, although teaching specific religious or sectarian doctrines or practices in the public schools is not.[22]

Biblical Christians are not capricious in making such truth claims. They base their conclusions on epistemological foundations rooted in the writings of seventeenth-century philosopher Francis Bacon and eighteenth-century Scottish Common Sense philosophers. Bacon's inductive method is the starting point. Disagreements or differences of opinion that arise about particular interpretations of facts can be resolved by "getting the facts right." Bacon's method provides three steps toward accomplishing this end: (1) carefully observing the facts, (2) accurately describing them, and (3) properly classifying them according to their characteristics. When this method is applied conscientiously, a coherent picture of the structure of the world emerges.[23] When the facts are not carefully observed, described, and classified, a false picture of things arises. The key to Bacon's method rests in the way it classifies facts. According to biblical Christians, the Bible provides categories and standards to classify facts. The argument follows a logical progression. God created the world and built into the creation divinely ordained structures, revealed to humans in the Bible. Humans apply these categories and classifications to the data. Disagreements about particular facts disappear when we see the data within the context of God's creation and plan for humanity. Those who do not observe the data using the perspective of the divine categories simply misperceive the world. Any conclusions or inferences drawn from those misperceptions are themselves necessarily flawed because of their defective foundation. Because nonbiblical Christians lack the proper assumptions about the way things are, they may not even be aware of the true nature of what they are doing. What appears to be legitimate from the perspective of defective knowledge may, in reality, be something entirely different. What appears to a science teacher, for example, to be a rudimentary demonstration of oxygen depletion by placing a bell jar over a candle may turn out to be, from the perspective of a Christian Right activist, a satanic ritual.[24]

To tighten the connection between the divine structures of creation and the human capacity to interpret the Scriptures with absolute certainty, biblical Christians turn to the epistemological assumptions of Scottish Common Sense philosophy. Common Sense philosophers such as Thomas Reed and Dugald Stewart argue that the mind operates through innate structures that are similar in everyone.[25] In order for humans to know God's plan through the Scriptures, God shaped the processes of the human mind to operate in ways that are consistent with God's created order. When allowed to operate freely, these mental structures help humans process information in ways that lead to inevitable conclusions about reality—"common sense" knowledge, which is available to all persons when the facts are correctly observed and classified. Thus, when humans read the Scriptures unencumbered by modernist thought, they can be sure that the truth they encounter is God's truth. Significant differences in interpretation result when nonbiblical Christians or non-Christians allow their understandings of the Scripture to be clouded by modern or secular thought.

When combined, Baconian methodology and Common Sense episte-mology form the basis for a highly rational intellectual tradition. A. A. Baker, vice president of Pensacola Christian School and a leading pub-lisher of Christian school textbooks, explains how these approaches work in conjunction with the Bible to provide teachers with the resources they need to do a good job in the classroom:

> The sources for understanding how human beings think and, therefore, how they ought to be taught are common sense, philosophical thinking grounded in common sense, and the Word of God. . . . The methods that common sense and the Scriptures call for . . . would make full use of any modern tools of technology that common sense says would be truly help-ful. Common sense would also tell the good teacher . . . [to treat them] as a complement of the primary methods, to be used whenever common sense calls for them.[26]

Christian Right critics are seldom the irrational anti-intellectual foes their critics paint them as being. They often ground their concerns in a solid intellectualism that values rational thought and careful analysis. Christian Right intellectuals and organizational leaders value truth. They believe that it is clearly understood and that it does not change according to situations or the latest cultural development. The reason rational dia-logue seldom works in bringing public school educators together with their Christian Right critics is that the presuppositions upon which the two sides approach the issues are vastly different and, in many ways, irrec-oncilable. The differences are not minor. They go to the depth of reality assumptions and the ways in which humans are capable of discovering the truth about the world in which we live.

Almost all Christian Right complaints about contemporary American public education rest on these foundations. Guided by speculative, skeptical, and relativistic philosophies (i.e. modernist thought), the American educa-tional elite simply have misunderstood the problems because they have not relied on common sense observations to accurately determine the facts and have not used the proper categories by which to structure those facts.[27] Be-cause Christian Right critics conclude that the entire foundation of public education rejects these presuppositions about the nature and certainty of truth, the schools cannot be saved by this or that specific adjustment. The correction to the problem of contemporary education demands, as the COR education sphere document suggests, an affirmation of the divine basis of all education. Only then can true knowledge be taught in the public schools.

Difficulties for public educators do not end here, however. A final set of biblical Christian assumptions about the nature of truth deeply impacts Christian Right analysis of America's schools. In addition to being biblically based, applicable to all aspects of life, and knowable with absolute certainty, truth, according to Christian Right presuppositions, is also revealed, propositional, and ahistorical. Each of these assertions is closely connected to the deeper pedagogical and curricular protests Christian Right activists have leveled against the public schools.

The claim that truth is revealed has specific pedagogical implications. The key contrast here with dominant contemporary educational methods is that truth is received, not discovered, by humans. This redefines the proper relationship between teacher and student. The role of the teacher is to reveal truth to students; students have the responsibility to accurately and fully receive what the teacher reveals to them. When one school district in Michigan came under fire, Christian Right activists submitted a petition to the board requiring that all desks and chairs in the district be permanently affixed to the floor in straight rows.[28] Group work or peer collaboration is highly suspect because students have not yet mastered the necessary biblical principles, standards, and categories or the logic of their application to the materials before them. Some activists, such as Dobson and Simonds, seem to accept more open-ended pedagogies, but they require the watchful eye of a properly informed teacher who is skilled in directing student explorations toward uncovering accepted truth.

Maintaining a highly structured classroom is not itself sufficient to establish an acceptable educational environment. Dobson's comments about the *Quest* materials remind us that even when some of the learning content is consistent with Christian principles, there is still the danger that a teacher whose thinking is not in complete conformity to biblical truth may misinterpret and misapply the materials. The only way Christian parents can be assured that teachers convey the correct truth is to make sure that they are biblical Christians. Failing that, the role of the teacher should be restricted to simply conveying factual material to children or developing their basic skills, leaving the construction of those facts into truth statements and the application of those skills to specific problems to be done at home by Christian parents.

The idea of the "propositional" nature of truth follows closely from its revelatory nature. The truth contained in the Scriptures appears in the form of true and precise "propositions," statements or claims of fact.[29] These propositions provide the standards by which all other truth claims should be judged. New discoveries or truth claims do not stand or fall on their own merit. Nor is rational deliberation productive in determining the status of truth claims. Since discoveries, human experience, and rational deliberation are subject to error or historical contextualizing, none of these sources provide a secure basis upon which to rest truth claims. Humans determine the truth or falsity of knowledge statements by measuring such claims against the biblical propositions revealing the universal laws of God. In *Escape from Reason,* Francis Schaeffer makes this point explicitly. Schaeffer argues that God's communication of propositional truth in the Bible provides the proper basis for truth. It does not rest in human experience.[30]

The revealed and propositional quality of biblical truth claims favors a pedagogical method in which truth is disseminated to students, not discovered by them. The responsibility of students is to learn what is true and what is not. At the younger ages, the appropriate methodology is rote memorization. As students get older, however, more sophisticated learning strategies may be required. One strategy that is recommended by several Christian Right educational critics is critical thinking. But the form of critical thinking advocated by these activists is not the same as that advocated by mainstream public educational reformers. In Christian Right circles, critical thinking means examining and mastering the internal logic structure of complex truth claims. Students should learn to recognize the connections between propositions and master the logic of how those propositions lead to particular conclusions about a given issue. Though open-ended exploration may be acceptable to Christian Right activists, it must be followed by a review by the teacher to show which explorations correctly trace out the logical inferences of biblical propositional statements and which ones do not.

The final quality that biblical Christians typically ascribe to the nature of truth is its ahistoricity. Truth, being from God, is eternal and immutable. It is not subject to change. As Cornelius Van Til argues, "there can be no new knowledge for God, about either Himself or the universe. His knowledge is analytic. God does not learn, for He is Himself the source of all that can be learned. . . . He does not progressively add to His knowledge. To think of God's knowledge in any other way leads to the insertion of the temporal into the eternal."[31] Paul Parsons makes a similar point in his analysis of a textbook prepared for Christian school children. "'The Bible is without doubt scientifically accurate,' states a Christian school science textbook. 'Because God is its author, we can depend upon it to be true, accurate, and unchanging. It sometimes takes science many years to catch up with the Bible, but true science and the Bible are always in perfect agreement.'"[32] Biblical Christians argue that what changes is human perceptions of truth when those perceptions are not grounded in biblical truth. The appearance of change is related to the concept that humans rely on progressive discovery of truth through "human digging, imagining, sifting, and assessing."[33] The fact that these conceptions of truth are derived from human discovery, not divine revelation, accounts for their error. Culturally and historically bound conceptions of truth that are not in harmony with biblical truth—and therefore are flawed—reflect the failure of those cultures and historical periods to recognize the way things really are. Despite cultural and historical errors that seem to suggest the relative nature of truth, biblical Christians believe that truth remains steadfast and unchanging.[34]

These three closely related presuppositions about the nature of truth—its revealed, propositional, and ahistorical nature—combine to provide contemporary biblical Christian pure religionists with a steady compass in a culture that seems to them to be adrift and rudderless. Furthermore, these elements of truth suggest to them that it is possible to build a civilization that stands firm against the relativism of modern and postmodern culture. Joining the revealed, propositional, and ahistorical nature of truth with the presuppositions of its divine origin and its applicability to every sphere of human life, Christian Right activists are about the task of building a civilization grounded in the eternal verities and functioning to a greater or lesser degree in harmony with God's will and plan for humanity. To fail to do so brings with it the promise of continued strife, conflict, and moral decay.

Responses to the Way Things Are

In evaluating the adequacy and implications of the biblical Christian concept of truth for public education, we need to remember that things are not always as they appear to be. What I have painted is an ideal representation of the biblical Christian perspective. I have also pointed out some important implications of this point of view for public educators. But we must remember that few local critics bring such a well-ordered and well-formulated perspective into their public discourse. Many Christian parents are simply uncomfortable with what they have heard about the public schools and fear that some of the dangers identified by Christian Right activists may have infiltrated their schools. They also have a growing realization that the content of some of their children's education is inconsistent with their religious beliefs. Their concern is with their children. They have no intention of imposing their religious beliefs on the school district or working toward bringing the school closer into conformity with biblical principles in all areas of its operation. Many of these parents find comfort when their concerns are taken seriously and provisions are made by the schools to give their children relief from certain activities and topics.

Such biblical Christian parents find a great deal of support within the subculture of conservative evangelical Protestantism among people who oppose any efforts to force biblical mandates on the larger culture. These conservative evangelicals find such attempts to restructure the culture along the lines described in the COR documents to be inconsistent with their place in a democratic pluralistic society. They may agree with the COR documents that such a widespread application of Christian principles is desirable in a Christian culture, but they refrain from joining the Christian Right out of respect for and recognition of the democratic and pluralistic nature of American society. They conclude that America is not a Christian culture and should not be restructured on a biblical basis.[35]

We must further be aware that a substantial number of conservative evangelicals find discomfort in the absolutist nature of biblical Christian truth assumptions. Conservatives such as Mark Noll, a highly respected professor of Christian thought at Wheaton College, argue that such truth assertions do not serve conservative Christianity well if Christians ignore completely the widely accepted knowledge base of the larger culture. In *The Scandal of the Evangelical Mind,* Noll faults absolutist biblical Christians for their lack of intellectual rigor. Noll here is not referring to the long tradition of anti-intellectualism that has been characteristic of much of the American evangelical subculture. He pointedly addresses his comments to those within the evangelical community who sometimes vigorously prosecute the wrong sort of intellectual life.[36] Biblical Christians, Noll suggests, have often tended toward an oversimplification of issues because their religious orientation does not lead them to deeper, more sophisticated, analysis. The consequence for biblical Christians is that they find themselves almost completely adrift "in using the mind for careful thought about the world."[37] The problem for these pure religionists is not with their faith nor even with its scriptural basis. The problem is in the way some biblical Christians have used Scripture to justify particular truth assumptions that Noll believes "fundamentally contradict the deeper, broader, and historically well-established meanings of the Bible itself."[38]

The ultimate irony of the biblical Christian truth claims described above is that they are neither absolute nor ahistorical. They are products of two particular historical contexts. Most notably, the underpinnings of the doctrine of biblical inerrancy are closely related to the revolutionary changes in scientific epistemology—particularly in its Newtonian form— that occurred in the seventeenth and eighteenth centuries. The principle of biblical inerrancy is firmly grounded in reason and the construction of rational links or "correspondences" between observable events and biblical truth. Charles Hodge, the intellectual ancestor of the modern conservative evangelical worldview, stated it this way: "Facts do not admit of denial. . . . To deny facts, is to deny what God affirms to be true. This the Bible cannot do. It cannot contradict God. The theologian, therefore, acknowledges that the Scriptures must be interpreted in accordance with established facts."[39] The resulting irony runs full circle. Biblical Christians argue that the Bible is without error because "Jesus says that the Bible is without error, Paul says so, Peter says so, and generally all biblical writers who are in a position to say anything about the matter say so."[40] Yet, the intellectual foundation upon which their claim for authority rests is derived from the nonscriptural source of Newtonian science with its reliance on rational correspondences.

One example of this irony comes from the history of the creationist movement. Beginning in the nineteenth century, debates about the inerrancy of the biblical record of creation were peppered with discussions of the overwhelming scientific evidence that was accumulating. The particular points upon which the discussion centered were the age of the earth and the speed with which God created the world. For example, geological evidence overwhelmingly grew to support the conclusion that the age of the earth was far older than the twelve thousand years allowed by the eighteenth-century Anglican defender of revealed religion Bishop Butler. In response, conservative evangelical scholars began to replace literal readings of the relevant biblical passages with more allegorical or metaphorical interpretations that allowed for a greater passage of time.

Even as they modified their conclusions, however, they remained stead-fastly committed to the doctrine of biblical inerrancy.[41]

What is particularly significant about such changes is that biblical Christians unconsciously began to change the basis upon which their truth claims rested. In effect, they abandoned their religious foundations for more materialistic conceptions of truth clearly derived from nontheistic natural science. For example, the facts that prove biblical inerrancy with respect to the flood of Noah are empirically verifiable facts. They include the geographical location of Mount Ararat, geological evidences of flooding, the economy of the species, and so forth. The acceptance of this methodological approach to truth led biblical Christians to operate in a way that confirmed that "facts precede interpretation," even if it did not appear that way to garden-variety lay conservative Christians. The correct scriptural interpretation accepted by biblical Christian scholars, the one chosen from among various possibilities, was the one that established a correspondence between the biblical text and the empirical fact.[42]

Biblical Christian claims regarding scriptural truth are closely connected to modern scientific assumptions in another way as well. Historical and literary critics of the Scriptures do not raise the question of the truth or error of the biblical accounts. They accept Scripture as the product of particular historical periods and authors. Scriptural investigation of this sort is concerned with meaning and significance. Questions relating to the truth or error of scriptural passages come from conservative evangelical biblical scholars and theologians who adopt an empirical understanding of the nature of truth. Facts in the empirical sense are either true or false, depending on the evidence that can be used to substantiate the claim.[43] Thus, biblical Christians express continuing interest in locating Noah's ark on Mount Ararat in order to confirm the truth of the Scriptures. This suggests that methodologically, although many biblical Christian scholars claim to read the Bible literally, the truth they ascribe to a particular passage comes not from common sense but from the amount of evidence they can garner to support such a reading.[44] In this sense, inerrancy is more important than biblical literalism.

A final indicator of the inconsistency of biblical Christian truth claims relates to the way in which pure religionist Christians have appropriated modern technology to advance their cause. Although theologically committed to a premodern worldview, biblical Christians in general and the Christian Right more specifically freely utilize a communications technology firmly rooted in a modern scientific woldview. Technologically, they are on the cutting edge in terms of their use of computer technology, public relations, the media, political analysis and strategy, and symbolic rhetoric. Most Christian Right organizations, for example, have elaborate interactive web sites on the Internet that facilitate communication and development of mailing lists. Most take full advantage of cable television and mainstream news media by providing spokespersons armed with talking points. Perhaps the best example of the use of cable to advance the Christian Right agenda is Paul Weyrich's "America's Voice" (née National Empowerment Network) cable channel. Organizations such as the Eagle Forum, Focus on the Family, the Christian Coalition, and the Family Research Council provide regular fax messages for informing and preparing their constituents to respond at the local level to national issues. During his days at the Christian Coalition, Ralph Reed used focus groups and target surveys to test how various rhetorical strategies and political positions would play in Peoria. Political scientist Matthew Moen argues that this increased technological sophistication of the Christian Right was one of the most important factors in explaining their rise to prominence in the last third of the 1980s.[45]

By pointing out these inconsistencies I do not mean to suggest that biblical Christians are intentionally disingenuous in their truth claims. Rather, when taken literally, the premodern worldview from which the Scriptures were written creates so much incongruity with the way biblical Christians now experience the world that a modification in the biblical worldview is absolutely necessary. For example, whereas the Bible describes a three-tiered universe with God at the top, modern space exploration and astrophysics clearly challenge that conception. When one of the early Soviet cosmonauts commented after orbiting the earth that he had seen neither God nor heaven, biblical Christians dismissed the evidence by spiritualizing or allegorizing the realities or by projecting them further out than science was able to detect. Such adjustments might appear minor, but they are adjustments to present-day realities nevertheless.

These inconsistencies are not insignificant. In particular, they bear directly on many Christian Right grievances with public education. From the early beginnings of Fundamentalism in the nineteenth century, proponents viewed modernism as the enemy. They blamed it for creating all the necessary and sufficient conditions under which departures from absolute truth became possible. Its philosophic presuppositions resulted in the rise of secularism. In turn, secularism pushed religion out of the public sphere. The resulting loss of respect for biblical authority created the conditions

4

Christian Right Foundations

When conservative Christian voters helped elect Ronald Reagan to the presidency in 1980, they began a rocky marriage with the Republican Party. After failing to achieve its social agenda during the Reagan-Bush Administration, the politically empowered Christian Right shifted its attention to the local and state level. This new strategy worked when the Republican Party, with the strong support of the Christian Right, took control of the Congress in 1994. With that victory, movement activists became a major factor in the Republican Party in many states. By 1996, Christian Right power was sufficient to impose its agenda on the party's presidential platform even though the party's presidential candidate, Robert Dole, expressed discomfort with a number of platform planks. Yet, although conservative Christian voters constituted the largest single voting block within the Republican Party, their power from 1994 to 1998 was not sufficient to move the party to advance their social agenda. By the 1998 midterm elections, many Christian Right leaders were convinced that the party's leadership was ignoring their agenda by failing to structure the Republican midterm strategy on movement issues.

The midterm election results sent shock waves through the Christian Right. Although activists managed to defeat a number of ballot initiatives in various states, many of their candidates lost. Among the favored torch-bearers of the movement, the most significant casualties were senatorial candidates in Washington and North Carolina and gubernatorial incumbents in Alabama and South Carolina. The defeat of Fob James in Alabama was particularly noteworthy because he had become a symbol of Christian Right stridency. In the eyes of movement activists, James had struck a blow for religious freedom when he defied the liberal power structure by adamantly defending an Alabama judge who refused to remove the Ten Commandments from his courtroom when ordered by another court. In the election's aftermath, an exit poll commissioned by the Christian Coalition revealed the truth. Although self-described religious conservatives accounted for 29 percent of the electorate, only a little more than half voted for Republican candidates. This was a drop of 13 percentage points from 1994. More significantly, Democratic candidates received about a third of the votes of religious conservatives.[1]

The Christian Right leadership argued nearly in unison that the Republican decline was a direct result of the party's decision not to focus the campaign on issues important to Christian voters.[2] They claimed this proved what the leaders had said for several years, that the current leadership of the Republican Party cared more about compromise than issues. To further advance the Christian Right cause, the most influential movement figures demanded and received the head of Newt Gingrich. Gingrich resigned both from his position of Speaker of the House and from the House itself. The resulting shakeup of the party's leadership in Congress brought the Republican side of the aisle closer to the Christian Right. When the Republicans announced the new House leadership for the 106th Congress, all the top positions were filled by representatives who had received perfect ratings from the Christian Coalition in 1998.[3]

Clearly, the vanguard of the movement at the national level wanted more from Congress than a strong conservative economic and foreign policy agenda. What did they want? What would an America more in line with the Christian Right vision for the country look like? To answer these questions, we must move beyond the biblical Christian worldview of many religious conservatives to the distinctive vision of the Christian Right.

The Way Things Should Be

A visit to the Internet web site of almost any Christian Right organization provides a clear answer to these questions—and most other Christian Right web sites give the same answer. The movement is working to bring the culture and its social and political organs more into line with biblical principles. With that purpose, it stands in the long tradition of the New England Puritans, who hoped to establish a holy commonwealth in America. Establishing a Puritan holy commonwealth or a Christian Right Christian culture on the basis of biblical principles is not equivalent to creating a theocracy. Like the Puritans, the vast majority of Christian Right leaders do not want to establish a theocracy, which, by definition, involves the rule of the clergy or the church over civil government. Although the Puritans restricted the political franchise to church members, they clearly separated the responsibilities of the clergy and the magistrates. The role of the ministers was to interpret the Bible and to draw out clearly the implications of the Scriptures for public as well as private life. The Puritans gave responsibility to the magistrates to govern the society in accordance with biblical principles. The Bible rather than the church or the clergy became the basis of government. What the Puritans sought to establish was a *bibliocracy*,[4] not a theocracy. Contemporary Christian Right activists have a similar goal. With the Puritans, they believed that the Word of God provides the foundation for all spheres of private and social life, including government.

Christian Right historians use the Puritans as their model of colonial American life, yet in reality the Puritans were only one of many religious groups that helped define colonial and early national life. The Puritans were different from many of the other Christian groups who hoped to create a regenerated society in the American colonies. Only the Puritans fused biblical texts with the official policies of the government to attempt to bring all people in the society under the authority of the Bible. Whereas other religious and secular leaders in the colonies based their vision for the future nation on Enlightenment principles such as the rights of man, the Puritans rejected any concept of rights that found its justification in any other source than their Calvinist theology. Given the Puritan view of the sinful condition of humanity, human-centered Enlightenment ideas of natural rights could never provide an adequate base upon which to build a holy commonwealth.[5]

The contemporary Christian Right continues or, perhaps more accurately, attempts to resurrect Puritan hopes for a biblical commonwealth in America. In good Puritan fashion, the movement legitimates its efforts through appeals to biblical passages and seeks to extend the authority of the Scriptures to all spheres of society. Christian Right intellectuals and organizational leaders express their vision for America in a concept that the movement elite call the "dominion principle." It is the single most characteristic feature of the movement.[6] At its most basic level, dominion refers both to God's sovereignty over all creation and to the charge God has given to humans to bring the world under God's sovereignty. Two scriptural passages provide the basis for this principle. The first is drawn from the book of Genesis (Gen. 1:26–28) and the second from the Gospel of Matthew (Matt. 28:18–20). According to the Revised Standard Version (RSV) of the Bible, Genesis 1:26–28 says:

> Then God said, "Let us make man in our image, after our likeness; and let
> them have dominion over the fish of the sea, and over the birds of the air,
> and over the cattle, and over all the earth, and over every creeping thing that
> creeps upon the earth." So God created man in his own image, in the image
> of God he created him; male and female he created them. And God blessed
> them, and God said to them, "Be fruitful and multiply, and fill the earth and
> subdue it; and have dominion over the fish of the sea and over the birds of
> the air and over every living thing that moves upon the earth."

Most mainstream Christians, from the redeeming right to the liberal left,
tend to interpret *dominion* as human stewardship over all aspects of the
nonhuman creation. In Christian Right circles, however, theorists interpret the passage as justification for movement efforts to extend dominion
to the human sphere. They read the passage as a divine charge to bring
every institution and organ of civil society into conformity with God's
will. From their perspective, this mandate is given not to humanity in general but specifically to those whose minds and wills are faithful to God.
Dominion is reserved for those who remain the spiritual and moral heirs
of the Judeo-Christian tradition.

To reinforce their interpretation of the Genesis passage, Christian
Right sources turn to the verses in the New Testament Gospel of
Matthew commonly referred to as "the Great Commission." The RSV
reads, "And Jesus came and said to them, 'All authority in heaven and earth
has been given to me. Go therefore and make disciples of all nations, bap-
tizing them in the name of the Father and of the Son and of the Holy
Spirit, teaching them to observe all that I have commanded you; and lo, I
am with you always, to the close of the age'" (Matt. 28:18–20). Christian
Right writers interpret this commission in political and social terms.
Movement theologians make a careful distinction here between the power
of humanity to bring the world under God's sovereignty and the power of
God to do it. Standing in the theological tradition of Calvinism, Christian
Right intellectuals reject the power of humans alone to accomplish the
task because of human sinfulness. What they hope is that God will work
through them spiritually to regenerate others. They are confident that the
mission upon which they have embarked has God's blessing and assistance.
They believe that God has called them to a higher responsibility for the
task of regenerating American culture.

The COR manifesto, cited in chapter 3, makes this interpretation of
the divine directive explicit: "We affirm that the Great Commission is a
mandate by our Lord to go forth into all the world and make Bible-obey-

ing disciples of all nations." The manifesto continues: "Getting men's souls saved is only a preliminary part of fulfilling the Great Commission. Our work is incomplete unless we teach them to obey all He commanded. The words of the Lord's prayer for God's will to 'be done on earth as it is in heaven' are another way to state the essence of the same Great Commission.[7] Most Christians, from the redeeming right to the liberal left, do not share the Christian Right's social and political reading of this passage. For most believers, the Great Commission refers to a Christian duty to spread the gospel through mission work in foreign lands and through evangelism at home. The frequently stated goal of such endeavors is to make Bible-believing, rather than Bible-obeying, Christians of all the world.

A discussion of the historical development of the dominion principle and the assumptions on which it is based will help elucidate the full implications of the idea for the Christian Right. According to Christian Right theologians, the dominion principle begins with Jesus and continues through the writings of the fourth-century Bishop of Hippo, Augustine, and later comes to its fullest expression in the theological system of the sixteenth-century reformer John Calvin. This lineage is consistent with the orthodox Calvinist tradition. The Christian Right's deviation from the mainstream of that tradition begins in the nineteenth century with the writings and work of four Dutch Calvinist thinkers: Guillaume Groen van Prinsterer, Abraham Kuyper, Hermann Dooyeweerd, and Cornelius Van Til. The basic principles of their teaching laid the foundation for the contemporary Christian Right. But even though these four thinkers provide important starting points for our understanding of the Christian Right, movement theoreticians have modified each of the four's contributions.

Guillaume Groen van Prinsterer (1801–1876) sets the intellectual stage for the dualistic tendencies of the three later writers. He argued that all major philosophic tendencies in the modern period derived from one of two sources: Enlightenment humanism and the Protestant Reformation. He identified the former with the French Enlightenment with its tendency to rely on human reason and its denunciation of religion.[8] He identified the latter primarily with the theological insights of John Calvin. He also recognized the debt the Reformation owed to Martin Luther. Groen van Prinsterer's teachings provided Francis Schaeffer with the theoretical structure that he applied to his analysis of Western civilization. According to Schaeffer, the march of Western civilization has proceeded through a continual battle between human-centered and God-centered worldviews.

Abraham Kuyper (1837–1920) was an enormous figure in Dutch Calvinism. He played a singularly important role for the Christian Right in defining the political implications of Christianity. Kuyper, the foremost Calvinist leader in the Netherlands from 1880 to 1920, was a theologian-politician who rose to the position of prime minister of the Netherlands from 1901–5. Kuyper made several important contributions to the development of Calvinist thought. Building on Martin Luther's doctrine of the priesthood of all believers, Kuyper extended the sovereignty of Christianity into all areas of public life. But his approach was not theocratic. He argued that divine principles revealed by God provided the foundation upon which every aspect of the social order should be built and upon which the public actions of the citizenry should be defined. He referred to this as the theory of sphere-sovereignty.

According to Kuyper, society is properly understood in terms of a series of spheres or domains, each with its own institutions, which are limited in both authority and responsibility. Society functions best when all these organs operate in conformity with God's divine will as revealed to humanity. Society falls apart when these spheres either fail to operate in accordance with divine principles or expand beyond their limited authority and responsibility. For example, the church errs when it confuses its role with that of the state. The former is restricted to proclaiming and advancing the gospel; the latter is limited to restraining and restricting evil. Kuyper referred to this negative function of the state as "common grace." By limiting human sinfulness, the state extends God's peace and comfort to people in the temporal realm. However, the common grace of the state should never be confused with God's saving grace.

Kuyper also followed Groen van Prinsterer's division of worldviews into two types, one arising from the French Enlightenment, the other from the Protestant Reformation. From this starting point, Kuyper developed his theory of presuppositionalism. He held that all ideas, social developments, and political platforms rested upon foundational assumptions he termed presuppositional principles. As basic notions about the nature of things, presuppositions condition everything "from the simplest handicraft to the study of philosophy." For Kuyper this meant that objective scholarship was not possible. All disciplines, he believed, rest on faith presuppositions grounded in either God or humanity.[9] This implied that not all faith presuppositions are equal. Because of human sinfulness, people who based their lives on nonbiblical (i.e., unregenerate) foundations were necessarily inferior to Christians who structured their lives according to divinely revealed presuppositions. Since the two foundations were so radically differ-ent, Christians should not compromise with unregenerates.[10] Accommo-dation by Christians to non-Christian ideas would necessarily force Christians to abandon the presuppositions they knew were true for ones that were based on a faulty foundation.

In Kuyper's judgment, Western culture was in a state of tragic demise that had begun with the Enlightenment. He argued that the Enlighten-ment's rationalist challenge to Christianity constituted a challenge to the divine order of things. As a result of the Enlightenment, Christians found themselves pitted in a battle against humanists for the control of the cul-ture. Since presuppositions conditioned all human activity, any political, social, economic, or educational structures that emerged from the triumph of humanism were direct threats and roadblocks to the Christian world-view.[11] Through the European political movement known as the Christian Democrats, which he helped found, Kuyper encouraged Christians to be politically active in their societies in order to challenge the dominant En-lightenment assumptions that were misguiding Western European soci-eties.

In order to achieve his vision, Kuyper was actively involved in reshap-ing Calvinist education in the Netherlands. He argued that the state should charter free schools (free from state religious control) so that the various religious constituencies could establish their own curricula with state support. In such a situation, Calvinist schools would be free to teach all disciplines exclusively from presuppositions grounded in the biblical faith. Attempts by others to merely put a Christian veneer on an otherwise secular education contributed to the demise of Western culture, in Kuyper's estimation. If Christians were to take responsibility for influenc-ing the social and political orders, they needed to be taught how to ana-lyze and respond to social issues from a Christian perspective. Christians so trained should accept their calling to become actively involved in poli-tics, commerce, science, education, and the arts in order to help society grow and develop.[12]

Hermann Dooyeweerd (1894–1977) took Kuyper's presuppositional-ism to the next step. Dooyeweerd was an educational theorist in the Netherlands who developed an educational method called cosmonomic philosophy. Dooyeweerd denied the possibility of secular thought, that is, thought divorced from religious presuppositions. He believed that the hearts of all people were religious in the sense that they all attempted to ground their perspectives in the highest form of truth that exists. His complex system identified fourteen levels of spheres of being, beginning with time and then space, eventually arriving at ethics and faith. The purpose of his system of philosophic investigation was to move people toward the higher states of existence until they revealed their ultimate faith presuppositions. Dooyeweerd applied his method to education. His method presumed that Christians had a better interpretation of faith or a more consistent understanding of it than non-Christians. Therefore, wherever Christians implemented the method, it would lead people to recognize the superior force of the Christian faith.[13]

Although the presuppositional elements of Dooyeweerd are important to the formation of the Christian Right worldview, his particular cosmonomic method of education is not a model I have seen targeted for implementation in Christian Right materials. In fact, Dooyeweerd's attempt to redefine the worldview argument in philosophic rather than theological categories has been criticized by those in the Kuyperian–Van Tilian line. Dooyeweerd's particular contribution is his assertion that all perspectives are ultimately religious. Legal attempts by Christian Right activists to have secular humanism declared a religion by the courts reflect this dimension of Dooyeweerd's thought. Such presuppositions are crucial to Christian Right claims that the schools are not neutral. That much can be established through Kuyper's work. What Dooyeweerd contributes is the notion that the very idea of a secularist perspective is impossible. This means that schools are in fact teaching religion whether or not they claim to be neutral or objective.

Of the four Dutch Calvinists who built the theological foundation for the Christian Right, Cornelius Van Til (1895–1987) had the most direct influence. Van Til taught Christian apologetics at Princeton Theological Seminary until 1929. When the seminary board of trustees fell into more liberal hands that year, Van Til, along with J. Gresham Machen and two other professors, moved to the newly organized Westminster Theological Seminary in Philadelphia. He remained at Westminster as professor of Christian apologetics until his retirement in 1975. At Westminster, Van Til instructed his students in line with the theories advanced by Kuyper and Dooyeweerd. He agreed with Dooyeweerd's contention that Christians could make no peace with secularization because the worldview that grounded secularization was based on fundamentally different faith presuppositions than Christianity. He also accepted Kuyper's and Dooyeweerd's conclusion that no one (including educators and students) could simultaneously hold contradictory presuppositions. In the dualistic mind-set of these three thinkers, a person adopted either a Christian or a non-Christian worldview. There was no middle ground, nor was there any desire or possibility for compromise. To adopt a Christian viewpoint meant to place oneself in subjugation to the autonomy and sovereignty of God as revealed in the Scriptures. To adopt a non-Christian viewpoint meant to place oneself in subjection to free independent human autonomy.[14]

Van Til did not remain neutral in terms of giving humans a choice between the Christian and the humanist worldviews. Along with Dooyeweerd, he held that "thought must be constrained to acknowledge its dependence upon the God-given order of reality and to realize that this order is understood only in the light of divine revelation."[15] Van Til developed an apologetic method closely related to Kuyper's presuppositionalism in order to force people to acknowledge their dependence on God-given reality. He also called his method presuppositionalism. Van Til's modification of Kuyper's approach was to move it in the direction he called transcendental. By this he meant that presuppositional investigation began with an analysis of the way things presently are and moved back to the conditions or foundations that explained them. This method applied not only to Christians in their own lives, but also to Christians in relation to unregenerates. Believing that the only way in which reality made any coherent sense was through God's divine sovereignty and truth, Van Til urged his students to press those opposed to the Christian worldview back to their grounding presuppositions.

If Christians were to break the hold of humanists on the culture, Van Til argued, Christians must take control of the culture. For him, however, the struggle was not political. The battle was to be won in the marketplace of ideas, not at the ballot box. In order to be successful, Christians must break down the presuppositions that prevented others from accepting biblical principles. Secularists would not be convinced by biblical or theological arguments, because their presuppositions protected them from attacks from that direction. The most effective way of undermining the secularist dominance of the culture, Van Til opined, was to create arguments and gather data from the secularist perspective to show how evidence derived from such sources weakened rather than supported humanist presuppositions.

This aggressive analysis of the secularist's position would eventually lead the non-Christian to an understanding of the inevitable consequences of holding falsely grounded ideas. There was no need initially for the Christian to argue *for* Christian presuppositions. The proper starting point was to push the opponent's position as far as possible back to its basic foundation and then show the weaknesses in that foundation. Only after the opponent's trust in his or her own worldview was broken, would he or she be ready to acknowledge the truth and superiority of the Christian perspective.

Van Til advocated his presuppositional method as the best means possible of wresting control of Western culture from the grasp of the humanists. Like Dooyeweerd, he believed that the way to begin undermining humanist control of the culture was through education. He broke with Dooyeweerd's contention that the educational method should begin by investigating the lower foundation of humanity's religions and then moving to the higher rather than beginning and ending with the highest—faith in God.[16] For Van Til, proper education proceeded from a Christian standpoint and critically assessed all other truth claims or philosophic assumptions from that perspective. Any other form of education gave students a false understanding of reality that moved them to contribute to the demise of Western culture. In this regard, Van Til was in firm agreement with Kuyper.

Most Americans have never heard of any of these four thinkers, but their influence within conservative evangelical intellectual circles is enormous. Kuyper, for example, has been described as "the patron saint of the 20th century evangelical resurgence in politics."[17] The influence of this lineage of Dutch Calvinists has been acknowledged by such contemporary leaders as C. Everett Koop, John Whitehead, and better-known figures such as Cal Thomas, Jack Kemp, James Dobson, and Ralph Reed.

The four Dutch Calvinists, however, differ in significant ways from present-day Christian Right thinkers. This means that evangelical Christians may fall into the Kuyperian or Van Tilian camp, for example, without necessarily identifying with the Christian Right. We find one example of this phenomenon in a movement among certain Calvinist Christians to reform Christian schools to conform to Kuyper's presuppositional theory of Christian education. Troubled by what they conclude are secular schools with a Christian face, these activists seek to restructure the curriculum of Christian schools to view every discipline from biblically grounded faith presuppositions. Although those active in this movement hope that their graduates will bring that perspective into the social order and work to transform people's understanding of things from their positions of influence, they do not accept the overtly political and transformational approach of the contemporary Christian Right as a social movement.[18]

The line of thought from Kuyper to Van Til is not incidental to the development of the much more coherent Christian Right that emerged in the late 1980s. Van Til schooled two students at Westminster Theological Seminary, Francis Schaeffer and Rousas John Rushdoony, who became essential to the progression of the Christian Right as a religiously grounded social movement. Schaeffer provided the contemporary activists with a theology of culture, and Rushdoony's writing contained the clearest articulation of the Christian Right's political theology. Beginning in the 1970s, these two enormously influential voices emerged in conservative evangelical circles to provide the movement with the systematic theological foundation that gave the Christian Right definition, purpose, and direction. Behind them stood their teacher, Cornelius Van Til, as well as other Reformed theologians from the same camp. What resulted was a growing shared consciousness among Christian Right leaders of a systematic theological analysis of culture, a systematic theological vision of the political order, and a systematic, theologically grounded understanding of the relationship of the Christian to the larger culture. In turn, the new theological coherence contributed greatly to the formulation of new symbol systems through which the leaders communicated to their constituencies and to the larger marketplace of ideas. The theocultural movement that emerged became a powerful force in providing religious structure, meaning, and purpose to those whose Christian worldview put them in tension with the larger culture.

Christian Right Foundations: The Mythos of Francis Schaeffer

Francis A. Schaeffer (1912–1984) is the single most important figure in the development of the contemporary Christian Right as a coherent religious movement. His contribution was enormous in three vitally important areas. Schaeffer's passion in opposition to abortion mobilized a largely apolitical evangelical community into social action around a single defining issue. His popularization of Van Til's presuppositionalism provided the newly mobilized constituency with a strategic blueprint. His magnum opus, *How Should We Then Live?* identified the cause of moral decline in Western culture and traced its development from the time of the ancient Greeks forward. This furnished the movement with its orienting mythos.

Schaeffer was a very unlikely figure to have had such a major impact on the rise of the Christian Right. As a child, he did not have a religious home life. When he did convert to Christianity as a teenager, it was into the Bible Presbyterian Church, a group that stood at the fringe of evangelical Protestantism. He attended Westminster Theological Seminary in Philadelphia but left before he graduated to help found the more conservative Faith Theological Seminary. After pastoring several churches in the United States, he went to Europe as a missionary of the Bible Presbyterian Church. There he had his first success, running L'Abri Fellowship, a faith community that, at first, attracted mainly Swiss university students.

In prolonged conversations with those students, Schaeffer began to understand at the deepest philosophical levels what he concluded to be the main weakness of contemporary culture—a pervasive materialistic worldview that had infected every aspect of Western civilization from art to politics, from science to philosophy. Building on the presuppositional method of Christian apologetics taught to him by Cornelius Van Til at Westminster, Schaeffer began to construct a theology of culture that was to rock American evangelicalism to its core. He argued that a fundamental opposition existed between the materialistic worldview of contemporary culture and the Christian worldview. Echoing Kuyper and Van Til, he concluded that because of the chasm between the two worldviews, Christians could not live in both worlds. Rather than preaching separation from the world, Schaeffer argued that contemporary Christians must understand both perspectives at the most basic level of their presuppositions, learn where the weaknesses in the materialistic worldview existed, push those presuppositions until people could no longer hold on to them rationally, and then provide an alternative perspective that did not rest on such internal contradictions. Like Christian Right leaders, Schaeffer claimed the Bible as the source of the Christian worldview.[19] He affirmed the inerrancy and absolute truth of the Scriptures, rejecting any suggestion that the Bible's truth be restricted to theology or narrowly conceived religious spheres of life. Arguing for the unity of truth, Schaeffer insisted that the Bible's history and science were just as true as its theological claims.

Schaeffer brought his analysis of culture to the United States in 1965. In a series of lectures at Wheaton College in Illinois, he challenged what he believed to be the complacency and comfort of American evangelicalism. His critique engaged culture at a time when evangelicals were avoiding it. As one commentator described it, Schaeffer was offering critiques of films by Bergman and Fellini while the students were fighting for permission to show Bambi. As the administration at Wheaton was struggling to keep textbooks free of references to existential philosophy, Schaeffer was discussing the writing of Camus, Sartre, and Heidegger, the art of Dali, the poetry of Dylan Thomas, and the music of the Beatles and John Cage.[20] Schaeffer's lectures and books convinced many young evangelicals of the baby boomer generation that they needed to engage the world on its own terms if they were to have an impact on society.

Schaeffer presented his mythic interpretation of Western culture in 1976 in his book and film series *How Should We Then Live?* It is epic in both its scope and its breadth. Beginning with the ancient classical civilizations of Greece and Rome, it moves through the course of Western history, tracing the development of Western science, philosophy, and art. The journey is marked by a number of crossroads where, because culture took one turn rather than another, the entire character of the culture changed. These pivotal periods Schaeffer defined as the early church, the Middle Ages, the Renaissance, the Reformation, the Enlightenment, the romantic era, and modern and contemporary culture.

Each crossroad presented Western culture with only two alternatives from which to choose. Humans could turn to either the God-centered worldview of biblical Christianity or the human-centered worldview of humanism. The God-centered worldview led to a happier, freer, and more fulfilling life. The human-centered worldview led to a life devoid of any possible solution to the problems humans faced in the present world. According to Schaeffer, the God-centered worldview was synonymous with the biblical worldview of orthodox Calvinism as taught by J. Gresham Machen and Van Til at Westminster. Schaeffer consigned every religious viewpoint that stood outside that narrowly defined tradition, Christian or non-Christian, to the humanist camp.

According to Schaeffer, the God-centered or biblical Christian worldview begins with the knowledge that God exists, that God is sovereign over all creation, and that absolute truth can be known by humans with certainty through the Bible. It asserts the truth about humanity and the divinely created cosmos. Humans are created by God and in the image of God. This gives humanity ultimate worth, dignity, and significance. As God reveals to humanity the purpose of creation, humans come to understand the ultimate meaning of life. Because God gives them absolute moral values, they have a rudder to guide them through the morass of human existence. Thus they have true freedom to fulfill their divine calling in their chosen avenue of life. Finally, God gives to humanity Jesus Christ in order to redeem humanity from its fallen condition. As a result, redeemed

Christians have the power and the necessary resources to get themselves and their culture back on the right road.

The human-centered worldview begins, according to Schaeffer, with the assertion that humanity is the measure of all things. Since this presupposition, from Schaeffer's perspective, is based on a distorted conception of the world and a flawed view of human nature, it cannot possibly speak with any assurance to the problems people face in life. The problem with the humanist idea of the world is that it fails to recognize the divine origin, purpose, order, and significance of the cosmos. By denying the divine nature of the cosmos, people cut themselves off from any chance of understanding the world in terms of ultimate meaning, value, or significance. They are left with a world that has no meaning, value, or significance beyond mere existence or the meaning, value, or significance that humans impose upon it. The problem with the humanist conception of human nature, as Schaeffer explains it, is that it fails to recognize the full implications of the consequences of the Fall. Because they do not recognize that the Fall left humanity in a condition of total depravity, humanists place false confidence in humanity and conclude that they have the necessary resources within their power to create a happy, free, and fulfilling life. The eventual cultural consequence of the human-centered worldview is that autonomous humans are alone in the world without the resources they need to solve their problems.

Although Schaeffer described the two paths as going in two distinctly different directions, he was too informed by history to judge either path as entirely good or bad. There were dangers and beauty on both paths. On the road of biblical Christianity, the chief danger was compromise with those treading the other path. Beauty was found in the true freedom Christians and Christian culture enjoyed through obedience to God's absolute truth. On the road of humanism, Schaeffer found the chief beauty to be the technical contributions humanists made in various fields and time periods. He located its chief danger in the inherent threat to God that was implicit in the humanist worldview.

In *A Christian Manifesto,* Schaeffer called biblical Christians to action. He argued that because these two worldviews were incompatible, no compromise was possible. Therefore, Christians must choose between the two. To choose the biblical worldview meant to engage in a far-reaching transformation of the entire culture into a "Christian cultural consensus." In such an environment, religious pluralism might exist on the private or individual level, but in the public arena every institution of society would be redefined to bring it into harmony with biblical principles. We saw this idea expressed before in Robert Simonds's call for the creation of "Christian worldview schools."

Schaeffer called Christians to bring the nation back to a biblical Christian cultural consensus. Before that could occur, he argued, two problems needed to be addressed. On the one hand, too many evangelical Christians did not understand the degree to which being a Christian required them to apply biblical principles to all areas of their personal and social lives. On the other hand, too many Americans did not realize that the only solution to their cultural problems was to orient themselves to a biblical Christian perspective. Schaeffer argued that only by making the biblical Christian worldview the starting point for being in the world could the truth be known about the world and oneself. Only by applying this truth to our problems could the cultural decline of Western civilization be reversed.

Schaeffer attributed America's moral decay to a collapse of the nation's Christian center. He viewed abortion with particular alarm. Through his presuppositional method, Schaeffer hoped to move Christians to an awareness of the problem and call them to their responsibility to do something about it. Schaeffer's early works *Escape from Reason* (1968) and *The God Who Is There* (1968) asserted that evangelicals both have failed to take the culture seriously and have failed to extend the Christian worldview to their situation in life.[21] Eight years later, Schaeffer's *How Should We Then Live?* (1976) provided evangelicals with a historical map by which they could recognize the forces that had led them to their twofold failure. *A Christian Manifesto* (1982) called them to repent of their sins and to transform the culture. In all these works and in his public speaking, Schaeffer's focus remained steadfastly directed to evangelical Christians. He spoke in-house. Because this was his focus, few outside the evangelical subculture in America have even heard of Francis Schaeffer.

Schaeffer did not view himself as an intellectual. His purpose was not merely to explore ideas. He was an evangelist, and there was a sense of urgency to his evangelism. As cancer consumed more of his health, Schaeffer issued a broadside to evangelical Christians. In *The Great Evangelical Disaster* (1984), he made his strongest case for a transformation of evangelical Christians. This jeremiad, along with his early works, called for a conversion among Christians to act in defense of God-centered Christianity in the face of the overwhelming attack on human worth, freedom, and dignity that the abortion issue represented. Schaeffer saw the battle over abortion in a cultural as well as a universal context. He wrote, "But the

Scriptures make clear that Bible-believing Christians are locked in a battle of cosmic proportions. It is a life and death struggle over the minds and souls of men for all eternity, but it is equally a life and death struggle over life on earth."[22] Though the issue was abortion, for Schaeffer, the public schools represented the ultimate battleground of the losing war against apostasy.

In a presentation at D. James Kennedy's Coral Ridge Presbyterian Church in Fort Lauderdale, Florida, Schaeffer made explicit the connection between the nation's moral decline and the public schools. Schaeffer understood well the degree to which the schools impacted the worldview of the students and, later, the society. The problem with the public schools, according to Schaeffer, was that they had come under the control of secular humanists, who taught a human-centered materialistic philosophy that offered no hope to people. Yet, the humanist control had become so great in the schools that the secular humanists could use their power to exclude any other perspectives. Schaeffer told the audience, "A good illustration is in the public schools. This view is taught in our public schools exclusively—by law. There is no other view that can be taught . . . and that is that the final reality is only material or energy shaped by pure chance."[23] From his perspective, the crisis in public education centered on the degree to which the schools had become the active agent of humanists in the humanists' efforts to destroy the Christian cultural consensus and replace it with their own. Humanists were so successful, Schaeffer argued, that both the content and the processes of public education were antithetical to the Christian worldview. Only a complete reorientation of public education could reverse this reality.

In his remarks at Coral Ridge, Schaeffer was more concerned with the immediacy of the abortion issue. After all, abortion was the issue that brought most of the early activists into the movement. But he took the opportunity at Coral Ridge to begin planting the seeds for the systematic criticism of public education that was to follow years later from Christian Right sources. Those who listened to Schaeffer could not help but draw the connection to education. The tapestry he wove was so tightly knit that the mythic pattern became clear to everyone. His analysis of the current state of public education in *How Should We Then Live?* contained the framework on which virtually all current Christian Right criticism of America's schools was built.[24] Schaeffer's argument about the course of Western civilization was so essential to his critique of education that it deserves a detailed presentation.

The epic dimension of the history of Western culture that Schaeffer dramatized in *How Then Shall We Live?* described two opposing forces locked in a battle for the control of culture. He began his mythic tale with the ancient Greeks, because, according to Schaeffer, Western culture owed its heritage to the Greco-Roman worldview. From the composite Greek and Roman worldview, Western culture received the "classical" basis of its intellectual life. As in most historical eras, Schaeffer found strengths and weaknesses in this early period. The glory of Greece and Rome was that they sought integration of all aspects of religious and social life. This desire for unity in all spheres of life gave birth to the concept of "culture." The failure of the Greeks and Romans was twofold. By organizing their social life around the *polis,* the Greeks placed unfounded confidence in the human ability to be self-governing. The Romans complicated the problem when they attempted to place humanity on the same level as God by divinizing the emperor. Schaeffer concluded that the Greco-Roman conception of human nature was too large and its gods too small. Thus, classical culture was incapable of rescuing Greek and Roman civilization from the seeds of its own destruction.

Schaeffer next turned his attention to the early Christian church. The glory of first-century Christianity was that it provided humanity with the only real alternative to Greco-Roman humanism, a Christian worldview. Existing in the midst of Roman civilization, early Christians realized that they must choose one or the other stance toward the world. They courageously chose to orient their lives to the teachings of the New Testament, to God's divinely revealed absolute truth. By refusing to worship Caesar, the early church demonstrated that it understood the social and political implications of its decision to worship God. The refusal of the early Christians to compromise with Caesar provoked the Roman authorities to persecute them, and they proved their courage and the strength of their faith by standing up to these persecutions. By centering their lives on the teachings of the New Testament, the first-century Christians found the necessary rudder to guide them through their suffering at the hands of the humanists. Schaeffer viewed the Christianity of the early church period as "pristine Christianity" because of these qualities.[25]

The Christian church sustained this pure or biblical Christianity through the leadership of Jerome, Ambrose, and Augustine, until the early Middle Ages. These giants of the Christian faith took Hellenistic culture seriously without compromising with it. Their solution to classical thought was to integrate it into a Christian worldview, thereby transforming classical thought.

This, in Schaeffer's words, "domesticated" classical thought and redeemed it.[26] The church of the Middle Ages followed. It did a number of good things. It placed culture on a Christian, if not always biblical, foundation. Schaeffer cited Charlemagne, in particular, for making Christianity a more general cultural force within the Holy Roman Empire. As Schaeffer described it, Charlemagne saw the implications of the Christian worldview for every aspect of culture and sought to bring every sphere of culture into harmony with the Christian worldview. The medieval church also contributed to the growth of the Christian worldview by providing some limitations to material excess among the populace, even if the church sometimes failed to achieve the same modesty in its own affairs. The monastic ideal of poverty provided an ideal moral counterbalance to the tendency of fallen humanity to seek first its own happiness without compassion for others. Finally, to its credit, the church asserted the authority of God over that of the state, even if it sometimes confused its own interests with God's. In restricting the power of the state, the church laid the foundation for the principle of limited governmental responsibility.[27] The medieval church was not without its faults, however, It departed from a God-centered worldview when it placed ecclesiastical or priestly authority over biblical authority. Rather than allowing the Bible to provide the final truth on all matters, the church depended on its own hierarchy and the Pope. The church also departed from a biblical worldview when it began to see merit in works-righteousness. This implied that humans could do good works even outside the redeeming grace of God.

The seeds of humanism, planted by the Greeks and Romans, were nurtured during the early Middle Ages by the Arabs and the Eastern Orthodox Church, which preserved some of the classical texts. But the demise of Christian culture began from within the Western church, when humanism flowered in the writings of Thomas Aquinas and the Scholastic philosophers. Aquinas had a partial view of the Fall. Schaeffer wrote that according to Aquinas, though the will was corrupted by the Fall, the intellect was not. This implied that humans had the capacity to discern truth through the use of human reason alone. Because of Aquinas's flawed conception of the Fall, he placed the truth claims of classical thought on the same level as those of Christianity, leading medieval Christians to a disastrous situation as they came to view the thought of the ancient Greeks and, in particular, Aristotle as a legitimate source of truth independent of scriptural standards. The mistake Aquinas made was his failure to submit the truth claims of classical thought to biblical standards.

The church's compromise with the human-centered worldview led slowly but directly to the Renaissance. In the Renaissance, humanism reached full bloom with the celebration of human reason, human potential, and human autonomy. Despite these dangerous developments, the Renaissance made valuable contributions to Western culture. Its emphasis on the physical reality of nature and humanity corrected some of the idealized distortions that had crept into the church during the Middle Ages. Further, the earlier Greek drive to see the unity of all things led to the development of the Renaissance idea of versatility in interests and learning. The failure of the Renaissance, like that of the medieval church under Scholasticism, derived from its overly optimistic view of human nature. By making humanity the measure of all things, the Renaissance stripped Western culture of any ultimate meaning and value. The emergence of Renaissance humanism as a viable alternative to the God-centered worldview placed European culture at a crossroads. In southern Europe, the High Renaissance took the road of humanism. In northern Europe, the seeds of cultural discontent with humanism that had been growing for several centuries erupted into the flowering of the Protestant Reformation.[28]

The paramount cultural contribution of the Reformers was their attempt to reestablish the biblical foundation of culture by removing the distortions in Christianity that had crept into Western culture through the Middle Ages and the Renaissance. The basis of the Reformation was Martin Luther's principle of *Sola Scriptura,* that Scripture alone was the basis of all authority.[29] By returning to the ultimate source of authority, humanity could once again with certainty know truth, know the absolutes and universals. Whereas humanism left southern Europe without any source of true knowledge about humanity and the cosmos, the Reformation provided northern Europe with absolute truth about both. Because biblical revelation gave humanity absolute truth about God, the creation, and humanity, it provided the only reliable standard against which to judge all truth claims. Thus, biblical Christianity was the only trustworthy foundation upon which to rest culture. This was the most important cultural contribution of the Reformation. Beyond bringing Christians back to their biblical foundation, the triumph of Protestantism in northern and western Europe and later America, was that it created a Christian cultural consensus.

The birth of modern science and technology, according to Schaeffer, came as a direct result of the Reformation's reestablishment of the Christian cultural consensus. Schaeffer argued that though science existed prior to the Reformation it found its proper basis in biblical Christian doctrines.

> To say theoretically that the Greek tradition would have been in itself a sufficient stimulus for the Scientific Revolution comes up against the fact that it was not. It was the Christian factor that made the difference. Christianity is the mother of modern science because it insists that God who created the universe has revealed himself in the Bible to be the kind of God that he is. Consequently, there is a sufficient basis for science to study the universe.[30]

According to Schaeffer, until the Reformation, science rested on Aristotelian logic, which provided an insufficient base because it focused on relations among particulars, or individual things, rather than seeing those particulars in the context of the absolutes and universals that gave the particulars meaning. Biblical Christianity supplied a firmer foundation for science by testifying to the ultimate order of things and providing, through the Scriptures, the assurance to humans that order could be known with certainty.

Schaeffer asserts that modern democracy was also a product of Reformation Christianity. The democratic principles of the limitation of the power of government over the people and the inherent equality of all people both grew out of a God-centered worldview. Samuel Rutherford's *Lex Rex* provided the theoretical basis for democracy with his argument that neither the king nor the will of the majority stood above God's law. Schaeffer's opinion on this matter was so thoroughgoing that he argued that Thomas Jefferson was able to contribute significantly to the design of the American democracy because he lived within a Christian cultural consensus, not because he was an Enlightenment deist.[31] What both Thomas Jefferson and John Locke contributed to American political theory, in Schaeffer's estimation, represented a secularized version of the Christian cultural consensus. Though Jefferson and Locke framed the particular articulations of democratic principles in secular terms, the substance of those principles was Christian because they were products of the Christian cultural consensus.

As these comments suggest, Schaeffer's treatment of the Enlightenment was partial, at best. He associated the Enlightenment almost exclusively with the form it took in France, completely ignoring its American counterpart. This put Schaeffer in the advantageous position of being able to attribute all of the immoderation of the Enlightenment to southern European humanism while ignoring its more positive effects in America. In his discussion of the Enlightenment, Schaeffer focused on the Enlightenment excesses and repression of Maximilien Robespierre and Napoleon Bonaparte in France. From France, Schaeffer then drew a direct line from the Enlightenment to the repression resulting from the activities of Vladimir Ilyich Lenin, Karl Marx, and Joseph Stalin in Russia; Benito Mussolini in Italy; and Adolph Hitler in Germany.

According to Schaeffer, the history of Western culture from then up to the present time is a record of the gradual ascension of the human-centered worldview and the decline of the God-centered one. Science fell from grace in two ways. By adopting an exclusively materialistic view of reality, science stripped the creation of its ultimate meaning and significance. Thus, science was left fulfilling the wants and needs of autonomous human beings who sought to raise themselves to the place of God. By extending the domain of cause and effect to humanity, psychology and sociology stripped humanity of any ultimate worth and dignity and made humanity just another part of the machine or organism. Modern philosophy also fell from grace. When humanists discovered the insufficiency of rationalism, they turned to romanticism and the glorification of experience over truth, process over content. In terms of education, these romantic notions came to full expression in the progressive movement, in the persons of John Dewey and his disciples. The fall from grace of rationalism eventually led to the absurdity of existentialism and the absence of any meaning except that asserted through the actions of the individual.

Gradually, with the loss of absolutes in all areas of modern thought, the Christian cultural consensus began to die. Modern thought with its emphasis on the individual, reason, experience, and relativism replaced it but without any ultimate basis upon which to organize human society. The danger of the present situation, according to Schaeffer, was that unless the Christian cultural consensus was restored, the social vacuum would result in a tyranny of either the elite or the majority; in the latter case, the state would become the absolute. Divorced from true absolutes, neither alternative had any capacity to solve the problems of contemporary Western culture.

Christian Right Foundations: The Symbolic Web of Rousas John Rushdoony

As Francis Schaeffer provided the contemporary Christian Right with its mythic framework through his theology of culture, Rousas John Rushdoony articulated the symbolic web that defined the movement's transformed culture politically and socially. The symbols Rushdoony used to weave this cultural web of significance included secularism (the chief representation of evil) and the divinely ordained institutions of the individual, the church, the state, and the family. The end product, in Clifford Geertz's words, was a complex set of symbol systems woven into webs of significance that tied every aspect of culture to every other aspect.[32] These deep symbols, as Edward Farley described them, became god-terms.[33] God-terms expressed the foundational presuppositions upon which culture rested by linking cultural ideals to transcendent and ultimate realities. They provided the compass that oriented people to the world with their directional markers. The writings of Rousas John Rushdoony presented the clearest and most systematic discussion of these deep symbols within the Christian Right.[34] By understanding the specific meanings Rushdoony gave to the basic symbols of the Christian Right, we will begin to understand the nuances of Christian Right critiques of public education.

The central symbol of Rushdoony's political theology is God. God, for Rushdoony, is the symbol humans use to designate what they take to be the ultimate or absolute dimension of existence. Religion is the form through which humans express these ultimate concerns. All worldviews are religious insofar as they all point to something humans take to be ultimate.[35] In this sense, as Dooyeweerd argued, both the biblical Christian worldview and the humanist worldview are religious.[36] However, only the God-centered worldview of biblical Christians identifies the true God as god. Although human understanding of God may be partial and finite, Christians have in the Bible true knowledge about the true God.

Rushdoony focuses on three important characteristics of his symbol of God. Christians can know them with certainty. The first characteristic is the creative aspect of God. God is the author of all creation, and all creation derives its meaning, purpose, and significance from this fact. The second characteristic is the redemptive aspect of God. Through Jesus Christ, God provides humans with the only possibility of redemption. When redeemed, Christians have the ability to see and understand things that are hidden to others. This puts redeemed Christians in a better position to know and execute God's will on earth. The third characteristic is the sovereignty or absolute authority of God. God is in control of the universe and has structured the creation in such a way that humans, when living in harmony with that structure, can achieve real happiness, peace, and freedom.

All of the remaining deep symbols Rushdoony employs derive from this understanding of God. In terms of Rushdoony's political theology, and that of the Christian Right, the most important of these symbols are the individual, the state, the church, and the family. Taken collectively, these are known within Christian Right circles as the divinely ordained institutions. All of them operate with a structure that begins with the Triune God, is revealed through the Bible, and operates within a covenant of grace. The holy commonwealth, or a society in harmony with God's purposes, exists as a collection of various institutions, each with its own limited and separate powers. Society functions well when each institution acts only in its proper sphere and for the purposes for which God designed it. When any institution oversteps its limited or denominated powers, society can no longer fulfill its proper role.

The Individual

Not all Christian Right leaders class the individual as a divinely ordained institution. Yet, along with the other deep symbols identified above, the individual has limited and unique powers and responsibilities. Moreover, for Rushdoony, at least, *the individual* is a god-term in the sense that its meaning and significance derive from his symbol of God and cannot be understood outside that context. Finally, the other deep symbols of the Christian Right presume a prior understanding of the individual. Though Rushdoony's concept of the individual is quite similar to that of Francis Schaeffer, described above, a brief discussion here will set the context for our consideration of the state, the church, and the family.

The starting point, as in Schaeffer's system, is with God the creator. Humans are created in the image of God and therefore have inherent worth and dignity. However, as a consequence of the Fall, humans have been totally corrupted by sin. As a result, autonomous humans are incapable of solving their own problems. Nor are they able without the Bible to understand their proper relationship to God, to God's creation, and to each other. The purpose of human life is the glorification of God. Humans glorify God by bringing their personal and social lives into conformity with God's divinely ordained institutions for human society. Through such an orientation in life, humans experience the only true freedom and happiness available to them.

> For those who believe that liberty is the concomitant of law and of order, the answer rests clearly upon man to accept, instead of the genetic fallacy, the sovereignty of the ontological trinity, God, the sovereign creator and redeemer. God, the self-determined one, has created man in His image, and man's self-government and responsibility under God in Christ is a restoration of liberty and order to a fallen world. Men who truly know themselves to be bought with a price and adopted into the glorious liberty of the sons of God will not become the slaves of man and of the state.[37]

As creatures of God created in the image of God, humans have God-given rights. Rights, in this sense, refer to the principles of personal responsibility and obligation in upholding God's law. In other words, humans have the right to live in conformity to God's will, and any action that diverts them from that conformity necessarily robs them of both their rights and their freedoms.[38] When the state oversteps its bounds and prevents individuals from living in conformity to what Rushdoony refers to as God-law, humans have the obligation to call the state to account. Ultimate authority, therefore, rests not with the individual or the state but with God-law.

The State

The state for Rushdoony is the basis for all human social order. It is "the social organization of the creed, the legal structuring of the moral system of a society."[39] As such, the state is inherently religious and therefore can never be religiously neutral. When the state claims to be religiously neutral, it engages in deception, either of itself or the people it governs. What really occurs when the state claims religious neutrality is that, in effect, it establishes the existing religion and its social order in order to protect that order from religiously grounded challenges to its authority.[40] Since the dominant cultural consensus in the contemporary United States is based on a humanistic worldview, present-day government claims of religious neutrality are specifically aimed at denying a foothold to the God-centered worldview within the existing social structure. The same is true of the schools. As social institutions under the control of the state, efforts of the schools to remain religiously neutral are really aimed solely at keeping out the biblical Christian worldview.

The state is the divinely ordained sovereign power over the people. The critical issue is not the state's power and its legitimate exercise, but upon what authority the state bases the exercise of its authority. There are two options. Either the state can view itself as sovereign, thus excluding God, or it can view God as sovereign. In the first case, the authority for the state rests in humanity. In the second case, the authority rests in a transcendent and absolute God. The first position leads to moral collapse because humans have nothing more than their own flawed selves to rely on. The second position leads to freedom and a just social order because humans rest their social order on transcendent principles. The purpose of the state, from the perspective of biblical Christianity, is to employ a concept of justice in which restitution is the fundamental principle of law. Law, not salvation, is the basis of the social order. The state misinterprets its role in human affairs when it seeks to save the people it serves or to provide them with the means to their own happiness. Because humanity is fallen, the state cannot save its citizens. Its only purpose is to seek from its populace conformity to God's law. Law and its enforcement in conformity to God's will are the only divine mandate God has given the state.[41]

Since the state exists under the covenant of grace, it is not without compassion. Its mercy, however, is limited to the proper exercise of its denominated power. True freedom and happiness cannot come from a social order that places its faith in humanity; the only possibility of freedom and happiness comes from Christianity. Thus, the compassion appropriate to the state is best expressed when the state promotes Christianity so that true restitution of the individual by God can take place.[42] This means that the only allowable educational function for the state is to educate children in the biblical Christian worldview. When the state fails to do that, it fails to fulfill its divinely ordained purpose. In order to prevent such failure or to restore the state to its proper function after it has failed, Christians must seek to gain control over the social order, not to save the unregenerated sinners but to structure the social order so that it conforms to God's law.

The implications for public education are profound. The danger of the public schools is not related to their lack of symbolic prayer or references to religious groups and events in history courses. It is found in their humanistic grounding presuppositions, the dangerous consequences of those presuppositions, and the evangelistic fervor with which the public schools promote them. This means that the schools as extensions of the state are illegitimate. The only alternatives Christians have left to them are to defund public education so that it can no longer act illegitimately or to transform the schools into what Robert Simonds calls "Christian Worldview Perspective Schools."

The growing influence of Rushdoony's thought among purist Christian Right leaders has important implications for the public schools. Previously, Christian Right controversies and criticism tended to be more issue-based than systemic. Now they are framed within this biblical Christian presuppositionalism that locates each of the particular issues within an entire symbol system. As long as the state is involved in public education, the ground point for criticism of public education from the purist camp of the Christian Right will be the presupposition of the nature of the state and the other divinely ordained institutions discussed here.

The Church

The function of the church is not to govern the people. Rushdoony and the Christian Right do not advocate a theocracy. The responsibility for governing, as we have seen, is reserved for the state only. The church oversteps its limits when it seeks to have a role in governing the populace. The main function of the church as declared by God is "to serve as the agency through which faith would be nurtured and sins forgiven." It remains true to its purpose only insofar as it preaches true doctrine and administers the sacraments according to Christ's institution.[43] Rushdoony pays proper respect to the role of the minister, but much of his attention in discussing the operation of the church as it fulfills its divine mandate is focused on the office of the elder.

The main function of the elder within the church is to assist the minister in maintaining and extending the gospel in the lives of the members of the congregation.[44] The elder, an older male, has demonstrated Christian virtue in his own personal life and in promoting such virtue in others through his role as the head of his household. Having demonstrated such virtue, he is worthy of performing the same function among the members of the congregation. Although his function then is similar to law, because he restrains evil and brings peace and harmony to the congregation, he should exercise his authority in a way that helps "train his charges into a way of life." The preferable means used by the elder are teaching, quiet conversation, and moral persuasion. To accomplish this end, the elder is expected to keep a careful watch over all aspects of the members' lives in all spheres of public life. Thus, the elder's instructions extend to helping members come to understand the principles that ground a Christian life, the requirements this places upon them, and the expectations for a consis-

is naturally prior to the state. Its priority derives from the immediacy of the personal bonds that hold the family together in service of God and obedience to God's commandments. In this sense, the family is even prior to the church. In its God-centered origin and function, the family is part of God's intended purpose for humanity. It is perhaps the most necessary institution through which humans can realize their full purpose and potential. As in the state and the church, such fulfillment derives from obedience to God's law through the ordering of the life of the individual in order to bring it into conformity with God's will. Primary responsibility belongs to the husband as the head of the household: guided by the elders of the church, he exercises authority over the family to ensure that the members of the family are led to a Christian way of life. This requires, particularly on the part of the husband, a willingness to "do battle for the Lord" outside the home in order to bring the outside world into the dominion of Christ. The exercise of dominion is more central to the divine function of the family than even procreation, according to Rushdoony. "The meaning of the family is thus not to be sought in procreation but in a God-centered authority and responsibility in terms of man's calling to subdue the earth and to exercise dominion over it."[50] Writers like Tim La-Haye tend to put greater emphasis than Rushdoony on the sexual and procreative character of marriage; nonetheless, LaHaye and others also accept the larger function of the family as the place where individual Christians live according to biblical principles and as the place that grounds their efforts to extend those principles into the larger society.

The sexual and procreative side of the family generally receives its fullest discussion in terms of the role of the wife rather than that of the husband. Tim and Beverly LaHaye, two of the most popular Christian Right authors on marriage, follow that pattern. The LaHayes emphasize that sexual energy is natural to men and caution wives not only to be aware of this energy, but also to give it every opportunity to be released. Thus relieved of sexual pressures regularly, husbands are free to devote their attention to matters of dominion and the proper exercise of authority over their family. The LaHayes hold women primarily responsible when their husbands stray from their marriage vows. Presumably, many men who seek comfort outside the marriage bed have not had their sexual needs properly met by their wives.[51] Citing George Gilder, Phyllis Schlafly echoes this view of women. Men are sexual predators who use violence to achieve sexual satisfaction. However, within the confines of marriage, the husband's sexuality can be controlled by the wife. The family is made stable and secure as the potentially destructive tendencies in men are curbed so that the energy may be redirected to Christianize the social order.[52] Women need that stability and security because of their more nurturing nature. As nurturers, women are vulnerable to others. Within the boundaries of a Christian marriage, however, women find the necessary security and stability to use their nurturing powers to their fullest and proper ends—imparting God's love to their husbands and to their children.[53]

The view of children that predominates within the Christian Right is one of moral weakness and sinful tendencies. Though children are creatures of God and therefore have inherent dignity, in their youthful state they are impressionable and easily swayed away from biblical principles. Lacking a firmly developed moral character and a proper understanding of things, they have no absolute standards against which to judge alternatives presented to them. They should therefore remain under the authority of their parents and be raised in conformity with Christian values so that they can gradually come to an understanding of themselves, their tendency toward sin, God's purpose for them, and the nature of the lives God wants them to live. To accomplish this, Van Til, for example, argues that Christian teachers have as their prime responsibility teaching students to submit to God's eternal purpose for them.[54] Since that is the proper function of education in any form, the primary responsibility for the education of children lies by divine mandate in the hands of the parents. Any role the state may play in education is merely to reinforce parental authority in guiding children to a submission to God's will. What is particularly dangerous in children is a strong will and a false sense of self-worth. Strong-willed children pose a danger to proper education because they resist submission to God's will and to the authority of their parents. A false sense of self-worth, one not derived from their submission to God's will, leads them to a false sense of security and a distorted self-understanding. This tendency of children to resist biblical principles and a true concept of their self-worth provides Christian Right authors with their primary justification for parental exercise of authority over children.[55]

A word of caution may be in order here. The descriptions of Schaeffer's theology of culture and Rushdoony's political theology represent an ideal type of the Christian Right perspective that is not articulated so clearly and completely by other movement leaders. Others express these ideas and concepts in a number of different ways, most of them giving greater emphasis to some parts of the mythos and the symbolic web than to other parts. Behind those variations, however, the dominion principle, expressed by many Christian Right leaders in terms of biblical principles, is the sine qua non of the movement. The secular humanist mythos and the symbolic web of the divinely ordained institutions give the movement its depth and direction. In this light, the movement's character has changed because of the degree of influence that Schaeffer and Rushdoony enjoy within Christian Right circles.

5

The Christian Right as a
Social Movement

In rallying the Christian Right troops at the 1994 Reclaiming America Conference in Fort Lauderdale, Florida, conference sponsor D. James Kennedy proclaimed the purpose of the conference to the gathered faithful: "We founded America." "It's ours. We want it back!" The response from the converted was predictable. A loud roar of approval filled the Coral Ridge Presbyterian Church.[1] As I sat in the audience and reflected on Kennedy's words, two questions came to my mind. Who is the "we"? And from whom do they want to take America back? Kennedy has quite clear answers to those questions. The "we" are biblical Christians. The forces of evil from whom he wishes to rescue America are the secular humanists.

At one level, Kennedy's appeal to take America back from the secularists seems absurd. By many measures, America is one of the most religious countries in the world and certainly the most Christian. Over 90 percent of Americans believe in God, and about 40 percent attend religious services regularly—approximately the same percentage as in the late 1930s.[2] Nearly 85 percent of Americans identify themselves as Christians. Of those, Protestants outnumber Roman Catholics by a bit more than a two-to-one margin. On the face of it Christians and people of faith firmly outstrip secularists. Even if we combine the number of secularists with other people claiming no religious affiliation, only about 7 percent of Americans would fit into Kennedy's "they" category.[3] Given such figures, it is hard to accept Kennedy's charge that a secular humanist conspiracy has gained control of America.

At a deeper level, however, Kennedy's charge makes sense, at least within his religious subculture. Biblical Christians are in a minority in the culture. If we restrict the meaning of biblical Christians to the definition provided previously, by most measures that reduces the percentage of Kennedy's "we" to about 35–40 percent of Americans at most. From their perspective, they have lost control of the culture. But even narrowing the definition to biblical Christians does not establish Kennedy's claim that the secular humanists are in the majority. To reach that conclusion, we must recall the Christian Right assertion that only two opposing worldviews exist and that they are completely incompatible with each other. The God-centered worldview includes only biblical Christians. Other Christians who hold a modified religionist perspective, adherents of other faith traditions, and nonbelievers all fall into the human-centered category of secular humanism. Thus, the category of secular humanism, as used by Kennedy, includes all religious movements within the Christian tradition that incorporate into their beliefs any Enlightenment or modernist principles. True Christians are those who have remained faithful to biblical absolutes in spite of the onslaught of modernism.

Kennedy's clarion call to biblical Christians for cultural transformation reflects a change in the redeeming right's attitude toward society. Until the early 1980s, biblical Christians assumed a primarily defensive posture toward the culture. In defense of the faith, they stood ready to protect themselves from Goliath. They were sustained in this defensive action by a theological orientation that brought meaning and hope to their lives as the culture around them collapsed. Since God is ultimately in control of events, they argued, in the end times, Jesus wins! Although biblical Christians throughout the years engaged in some skirmishes with the larger culture and its public schools, these actions were scattered and poorly organized. Since the 1980s, there has been a drastic change. Many biblical Christians have adopted a more aggressive stance toward the culture, one that seeks transformation, not protection. Through the use of highly sophisticated organizational strategies, cutting-edge communications technologies, and effective political involvement, the biblical Christians who want to "take America back" have become one of the most significant social movements in the last half of the twentieth century.[4] These socially conservative Christian pure religionists constitute the most significant religiously grounded social movement since the battle over civil rights in the third quarter of the twentieth century.[5]

Social Movements and the Christian Right

In describing the Christian Right as a religiously grounded social movement, I want to clarify my definition of social movements and suggest some of the specific characteristics of such forces when they are religiously informed. Social movements arise at times of situational incongruity, and they seek to resolve the incongruity in a number of ways depending on what type of movement emerges. Some movements depend upon strategies of personal transformation.[6] Individual change may be a complete personal transformation, such as the jail-house conversion of Watergate convicted felon Charles Colson; or it may be partial, as expressed in merely signing a petition against the inclusion of a particular book in the local school library. Other social movements seek supraindividual transformation. Of these, reformative movements focus on partial change such as in textbook adoptions, whereas transformative movements seek total change in the culture.[7] The Christian Right is a transformative social movement.

Conflict is essential to both the birth and the growth of social movements.[8] Social groups that desire to change the existing social arrangements use conflict to construct meaning and identity, and in that respect conflict has a positive dimension.[9] The question that often confronts people who are drawn to social movements is whether they are worthy to play a positive role in changing the existing system.[10] Insofar as social movements provide individuals with a justification for participation, they perform a redemptive function. The redemptive power emerges from the involvement of the individual in the process of social transformation, and the involvement of the person in the conflict constitutes a ritual process of transformation.[11] The most significant difference between social movements grounded in secular or political motivations and those rooted in religious motivations is the source from which movement architects draw their justifications. Religiously grounded social movements locate that source in the transcendent sacred order as divinely revealed to movement leaders. The meaning and identity generated by such movements resolve the existing incongruity within the context of reality itself. In the process, the social transformation brings the existing culture into harmony with divine realities.

Social movements tend to have both structural and ideational components. At the structural level, they exhibit some degree of organization designed to engage people in collective or joint actions directed toward change-oriented goals. Engagement occurs through a mixture of both extrainstitutional and institutional activity. That is, people engage the present situation both through informal activities such as protesting in the streets and through more formal institutional activities such as political lobbying.

Through those activities, social movements build a sense of cohesion, hope, and shared identity among the participants.[12]

At the ideational level, religiously grounded social movements construct the sacred canopy and provide the necessary tools to expand it and keep it in good repair. Among the most important tools available to movement leaders are myths, symbols, and rituals. The rise of the contemporary Christian Right occurred in the last decades of the twentieth century when movement leaders opened the toolboxes of Francis Schaeffer and Rousas John Rushdoony. Not only did the writings of these thinkers provide the movement with its mythos and symbolic web, but through the presuppositionalism Schaeffer and Rushdoony learned at Westminster Theological Seminary under the guidance of Cornelius Van Til, the movement also discovered its strategic blueprint.

At the structural level, social movements depend on institutional resources to generate momentum and provide direction. Theoreticians working through organizational structures identify and interpret incongruities, construct meaningful symbolic webs, promote the cause, and enable people to operate in a coordinated manner to achieve clearly defined ends. The organizations play a vital role in legitimating and maintaining the movement's sacred canopy. In a well-developed operation, this occurs at three different levels, according to Peter Berger and Thomas Luckmann. Each of the three levels functions well in the Christian Right. The first level is that of the cultural elite. Here the movement's intellectuals form the plan of attack and bring the various targets into the coherent mythic and symbolic frameworks. These are the scholars and intellectuals who shape the symbols that define the public discourse.[13] They operate at the conscious level of worldview construction, legitimation, and maintenance and tend not to be well known to the masses. The cultural elite also develop the ideological rhetoric or master protest frames that give the movement ideational coherence. The tactical coordinators among the knowledge workers also function at this level, bringing together the resources needed to implement their agenda and coordinate their efforts.

At the second level, knowledge workers frame the work of the cultural elite into the popular symbol systems, practical activities, and moral norms familiar to the average person. Knowledge workers provide two essential services to the movement. Through their communications with their constituents, they generate a sense of purpose and belonging: a movement culture. Knowledge workers also produce what the masses within the movement come to identify as common sense knowledge, knowledge that is taken for granted. Thus, knowledge workers stand between the intellectual elite, who deal explicitly with the presuppositions that ground the movement, and the grassroots activists, who implicitly accept these basic ideas at an unconscious level. At the third level, the movement's foot soldiers carry out the designs and targeted actions of the knowledge workers. They are the heart and soul of the group; they tend to look to specific organizational leaders to guide and inform them. In a movement as complex as the Christian Right, the grassroots activists look to a number of different leaders to push them into action and to coordinate their efforts.

The Christian Right's Cultural Elite

The Christian Right's cultural elite provide the movement with both its intellectual and its strategic leadership. The elite, staying well behind the front lines in a cluster of centers, coalitions, and alliances, frame the lines of attack using the grounding presuppositions expressed by Schaeffer and Rushdoony and bring together the movers and shapers who have the resources to put their plans into action. Although diversity characterizes the overall composition of the Christian Right, at the level of the intellectual elite most of the scholars seem to fit comfortably in the theological tradition that begins with Abraham Kuyper and Cornelius Van Til. Kuyper describes this strand as "neo-Calvinism."[14] Although the Christian Right intellectual elite identify with a number of different conservative denominations, the most consistent and sophisticated proponents of dominion neo-Calvinism operate from within several small denominations in the Presbyterian-Reformed tradition.

The Center for the Advancement of Paleo Orthodoxy (CAPO) in Oak Ridge, Tennessee, is a good example of this phenomenon. Primarily drawing on intellectuals in the Presbyterian Church of America (D. James Kennedy's denomination) and the Orthodox Presbyterian Church, CAPO bills itself as an umbrella organization that provides the resources for a cluster of seven institutes, each dedicated to articulating a dominionist Christian worldview in a particular sphere of society. The Kuyper Institute for Politics defines its mission as "applying biblical standards to politics, particularly House and Senate races." In this regard, it claims to be unique; it was "created and developed to promote a distinctively Christian critique of modern politics."[15] Other CAPO arms include the Van Til Institute for Apologetics, the Groen van Prinsterer Institute for History, the Burke

Institute for Economics (named after the eighteenth-century economist Edmund Burke), and the (Isaac) Newton Institute for Science. CAPO is quite an obscure organization in the larger culture, but its "fellows" include a number of theoreticians who carry considerable weight within the lofty arena of the Christian Right intellectual elite.[16]

Two other loose organizations illustrate the organizational direction of the Christian Right intellectual elite, the Coalition on Revival (COR) and the Council for National Policy (CNP). Both were formed in the early 1980s, and each performs a specific function. COR, which appeared in 1982 with Dr. Jay Grimstead as its coordinator/founder, is designed as an umbrella organization to unify and coordinate Christian Right efforts in developing the theoretical models for transforming every sphere of American society. A 1990 COR publication describes the organization as a "'Bible obedience, holiness movement' that crosses denominational and theological lines." COR's stated purpose is to turn America around so that it can "once again function as a Christian nation."[17] Among the most significant work COR produced were Grimstead's *Manifesto for the Christian Church* and COR's *Christian World View Documents,* mentioned earlier.

Even though COR is not well known outside the Christian Right, it has had great influence within the movement. The list of steering committee members, document authors, and supporters of COR principles included in the COR worldview documents reads like a "who's who" of the Christian Right elite.[18] Although there are some important omissions from the list, Focus on the Family being the most significant, the list represents both the wide doctrinal and confessional diversity of the movement and its range of special purpose groups. During the mid-1980s, when the Christian Right leadership emerged with a unified and powerful plan for social transformation, the Coalition on Revival was among the most important forces for the theological transformation of the movement. In terms of the impact COR had on framing the lines of attack on American public education, we must note that NACE/CEE's Robert Simonds was the cochair of the sphere document on education. Perhaps COR's greatest contribution at the time of its highest influence was the unequivocal manner in which it expressed the dominion principle and applied it to seventeen spheres of society. The cumulative picture these documents provide represents the clearest vision of transformed Christian Right culture.

In the early 1990s COR's influence began to wane as its founder Jay Grimstead moved closer to some of the more extreme views of Rousas

John Rushdoony. Among these was the most controversial aspect of Rushdoony's thought, his precise description of a reconstructed America functioning on the basis of literal Old Testament biblical law applied to all aspects of the society. Among Christian Right knowledge workers, Simonds and the American Family Association's Donald Wildmon publicly distanced themselves from Grimstead but continued to utilize the basic blueprint developed by COR. COR's influence did not completely disappear, however. As Focus on the Family's James Dobson moved closer to Howard Phillips's United States Taxpayers Party beginning in 1996, he increasingly used the dominionist rhetoric of COR principles. Phillips is a self-identified reconstructionist. Another group, called the Alliance for Revival and Reformation, continues to list COR documents on its web page as its primary statement of principles. Among its activities, the Alliance sponsors Conferences on Revival throughout the country. Antiabortion leader Randall Terry is listed among the conference leaders.[19] CAPO also acknowledges strong ties to COR. CAPO identifies E. Calvin Beisner as a CAPO Fellow. When COR, under the leadership of Grimstead, produced the documents mentioned above, Beisner was the assistant editor. Though such structural links to the enduring influence of COR are not widespread in the leadership of the contemporary Christian Right, COR's real continuing influence exists in the ideational dimension of the movement. Most of the contemporary leaders have been shaped by participation in COR or by the adoption of COR's main principles.

The Council on National Policy (CNP) plays an equally important, but quite different role within the Christian Right's cultural elite.[20] It is a major coordinating body and funding mechanism for Christian Right projects.[21] Tim LaHaye founded the council in 1981 in conjunction with T. Cullen Davis and Nelson Baker Hunt. From its founding, CNP's purpose has been to bring together religious leaders, financiers, and politicians to promote cooperation and coordination among political and religious conservatives. Hunt is a former council member of the John Birch Society.[22] In the mid-1990s, James Dobson and Phyllis Schlafly cochaired the council's Committee on the Family,[23] and Schlafly continues in that role. The list of CNP members includes the entire range of top Christian Right leaders.[24] Howard Phillips, one of the founders of the Christian Right as a mass movement in the late 1970s,[25] describes the council in the following way: "CNP is an organization which has been effective in developing links among people who ought to know one another, who are moving in the same direction. But who, but for the fact that these meetings occurred, would simply be ships passing in the night."[26] The council meets three times a year. Neither the meeting place nor the agenda are public information. According to reports, the council's rules state, "Meetings are closed to the media and the general public" and "Our membership list is strictly confidential and should not be shared outside the Council." The rules further prohibit members from divulging the content of the discussions without permission and require members "to keep in their personal possession their registration packets and other materials distributed at the meeting."[27]

Former Reagan attorney general Edwin Meese, a past CNP president, claims that the "Council encourages its members to be activists. And, that is not just to learn something about the issues, but do something about it. It is so important to get involved." James Dobson, who returned to council membership in 1998 after several years' absence, notes, "There are very few organizations left that say 'yes, we believe.' And, we're out to implement that policy in every way we can. We need those people out there who are considering linking hands and arms with us in this battle. I do hope they'll join us."[28] Membership in the council numbers about five hundred, and new members are admitted by invitation only. Ralph Reed began attending CNP as a youth delegate while still in college. All of the following Christian Right organizations are represented on the Council: the American Family Association, the Eagle Forum, Concerned Women for America, Focus on the Family, the Family Research Council, Chalcedon, the Rutherford Institute, the Traditional Values Coalition, the Christian Coalition, and the American Center for Law and Justice. Past presidents include Rich DeVos of the Amway Corporation (two terms), Pat Robertson, and Tim LaHaye.[29] Among the educational issues the council promotes are "schools of choice," school prayer, and school vouchers.

These centers, coalitions, alliances, and councils provide the Christian Right with the necessary intellectual, financial, and political resources to advance its cause as a social movement. The list of leaders mentioned is not exhaustive. One of the movement's characteristics is that it is comprised of a large number of persons and organizations, most having specific focuses and concerns. For example, Henry Morris of the Institute for Creation Research develops intellectual challenges to evolution in support of creationism; David Barton of Wallbuilders and Rus Walton of the Plymouth Rock Foundation provide researched arguments for the Christian foundation of the American nation; George Grant, former associate of

D. James Kennedy at the Coral Ridge Presbyterian Church, writes extensively on economic issues; John Whitehead and the Rutherford Institute focus on the theological foundation for constitutional arguments regarding religious freedom; and Regent University's Robertson School of Law and Government provides a similar legal function.

A number of colleges, universities, and seminaries provide the Christian Right with another type of institutional structure. Perhaps the best known of these are Jerry Falwell's Liberty University and Pat Robertson's Regent University, both in Virginia, and Trinity International University in southern California. Examples of theological seminaries include Westminster, with one branch in Philadelphia and the other in California; D. James Kennedy's Knox Theological Seminary in Florida; and the Reformed Theological Seminary in Jackson, Mississippi. These institutions are positioned to develop a theologically well-trained leadership corps for the Christian Right into the future.

The final type of institutional structure that functions at the level of the Christian Right cultural elite includes numerous secular conservative think tanks and coordinating organizations, which offer secularized symbolic, financial, and strategic support. Examples of this leadership include Samuel Blumenfeld, a home schooling advocate closely related to the John Birch Society; and the intellectuals associated with think tanks such as the Heritage Foundation, the American Enterprise Institute, the National Right to Work Committee, and the Institute for Educational Affairs. Most of these intellectuals have strong ties to libertarian, anticommunist, free enterprise ideological traditions within American conservatism. Because of their backgrounds, they draw their sources of legitimation from secular rather than theological intellectual traditions. Thus, their significance for this study is limited. Any ideas deriving from these sources would still need to find theological legitimation from the religious viewpoint of the Christian Right.

Knowledge Workers

One level below the movement's cultural elite, Christian Right knowledge workers bridge the gap between the vanguard and the grassroots foot soldiers. Knowledge workers reduce the systematic and complex arguments of the theoreticians to common levels of understanding. They maintain and legitimate the worldview at the level of most ordinary people by framing the knowledge structures within symbol systems, practical activities, and moral norms that are familiar to the average person. They also motivate and mobilize their constituents to implement the movement's overall strategy. The knowledge workers operate in the context of what Robert Wuthnow calls special purpose groups (SPGs). SPGs differ from other special interest groups because of their uniquely religious character. They arise from religious communities and advocate in the arena of public opinion and politics from the perspective of a religious worldview. They also have a narrower purpose than secular advocacy groups insofar as they either represent a particular segment of the faith community or limit their advocacy to specific issues.[30]

One of the most important functions of knowledge workers is to provide synthesized and simplified information that calls their followers to action on particular issues or at certain events. Often referred to in the literature as "talking points," this distilled synopsis constitutes "recipe knowledge."[31] Using the metaphor of cooking from a recipe, Leigh Schaffer suggests that such organizations provide their members with step-by-step interpretations and tactical strategies. Because most people at the grass roots remain unaware of the entire theoretical framework that constitutes the Christian Right worldview, knowledge workers condense it into formula knowledge that can be understood, applied, and argued at a simpler level. Their mass-mailing solicitations and organizational publications give people enough information, symbolic connections, and rhetorical devices to argue the points at the local level without the need to understand anything of the deeper complexity of the issues or the grounding presuppositions that stand behind them. Conflict is important in generating and sustaining movement cultures. Knowing this, knowledge workers attempt to instill in grassroots activists the belief that local response to a real crisis in their community on a particular issue is called for.

Because they operate from recipe knowledge, activists at the local level do not always see their actions as part of a much larger coordinated effort to implement a presuppositional strategy or to achieve a much larger cultural transformation. They simply rely on the recipe, using its preformulated criticism, either as they receive or slightly modify it, to speak directly and specifically to local issues. This explains why controversies at local school board meetings sometimes move toward bizarre discussions of topics unrelated to the issue at hand, whereas at other times they seem to be precisely focused on the relevant issue. Because recipe knowledge reduces issues to their simplest forms, it militates against serious discussion of important controversies in two ways. It breeds an incipient anti-intellectual-ism, so that discussion seldom gets beyond slogans and preformulated objections. It also raises fears in people at the local level because its primary use by knowledge workers is motivational. That is, it is not designed to provide in-depth understanding but to move people toward two types of action—involvement in local politics and financial support for the special purpose group. To accomplish these ends, SPGs frequently sensationalize topics in ways that raise the stakes to the emotional level, where ordinary people express fears rather than concerns.[32]

Tracking Christian Right special purpose groups is not an easy task. One difficulty relates to their sheer number. Even on such a narrow topic as public education, at least two dozen groups actively promote the Christian Right agenda, issuing periodic position papers in addition to articles and news notes. Finding, organizing, and distilling the large volume of material generated by these SPGs takes considerable time. Yet, distilled to their essential points, the voluminous materials show a great deal of commonality at both the presuppositional and the rhetorical levels. A letter to the editor on school vouchers in a newspaper in Helena, Montana, will look and sound very much like a letter on the same issue sent to a newspaper in Merrimack, New Hampshire.

Another challenge in tracking the Christian Right as a social movement concerns the fluid nature of the movement's SPGs. New groups constantly emerge, attempting to fill a narrow niche in the movement's overall strategy. Two fairly recent examples are Of the People, which focuses on parental rights, and the National Council on Bible Curriculum in Public Schools, which promotes sectarian religion courses in the schools. Local communities confronted by Christian Right challenges can never be sure which groups might be operating and influencing the grass-roots activists in a given controversy. Just because local critics claim no affiliation with the Christian Coalition or the Family Research Council, for example, does not mean that their challenges are not informed and directed by the Christian Right movement.

This discussion of Christian Right special purpose groups examines only one of two types of Christian Right SPGs—the advocacy groups that cultivate national constituencies. Legal-oriented SPGs, the second type, also play a major role in shaping and generating educational issues, but in general they emerge on the local scene only infrequently and then do not establish either local chapters or continuing relations with grass-roots activists. Consequently, they are not very important to this study.

These comments are framed within the context of the overall religious environment of the Christian Right worldview. Because the SPGs generally accept Schaeffer's claim that a Christian worldview impacts every aspect of culture, including education, the purpose of their criticism of public education includes a presuppositional strategic component. Such criticism is designed in part to weaken public support for schools so that the Christian Right can extend its influence into as many areas of instruction as possible. Most of the SPGs also accept Schaeffer's interpretive model of two mutually incompatible worldviews, identifying themselves with the God-centered perspective and the public schools with the human-centered stance. Further, they accept, in some form, the dominionist position that all aspects of education must be brought into conformity to biblical principles under the divinely ordained responsibility of parents. Finally, they tend to view the present situation as a culture war in which they represent the side of righteousness and the educational establishment is the occupational force to be removed or destroyed. In this sense, the movement exhibits prophetic and apocalyptic characteristics.

The two most important Christian Right special purpose groups are Pat Robertson's Christian Coalition and James Dobson's Focus on the Family. They are the largest both in financial resources and in constituency. When Ralph Reed announced his resignation as the executive director of the Christian Coalition in April 1997, he claimed a membership for the organization of 1.9 million members and two thousand local chapters.[33] According to the Coalition's web site home page, however, the membership was "only" 1.5 million with fifteen hundred local chapters in all fifty states.[34] Dobson's Focus on the Family does not list a membership figure, but its 1996 budget of $115 million is significantly larger than the Christian Coalition's revenues of $26 million for the same year.[35] Moreover, Dobson's radio audience and communications to his Focus on the Family organization suggest a far larger following than the Christian Coalition has. It seems curious that most scholarly writers who focus on the Christian Right, and the media, give much more attention to Robertson than to Dobson.

The Internet web pages of both Robertson's and Dobson's special purpose groups make it clear that they fit into the parameters of the dominion principle described in previous chapters. This is reflected in their commitments to make biblical principles the foundation of every sphere of public life in the United States, including the government and the public schools. Since the departure of Ralph Reed from the Christian Coalition, its rhetoric has taken on a sharper dominionist edge. Speaking to the 1998 Road to Victory Conference, Coalition president Don Hodel told the audience that they were the hidden army poised to take over the United States. Republican House Whip Tom DeLay made the point even more clearly. "[Many Americans] don't understand the Constitution of the United States . . . is a model of the Bible, comes directly out of the Bible."[36] Robertson's Regent University promotes itself as an advocate of the biblical Christian worldview applied to all aspects of society. The mission of the university's Robertson School of Government is

> to restore a Biblical foundation and renew the Christian witness in public affairs in the United States and the nations of the world. Governance and public policy issues are addressed using principles drawn from Scripture and the humanities and sciences in a rigorous interdisciplinary endeavor. The School seeks to equip men and women for twenty-first century leadership in government, policy-making and politics.

The School of Education seeks "to prepare leaders from a biblical perspective in order that they might significantly impact education worldwide, particularly in the areas of educational administration, at-risk populations, special education, and educational policy." The Institute for Educational Policy, within the School of Education, works with the Robertson School of Government to "develop position papers and sponsor conferences and lobbying activities to be used in an effort to generate and influence educational policy decisions in the U.S. and abroad." The School of Education also promotes biblically based programs for effective discipline and character development. According to Regent University, these programs are being piloted in public and Christian school settings.[37]

Dobson is also becoming more directly dominionist in his rhetoric. In a speech to the 1998 spring meeting of the Council on National Policy, Dobson told the audience that "to understand my worldview and the way I see things, politics and every other aspect of life, you have to go to this book [the Bible], because that's the foundation of everything I care about." He went on to describe the absolute nature of the moral law of the universe and its application to government and to discuss his vote for Howard Phillips of the United States Taxpayers Party in the 1996 presidential race. Commenting on the reconstructionist Phillips, Dobson declared, "I voted for him because he stands for the principles and values that I believe in, and nobody else did." Dobson ended his speech by reminding the faithful that there were only two, incompatible, ways of looking at life—the way of God that leads to life and the way of humanity that leads to death.[38] Dobson's embrace of the secular humanist conspiracy argument also emerged in the October 1998 edition of *Teachers in Focus* magazine. Francis J. Beckwith, an established dominionist, told teachers in an article there that they should take aggressive action to include supplemental materials in their classes in order to combat the rampant secularism of public education. Beckwith also advised them to change assignments, distribute additional readings, and present alternative viewpoints to those of the secularists. Since Beckwith subscribes to the neo-Calvinist theory of dueling worldviews, he asserts that the only real alternative open to teachers is to explicitly teach biblical Christian principles in the public schools.[39]

In promoting the political dimension of their agenda, Robertson and Dobson are split on their favorite candidate for president in 2000. Robertson and the Christian Coalition supported Sen. John Ashcroft (R-Mo.), whose pentecostal background in the Assemblies of God is close to Robertson's religious stance, whereas Dobson prefers his own associate Gary Bauer, from the Family Research Council (FRC). Ashcroft's withdrawal from the presidential race leaves Robertson without a favored candidate.[40] Bauer's entry into presidential politics reflects Dobson's gradual movement into the dominionist camp. Dobson started the FRC in 1988 to increase his political clout in Washington. In 1992, Focus on the Family formally severed connections with the council for tax reasons. Nevertheless, Dobson and Bauer remained extremely close, and Focus's *Citizen* magazine continued to feature a regular column by Bauer until Bauer announced his candidacy for president in early 1999.

The Family Research Council offers a variety of publications on issues related to public education. Among the stated goals of the council is to "inform and educate citizens on how they can promote Biblical principles in our culture." To this end, the council provides position papers, media spokespersons, and expert congressional testimony on such issues of interest to educators as parents rights, school choice, tax vouchers, sex education, Goals 2000, educational reform, and school prayer, and it promotes "Classical Education." Before he became the FRC's executive director, Gary Bauer held several positions in the Department of Education during the Reagan administration.[41]

Robert Simonds's National Association of Christian Educators/Citizens for Excellence in Education also continues to promote the dominion principle in American education. Although his impact has diminished, his newsletter commenting on contemporary educational issues still circulates among the many local chapters of CEE. Simonds claims that his CEE parents' group has more than 350,000 parents involved in fifty states, with 1,680 active chapters.[42] Like most other Christian Right special purpose groups focusing on education, Simonds's group gives particular attention to school voucher initiatives and parental rights legislation. Simonds also produces a radio program called *CEE's Issues in Education Radio Show*, hosted by Bob and Geri Boyd. The Boyds believe that America has surrendered to pagan forces, and they dedicate their show to motivating Christians to take it back. In one broadcast, they argue that Christians should be involved in the political process to make this America "one nation under God." In the context of the dominion principle, their vision of one nation under God has far different implications than did the vision of the nation's founders. To make their meaning clear, they cite George Grant's *Changing of the Guard:*

> God called Joseph, Gideon, Deborah, Samuel, Nehemiah, Daniel, David and Josiah into the ministry of political action. Each of these heroes of the faith understood clearly that there was no wall of separation between God and the state. They knew that God had ordained and established civil government just as surely as He had the family and the Church. So they looked upon political action as a holy calling.[43]

In their commentary, the Boyds provide a perfect example of recipe knowledge being transmitted to their listeners. Although they couch their arguments in a set of broad-based references to past political and religious leaders, they move their audience toward action not by explicitly promoting the dominion principle, but by simply relating Christian duty to political action.

Several other Christian Right SPGs also play significant roles in the educational arena. One of the more important and long-established groups is Phyllis Schlafly's Eagle Forum. Schlafly, a longtime Roman Catholic conservative activist, founded the Eagle Forum in 1972 to counter liberal efforts to pass the Equal Rights Amendment. Since then, the Eagle Forum's focus has expanded into the area of education. Two monthly Forum newsletters called the *Phyllis Schlafly Report* and the *Education Report* address education issues.[44] Schlafly also writes a nationally syndicated newspaper column. In the years 1995–97, about one-third of her columns dealt with topics related to education. Her commentary is heard on 270 radio stations. Eagle Forum membership in 1996 numbered eighty thousand.

The Eagle Forum's mission is "to enable conservative and pro-family men and women to participate in the process of self-government and public policy making so that America will continue to be a land of individual liberty, respect for family integrity, public and private virtue, and private enterprise." Its efforts are designed to "affect government policies in Congress, state legislatures, city councils and school boards; elect candidates at every level; and articulate conservative and pro-family policies through the media."[45] The name Eagle Forum refers to a biblical passage (Isa. 40:31), not to the patriotic symbol of the eagle. The verse reads, "They that wait upon the Lord shall renew their strength; they shall mount up with wings as eagles; they shall run, and not be weary; and they shall walk, and not faint" (King James Version). This suggests that Schlafly sees her organization's participation in the political arena as an extension of her religious, rather than secular, conservative motivations.

Education stands at the forefront of the Forum's interests. Its self-description begins with the following commentary on education:

> EAGLE FORUM stands for the fundamental right of parents to guide the education of their own children. Parents should have the right to choose private schools or homeschooling without oppressive government regulation.
>
> In public schools, parents have the right to expect that schools
> *educate* children in factual knowledge, true history, and academic skills (reading, writing, arithmetic), with an overall purpose of encouraging excellence—not mediocrity. We oppose the "dumbed-down" system called Outcome-Based Education.
> *respect* the religion and values of parents and children. Schools should not deprive children of their free-exercise-of-religion rights, or impose on children courses in explicit sex or alternate lifestyles, profane or immoral fiction or videos, New Age practices, anti-Biblical materials, or "Politically Correct" liberal attitudes about social and economic issues.
> *obey* the Protection of Pupil Rights Amendment restrictions about psychological testing or treatment. Schools should *not* use children as guinea pigs in experimental courses in "self-esteem" or "decision-making," or administer privacy-invading surveys.[46]

Columns by Schlafly emphasize opposition to national testing, gifted and talented programs, the National Education Association, the Department of

Education, school-to-work programs, sex education, school-based health programs, and psychological testing.

The National Council on Bible Curriculum in the Public Schools (NCOBCITPS) was formed in Greensboro, North Carolina, in 1992 by Elizabeth Ridenour. Its goal is to encourage schools to acknowledge the Bible's important place in history and its continuing influence on society. To do this, the NCOBCITPS attempts to persuade public school boards throughout the United States to offer a high school class "to study the Bible as a foundation document of society . . . [and the] foundation and blue print for our Constitution." The NCOBCITPS offers schools the outlines and materials for two courses with two-semester curricula. The first focuses on the Old Testament, and the second centers on what NCOBCITPS describes as "the life of Jesus of Nazareth and the origins of Christianity." Part of the council's purpose is to use these materials to convince public school children of the Christian nature of the nation and its origins.

The NCOBCITPS provides a large packet of legal information to parents, teachers, and school board members who seek to adopt their curriculum. Although the packet includes a letter from Jay Sekulow, chief counsel of the American Center for Law and Justice, attesting the legality of the curriculum, a U.S. District Court in Florida held in 1997 that a course sequence based on NCOBCITPS materials would not be constitutional. The source of the court's concern was that the proposed course assumes a literal interpretation of the Bible in which all events qualify as "historical facts."[47]

A number of other Christian Right special purpose groups also provide recipe knowledge about educational issues to their constituents. Among the most important in terms of the impact they have had on the national scene are Beverly LaHaye's Concerned Women for America, D. James Kennedy's Coral Ridge Ministries, Lou Sheldon's Traditional Values Coalition, Donald Wildmon's American Family Association, and Jeffrey Bell's Of the People. All mirror the objections to public education found in the other Christian Right groups. The issues of choice are secular humanism and New Age religion, Outcome-Based Education, school choice, school vouchers, and parental rights. The most important legal defense associations are Pat Robertson's American Center for Law and Justice, John Whitehead's Rutherford Institute, Donald Wildmon's American Family Association Law Center, David Llewellyn's Western Center for Law and

Religious Freedom, Alan Sears's Alliance Defense Fund, and Michael Farris's Home School Legal Defense Association. Though acting independently of each other, all these Christian Right special purpose groups, both the advocacy and the legal organizations, share the overall goal of transforming American culture to bring it into closer conformity with biblical principles. Each of them has made a significant contribution to the movement's agenda. As extensive as this list of contributions is, it does not include any of the many secular conservative advocacy groups that continue to build a case for a total restructuring of America's public schools.

The Grassroots Level

Even with all the resources of the above groups, the Christian Right as a social movement cannot hope to achieve its agenda without mobilizing millions of foot soldiers at the grassroots level. In addition to the mass mailings done by the advocacy special purpose groups to build the movement, many organizations have state and local chapters that receive the recipe knowledge prepared by the knowledge workers and apply it to local circumstances. People at the grass roots often have little understanding of the theological presuppositions and foundations of the Christian Right movement. Many activists simply respond to the fear-laced alarmist rhetoric included in the materials sent by the knowledge workers. These materials are particularly powerful when linked to the symbolic web that already constitutes the local activists' common sense understandings.

The alarmist rhetoric of the SPGs is not unintentional. Since so many national special purpose groups compete with one another for support at the grassroots level, their solicitation materials must convince the recipient of the urgency of contributing to that particular organization. This has led to the use of increasingly polemic language in communications from SPGs to their local constituencies. The result in local controversies is that sometimes unsubstantiated allegations are made against a particular school initiative. People at the local level may also attribute conspiratorial motives to educators and school boards when an innocent explanation would suffice. Many educators report that criticism directed against them simply was not relevant to the curricular reforms or pedagogical changes that were being introduced by the educational establishment in that location. Competition among organizations and their leaders also keeps national

SPGs independent and distinct from one another in order to retain their constituency. The impression is often conveyed that the Christian Right is much more uncoordinated and indefinable at the national level than it is.

Although mailings to activists may compete with each other, they also reinforce each other when they identify the same issues and employ the same rhetoric. This is understandable given the likelihood that the knowledge workers draw their interpretations from the same pool of intellectual analysts, but the shared reservoir of knowledge is seldom made public or explicit. Because different groups make the same claims, grassroots activists interpret such overlapping analysis as proof of the legitimacy of what they hear and read. The interpretation becomes objective knowledge. Having come to such conclusions, the local activists approach the public arena with the confidence that their concerns are based on authoritative factual knowledge. For example, if Beverly LaHaye, Pat Robertson, James Dobson, and Phyllis Schlafly all agree that Goals 2000 is a conspiracy on the part of big-government liberals to control the schools from the national level in order to promote a homosexual agenda, then many people at the local level will believe them and seek to discover that connection in their local schools.

The controversies generated at the grassroots level by the knowledge workers constitute another way the Christian Right functions as a social movement. By engaging people at the local level in conflict, the movement creates a sense of meaning and identity among the respondents. Through the conflict, the participants gain a sense of being part of a movement, and that perception helps build a movement culture that advances the movement and draws others into it. The controversies themselves become the means by which the movement achieves its status as a social movement. Insofar as those conflicts are successful, people at the local level begin to feel empowered and use that empowerment to advance the movement even further toward its goal of cultural transformation.[48]

Whatever the effects of the special purpose groups at the grassroots level, they all seek to motivate activists toward the movement goal of bringing the various civil institutions of our society into conformity with biblical principles. The goal of the knowledge workers is not merely to defend religious liberty or to assert equality of religious persons within the public arena. The objective is to gradually transform American society into conformity with the Christian worldview in order to redeem the culture. The means the strategy organizational activists often employ derives from Francis Schaeffer's observation that the best way to accomplish this end is to undermine the presuppositions upon which the larger society's confidence in its social institutions rests. Once knowledge workers shake public confidence in existing institutions, the general citizenry may be more receptive to their prescriptions. With respect to public education, for example, the real issue is not improving the academic quality of America's schools. The issue is whether Christian Right special purpose groups can create the perception of the failure of America's schools in the minds of the general public so that the public is more receptive to Christian Right alternative strategies, strategies derived from a quite different set of premises.

The Christian Right Constituency

Who are these local Christian Right activists? The vast majority of them are drawn from the various religious traditions commonly identified as conservative evangelical Protestantism, the term most often employed by political scientists in tracking the political activities of the Christian Right. This larger umbrella label, however, masks the religious diversity within the movement. The fact is that most of the foot soldiers come from five distinct religious traditions within conservative evangelical Protestantism as well as the conservative wing of American Catholicism. The five Protestant branches are fundamentalists, holiness Christians, pentecostals/charismatics, the somewhat ill-defined category born-again Christians, and Reformed Christians.[49]

These distinctions have particular significance with respect to the specific SPG to which a local activist might be connected. Though personality may be important when it comes to the leaders of the largest organizations, to some degree people within particular religious groups may be attracted to one leader more than another because of a mutual religious orientation. Because each of these six traditions has distinctive theological and cultural characteristics, the flavor of an SPG associated with one tradition may be quite different from that of another group. Perhaps the best example of such peculiarities is found in the contrast between the militant rhetoric of fundamentalist Jerry Falwell and the comforting counsel of Nazarene James Dobson. An overview of each of the six constituencies will better define the religious contours of the Christian Right.

We begin with fundamentalists because they provided the earliest political expression of the Christian Right, dating back to the first decades of the twentieth century. This branch of conservative Protestantism is named after a series of twelve documents known collectively as *The Fundamentals: A Testimony of Truth,* published between 1910 and 1915. Written mainly in defense of the theologically conservative doctrines of the Reformed tradition, they contain Fundamentalism's early statements of belief. The more than ninety articles in the documents specifically defend Christianity against the forces of theological modernism that had developed and gained favor in American Protestantism in the last quarter of the nineteenth century. In particular, the publications opposed any modified religionist adaptation of established Christian doctrines to modern scholarship in the areas of history, biblical studies, literature, and the natural sciences. The willingness of modernists within all of the mainline denominations to accommodate Christianity to these new teachings provoked a backlash against the modernists among the people who came to be known as fundamentalists.[50] Although *The Fundamentals* contained articles by scholars who did not insist on the complete inerrancy of the Scriptures, that doctrine later became a theological cornerstone of the movement.[51] Other distinctive doctrines of Fundamentalism include insistence on the Virgin Birth, the miracles of the Bible, the bodily resurrection of Jesus, and the power of Jesus' sacrificial death to remove the stain of sin from us. Fundamentalists also agree that an explicit conversion experience marks the life of a true Christian. The fundamentalist emphasis on doctrine in defining the boundaries of the Christian faith suggests that it tends toward the cognitive dimension of religion, discussed in chapter 2.

Although fundamentalists carried the banner of the Christian Right for decades, Fundamentalism's centrality to the movement began to fade in the last years of the 1980s. Its decline related, in part, to the militaristic and strident rhetoric characteristic of fundamentalists doing battle for the Lord. Because its tone breached the boundaries of civil discourse, this form of the Christian Right had little appeal to potential constituents outside fundamentalist circles. The social movement of the fundamentalists during this period was reformative rather than transformative. It aimed at partial change and focused on specific issues such as creationism and school prayer. One reason for the limited scope of the fundamentalists' effort was that popular Fundamentalism never developed a theological critique of the culture. Nor were the arguments they did offer very sophisticated. For these reasons, Christian Right fundamentalists gradually relinquished their power to nonfundamentalists such as James Dobson, Pat Robertson, Phyllis Schlafly, and D. James Kennedy.

The holiness family of denominations represents a second major constituency for the Christian Right. Unlike fundamentalists, who define Christian purity in terms of right belief or correct doctrine, the holiness tradition emphasizes religious behavior and the moral life as the marks of a true Christian. They reflect more the volitional dimension of religion. The movement derives its name from a belief in the possibility of spiritual and moral perfection in this life through the blessing of the Holy Spirit. It draws upon three distinct and disparate sources.[52] The exact nature of that blessing and the specific character of perfection are described differently by the three wings of the holiness movement, but all three share a belief that a life of moral and spiritual holiness provides the surest evidence of Christian perfection. The largest holiness denominations are the Church of the Nazarene, the Wesleyan Church, the Free Methodist Church, the Salvation Army, the Church of God (based in Anderson, Indiana), and the Christian and Missionary Alliance.

The purest Christian Right example of the holiness tradition is James Dobson. His homey counsel reflects a highly idealized description of family life, as do his personal memories of his own home life.[53] Dobson's defense of the home and family values harks back to previous generations when holiness Christians viewed the home as a protected place of safety in a hostile world. His message is well received by those who share his vision. Dobson's personal life represents the holiness connection with the Christian Right in another way. As he became more involved in the cultural mainstream, he discovered that the home had come under enormous pressure and could no longer provide a safe haven from society. The politicization of James Dobson came with his movement into the socioeconomic mainstream.

Pentecostal/charismatic Christianity comprises the third major religious family from which the Christian Right draws its support. It is closely related historically and theologically to the holiness movement. The distinguishing theological characteristic of the pentecostal/charismatic movement is its insistence on the reception by the individual of the "gifts of the spirit," signaled by the experience of speaking in tongues at the moment of baptism, even if the individual never has the experience again.[54] Because pentecostals place so much emphasis on this manifestation of the gifts of the spirit, they exemplify the affective dimension of religion. Pentecostals differ from charismatics only in that, although both practice pentecostal-style worship, pentecostals do so within pentecostal denominations and charismatics engage in those practices within denominations not normally characterized by ecstatic worship. Pentecostals also tend to accept a quite militant form of premillennialism. The two largest pentecostal denominations are the predominantly white Assemblies of God and the predominantly African American Church of God in Christ. The most prominent pentecostal Christian Right leader is Pat Robertson.

The fourth Christian Right constituency, born-again evangelicals, constitutes the largest group from which the Christian Right draws its supporters. It is also the least clearly defined segment of conservative Protestantism in the United States. Like other representatives of the redeeming right, born-again evangelicals remain solidly committed to protecting biblical authority, religious supernaturalism, and New Testament Christianity. They also accept most of the doctrines associated with Fundamentalism and the spiritual and moral emphasis of the holiness movement. Their name, pointing to a born-again experience of personal salvation, reflects an emphasis on the affective dimension of religion. This conversion experience marks the moment they are "saved" and enter the kingdom of God's remnant on earth. They differ from holiness and pentecostal Christians on theological issues related to human perfection and speaking in tongues as the true mark of the Christian life. Perhaps the most purely "evangelical" denomination is the relatively small Evangelical Free Church in America. The single largest block of born-again evangelicals are found within the nonfundamentalist segments of the Southern Baptist Convention, in other Baptist churches, and in the conservative wings of mainstream Protestant denominations.

Roman Catholics comprise a fifth constituency of the Christian Right. In 1996, Ralph Reed estimated that Catholics accounted for about 16 percent of the Christian Coalition membership.[55] The Catholic Alliance, formed as an extension of the Christian Coalition in 1995, was designed to bring more American Catholics into the fold, but by 1998 it had not been very successful. The most visible Christian Right Roman Catholics are Phyllis Schlafly, Pat Buchanan, William Bennett, and Henry Hyde. Several factors hamper Christian Right efforts to recruit substantial numbers of Catholics into the movement. Perhaps the most significant is the history of hostile rhetoric and sometimes violent nativistic fervor directed against Catholics by conservative Protestants from the last half of the nineteenth century onward. Theology is another important barrier. On key issues such as biblical literalism and creationism, the Catholic Church stands in opposition to conservative Protestantism. In the political arena, Catholics are among the most liberal voting blocks in America. Next to African American Protestants, they are the strongest religious block within the Democratic Party. The majority of Catholics have views very different from the Christian Right on such key issues as social justice, women's roles, and economic policy.

Despite these differences, there are some points on which a fairly close alliance is possible with socially and religiously conservative Catholics. Perhaps the most visible points of contact are on the issues of abortion and public funding of religious schools. At a less visible, but nevertheless significant, level is the common cause antimodernists within the American Catholic tradition have with Protestant conservatives. The most important points of contact here are a spirited defense of supernaturalism and moral absolutism, support for traditional family values, and a critique of progressive educational pedagogy. Conservative Catholics tend to draw their conservatism from two sources, neither necessarily related to the other. Liturgical conservatives point to the reforms of Vatican II as their source of contention with the church.[56] These conservatives are just as likely to fight their battles within the church as in the larger society. Prolife conservatives embrace the issue of abortion and are much more likely than other Catholics to find commonality with the Christian Right on other social issues related to family values and the importance of religion in public life. Though prolife conservative Roman Catholics are often quite willing to stand together with the Christian Right on specific issues, and though they both tend toward a pure religionist stance toward culture, on the defining cultural and political theology of the Christian Right, conservative Catholics are not likely to find themselves in full agreement with the movement.

Reformed Christians make up the sixth constituency of the Christian Right. That tradition draws its defining characteristics from the theological teachings of John Calvin. Of the six camps, Reformed Protestants clearly constitute the smallest potential constituency. Yet, because of the influence of Francis Schaeffer and Rousas John Rushdoony, this segment has had the greatest influence on shaping the religious contours of the Christian Right as a social movement. With the exception of Roman Catholicism, the Reformed tradition is the only constituent group that has an explicit and distinct political theology. Therefore, as the movement has coalesced in recent years around Schaeffer's theology of culture and Rushdoony's political theology, the leadership of the other branches of the movement has gravitated toward Reformed principles. Perhaps the most public Reformed Christian Right leader is D. James Kennedy, who pastors one of the largest congregations in the Presbyterian Church in America. Other Calvinist denominations from which the Christian Right draws support are the very conservative Orthodox Presbyterian Church and the ultraconservative Bible Presbyterian Church, Schaeffer's denomination. Members from more mainstream denominations such as the Reformed Church in America and the Christian Reformed Church in North America also provide some support to the Christian Right.

When D. James Kennedy told his listeners at the Reclaiming America Conference, "America is ours, we want it back," he was speaking to a very specific audience. "We" refers to biblical Christians who accept the Christian Right goal of restructuring American society on the basis of biblical principles. As we have seen, this message receives its greatest support in six core constituencies within American Christianity. With the exception of conservative Roman Catholics, all are Protestant. We have also seen that within each of these traditions there exist substantial reasons why these believers might not associate with the Christian Right. The Christian Right holds attraction for adherents to these traditions, but unless Christians subscribe to the cultural and political theologies that provide the movement's presuppositions, they are not likely to be counted among the Christian Right faithful. Nevertheless, the three-tiered organizational structure of the movement and the efforts by the leaders to coordinate their efforts and resources do give the Christian Right the necessary resources to develop the most significant social movement in America today.

Because of the fluid nature of the Christian Right, it is difficult to assess its numerical strength, but a good estimate is about 15 to 20 percent of the American population. This assessment is based on two sources. A 1996 *Times-Mirror* poll estimates the percentage of "moralists," as they call them, at about 15 percent of the adult population and 18 percent of "likely voters." The poll describes "moralists" as "middle-aged, middle-income, predominantly white, religious (more than half are Evangelicals). This core Republican group is also socially intolerant and anti–social welfare, militaristic, anti–big business and anti–big government."[57] Another 1996 survey asked respondents how close they felt to the Christian Right. Sixteen percent chose "very close," and another 17.5 percent said "somewhat close."[58] If we assume that those selecting "very close" reflect the core constituency of the movement and that the second figure represents those

6

Strategies for Change

In the spring of 1993, I was invited to Denver, Colorado, by the Institute for the Development of Educational Ideas to present a keynote address on the Christian Right at a national conference for educators. The overwhelming majority of those present at the session had been involved in the past year or so in religiously motivated controversies in public education at the local level. They were some of the earliest frontline casualties in the educational theater of the culture war. In my opening remarks, I stated, "My research and involvement in the present defense of public education leads me to the conclusion that the goal of the Christian Right leadership is the destruction of the current educational system in this country."[1] The reaction of the audience was surprise and disbelief. Although the conference participants had come because they were interested in understanding Christian Right challenges to public education, they remained supremely confident that the existing structure of public education was strong enough to survive Christian Right challenges.

In talking with the participants after my presentation, I discovered that they viewed their local controversies as relatively isolated from similar challenges elsewhere. The conferees also believed that defusing the crisis back home revolved around resolving one or two specific issues. They based their assessment, I believe, on a flawed understanding of the strategic method employed by movement leaders and the strategy's connection to their local situation. That strategy, like much of the Christian Right worldview, was based on the presuppositionalism of Abraham Kuyper, Cornelius Van Til, and Francis Schaeffer. What surprised me in subsequent years about my own claim was the speed with which the Christian Right brought the American people to the brink of completely reshaping our nation's public schools. The ability of the movement to swiftly undermine public confidence in the American system of education testifies to the power of the presuppositional strategy that the Christian Right has adopted.

Presuppositional Strategy

The presuppositionalism of Cornelius Van Til was perfectly suited for advancing Christian Right attempts to gain control of public education. As taught by Van Til, presuppositionalism had both social and personal implications for conversion. Francis Schaeffer and Rousas John Rushdoony picked up its social dimension and developed it into a strategy for cultural conversion. Rushdoony's impact on the Christian Right, although substantial in terms of the movement's defining symbols, was diminished by his extreme views on the application of literal Old Testament law to contemporary social institutions. Schaeffer's teachings gained a much more central place in the Christian Right during the 1980s because of the substantial role he played in the prolife movement. Not only did Schaeffer call evangelical Christians to account for not doing more to oppose abortion, but his presuppositionalism also became the core strategy of the prolife movement. Since abortion was the single most important social issue for Christian Right activists in the 1980s, the activists who cut their teeth on the prolife movement naturally took Schaeffer's presuppositional strategy into other areas when new issues such as education caught their attention. Eventually, presuppositionalism became the characteristic strategy of the Christian Right.

Basing his approach on the basic incompatibilities Van Til identified between the presuppositions of the Christian and the human-centered worldviews, Schaeffer developed Van Til's presuppositionalism into an effective, uncompromising strategy for social transformation. Schaeffer's method exploited that incompatibility by using it to define the human-centered worldview's weaknesses. In some cases, this was at the level of basic assumptions. In most cases, however, it simply played on the lack of awareness in the general public of the basic presuppositions that grounded mainstream American life. By attacking these contradictions or hidden assumptions, Christian Right strategists began to learn how to put those outside the movement on the defensive. The purpose of their onslaughts was not to debate the issues with the general public, but to weaken the public's reliance on, or commitment to, nonbiblical Christian presuppositions. Thus, Christian Right attacks against the public schools for failing to teach Johnny how to read were not designed to make better schools or improve public education. They were an initial step in a larger process that involved building the movement and dismantling the existing system of public education. If the Christian Right could accomplish these two goals, then movement leaders hoped that their solutions would find increased receptivity in the larger culture.

The presuppositional strategy was never intended to win this or that local skirmish. Local skirmishes were designed to achieved two larger ends. They were to put in motion a ritual process through which conflict might bring people into the movement. Their purpose was also to erode the public's confidence in public education. As suggested by David Berliner and Bruce Biddle, beginning with the publication of *A Nation at Risk,* the Christian Right in conjunction with social conservatives manufactured the contemporary crisis.[2]

As Schaeffer so often reminded his followers, his interest was conversion, not dialogue. His goal was to convert the culture to the biblical Christian worldview. To achieve this, Schaeffer advocated pushing people to a "point of pressure" where their presuppositions collapsed, leaving them without any protection against the world. Schaeffer called this breaking point "taking the roof off." It was designed to strip people of the sacred canopy that protected them at the very time they were being pressured to defend it most vigorously. Schaeffer admitted that such a strategy had potentially dangerous consequences for the individual because of the degree of stress and pain it produced. But according to his rather utilitarian calculations, he concluded that it was better to put people through suffering than to leave them comfortable in their misdirected lives. Schaeffer wrote, "We confront men with reality; we remove their protection and their escapes; we allow the avalanches to fall. If they do not become Christians, then indeed they are in a worse state than before we spoke to them."[3] Such a strategy was neither torture nor human experimentation when used by the Christian who had prayed that the Holy Spirit remain in control of the process.[4]

Schaeffer's presuppositional method of social transformation received widespread support among Christian Right leaders in the 1980s, particularly in the movement's crusade against abortion. Operation Rescue's Randall Terry, Moral Majoritarian Tim LaHaye, and constitutional lawyer John Whitehead publicly acknowledged Schaeffer's influence in their work, particularly in using Van Til's presuppositionalism as the model for effecting social change. Schaeffer's jeremiad *A Christian Manifesto* (1981) put forth the parameters for this strategy. He compared the present cultural situation to the situation the early Protestant reformers faced in previous centuries. The reformers' political radicalism, Schaeffer argued, proceeded from the basis that all authority was derived from the Bible. Thus, if contemporary evangelicals wanted to change the present culture, they must follow the lead of the early reformers and reconstruct the civil government on the basis of God's law as given in the Bible.[5]

Schaeffer pointed to Samuel Rutherford's *Lex Rex; or, The Law and the Prince* (1644) as the classic statement of the radical social implications of the Reformation. Noting that Rutherford advocated resistance based on the Christian moral obligation to oppose tyrannical rule, Schaeffer emphasized the "right of resistance" within Reformed Christianity. "While we must always be subject to the *office* of the magistrate, we are not to be subject to the *man* in that office who commands that which is contrary to the Bible."[6] Following Scottish reformer John Knox, Schaeffer extended this right of resistance and civil disobedience to the common people. When government officials acted in ways contrary to the Bible, Christians, according to Schaeffer, had the right and the duty to disobey and rebel. "In almost every place where the Reformation flourished," Schaeffer observed, "there was not only religious noncompliance; there was civil disobedience as well."[7] This Reformation model was particularly important for Christians who found themselves in a human-centered civilization.

In the *Manifesto,* Schaeffer urged biblical Christians to use the political processes, but he also cautioned them not to limit themselves to that front. Since they were to fight the battle at the level of presuppositions, not at the ballot box, Christians ought to take their arguments into all spheres of society and use all avenues of influence available to them to pressure the society to the breaking point.[8] This included shaping public opinion, litigating grievances through the courts, using the media, and, as a last resort, engaging in civil disobedience to oppose the existing social order. Schaeffer sanctioned force, but only after all other avenues had been exhausted and after a long series of abuses.[9] "When discussing force," Schaeffer cautioned, "it is important to keep an axiom in mind: Before protest or force is used, we must work for reconstruction. In other words, we should attempt to correct and rebuild society before we advocate tearing it down or disrupting it."[10]

Schaeffer cautioned that the use of force can be dangerous to Christians. In the hands of the wrong people, it can become destructive to the long-term goal of social reconstruction. Christian Right leaders have been much more willing to use force in the abortion arena than they have in the debate over the public schools. One example of the willingness to use force is Operation Rescue, particularly under the leadership of Randall Terry. One reason for the greater tendency to use violence in the abortion wars than in the school wars is that the Christian Right does not sense the same kind of moral urgency toward public education as they do toward abortion. Abortion remains the strongest issue bringing the movement into collective action. Another reason Christian Right tactics have been more moderate in education than in the abortion debate is that transformation of the public schools is a much more long-term objective. It is not that education is any less important an issue. In some ways, it is more important because of the breadth of education's influence in the culture. But because life itself is not at stake in the same way as in abortion, the movement elite can adopt interim strategies and goals without using force to attack public educators directly.

The Christian Right eagerly adopted interim strategies for the transformation of the public schools for several reasons. Most importantly, the elite recognized that a much greater consensus regarding the nature and importance of public schools existed in the mind of the general public than regarding the issue of abortion. Therefore, a full frontal attack on the public schools might provoke a negative response toward the Christian Right on the part of the very constituency they were trying to convert— mainstream Americans. Furthermore, the issue of public education simply did not provoke the same level of moral anger and passion among the Christian Right's religious constituency. Although socially conservative evangelicals might have been concerned about the quality of public education, they were not as likely to take to the streets and engage in militant actions as the abortion protesters were. Finally, the movement's vanguard remembered the degree of resistance the general public showed in the mid-1980s to the intolerant and provocative rhetoric of the Moral Majority. Christian Right leaders learned from that experience that strident, confrontational rhetoric was not an effective strategy. They concluded that a successful presuppositional strategy must bury its own grounding principles and express its concerns without using explicitly religious deep symbols to frame the protests. Such an approach needed more time to develop. From presuppositional foundations, the Christian Right constructed a long-term incremental three-tiered strategy. Movement leaders also invoked a game plan of using all peaceful avenues available to them to accomplish their end of transforming the public schools—local controversies, the courts, the mass media, and legislative activism.

Inclusion, or "A Place at the Table"

At the first tier, the Christian Right presuppositional strategy sought inclusion in public discourse about the major social issues of the day. Ralph Reed expressed this sentiment in *Politically Incorrect* when he argued that conservative evangelicals were only asking for "a place at the table in the conversation we call democracy."[11] Movement activists applied the strategy of inclusion to educational issues at three different levels of discourse. At the highest level of national politics, they wanted to be included in policy discussions related to the future direction and content of America's schools. At the middle level, they wanted to be part of the same conversations with the educational establishment, including the various professional organizations that informed and advised teachers, administrators, and board members. At the local level, they wanted to be consulted about textbooks and curricula, counted among those who served on task forces for policy development, and involved in school board deliberations.

To pursue these objectives, Christian Right knowledge workers began to portray their constituency as a beleaguered minority who merely wanted their concerns about education to be given a fair hearing in a society that purported to value inclusion and fairness. This depiction was not entirely without justification. The whole educational hierarchy historically had frequently dismissed religiously motivated critics of public education. This kind of exclusion became increasingly evident in the early 1990s when the controversies over educational reform arose throughout the country. Many educators initially characterized their critics as extremists and religious fanatics and simply tried to exclude them. Professional associations like the Association for Supervision and Curriculum Development and the American Association of School Administrators at first simply ignored them. Other professional organizations, such as the National Education Association, expressed outright disdain for the activists. At the local level, school officials and teachers often either dismissed parent complaints about books or curricula on religious grounds or they created committees whose recommendations had the same effect.

Christian Right leaders understood that if they were to achieve inclusion, they had to overcome resistance at every level. Their hopes for a greater voice in the society soared with the election of Ronald Reagan to the presidency in 1980, but their high expectations quickly deflated when they realized that those within the Reagan Administration during the 1980s did not share the Christian Right's concerns about education. For the most part, the Reagan educational appointees were politically conservative ideologues and libertarians more interested in with limiting the power of the federal government in public education than in changing the entire structure of the system.[12] With the notable exception of Edwin Meese, who was sympathetic to the Christian Right, Reagan and his associates believed that the schools did have a positive secular public role. Reagan's attitude toward the public schools reflected a belief that the schools, in order to sustain in future citizens a commitment to democratic republicanism, had a civic responsibility to transmit the cultural, moral, and political values of the nation.[13] In this sense, Reagan stood squarely within the cultural mainstream. Mainstream Americans have long exhibited widespread support for the role of the public schools in transmitting the values of democracy and classical liberalism.[14] If the Christian Right was to move beyond the modest reforms proposed by Reagan and his followers, the leadership knew it had to press its cause in terms of mainstream values, not in opposition to them. The reality they faced was that neither their favored president nor the general public viewed public education from the Christian Right perspective. Movement theoreticians became convinced that, under such conditions, the reforms proposed by the Reagan administration would never achieve Christian Right goals.

The leaders concluded that the only solution available to them was to adopt the rhetoric of democracy and classical liberalism. In essence, they would use the symbols of freedom, tolerance, and rights to overcome public support for democracy and classical liberalism. To begin the process, they took advantage of Reagan's lack of attention to public education. Edwin Meese carried their banner at the highest level within Reagan's inner circle.[15] Within the Department of Education, movement activists were able to secure relatively high administrative posts, which they used to turn up the heat on public education. Gary Bauer, the former executive director of the Family Research Council, became the most visible of those appointees.[16] As undersecretary of education and later domestic policy adviser to Reagan, Bauer was on the inside when the educational establishment started to develop its reform initiatives in response to the 1983 release of *A Nation at Risk*. He was in the perfect position to frame Christian Right responses to those reforms. When the reforms in education hit the public schools and the state departments of education in the late 1980s and early 1990s, the Christian Right was prepared.

The report of the President's Commission on Educational Excellence gave the Christian Right's long-term presuppositional strategy a huge

boost at the very time the movement was searching for a way to undermine the educational establishment. Though the commission itself was bi-
partisan, the report it issued was not entirely free from political bias. Feeling the pressure for ideological conformity within the Reagan administration, Education Secretary Terrell Bell accepted the report not on its
merits, but because he felt that it would be acceptable to President Reagan. The report, without presenting any documentation or source citations,[17] concluded that America's schools were not competitive with those
of other nations. As a consequence, the report argued, the long-term security of the nation was in jeopardy. America's schools "are presently being
eroded by a rising tide of mediocrity that threatens our very future as a
Nation and a people," it said.[18] The dangers the report identified and the
remedies proposed therein were clearly consistent with mainstream cultural and economic values. The chief danger identified by the study was
that the shortcomings of the schools were undermining the nation's economic competitiveness. After the report's release, other publications, many
issued by conservative think tanks, came to the same conclusions. America
was at risk because of the failing condition of the public schools. Thus,
though not ideologically aligned with the Christian Right, the commission's conclusions did enhance the effectiveness of the movement's presuppositional approach.

The remedies called for by the commission were disappointing to the
Christian Right. The report called for continued federal involvement in
public education rather than a complete privatization or public funding
of religious schools. Using classical liberal arguments, the commission argued that such involvement was necessary to protect students who might
be the targets of discrimination and to provide assistance for poor students as well as the gifted and talented. Nowhere did the report include
any specific references to school prayer, tuition tax credits, vouchers, or
public funding of private schools.[19] However, at the press conference an-
nouncing the release of *A Nation at Risk,* Reagan ignored these recommendations and instead called for "the passage of tuition tax credits,
vouchers, educational savings accounts, voluntary school prayer, and the
abolishment of the Department of Education."[20] The surprising content
of Reagan's remarks came about because (1) Reagan had not read the report, so he did not know what its recommendations were; and (2) Edwin
Meese inserted the comments into Reagan's remarks, without the approval of either Secretary Bell or the commissioners.[21] The fact that some
commission members later expressed dismay over Reagan's statements

became irrelevant in the larger discussion that ensued. Through Meese, Reagan legitimated some of the most important stepping stones the Christian Right sought to lay in its efforts to transform American public education. The Christian Right did not win a place at the table in the Reagan administration, but the voices of their leaders at least gained recognition for being in the room.

Putting aside the issue of whether the commission's report and other similar findings issued by conservative think tanks were valid, the discussion that followed *A Nation at Risk* began to redefine the parameters of public discourse about education. For a number of years, Americans in general had been growing frustrated with the inability of the public schools to solve many of the nation's social problems. Beginning in the 1950s, Americans increasingly turned to the public schools to remediate the problems of segregation and poverty. The federal government funded countless programs designed to level the playing field for minorities and the poor. Through school health services, counseling, Head Start, school lunch and breakfast programs, before- and after-school care, special education, and similar efforts, the schools had evolved into one of the primary institutions for social equality and change. The failure of the schools to resolve the problems of poverty, racism, and social inequality led to a gradual decline in faith in the power of education among the general public. The release of *A Nation at Risk* provided the Christian Right with a valuable window of opportunity. In conjunction with the conservative think tanks' own economic agenda for public education, Christian Right leaders fanned the public's growing disenchantment into dissatisfaction with the public schools. They used the opportunity to advance their long-term objectives, employing alarmist rhetoric, symbolic language appropriated from the larger culture, and questionable data.

The campaign began in 1985, when Education Undersecretary Gary Bauer issued a report to the National Consultation on Pornography linking the rise in public obscenity to the Supreme Court's 1962–63 ban on school prayer. Blaming the schools for failing to teach sound values, Bauer argued that the absence of prayer in the public schools had been a major cause of what many Americans perceived to be a moral decline in the culture.[22] Several years later, Beverly LaHaye's Concerned Women for America (CWA) was more explicit. A 1988 CWA book claimed that "removing prayer and the acknowledgment of God from our classrooms has been the *primary cause* of the devastatingly serious decline in the lives of students, their families, the schools, and our nation."[23]

To repair the damage done by the Court, Bauer transformed Secretary of Education William C. Bennett's call for restoring the three "C's" of education—character, content, and choice—into support for the Christian Right agenda.[24] Bennett's statement helped the Christian Right form the symbolic link that connected the problems faced by America's public schools, the perceived moral decay of the culture, and the Christian Right worldview. These symbols, being fluid, allowed for multiple interpretations without confronting the specific presuppositions in which different segments of the society grounded the symbols. By using the symbols of character, content, and choice, the Christian Right could advance their cause without playing their hand.

Recognizing the advantage of creating such imprecise symbolic links, the Christian Right moved to recast its arguments in the traditional secular mainstream values of democracy and classic liberalism. In November 1990, the conservative Heritage Foundation sponsored a meeting with the Christian Right leadership in Washington, D.C., to develop this new rhetorical strategy. The conversation at that gathering revolved around an article written by former Robertson staff member Thomas C. Atwood for *Policy Review,* the Heritage Foundation house organ. Atwood accused the Christian Right of ignoring the basic rules of politics, suggesting that its leaders "often came across as authoritarian, intolerant and boastful, even to natural constituents." Atwood suggested that the movement appeal to more mainstream values such as "common sense." In summing up his thoughts, he stated, "The best thing that could happen to the movement is for it to be less identifiable as a movement and have its people and its ideas percolate through the system."[25] Thus was born the stealth dimension of the Christian Right's presuppositional strategy. By framing their objectives in the rhetorical clothing of democratic and classic liberal values, movement strategists hoped to exploit mainstream America's presuppositions in order to weaken mainstream power over education.

By 1993, the strategy was in place. Former Moral Majority leader and syndicated columnist Cal Thomas acknowledged the intentionality of the rhetorical shift and the wisdom behind it in an article entitled "Religious Expression Is a Free Speech Issue." Thomas applauded the success of the shift from religious arguments to the rights language of classic liberalism. In the column, he focused on two Supreme Court decisions that he felt exemplified the wisdom and success of the strategy shift. "Two recent Supreme Court verdicts represent important victories for those who usually have found themselves on the losing end of arguments over religious freedom in public schools. The attorneys for the religious plaintiffs finally got smart. Instead of arguing the cases on the basis of religion, they argued them on the basis of free speech."[26] The decisions to which he referred were *Lamb's Chapel v. Center Moriches School District* (New York)[27] and *Jones v. Clear Creek Independent School District* (Texas).[28]

In the Lamb's Chapel decision the Court extended to religious groups equal access to school facilities after school hours on the same basis as other groups. In the Jones case, the Federal Appeals Court for the Fifth Circuit ruled student-led graduation prayers legal. The Supreme Court refused to hear the appeal. Thomas interpreted the Court's decision not to certify the Jones case for review as an implicit endorsement of the appellate court's decision. Later in the article, Thomas provided constitutional legitimation for Christian Right legal challenges to public education. Quoting Justice Joseph Story, appointed to the Supreme Court by President James Madison, Thomas recalled that "the real objective of the First Amendment was . . . to exclude all rivalry among Christian sects, and to prevent any national ecclesiastical establishment which should give to a hierarchy the exclusive patronage of the national government." Thomas added, "The First Amendment was written to prevent sectarian conflict over the control of government, not to erect a wall that keeps people of religious faith from influencing government, as modern courts have misinterpreted it."[29] Thomas thus gave a conspiratorial cast to both the Lamb's Chapel and the Clear Creek cases. This move reflected the conspiratorial dimension of Christian Right arguments. In this protest framework, the Christian Right cast itself as a beleaguered minority oppressed by an intolerant majority for simply seeking a voice in public affairs. The Court's decisions seemed to reinforce the claim.

The inclusion strategy of the Christian Right at the national level thus had two prongs. On the one hand, the movement used it to legitimate its claim that its voice should be included in any public discourse about the nation's schools. In this framework, the claim appealed to the democratic values of fairness, inclusion, and tolerance. Placing their claim in this context, Christian Right leaders found a sympathetic ear among many mainstream Americans. On the other hand, the Christian Right could only appropriate these democratic values and rights arguments by stripping them of their common meanings and reframing them within the movement's worldview and long-term agenda of cultural control.

Having gained a place at the table at the level of national political discourse, the Christian Right still faced the not inconsiderable task of getting the attention of the educational establishment. They accomplished this in large part with the unintended cooperation of the educational elite. Acknowledging the concerns about public education identified in *A Nation at Risk,* the educational establishment began during the 1980s to formulate plans to restructure America's schools. The plans included, but were not limited to, site-based management, multicultural studies, cooperative learning, higher order thinking, whole language, and new approaches to reading, such as the aforementioned *Quest* series. President George Bush endorsed many of these innovations in his America 2000 initiative. The measure initially passed Christian Right muster only because movement lobbyists and sympathetic elected officials were able to incorporate such profamily measures as tax credits and parental choice into the bill.[30] By the early 1990s, most state level departments of education had developed reform initiatives based on the advice of the educational establishment, and the establishment's educational reform movement was in full gear.

Christian Right support quickly turned to opposition when the profamily provisions ran into trouble in Congress. Movement strategists seized upon the establishment's reform initiatives and brought to bear the full measure of presuppositional pressure. Christian Right activists were aided by the fact that few educators at the local level really understood the reforms either in terms of their implications for the classroom or the research base upon which they had been developed. This confusion among educators, administrators, and school board members provided the perfect opportunity for the Christian Right to turn up the pressure. Activists such as Phyllis Schlafly, Robert Simonds, and James Dobson attempted to transform their concerns about secular humanism into opposition to Outcome-Based Education (OBE). Although OBE had specific reference to the educational reform package marketed by William Spady, Christian Right tacticians used it as an umbrella term for all of their objections to public education.[31] The uncertainties present in the public's mind about OBE opened the window of opportunity sought by the Christian Right. In this way, the educational establishment provided the Christian Right with the symbolic wedge that the movement's long-standing protests against secular humanism had failed to develop.

In 1992, Citizens for Excellence in Education began publishing a series of three books by Kathi Hudson that put forward many Christian Right objections to the reforms proposed by the educational elite. Hudson sounded the clarion call by describing OBE as "one of the most controversial and divisive educational trends of the decade."[32] The first volume focused on OBE. Hudson began her analysis by affirming the need for schools to change in light of a changing world, but she cautioned that such changes should not override the rights of parents "to instruct their children in matters of morality and religion. They have a fundamental right to pass on their values. That is non-negotiable."[33] She then outlined her case against OBE. The series of charges she leveled became the standard rhetoric of Christian Right educational critics from the national to the grassroots level. Hudson's objections focused on two key areas, both designed to provoke the fears of parents and thus turn up the presuppositional pressure. The first stated that the restructuring ideas were "completely experimental and unproven." Translated by movement knowledge workers into the phrase "Don't experiment with our children," the allegation became a rallying cry of grassroots Christian Right advocates. Hudson's second indictment of the reforms fit closely with the first. The schools were engaging in a vast social experiment designed to change the values and religious beliefs of school children. To accomplish this agenda, schools were abandoning the content emphasis of traditional education and substituting process-oriented OBE. Translated into the protest frames of the Christian Right, this meant that the proposed reforms were designed to change the students' beliefs and feelings into politically correct New Age ideology, rather than to require content mastery of the students.

To help parents understand how such seemingly innocent outcomes as higher order thinking and problem solving were in fact conversion motifs of New Age zealots, Hudson provided a description of three types of OBE. She built these characterizations on previous work by OBE guru William Spady. Hudson encouraged Christian parents to pursue the first type, Traditional OBE. She claimed Traditional OBE was what most parents thought about when they were told all education was outcome-based. Traditional OBE emphasized knowledge mastery. In this approach, course content determined the outcome.

The second type of outcome-driven model Hudson identified as Transitional OBE. It changed the focus of education by introducing process-related and interdisciplinary goals (e.g., critical thinking and communication). Testing of subject matter and information recall was generally replaced with performance-based assessments. This form could be acceptable to Christian parents, according to Hudson, if the outcomes sufficiently focused on content. She warned that it was potentially dangerous if the outcomes emphasized student beliefs and values. The third type, Transformational OBE, was the most dangerous. It was what educational reformers meant by Outcome-Based Education, according to Hudson. "It attempts to create 'competant [*sic*] future citizens' by equipping students with the knowledge, skills and *orientations* needed for an everchanging global society. Assessment is performance-based. All aspects of schooling— curriculum, asessment [*sic*], governance, school structure, etc.—must be structured to support the exit outcomes."[34] In this form, she argued, OBE substituted content for values. It engaged in social engineering by build- ing in students the unacceptable affective goals of tolerance for "'politi- cally correct' views on environmentalism, global citizenship (as opposed to national sovereignty) and multiculturalism."[35] In short, it moved students toward compromise and concession to the collective group decision in a problem-solving session instead of teaching them to stand up for their own convictions. Hudson's critiques became the rallying points for grass- roots activists. They were echoed by Phyllis Schlafly, Gary Bauer, and James Dobson and repeated by many other Christian Right organizations in communications to their constituents.

The anti-OBE campaign moved Robert Simonds to center stage in discussions of educational reform. By effectively training grassroots ac- tivists, CEE launched a crusade against OBE that brought William Spady's consulting business to near collapse. With such a groundswell against re- structuring, the educational establishment could no longer ignore Christ- ian Right pressures. Two indications that the movement had finally gained a place at the table of the educational elite appeared in the late fall and winter of 1993–94. In October 1993, the *School Administrator,* the maga- zine of the American Association of School Administrators (AASA) de- voted an issue to the "Far Right." Two articles appeared in that publication by Christian Right spokespersons Ralph Reed and Robert Simonds, who described in one of the articles "The Agenda of the Religious Right."[36] *Educational Leadership,* the house organ of the Association for Supervision and Curriculum Development (ASCD) followed suit in its December– January issue on "fundamentalists," which focused exclusively on Christ- ian Right concerns about public education and included an article by Si- monds.[37] For the first time, two major educational establishment publica- tions presented to their readers articles by Simonds and other Christian Right activists. ASCD later sought to further include Simonds and the Christian Right through a conference designed to seek common ground among Spady, the educational establishment, and Robert Simonds. Although he accepted the invitation, Simonds never appeared. In his place, he sent Arnold Burron, a NACE/CEE surrogate who taught in the School of Education at the University of Northern Colorado. Even through his absence, Simonds hoped to achieve parity for his Traditional OBE plan with Spady's Transformational OBE among the educational establishment. The ill-fated attempt at accommodation failed because neither Spady nor Simonds was genuinely interested in compromise. Spady and others in the educational establishment naively thought that dialogue could bring an end to the conflicts.[38]

This series of events was important for Simonds because an important organization within the educational establishment had given him a platform to voice movement concerns. By consistently raising their voices throughout the nation, Christian Right activists had achieved the movement's first strategic objective. From that point on, the educational establishment would have to take seriously criticism raised by Citizens for Excellence in Education, the Family Research Council, the Christian Coalition, the Eagle Forum, and other Christian Right special purpose groups. What was impressive about the movement's success was that it achieved it using mainstream discourse, thereby protecting its own presuppositions and strategic goals from public examination.

The fact that national organizations both inside and outside the educational establishment had granted Christian Right voices legitimacy did not necessarily translate into the movement's acceptance at the local level. Inclusion at that level often came through school board elections in which conservative evangelical candidates, often using stealth tactics, won seats. In 1994, Simonds claimed that Christians held a majority on 2,240 school boards nationwide, although he consistently refused to provide a list of them. He did boast, in regard to the Lake County, Florida, board majority that CEE helped elect, "We now own that school district."[39] Although there is no way to verify Simonds's claim about the number of school boards dominated by Christian Right activists, it is clear that their presence in many districts throughout the country did change the tenor and content of public discourse about education. This was equally true of state boards of education, where Christian Right activism turned the tide away from the reform plans of the educational establishment toward those of the Christian Right. By the mid-1990s, the Christian Right had won a seat at the table at all levels of educational discussion.

Exclusion, or "Safe Passage through the Schools"

Christian Right activism in the educational arena was never intended to stop at the level of inclusion. Framed in the dualism of two competing worldviews, movement strategists saw cultural legitimation only as a precursor to protecting Christian children from the onslaught of secular humanism that, in their minds, dominated the American system of public education. When given mainstream recognition, activists at the national, state, and local levels pushed for changes in the present system that would exclude from the public schools curricula and pedagogy that movement activists felt were a threat to their children and contrary to the worldview they held. These changes, according to Simonds, were necessary to create "safe passage through the schools" for Christian children who needed protection from secular humanism and New Age religion. Safety for their children was only a penultimate goal, however. To prevent the spread of secular humanist influence throughout the culture, the Christian Right intended to purge all classrooms of objectionable content and methodology.

The difficulty the Christian Right faced was that, though the general public might be sympathetic to claims for "safe passage" for the children of Christian Right parents, it did not agree that Christian Right parents should impose their alternative curricula and pedagogy on all school children. Most parents still had confidence in the public schools and did not "see what all the fuss was about."[40] The Christian Right faced the difficult task of convincing other parents and the general public that the curriculum and pedagogy now in place or being implemented through educational reforms not only was inferior, but that it would have disastrous consequences for the entire nation.

Robert Simonds, who, with CEE, had taken the lead in providing Christian Right grassroots activists with materials detailing the dangers of the establishment's educational reforms, also achieved prominence within the movement for CEE publications that taught local activists how to organize politically. The goal was to elect Christian Right members to school boards and thus turn up the pressure on the public schools. As early as 1985–86, CEE had initiated more curricular and textbook challenges than any other single organization.[41] By 1994, CEE's *Public School Awareness Kits* were in use in more than two hundred districts throughout the nation and Simonds was in constant demand as a workshop facilitator.[42] Other organizations contributed to the cause. Phyllis Schlafly's Eagle

Forum, James Dobson's Focus on the Family, Gary Bauer's Family Research Council, Pat Robertson's Christian Coalition, Beverly LaHaye's Concerned Women for America, Lou Sheldon's Traditional Values Coalition, and Christian Right spokeswoman Peg Luksik all took up the banner for Christian Right parents. It was Simonds and NACE/CEE, however, that had the biggest impact.

Christian Right leaders knew that, using presuppositional strategy, they had to convince the general public that the alarms they were sounding about public education were justified. The OBE controversy provided the opportunity to do that. If movement strategists could create concern in the citizenry about the presuppositions that guided the reforms, they could create skepticism about the reforms themselves. Peg Luksik, a previously obscure activist from Pennsylvania, took up that challenge. She began using conspiratorial language in making the case for the Christian Right as early as 1990. Her opposition to educational reforms framed within the context of populist distrust of the federal government, Luksik traveled throughout the country promoting an antistatist conspiratorial theory with respect to Outcome-Based Education and psychological testing of students. Her videotape, *Who Controls Our Children,* employed populist antigovernment and rights symbols rather than religious ones. Drawing upon John Birch Society rhetoric, Luksik claimed that the issue of educational reform was a matter of parental rights only, not religion.

> It's not a religious issue at all. . . . It's a "parents vs. the state" issue. . . . As far as public schools are concerned, parents have the right to raise their children in their own value system. It is not the right of public schools to remediate their child away from the value system of their parents. That's not a religious issue, that's a civil-rights issue.[43]

Despite her comments about religion, Luksik worked closely with Robert Simonds's NACE/CEE, even using his office in Costa Mesa, California, for a period of time as her contact point.[44] The Christian Coalition, among other Christian Right organizations, embraced and promoted Luksik's arguments.

By invoking the civil rights argument, Luksik demonstrated the growing ability of the Christian Right to reframe its rhetoric in symbols that drew on democratic values and classic liberal rights positions. Making use of the multivocality of symbols, the Christian Right appealed to the mainstream without revealing the specific meanings the movement leaders gave to the symbols. The strategists simply trusted that the mainstream would

interpret the rhetoric according to mainstream assumptions without raising any critical questions. Although Luksik was successful in generating
opposition to establishment reforms, the antistatist conspiratorial framework she employed kept her arguments from convincing many mainstream Americans.

To move the presuppositional strategy forward, tacticians began linking
educational reform opposition to patriotic motifs. Building on the nation-
alist fervor generated by the Reagan presidency, Christian Right knowledge workers connected the reforms to globalism and the one-world government of the New World Order.[45] They also exploited parental anxiety
about the new religious movements that had particular appeal to younger
Americans, linking these alternative expressions of religion to the more
violent and sexually explicit elements of pop culture. "New Age religion"
became a symbol that clustered Eastern religions, religious cults, pagan religion, religious humanism, and Satanism together. Such linkages seemed
at least tenable to mainstream Americans who had little familiarity with
either globalism or New Age religion.

As noted, many educators, administrators, and school board members
had a poor understanding of the reforms they were asked to implement by
state and national educational authorities. This fact aided Christian Right
presuppositional strategy at the local level. In the informational vacuum,
Christian Right interpretations often seemed to be the most coherent explanations parents and citizens received about the reforms. Because most
educators confronted by Christian Right explanations understood even
less about the symbols and rhetoric of the Christian Right, they often
were at a loss to refute the charges brought by the critics. A series of books
published by Christian Right knowledge workers that drew out the specific connections between the educational reforms and socialism or New
Age religion also aided local activists. One of the most important was Eric
Buehrer's *The New Age Masquerade: The Hidden Agenda in Your Child's Classroom*. The subtitle spoke to the fears of parents.[46] Although only a small
percentage of Americans identified themselves as New Agers, Buehrer's
book, and others like Pat Robertson's *New World Order*, made it appear
that New Agers, secular humanists, and anti-American globalists were behind every desk, textbook, and educational reform.[47] James Dobson's endorsement of Buehrer's work brought it into the Christian Right mainstream. Dobson also recommended Buehrer's Gateways to Better Education group in Lake Forest, California, as a valuable resource for Christian
Right teachers as they approached the Christmas season. Buehrer's organi-

zation offered strategies by which public school teachers could infuse biblical Christian dogma into classroom instruction.[48]

Having provoked the anxieties of mainstream parents about globalism and New Age religion, Christian Right knowledge workers utilized these symbols in two ways to achieve their goal of exclusion. First, they linked globalism and New Age religion to almost every aspect of public instruction and educational reform to which the Christian Right objected. Collaborative learning represented an attack on American individualism. Higher order thinking was linked to relativism and the lack of moral values in the culture. Books used in classes were connected to New Age writers and themes. Visualization techniques in writing and reading were reframed as New Age and Eastern religious meditation. Even a science experiment demonstrating the effect of depletion of oxygen on a candle under a glass bell jar was identified by a local activist as a satanic ritual.[49] Ultimately, the Christian Right used Outcome-Based Education to bring all these criticism together under a single symbolic umbrella. To the benefit of the Christian Right, the educational establishment sometimes appeared eager to provide the critics with legitimate targets.

For example, Christian Right literature was full of descriptions of state-mandated outcomes that, on the surface, appeared to the general public to have little direct relationship to the academic purposes of public schools. Robert Simonds told his constituency, "Humanist doctrine has been written into the Pennsylvania State School Code: Self Esteem, Self Worth, Wellness and Fitness, Adaptability to Change, Higher Order Thought, Learning Independently, Ethical Judgment, Appreciating and Understanding Others, the State supplanting the family, and all without discrimination or sexual orientation."[50] Peg Luksik pressured the governor of Pennsylvania to accept a compromise on the reforms that eliminated an outcome of "appreciating and understanding others."[51] The *Phyllis Schlafly Report* instructed readers on the dangers of outcomes such as "world citizenship and government (instead of patriotism), population control, radical environmentalism, and government 'solutions' for every problem." Other perilous outcomes detailed by Schlafly included those that

> concern values, attitudes, opinions and relationships rather than objective information. . . . OBE requires students to meet vague psychological objectives relating to self-esteem, ethical judgment, and adaptability to change. . . . OBE thus involves a major change in the school's avowed mission. Henceforth, its mission is to conform student beliefs, attitudes and behavior

to prescribed school-mandated social norms, rather than to provide an academic education.[52]

James Dobson informed his followers that outcomes such as "problem-solving," "effective communication" and "appreciating others" took away from the students' ability to master science, math, and literature.[53]

Christian Right leaders also linked other reforms and outcomes to fears of many mainstream Americans. Robert Simonds, for example, connected multiculturalism to anxiety in the general public about race wars and racial discord. In his *President's Report,* Robert Simonds wrote that multiculturalism led to the race riots in Los Angeles. Through the multicultural agenda of the schools, "children," Simonds charged, "will be induced with a radical guilt about racism (inciting riot wars in our cities)." He further asserted that mental health counselors in the schools cooperated with a special education interest in "classifying almost every student as 'mentally ill' in need of special education, re-thinking education and re-socialization." Simonds attacked environmental awareness as well. It was being used in the schools by New Age globalists to advance their agenda on unsuspecting parents and children through the fear of overpopulation and the resulting need for population control. Once that was in place, these "same globalist New Agers could promote abortion and sexual immorality in the classroom." Simonds argued that Earth Day, recognized by most schools, was "an annual program to introduce all children to worshipping the rocks, birds, plants, etc.—'you are God.'"[54]

Once the Christian Right successfully linked many of these outcomes to New Age religion, it turned its appeals to mainstream values such as religious freedom, equality, and fairness in pursuit of the exclusion strategy. Echoing the century-old assertions of Hermann Dooyeweerd, Christian Right leaders argued that secular humanism, as expressed in New Age religion and globalism, was a religion and that its presence in the public schools constituted an illegal establishment of religion. Their argument had some legal basis. Rutherford Institute's John Whitehead and Congressman John Conlan, for example, made a case for this interpretation in a coauthored article in the *Texas Tech Law Review;* they cited several precedents, including Justice Hugo Black's footnote in *Torasco v. Watkins* (1961) calling secular humanism a religion. They included a 1987 case by U.S. District Court Judge William Brevard Hand, even though it had been overturned a year later. In his decision Judge Hand wrote, "Humanism is, indeed a religion."[55] They drew a third reference from Justice

Potter Stewart's dissenting opinion in the so-called 1963 school prayer case *Abingdon School District v. Schempp.* In his comments, Stewart equated irreligion or secularism with religion. It followed then, Stewart argued, that "a refusal to permit religious exercises is thus seen, not as a realization of state neutrality, but rather as the establishment of a religion of secularism."[56] Since neither Stewart's comments or the ruling by Judge Hand had the force of law, it was clear that the article was aimed more at providing activists with legal citations than at accurately reflecting the legal state of affairs.

The tactic of arguing for fairness, equality, and religious freedom called upon the rhetoric and values of classic liberalism even though it was used to further ends that stood in stark contrast to those values. If humanism was a religion, and if it provided the presuppositional foundation for current educational practice, then, Christian Right activists argued, it would only be fair to include Christian instruction and religious activities in public school curricula. At the same time they argued this position, movement leaders waged a counterargument calling for enforcement of the separation of church and state. If humanism was a religion, the second prong of the argument ran, and if it provided the presuppositional foundation for current educational practice, then the Constitution required that every vestige of secular humanism be stripped from the curriculum. On the surface, such arguments had popular appeal, even though they appeared to be logically contradictory. What the Christian Right was saying was that either the courts take "their" religion out of the schools or they allow "ours" in on an equal basis.

These appeals to fairness and equality seemed to strike a chord in the general public. The strategy might have succeeded had the general public not learned of the specifics and the overall implications of what the Christian Right was asking from the public schools. Citizens at the local level were supportive of fairness and equality, but they objected to the overtly sectarian remedies posed by the critics. Officially endorsed sectarian prayer, creationism in science, and American supremacy curricula still seemed to be too far outside the mainstream for inclusion. Furthermore, in a number of instances, the credibility of Christian Right arguments began to fade when the activists became explicit and precise about their objections.[57] In other cases, local foot soldiers simply took the recipe knowledge provided to them by national organizations and made accusations against the schools even when none of the particular reform measures were being considered by the district under fire.

In the early 1990s, when the general public did discover the nature and extent of the changes Christian Right activists envisioned, opposition to the Christian Right and their tactics arose across much of the nation. In Pennsylvania, Colorado, and California, for example, citizen groups developed effective responses to Christian Right challenges. In Florida, Texas, and California, high-profile Christian Right school board takeovers were followed by recall elections and rejection of Christian Right candidates in subsequent contests. The obvious conclusion the Christian Right drew was that the general public was not yet ready to accept the exclusion strategy in the schools. The exclusion strategy did not fail, however. From a presuppositional perspective, the exclusion strategy "pushed up the pressure" on education nationally and at the grassroots level. In many cases, these controversies "ripped the roof off" public confidence in the schools. Combined with inclusion, exclusion worked to help build the foundation for the third-tier strategy of control of the schools.

Control, or "Christian Worldview Perspective" Education

The third tier of Christian Right strategies toward education focused on the ultimate goal of gaining control of America's schools. This approach took three forms. Movement leaders sought to (1) defund public education at the national level in order to eliminate the ability of the federal government to impose limitations on the local schools; (2) to reduce the influence of educational professionals at the local level through advocacy of parental rights and parental choice; and (3) to extend public funding of education to private, parochial, and religious schools through vouchers, tax credits, and "empowerment scholarships." In combination, the three approaches aimed at a total restructuring of public education to bring it more into line with biblical principles. The envisioned strategy was a long-term process in which advances would be made slowly and incrementally. In order to prepare the public for Christian Right control of the schools, the leadership knew they had to move the public along that road one small step at a time. Parental rights and choice led to schools of choice. Once the public became accustomed to choice, the idea of extending it to religious schools would not raise the same level of suspicion as if no preparations had been made. If the ultimate strategy was successful, Christian parents could feel safe in sending their children to publicly funded religious schools. Christian parents who kept their children in the public schools could demand changes from the schools by invoking parental rights in order to control curricular content and pedagogical methods. At the national level, the leadership intended to attempt to accomplish these same goals through the courts and the state legislatures.

J. R. Wynsma describes the confluence of these third-tier strategies in an article entitled "Educational Reform: The HELP Scholarships Amendment of 1997," published in the December 1997 issue of *Neopolitique*. Significantly, *Neopolitique* is the house organ of Regent University's (Pat) Robertson School of Government. Regent University is the academic wing of Robertson's Christian Right network. Wynsma's article is not unique, but rather is highly representative of Christian Right thinking at the level of the Christian Right's exclusionary strategy.[58] Variations of these arguments appear in the literature of Focus on the Family, the Family Research Council, the Christian Coalition, the Traditional Values Coalition, Concerned Women for America, and the Eagle Forum. But the arguments are seldom made so explicitly and coherently as in Wynsma's article.

Wynsma lists four specific goals for the Christian Right with respect to education: (1) eliminate the federal role in education, (2) increase parental and local control of the schools, (3) ensure a prominent role for religion and morality in educational reform, and (4) reform tax policy at all levels in order to favor religious and private schools. The article links together defunding the Department of Education, supporting the privatization of schools, promoting parental choice through schools of choice, and creating "Christian-friendly" public schools through charter schools. It also calls for the elimination of national educational standards and testing and the elimination of governmental funding of all school programs.

Wynsma constructs his argument from theological, legal, and pragmatic sources. Theologically, removing federal influence from the public schools is consistent with the Christian Right presupposition that families are divinely ordained to educate their children. Citing Ephesians 6:4,[59] Wynsma asserts that "the Scriptures teach that it is the responsibility of the parents to educate their children." Wynsma's legal argument notes that the U.S. Constitution nowhere enumerates education as one of the powers of the state. Christian Right legal scholars conclude that the federal role in public education has no legal basis; legal authority for education rests at the state and local levels. Because the federal government has usurped the prerogative of parents as well as citizens at the state and local levels, Christian Right leaders increasingly refer to America's schools as "government" rather than "public" schools. The Christian Right argument runs that the schools will not be truly public until the ultimate authority of the public schools rests with "we the people." Wynsma's pragmatic justification for Christianization of the public schools connects federal involvement in public education to the Christian Right claims about the decline in educational quality. Wynsma writes that the downfall of the "government education system" includes a "failure to equip children with the skills required to function in today's increasingly competitive world, lapses in technology, bureaucratic waste, hostility toward religion, disputes over 'common values,' violence, and drugs . . . [and] the inequality of opportunity that results from the monopoly system."[60] He attributes these failures to the progressive educational philosophy of John Dewey and the National Education Association (NEA). Rushdoony earlier made precisely the same connections in his writings.[61]

The linkage of declining quality in the public schools with progressive educational philosophy and the NEA is almost universal in the Christian Right.[62] According to this line of argument, the influence of progressivism and the NEA are so completely woven into the fabric of America's educational establishment that the elimination of one or several parts of the system will not correct the problem. Moreover, progressivism and the NEA are so opposed to biblical values and scriptural truth that the only solution is to get the federal government completely out of the way by eliminating its role. Once citizens eliminate federal government participation in education, parents can take control of the schools at the state and local levels and purge them of the influence of Dewey as well as the NEA.

Such a strategy leads logically and inevitably to Wynsma's second goal of increasing local and parental control of the schools. Specific tactics mentioned by Wynsma include electing candidates sympathetic to the Christian Right to school boards, protecting parents' values through curriculum review, and asserting parental oversight in the schools' decision-making processes. Here Wynsma returns to theological and pragmatic rationales. Recalling Rushdoony's arguments, theologically the only legitimate function the government can play in education is in promoting a biblical Christian worldview. Scripture requires this, as Wynsma explains. "Our children must be taught, among other things, that they are accountable to the Lord, that there are biblical moral absolutes, that self-government is essential, and that education is based on biblical reasoning."[63] Pragmatically, Wynsma notes, such changes in the educational system are much more easily effected at the local level where Christian Right parents and those sympathetic to them provide a solid voting block. Wynsma's article strongly suggests that by increasing local control, Christian Right leaders believe that they can begin to control the public schools, particularly in communities where a significant block of voters are sympathetic to their agenda. The Christian Right does not believe it is yet in a position to do this in all the nation's schools or in the educational establishment at the national level.[64] Further, at the practical level, Christian Right leaders believe that "parents' rights" arguments tap into the increasing frustration of parents who have seen their local schools lose authority for curricular matters to state and federal educational bureaucracies. Such a rights-based appeal fits comfortably into mainstream values.

Wynsma's third goal of increasing the role of religion in the public schools follows closely from the theological justification for the first two goals. If education is based on biblical reasoning, then schools must be forced to ensure that religion and morality play a prominent role in the design and execution of the school's educational mission. According to Wynsma, the problem rests with the nature of government schools. "Even if government schools were controlled by Christians, it would still amount to the same type of indoctrination that currently is happening with secular humanism."[65] Using appeals to freedom of religion and the natural link between religion and morality, Wynsma argues, "If religion and morality is an inevitable and vital dimension of education, then only when parents are free to choose and schools are free to teach, can this dimension function properly."[66] Like other Christian Right writers, Wynsma bases his conclusions on the statements of the nation's founding figures, legal documents such as the Northwest Ordinance, and the observations of the early-nineteenth-century French aristocrat Alexis de Tocqueville.

All of these sources join religion to morality and morality to the health of the democracy. The Northwest Ordinance, for example, includes a provision that, "religion, morality, and knowledge being necessary to good government, . . . schools and the means of education shall forever be encouraged." Christian Right leaders argue that this means that schools should not only accommodate religion, but they should also provide a religious foundation to education. Tocqueville is cited to support the same contention. From his visit to America, Tocqueville concluded that it was Christianity that largely provided the nation with the public virtues necessary for a strong democracy.[67] Tocqueville added that not all religions promote the virtues necessary to democracy. In such cases, Tocqueville observed, religion constructive to democracy must oppose tyrannical religion.[68] From these statements Christian Right theorists argue that America can and should be returned to the moral country it once was—which can only occur through reinstitution of a Christian cultural consensus, with schools bearing responsibility for the task.

The final piece of Wynsma's article focuses on tax policy reform. Speaking for the Christian Right, he writes, "Our goal must be to reduce the burgeoning tax burden and eliminate compulsory funding of government education. . . . Families who send their children to non-government schools are forced to pay government school taxes. The rationale given is that it is for the 'public good.' Analysis of the product suggests that this is an indefensible argument."[69] Although the tactics the author cites in this part of the article are consistent with his first point, defunding the Department of Education, they go beyond the earlier one to seek changes in the funding of public education in general at all levels. The tactics he identifies to accomplish that include conservative efforts to change the form of federal funding for education to block grants administered at the state level without federal strings. He also mentions tuition tax credits, school voucher programs, and charter schools, all designed to create in the general public the idea that choice in education is desirable and serves worthy ends.[70] Once choice in education becomes incorporated into the presuppositions of the general public, Christian Right activists are poised to gradually cloud the boundaries between public and sectarian education using the above-mentioned strategies. Their long-term goal is to eventually move the public to accept public funding of private schools accompanied by the defunding of public schools.[71]

What makes Wynsma's article particularly significant is that it is not an exercise in theoretical speculation. As the title of the article ("Educational Reform: The HELP Scholarships Amendment of 1997") suggests, he is commenting on Christian Right efforts to support and secure the passage of an important piece of federal legislation. The bill, House Resolution 2746, had as its stated purpose "to amend title IV of the Elementary and Secondary Education Act of 1965 to give parents with low-incomes the opportunity to choose the appropriate school for their children." Conservatives promoted the bill as an effort to combat the effects of poverty and racism in the society, goals that fit nobly into the presuppositions of mainstream Americans. Although it failed in the House, the real purpose of the legislation from the Christian Right perspective was as Wynsma describes, to "attempt to minimize the threat of increased federal regulation (i.e., teachers unions, national testing, curriculum control, government accreditation, and teacher qualifications) by including language to prohibit new regulations of private schools."[72] Three of the bill's specific provisions exemplify Christian Right efforts to control public education. The first prohibits anyone at the state or federal level from placing any requirements or regulations regarding religion on schools that receive this funding.[73] Another defines the scholarships as aid to parents, not to schools that choose to participate in the HELP program.[74] Both of these provisions are designed to avoid church-state constitutional challenges. A third provision forbids the secretary of education to exercise any control over school goals, personnel, curricula, programs of instruction, or administration.[75] These prohibitions include teacher certification and any mandatory religious practices, behaviors, or beliefs that administrators might deem necessary to fulfill the mission of their schools. The bill would, in effect, establish federal funding of religious schools and thereby begin to break down the barrier that separates the two in the minds of the general public.

The three-tiered strategy for control of public education is a product of long and serious reflection on the part of the Christian Right cultural elite. The tactics are designed to gradually gain the support of Americans so that the Christian Right as a social movement can accomplish its goal of a transformed culture. It is difficult to speak with any certainty about how intentional the movement was in developing this overall strategy in the manner presented. It is possible, however, to say with some confidence that the process is not only fully consistent with Schaeffer's presuppositional strategy, but it is also consistent with the groundwork laid out for him by Abraham Kuyper and Cornelius Van Til. These men intentionally developed a process for cultural transformation. Nonetheless, neither Kuyper nor Van Til envisioned the process unfolding precisely as it has done through the Christian Right.

My description of the overall strategy focuses on particular people and organizations who have led the fight or who have been particularly articulate spokespersons in making the connections. The discussion is not intended to be exhaustive either in terms of the large number of Christian Right leaders and special purpose groups at the national and state levels or in terms of the efforts by activists in particular states where variations of these strategies have been and continue to be employed. What I have done is to offer an interpretive structure, based on authoritative Christian Right

7

Cultural Transmission

In 1997, a high school principal in Colorado Springs, Colorado, denied two students permission to distribute religious literature in the school. In commenting on the case, Jay Sekulow, the lead attorney for Pat Robertson's American Center for Law and Justice, said, "It seems unnecessary to say it but high school students do not abandon their rights of free speech and free press just because they have walked onto a school campus."[1] On the face of it, Sekulow's comments seem reasonable. Why object to students who simply and innocently want to share their faith with their classmates? But when I read Sekulow's statement, given my research on the Christian Right and the source from which I took the account, I wondered how innocent the students were in sharing their faith.

I found the description of the incident on the web page of Summit Ministries. Summit Ministries, based in Manitou Springs, Colorado, conducts workshops and seminars for high school students to train them in the use of public schools and classrooms for evangelistic purposes. Summit Ministries drew the report about the Colorado Springs incident from *Caleb News,* a publication of the Caleb Campaign and its Colorado state director Bill Jack. The Caleb Campaign publishes a newspaper called *Issues and Answers* for high school students. The tenor of the stories suggests a presuppositional strategy. Many of its articles are directed to students outside the biblical Christian camp. The paper presents topics, especially creationism, from the biblical Christian perspective and is intended to be used by students as an evangelistic tool. Summit Ministries describes the publications as "underground newspapers [that] can be especially effective in getting the attention of students." Bill Jack distributed copies of *Issues and Answers* to attendees at his workshop group at D. James Kennedy's 1994 Reclaiming America Conference. The copies of the paper I saw there were, to put it mildly, provocative and seemed intended to undermine the credibility of the public schools and their teachers.[2]

The connection among Bill Jack, the Caleb Campaign, and Summit Ministries is no accident. All of them provide resources for high school students to help them turn their classrooms into arenas for evangelism. Students are taught how to ask disruptive questions in biology classes and how to use every class assignment as an opportunity to convert other students to Christ. The purpose of the activities is not to innocently share one's faith with other students. It is to frustrate the delivery of public education's secular humanist bias and to combat the schools' failure to ground instruction on biblical principles. In this context, Sekulow's question seems reductionistic. The issue is not simply the free religious expression of students. It raises the larger issues of whether the principal denied permission to the students because of the disruptive nature of the literature they sought to distribute and the way the students used the materials. Such reductionistic rhetoric, however, is part of the Christian Right presuppositional strategy to link the actions of its adherents to democratic symbols of personal and religious freedom.

Many Christian Right strategists target the public school classroom as an important theater of operation for their social movement. Given their presuppositional objections to the content and pedagogy of public education, movement leaders see disruption of school instruction as a necessary interim step until they can gain control of the schools and their content. In its criticism of curricular content and pedagogical method, the Christian Right uses the myths, rituals, and symbols that ground it as a social movement. The same critical categories can serve to structure an examination of the way the Christian Right attempts to use the schools to achieve its goal of cultural transformation.

Our previous discussion of movement presuppositions regarding the nature of knowledge and its relationship to truth places Christian Right criticism of the public school classroom in its broader context. Put briefly, for the Christian Right, knowledge is received from God through the Scriptures, not discovered through human investigation and logic. Truth is propositional, not open-ended. That is, truth comes in the form of statements to be accepted, not ideas or concepts to be explored. These presuppositions provide the foundation for all Christian Right protests against public school content and instruction. A Concerned Women for America Newsflash makes this point clearly in relation to the teaching of creation science in the public schools: "The focus of creation science is to establish the fact that what God says in the Bible is truth. A student who is taught that the Genesis account is false is bound to question the validity of the rest of the Bible." Instead of teaching biblical truth as truth, the statement continues, the public schools have attempted to indoctrinate the students to reject the Bible through the teaching of evolution. The result is that students "come out of the school system having no basis for right or wrong, and no real concept of God's unchanging truth as it applies today. They think they can decide truth for themselves, regardless of what their authority says."[3]

In a briefing to members of Congress on behalf of the Family Research Council, Linda Page declared that schools promote this reckless disregard for truth through such learning strategies as higher order thinking. Instead of teaching students "genuine" critical thinking, Page asserts, schools teach a form of critical thinking that promotes circular reasoning in order to justify whatever the student or teacher thinks or feels is right. She defines genuine critical thinking as "learning to discern and express what is true—to submit to *truth* and to a set of absolutes."[4] According to this interpretation, the purpose of education is to learn information, to master facts, to understand systems, and to give the information back to the teacher to correct. Critical thinking in this context means understanding the internal logic of the relationship of specific received truths to each other in an already established and accepted framework of meaning. Because schools have abandoned real critical thinking for an approach that allows more ambiguity and more possible alternatives, they are guilty of the "dumbing-down" of education in both the content and instructional methodology.

With specific reference to Outcome-Based Education, Phyllis Schlafly notes that "a high percentage of 'outcomes' concern values, attitudes, opinions and relationships rather than objective information."[5] Mastery of academic and factual subject matter has given way to vague and subjective learning outcomes. Instead of learning what is right and wrong in a given body of material, students are asked to solve problems, to work with each other in order to come up with viable alternatives, and to express their opinions regarding events. Nowhere is the question of truth more important for the Christian Right than in the transmission of the mythos of the American and Western cultural heritage from teachers to students.

The Mythic Dimension: History and Culture

Two closely related ideas supply the presuppositions that inform the preferred mythos of the Christian Right. The first is that the Bible contains the broad categories by which humans should interpret history if they want to understand its true course. To represent past events according to any other criteria is to give a false perspective on history. The second idea is that God has chosen the American people and nation for a particular role in the unfolding events of the divine plan for humans. To direct America's school children to any other reading of the past is to misinform them of our country's role and purpose and to undermine the true strength of the nation. For reasons related to that conception of truth, the movement's mythos tends to give positive voice only to the Christian strands of the complex cultures and religions that comprise the tapestry of our nation's heritage. Because of this exclusionary picture of history, the Christian Right mythos can be called the great American monomyth. It emphasizes the religious origins of the nation, particularly as represented in the Puritans, and transforms the history of the country into a religious destiny. David Barton's video *Our Godly Heritage* provides the movement's clearest statement on the issue.[6] The myth argues that the principle of separation of church and state is a fiction never intended by the nation's founding figures. By invoking First Amendment establishment arguments, secular humanists have erected an unintended wall that has kept America's teachers from presenting a true picture of the nation and its history.

In its mildest form, the monomyth simply seeks to reintroduce into public school curricula the Christian dimension of the culture and the defining role Christians have played in our history as a nation. This includes talking about the Christian vision of the Puritans. It means emphasizing the preeminent role the Christian faith and the Christian cultural consensus had in guiding the colonists, the nation's founders, and the early life of the nation. In a stronger form, the monomyth suggests that the positive dimensions of America's heritage are derived exclusively from Christian sources. According to this interpretation, the founders conceived the nation in Christian terms and drew upon explicitly biblical sources in creating the originating documents of the nation. Other influences are downplayed, such as the Enlightenment and the diversity of religious backgrounds of the founders. In Schaeffer's *How Should We Then Live?*, for example, the monomyth all but ignores the Deism of the most important contributors to our nation's origins and reinterprets their religious beliefs in terms much more consistent with Reformed Calvinism than Enlightenment Deism.

To promote the stronger version of the monomyth in public schools, Focus on the Family markets "Christian Heritage folders" through its

Teachers in Focus magazine. The folder contains "Christian America" materials that stress the Christian origin of the nation. For example, the packet states that America's founders intended the First Amendment only to prevent the establishment of a single national church, not to restrict the promotion of religion through public institutions. The resource lists for teachers reference Christian Right groups that promote Christian America viewpoints,[7] for example, the Rutherford Institute, Summit Ministries, and the Plymouth Rock Foundation. The folder is designed to be used in public school classroom instruction by sympathetic Christian teachers.

Concerned Women for America also participates in Christian Right efforts to promote its monomyth in our nation's schools. CWA endorses "unique holiday cards to help change the way educators teach about the holidays." Developed by Eric Buehrer's Gateways to Better Education, the cards include "a nonthreatening story encouraging the teacher to teach about the religious nature of the [Thanksgiving or Christmas] holiday. These cards also include legal documentation and constitutionally sound lesson plan ideas." An anecdote describing a "successful" use of the cards casts doubt on the CWA claim that these cards and lesson plans pass constitutional muster. "After receiving a card," the story explains, "one fourth-grade teacher had her class read the *historical account of Jesus' birth* in Luke 2, sing Christmas carols, analyze the lyrics of the carols, and draw nativity scenes for classroom display."[8] As noted earlier, Dobson's *Focus on the Family* magazine also promotes Buehrer's Gateways to Better Education materials.

In its strongest form, the Christian Right American monomyth emphasizes the role divine providence plays in guiding the American nation to its unique and superior status above all other nations. A popular U.S. history textbook prepared for Christian schools states as fact, "The United States is a special nation . . . because it, more than any other nation in modern history, has been founded and built upon biblical principles. Consequently, it has been unusually blessed by God."[9] This is what makes us stand apart, according to the authors. "No other nation has been grounded so thoroughly in religious belief and biblical truth. It is no accident that the nation eventually became the strongest and most prosperous on earth."[10] In *The Light and the Glory,* one of the most popular books on the subject among Christian Right activists, Peter Marshall and David Manuel write of America's special status: "In the virgin wilderness of America, God was making His most significant attempt since ancient Israel to create a new Israel of people living in obedience to the laws of God, through faith in Jesus Christ."[11] Tim LaHaye agrees. He argues that the Ten Commandments and the civil laws of the Old Testament "formed the basis for our laws and our Constitution."[12]

As these comments illustrate, the stories and symbols that define our identity as a people are a major point of controversy between the Christian Right and the public schools. Phyllis Schlafly's Eagle Forum mission statement makes the point clearly. "In public schools, parents have the right to expect that schools *educate* children in factual knowledge, *true history* . . ."[13] According to the Eagle Forum, under the guise of bilingual education and multiculturalism, schools are destroying the true history of the nation and reconstructing a new history that minimizes the greatness of America and emphasizes our weaknesses. Believing that true Americans accept the Judeo-Christian tradition as the basis of our national identity, Schlafly writes, "The United States is the world's most stunning example of a nation that has peaceably and successfully assimilated people from many disparate cultures." Referring to bilingual education, she asks, "So why are some people trying to separate us into factions, emphasizing what divides us instead of what unites us? This fad seems to be trying to get us to change our national identity from E pluribus unum (From the many, one) to E uno plures (From the one, many)."[14]

According to Schlafly and other Christian Right leaders, multicultural education as taught by the schools has the effect of dividing Americans, not bringing them together. By including other cultural heritages in history and literature courses, for example, teachers implicitly undermine the patriotism of their students. Multicultural education destroys respect for our nation's history and its institutions, promotes allegiance to foreign governments rather than the domestic government, and contributes to our cultural decline by destroying moral values among students. NACE/CEE's Kathi Hudson writes, "Rather than *promoting* diversity, a good multicultural program will help students to *understand* and *overcome* diversity. Multiculturalism should promote unity as Americans."[15] According to Robert Simonds, Hudson's father, the Los Angeles riots were a natural consequence of multiculturalism as the schools teach it. He argues that multicultural education led to the riots by inducing feelings of radical guilt in children about racism. Multiculturalism, according to Simonds, also divides Americans into warring factions that will seek redress from grievances through violence.[16] With presuppositions about America's cultural heritage so deeply grounded in Simonds's mind, NACE/CEE can argue that a "Model Policy for Teaching Multiculturalism and Diversity . . .

should be academically strong, not ideologically based. It will support de-mocratic, Western values and respect individual rights."[17] To Simonds, there is no contradiction in that statement.

From the Christian Right perspective, both bilingual education and multicultural instruction are part of the secular humanist plot to defraud American children of their cultural heritage. Christian Right leaders find evidence of the secular humanists' "deliberate rape of history," as Tim La-Haye calls it,[18] in the "National History Standards" proposed to Congress, and rejected by it, in the mid-1990s. The controversy began in 1994 when the National Center for History in the Schools at the University of Cali-fornia, Los Angeles, released America's new national history standards. Scholars developed these standards to improve student understanding of American history. The standards, which reflected an approach that was more inclusive of the nation's diversity than previous standards had been, struck at the very heart of the American mythos. Conservative critics im-mediately recognized the degree to which these new standards were in-clusive of a number of different cultural traditions not traditionally associ-ated with the accepted mythos. Such inclusions, said the critics, had the effect of advocating moral and cultural relativism, viewpoints that stood in clear opposition to Christian Right presuppositions about the absolute nature of truth.

Concerned Women for America told its constituents that "the standards had a clear bias in that they focused on only what is politically correct." (*Politically correct* is a derisive term used by conservatives to discount liberal interpretations and points of view.) Gary Bauer added, "It goes without saying that the history standards' emphasis on race, gender, and class forces young Americans to accept a secular world view."[19] CWA's specific criti-cism was typical of other Christian Right groups' objections. "The Amer-ican history standards mention the Ku Klux Klan 17 times but the Feder-alist Papers are scarcely noted. And while the Continental Congress re-ceives only a passing glance, the standards encourage students to study Mansa Musa, a West African king in the 14th century." CWA concluded, "The standards were both intellectually dishonest and politically propelled by a left wing agenda."[20] Gary Bauer described the magnitude of the problem these new history standards created: "If we adopt these amnesiac history standards, we will succumb to a kind of national identity crisis. We will cease to remember who we are and why it matters that there is an America."[21] Jennifer Marshall, policy analyst for the Family Research Council, put a somewhat more moderate slant on the criticisms. "The standards not only trivialize American history, but also present an exceedingly gloomy view of America. Nobody wants a history written through rose-colored glasses—but the standards go beyond an honest appraisal of national failures, replacing 'America: land of opportunity,' with 'America: land of oppression.'"[22]

Even after scholars rewrote the standards to accommodate some of the conservative objections, one feature particularly threatening to the Christian Right remained. The revised standards "included a provision that stated that B.C. and A.D. will no longer serve as the basis of the historic calendar. Instead, BCE (before common era) and CE (common era) were to be used."[23] B.C.E. and C.E. refer exclusively to the common era of Judaism and Christianity. Their substitution signified to the critics that the schools would be required to abandon purely Christian designations of time. Although Christian Right groups like CWA claimed they supported the idea that the Western cultural heritage grounding American national identity was "Judeo-Christian" rather than exclusively Christian, they objected when the designations for dating history were changed to reflect that wider reality. Because of these issues and others, when the national history standards came before the U.S. Senate, all but one member rejected them.

The issue of the larger Christian Right concern about the nature of truth and its relation to the teaching of history became the center of a set of legal controversies in 1997. Public school boards in Florida, Mississippi, and Texas proposed the adoption of Bible as history courses for their districts. Promoted by Elizabeth Ridenour's National Council on Bible Curriculum in the Public Schools (NCOBCITPS), based in North Carolina, these courses claimed to meet the constitutional standards for teaching religion in the public schools laid down in the majority opinion of the Supreme Court in *Abingdon v. Schempp*, the so-called school prayer case of 1963. Writing for the majority in that landmark case, Justice Tom Clark noted that nothing in the Schempp decision prevented schools from offering academic courses in religion or in the study of the Bible when teachers presented the materials objectively as part of a secular program of education.[24] Even though the NCOBCITPS curriculum refers to numerous biblical events as historical facts, Ridenour marketed the plan to the public schools. Adam and Eve are presented as historical persons and the covenant between God and Abraham, the parting of the Red Sea, and the reception of the Ten Commandments as historical facts. In the New Testament course, the Resurrection of Jesus, Jesus' miracles, and the Virgin Birth are historical events.

The issue came to a head in Lee County, Florida, in 1998 when community members objected to the Christian Right board majority's decision to include both courses as electives in the district's curriculum. Despite several legal opinions indicating that the materials were not appropriate, the board majority refused to compromise. The case eventually ended up in the legal system. In support of the board's decision, Jay Sekulow, chief legal counsel for the American Center for Law and Justice, defended the National Council's materials. He commented, "The Supreme Court has consistently held the Bible is appropriate for curriculum study. The Bible should not be a banned book."[25] Sekulow apparently believed that presenting theological interpretations as historical facts was consistent with the parameters established in *Abingdon* by Justice Tom Clark. The issue of what constitutes historical fact was never raised in the Lee County case. From the Christian Right perspective, the materials met the constitutional standards because the references were factual events for biblical literalists. Within the Christian Right frame of reference, the refusal of the community and the court to recognize the facticity of the course materials demonstrated that the schools and the courts remained hostile to Christianity. Although the National Council would not release precise figures, it claimed that a large number of school districts throughout the country used their Bible-as-history curriculum. Since the council actively promotes its curriculum, it is likely that these same controversies about the nature of history and truth will be repeated in countless school districts in the future.

Although Christian Right efforts to judge the propriety of content for history courses by the standards of biblical literalism may be problematic for history teachers, the criteria used by the court to decide the Lee County case suggest that that reason was set aside. In her decision, U.S. District Court Judge Elizabeth Kovachevich separated the two courses proposed by the board and drew a religiously controversial distinction between them. The first-semester course, entitled "Bible History: Old Testament," covered events in the Hebrew Bible, accepted by both Jews and Christians as divine revelation. The second-semester offering, entitled "Bible History: New Testament," centered on content exclusive to Christianity. Although the court seemed to distinguish the Jewish theological foundation for the "Old Testament" course from that of the Christian New Testament materials, the "Old Testament" designation for the first-semester course strongly suggests that the material was interpreted from a Christian rather than a Jewish perspective. If the material had been viewed from a Jewish perspective, the title would more properly have been "Bible History: The Hebrew Bible." Despite the court's acknowledgment that both courses rested on theological presuppositions, in her decision Judge Kovachevich concluded that the Old Testament course could be offered because it was "ostensibly designed to teach history and not religion." The New Testament course, however, was out because the judge found "it difficult to conceive how the account of the resurrection or of miracles could be taught as secular history."[26] Elizabeth Ridenour, president of NCOBCITPS, called the decision "blatant hostility toward Christianity." She vowed that her curriculum would never delete one item: "We will not take out the Resurrection."[27]

What is confusing about Judge Kovachevich's ruling is that it raises the obvious question why Old Testament passages qualify as history rather than religion, whereas the New Testament ones do not. The answer has to do with the way in which Americans view their larger cultural heritage. The court excluded the New Testament material because it rests on a theologically conservative Christian insistence on the factual truth of the Virgin Birth, for example. Most Americans agree that such a narrow interpretation of these events is religiously sectarian and therefore should be excluded from the public schools. The case for the sectarian nature of the Old Testament is less clear to many Americans. Granted, it views the scriptural accounts as historical fact. But it appears to be not so clearly sectarian because it contains many of the deep symbols of what conservatives call the wider Judeo-Christian tradition.[28] That Judeo-Christian tradition provides the majority of Americans with their sense of self-identity and national identity. Tim LaHaye makes this point when he argues that America was founded on biblical rather than exclusively Christian principles.[29] Liberals and conservatives share a commitment to the relevance of such biblical principles as compassion, equality, and liberty to the political order and to the significance of our nation. Both also agree that the same tradition provides a set of transcendent values and orientations against which the present realities of the country can be judged.[30] The vast majority of these principles and values appear in the Hebrew Bible, or the Old Testament. The same is true of the stories and symbols that provide the meaning and significance we ascribe to our country.[31] Thus, excluding the "Bible as History: Old Testament" course would irritate some of the deepest nerves and would reach to the very core of what most Americans accept as our national character. The second-semester course symbols, viewed by the court as more sectarian, apparently did not penetrate as deeply into our national identity.

In support of their monomythic interpretation of American history, Christian Right strategists have begun introducing American heritage bills in state legislatures. The bills "authorize or require the display and teaching of particular historic American documents" and "prohibit school officials from censoring the religious content in such documents as the Declaration of Independence, the Federalist Papers, and the Mayflower Compact."[32] The apparent purpose of this type of legislation is to promote greater appreciation for the religious dimension of American history and culture among the nation's school children. Such a concern on the part of the Christian Right for the inclusion of religious references in public school textbooks and curricula is justified. A review of most textbooks used in the public schools published before the mid-1990s suggests that schools present children with a "secularized" version of American history and culture. But the attempts by the Christian Right to advance its mythos in the public schools goes beyond accommodating religious preferences in the curriculum. The agenda seeks to instill in children the great American monomyth as the only, or at least the only correct, understanding of our nation's history and culture—a goal that is completely consistent with the presuppositions about truth, facts, and absolutes that movement leaders bring to their place at the table. Since the schools are the primary transmitters of our nation's cultural heritage, the Christian Right views the battle over the content in history, literature, and social science classes as one of mythic proportions for our children.

The Symbolic Dimension: The Family

If the fight in history classes is for control of the mythos of American education, the fight over the content and structure of sex education classes is over the symbols of the family. The deep symbol of the family provides Christian Right activists with their most common set of critiques of public education. For the Christian Right, the divinely ordained institution of the family reserves for the parents ultimate and exclusive authority over their children. Parents who entrust their children to public schools delegate to the schools authority over the students but only insofar as the schools promote values and curricular content that is consistent with the beliefs of the parents. When the content and pedagogy of the schools strays from the values of biblically principled parents, Christians have a duty to change the schools. Failing to change the schools, Christian parents have a responsibility to remove their children from the public schools and either enroll them in a Christian school or home school them. Since many Christian parents lack the necessary financial resources to take their children out of the schools, the priority for them must be to bring the public schools into conformity with their beliefs.

Because the schools are an extension of the family, the transmission of cultural values ultimately rests with the traditional heterosexual two-parent family, not the schools. In other words, the primary interest of the schools is not to serve the common good of society as the citizens define it. The main responsibilities of the schools are to transmit to students divine absolute values and to promote the preservation of the family and the other divinely ordained institutions. Through curricular content and instructional methods, the schools should emphasize and enforce values that "temper and restrain behavior" in students and promote reverence for parental authority.[33] In this way, the schools show respect for parental values.

Significant social problems result when either the parents fail to transmit these values to their children or the schools work in opposition to the parents. As noted above, Robert Simonds draws a connection between multiculturalism in the schools and the Los Angeles riots. According to him, the schools caused the riots because multicultural education inherently undermines the student's respect for moral absolutes and parental authority. When absolutes disappear and respect for authority diminishes, children lack any moral principles to temper and restrain their behavior. As a result, they give in to their own impulses and distorted priorities. The same consequences flow from the failure of the parents to provide the proper guidance for their children. In fact, according to Christian Right leaders like Tim LaHaye, James Dobson, and Gary Bauer, the failure of the parents to properly guide their children is the ultimate cause of the moral decay in our society.[34] Schools simply promote that decadence by taking advantage of parental failure to advance their own humanist and statist agenda. When the family fails in its responsibility to transmit absolute moral values, individual liberties diminish, because the government steps in and attempts to fill the vacuum. Such government usurpation of parental authority is one of the central dangers of a free society, and it is a present reality in public education. Christian Right authors, therefore, tend to refer to public schools as government schools to make the point clear. What is at stake for the Christian Right goes beyond whether or not the schools respect the sectarian values and beliefs of the parents. The loss of local control of the schools signals the continued corruption of the divine order of society and can lead only to cultural and moral decay.

The area of the curriculum where that parental failure and government displacement of biblical values is most evident is in a complex of curricular issues that fall under the category of sex education. They include human sexuality and HIV/AIDS instruction and diversity training. Christian Right leaders like Phyllis Schlafly and Beverly LaHaye use the term *diversity* to refer to what they perceive as the schools' legitimation of homosexual lifestyles.[35] According to critics, all of these curricular components play on the inherent moral weakness of children in order to promote the values of a human-centered worldview. Students are so morally defenseless against this type of instruction that the mere mention of alternative choices for students constitutes a legitimation and endorsement of the evils. Because of these weaknesses, the only appropriate sex education course that can be acceptable to Christian Right parents is an abstinence-only curriculum.

Although sex education constitutes only a small part of the curriculum in most public school districts, its mere presence, from the perspective of Christian Right critics, is enough to derail students from the more important academic components of their study. For example, Robert Knight, a Family Research Council policy analyst, asks, "How, indeed, can children keep their mind on arithmetic when they are exposed to sex in a big way? From kindergarten on, many children are learning the ABC's of sexuality, taught in a 'morally neutral' manner in state-mandated programs."[36] Knight's comments identify the three most important complaints voiced by Christian Right activists against current sex education instruction. The primary criticism is that sex instruction is included in public education at all, and especially in such early grades. A further objection is to the absence of any moral context with the instruction. By not emphasizing the sinful and dangerous nature of sexual activity outside the bounds of a traditional marriage, schools are telling students that they do not care whether or not students engage in premarital sexual activity. Finally, since the programs are state mandated, they have been removed from the control of parents and therefore reflect statist, not biblical, priorities.

Christian Right activists also challenge the research base of course content in sex education classes and the motives of Planned Parenthood, which they identify as the chief promoter of sex education in the public schools. Concerned Women for America, for instance, links the origin of sex education to the publication of the Kinsey Report on Human Sexuality. CWA claims that the Kinsey research is both flawed and criminal because of the subject pool from which the data was gathered. Since pedophiles and other sex offenders comprised the pool from which Kinsey collected the data, says CWA, the findings have no bearing on the sexual tendencies, needs, and urges of most Americans, especially children. Further, since pedophilia is illegal, the research itself constitutes promotion of a gross disregard of the law.[37] Planned Parenthood, Christian Right critics argue, continues the Kinsey deception and takes it to the next step by actually promoting sexual activity among school-aged children. Referring to a videotape developed by the Planned Parenthood Federation of America (PPFA), Phyllis Schlafly's Eagle Forum claims that the tape's main purpose is to energize Planned Parenthood's lagging sales of birth control products.[38] Also singled out as an enemy of biblical values is the Sex Information and Education Council of the United States (SIECUS) for their promotion of infant and childhood human sexuality.[39] Christian Right authors also blame SIECUS and Planned Parenthood opposition to abstinence-only sex education for blocking the attempts by parents to promote biblical values in the schools.[40]

For various Christian Right organizations, abstinence-only sex education is the only approach the schools should use. They oppose programs that are merely abstinence-based because they send mixed messages to the students. Though abstinence-based, abstinence-plus, and comprehensive sex education curricula may include an abstinence component, they are ineffective from the Christian Right perspective because they assume that teenagers will be sexually active outside of marriage, because they emphasize contraception and abortion, and because they include "affective decision-making (presenting abstinence as one of many options from which to choose)."[41] In such approaches, any abstinence message will be lost amid the other content of the course that works in opposition to parents' values. To prevent the abstinence emphasis from being weakened, Christian Right groups promote abstinence-only courses that "encourage young people to abstain from sexual intercourse, learn self-restraint, and self-discipline."[42]

The materials in abstinence-only curricula typically exclude all references to contraception, promote the value of postponing sexual activity until marriage, and stress the dangers of HIV/AIDS, STDs, and pregnancy.

Courses that discuss the "hows" of sexual activity are unnecessary, according to Tim LaHaye. Couples anticipating marriage can learn "all the basic ingredients (for sex) in two or three hours just prior to marriage." By contrast, sexual education outside of marriage can only lead to sexual experimentation or, even worse, "to an obsession."[43] To help parents make informed decisions about sex education curricula in their schools, Onalee McGraw provides them with a point-by-point comparison of legitimate abstinence-only programs and those that are mere pretenders. McGraw calls the first type "directive" and the second type "non-directive." As the label suggests, directive programs instruct students not to become sexually active by connecting personal desires and social needs to moral absolutes. Core values, as McGraw calls them, are taught as objectively true and good.[44]

Christian Right authors also argue that many sex education courses that are not abstinence-only are also dangerous to children because they tend to present homosexuality as an acceptable alternative lifestyle. Perhaps no issue has had greater impact on the destruction of the structure and values of the traditional family than homosexuality, according to the Christian Right. Though Christian Right writers do not often utilize "sin" language in their discussion of homosexuality, they do identify a number of consequences that they believe flow from including the topic in the public schools. The most morally neutral form that criticism takes is to argue that the time used to teach about "strange life-styles" in sex education classes should be more properly directed toward "reading, writing, [and] the history of this country."[45] More to the point, FRC's Linda Page argues that when schools teach homosexuality as a positive lifestyle and accept same-sex marriages as legitimate, they contribute to the destruction of public education. Including information on the same-sex marriage value system in school curricula negates moral absolutes of right and wrong. If moral absolutes are ignored, schools eventually will have to tolerate cheating and stealing.[46] Page's conclusions are based on Christian Right presuppositions about the lack of self-discipline in students and the absence of any proper moral compass as they develop into adults. Merely including such materials without condemning them creates in students the impression that these alternatives to the traditional marriage are acceptable. If they are acceptable, then curious students with strong sexual urges will choose to engage in such activities.

Diversity training and education are particularly dangerous in this regard. According to the Eagle Forum, President Clinton contributed to the moral decline in our culture when his administration endorsed grade school "diversity training" in November 1997. The particular peril presented by such instruction rests in the encouragement such programs give to students "to be tolerant of minorities, homosexuals and the disabled."[47] From the Christian Right perspective, tolerance suggests moral relativism and the absence of any moral absolutes. Tolerance means that there are no absolute standards against which to judge what is right and wrong, what is true and what is an aberration. The point here is not that the Christian Right typically views minorities and the disabled as unworthy of respect. Rather, they charge that humanists use tolerance for minorities and the disabled as a cover for their homosexual agenda. The Eagle Forum, for example, claims that "diversity has become a code word for implementing the homosexual agenda in the schools." Christian Right spokespersons base this claim on the observation that groups like the National Education Association typically include sexual orientation as one of the differences that should be included as acceptable in diversity education.[48]

Drug and alcohol abuse should be taught in the same manner as abstinence-only sex education courses, according to movement leaders. When those topics are presented outside the moral context of biblical principles, students get the same mixed message as with sexuality. "Just say no" works, according to the Christian Right. It must be at the center of any discussion of the use of illegal drugs and alcohol. To promote such instruction, Christian Right activists encourage "faith-based" treatment programs in and outside of the schools. In contrast to other programs that define drug and alcohol abuse as a disease, faith-based approaches emphasize the underlying moral and spiritual causes of such behavior. For example, Teen Challenge, the largest faith-based treatment network, states that addictions are "manifestation of larger problems brought about by sin and self-centered attempts to find meaning and fulfillment in life." The solution offered by Teen Challenge is to encourage the student to develop a personal relationship with Jesus Christ. Only through this relationship can the student overcome the "profound emptiness that is often filled with misguided and self-destructive efforts to achieve happiness."[49] The D.A.R.E. approach to drug education is particularly injurious, according to these writers. Although Christian Right sources quote studies that have shown that D.A.R.E. is ineffective, the real hazard of the D.A.R.E. program is the way in which it infringes on the family. Citing a *New Republic* article, the Eagle Forum claims that D.A.R.E. "has encouraged schoolchildren to inform on their parents, thereby breaking up families."[50] By asking questions about drug and alcohol use in the home, the schools intrude into the sphere of the divinely ordained family and turn children against their parents. When the government is involved in the collection of such data, as it is through the public schools, this information can then be used by statist humanists to further their efforts to control the society.

School lunch and breakfast programs also contribute to the erosion of the family by usurping for the government responsibilities divinely given to the family. From the Christian Right perspective, the destructive force of these programs outweighs any positive effect they might have on student performance. Christian Right authors have taken full advantage of the recent research that shows the primary importance of families in influencing the intellectual development of children. They use such studies to argue that time spent eating with families at home has a substantial impact on student academic performance. Family mealtimes also give parents an opportunity to find out what their children are doing at school as well as a chance to direct and broaden their children's educational and career horizons.[51]

The government also threatens parental influence over the career directions of their children through such educational initiatives as Goals 2000, CAREERS, and school-to-work legislation. The overall intention of these programs, according to Christian Right sources, is to promote the statist agenda by gradually removing from parents any control over their children both in the present and in the future.[52] "As School-to-Work attempts to steer children into slots deemed in the interest of regional labor market and economic development needs," Robert Holland noted in a speech on Capitol Hill, "it will become obvious how children are being cheated and deprived of a chance to realize their dreams and achieve their highest potential."[53] The implication for Christian parents, Holland continues, is that their children may be forced into career tracks that trample the parents' family values. Christian Right sources describe schools' tracking of students in terms of micromanaging children's specific career choices. Tracking does not just point students into areas that are consistent with their interests and at levels that are appropriate to their abilities. Rather than counseling students, the ultimate purpose of school-to-work legislation is government control over children.[54]

With the manipulation of Christian children and the destruction of family values so closely related to government-imposed curricula in the eyes of conservative Christian activists, they conclude that the public schools are no longer safe for their children. That conclusion has given strong impetus to the school choice movement. But not all Christian Right activists are equally convinced that the school choice movement will give them the opportunity to provide their children with Christian-based education. Most leaders caution that school choice legislation cannot be allowed to impose government mandates or standards on religious schools. The only accountability of these schools to the government must be based on standardized tests that are developed and administered by private rather than government organizations. In all other respects, federal moneys that might come to sectarian schools through vouchers or other school choice initiatives must be completely free from government restrictions. Legislation introduced at the federal level in both the House and the Senate in 1997–98 include provisions that prohibit the government from interfering with the conditions sectarian schools receiving federal moneys impose on students regarding religious beliefs and practices.[55] Using Schaeffer's presuppositional approach, Christian Right activists are carefully building momentum through charter schools, school vouchers, tuition tax credits, and school choice initiatives to weaken public resistance to the direct funding of sectarian schools. All these activities are designed to protect the integrity of the family. They are intended to preserve for the family the divinely ordained responsibility for transmitting to children the religious values of their parents and the Judeo-Christian cultural heritage of America.

The final public school curricular area that attracts attention from the Christian Right is the teaching of evolution in biology classes. Evolution is dangerous for several reasons, most of them falling under the umbrella of the advancement of secular humanism in the schools. Evolution, from the Christian Right perspective, is based on faulty presuppositions regarding the nature of truth. Derived from human reason and in contradiction with the biblical record, evolution undermines students' respect for absolute truth. Arguing that evolution requires a relativistic concept of truth, the American Association of Christian Schools President A. C. Janney identifies its danger for Christian parents: "Evolution is more than just a matter of where we came from; it's a whole attitude toward truth. Evolution says that we have simply evolved to a higher species of life from a lower, that evolution has a migration of truth, that is to say, that truth means one thing one day and something else the next."[56] In identifying the evolutionary presupposition that humans developed from lower species, Janney touches on another objection to the teaching of evolution in the public schools. By divorcing human origins from special creation in which God intervened direct and separately from the rest of God's creative acts, evolutionists remove the basis for the dignity and inherent worth of humanity. Creationists reinstate humans to their proper status by insisting that God created humanity in a special act and that humans therefore have no inherent biological relationship to lower forms of life. In a related point, evolution emphasizes a mechanical or organic view of the development of life that denies the teleological dimension of the creation. Without a final cause or a final purpose of creation, proponents of creationism argue, we are left with a universe stripped of God and operating by mere chance.[57]

Christian Right activists advance several arguments in their attempts to include creationism in public school curricula. The most common approach emphasizes fairness. If both creation and evolution are theories, then it is just a matter of fairness to give equal time in science classes to the two positions. The argument pivots both on invoking mainstream values of fairness and equality and on obscuring the disagreement between biblical Christians and scientists on the nature of truth and its relationship to the scientific method. Numerous court cases, including *Epperson v. Arkansas* (1968) and *McLean v. Arkansas* (1981), indicate that this difference in presuppositions about the nature of truth is critical in legitimating the exclusion of creationism from science classes.[58] In response to these rulings, Christian Right activists recast their arguments in a religiously neutral framework, and Creation Science was the result. Creation Science attempts to meet court objections to creationism by leaving aside the issue of the divine origin of creation and simply arguing for an alternative method of creation consistent with biblical principles. Arguing the deluge theory, that the fundamental changes in life occurred as a result of cataclysmic events, proponents try to undermine the authority of evolution scientifically so that teachers will open the discussion to alternative possible origins of life. The courts have not accepted the modification. In *Edwards v. Aguillard* (1987), the Supreme Court held that the presuppositions grounding Creation Science are religious, not scientific, and therefore it is not appropriate for public school instruction.

This brings us back to Summit Ministries, Bill Jack, and the Caleb Campaign. Having lost in the courts, Christian Right activists now train students to disrupt lessons that include evolution. In his presentation at the 1994 Reclaiming America Conference, Bill Jack distributed to participants in his workshop materials that described a strategy in which students were to ask a series of "four devastating questions which destroy evolution" during class instruction on evolution: "1. What do you mean by that? Question what everything means. 2. How do you know that to be true? 3. What difference does it make in your life? 4. What if you are wrong?"[59] By placing the faculty member on the defensive, the students weaken the authority the teacher brings to lessons on evolution. The faculty member who stifles the student asking the questions is placed in the position of appearing to prohibit discussion of the issues.

The Family Research Council promotes an alternative strategy that encourages parents to work with teachers so that they will "keep open lines of communication with parents, respecting their private beliefs but standing up for the right of students to encounter science as a process of inquiry that is driven by empirical evidence, not dogma."[60] The presumption here for the Christian Right is that its presuppositions regarding the nature of truth put creationism on the same empirical foundation as evolution. When teachers present all the evidence simply as facts, not wrapped in secular humanist religion, these activists assert that parents and students will find creationism more legitimate as an interpretation of human origins than evolution. Organizations like the Creation Research Society, the Bible Science Association, and the Institute for Creation Research stand ready to provide schools with the supporting evidence and arguments.

The Ritual Dimension: Pedagogy

Christian Right leaders agree with mainstream proponents of public education that schools should transmit to their students the cultural heritage and moral values that will contribute to the students' development into responsible adults. Difficulties arise when the two sides begin to identify the presuppositions they hold about the source and nature of those values and the ideal model of a responsible adult. Controversy also surrounds the structure of the pedagogy that is used to transmit the heritage and values. Again the arguments go back to differing conceptions of the nature of truth and the roles the teacher and students assume in its communication. Pedagogy, the Christian Right argues, ought to be consistent with the nature of truth, the weak moral condition of children, and the structure of the family, from which the schools gain their legitimacy. The schools, in both curriculum and pedagogy, need to create the proper environment, where students not only come to understand and master truth, but also do so in a way that is consistent with the divine nature of the creation. In the language of ritual studies, the methods of instruction must be coherent with the world we envision.[61] When the schools are able to create such an environment, then the ritual passage of students from childhood to adulthood is more likely to shape them into responsible adults who live in harmony with the desired order of existence.

One illustration of what the Christian Right envisions as the proper pedagogical environment comes from a controversy that occurred in a Michigan school district in 1991. After the school board, under pressure from a vocal Christian Right constituency, voted unanimously to withdraw from an educational reform project, the leaders of the pressure group submitted a petition to the school board demanding that all student desks in the district be permanently affixed to the floor in straight rows. Though the mainstream majority on the school board was caught off guard by the request, the petition was completely consistent with the pedagogical concerns of the Christian Right. Truth is revealed to humans in propositional statements that are factually accurate. The role of the teacher is to mirror the role of the minister in the sphere of the church and the father in the institution of the family as the authority from whom students receive truth. Students need to face the teacher, not each other, since it is from the teacher that knowledge is received. Since students are not capable of discerning truth for themselves, instruction should be by the teachers in the form of factual knowledge. Appropriate assessment, from this perspective, consists of measuring whether or not the students can reproduce the information correctly through tests that measure their factual knowledge.

Christian Right activists promote classical education, a method of instruction that is consistent with their presuppositions. Classical education differs from contemporary pedagogical fads and innovations. It returns to the form of education that provided the foundation of the development of the Western cultural heritage from the Middle Ages until progressives cast it aside. The Family Research Council credits Dorothy Sayers with the development of the contemporary model of classical education. Sayers's research leads her to the conclusion that the medieval model divides instruction into two parts, the first called the trivium and the second, the quadrivium. The trivium, the more relevant of the two to pedagogical issues, includes three areas of instruction: grammar, dialectic, and rhetoric. These are to be taught sequentially as the child develops mentally. Instruction begins with grammar, which is based on memorization and the mastery of basic facts. At this stage (usually ages 9–11), students are not yet capable of understanding the significance of things, so it is not important that they be instructed in anything but factual mastery. "This is the time to fill them full of facts: multiplication tables, geography, dates, events, plant and animal classifications—anything that lends itself to easy repetition and assimilation by the mind."[62] Language instruction is appropriate here because it requires a great deal of memorization of grammatical structures.

The dialectic stage of instruction (ages 12–14) recognizes the student's greater reasoning ability. At this level, it is appropriate for students to begin asking questions based on the information mastered in the grammar stage. Here instruction focuses on making logical connections among the wealth of facts. The role of the teacher is particularly important because students do not yet have a full enough understanding of the nature of things to be allowed to draw their own conclusions. The teacher's job is to see that the connections posited by the student correspond to the order and structure of reality. What students learn at this stage in Christian worldview perspective schools, for example, is a logical structure consistent with Christian Right presuppositions. "The American Revolution is no longer a mere fact in history," asserts a Family Research paper; "it must be understood in light of the child's whole scope of knowledge. For example, how are the actions of the American revolutionaries to be understood in relation to our responsibility to obey the governing authorities?"[63] Again, critical thinking is important to Christian Right leaders. They simply do not assign the same meaning to it as the public schools commonly do. Critical thinking means mastering the internal logic system of a given worldview. It does not include giving equal legitimacy to alternative possibilities. Other explanations can be used, but only to demonstrate their weakness in comparison to the Christian Right worldview.

The third stage of instruction (ages 14–16) focuses on teaching students how to present their arguments and conclusions in "a persuasive, aesthetically pleasing form." Having developed the necessary thinking skills and mental discipline, students can branch out at this point into areas of study of particular interest to them. The purpose of this level of study is to apply the worldview presuppositions learned at the second stage to various fields of inquiry of interest to the student and consistent with the student's natural ability. Some proponents of classical education permit students to work with each other at this level in order to hone their abilities and to question each other about the degree to which a particular interpretation of material corresponds with the previously established worldview. Ultimately, however, the teacher's assessment is the most important in judging the correctness of the application. Style is important here, as is the application of learning tools. Neither, however, is as important as whether the student is right or wrong in his or her conclusions and applications. Truth outweighs process.[64]

Not all Christian Right activists specifically promote classical education, but the model's pedagogical assumptions are widely enough accepted in the movement to provide a useful context for discussing Christian Right pedagogical concerns. Back-to-basics appeals are best understood in this light. As movement literature commonly uses the phrase, *back to basics* refers both to a renewed emphasis on the "three r's" and to an older model of instruction that emphasizes the authority of the teacher. According to the Christian Right, John Dewey and the progressive movement in education are the secular humanists who moved education from its classical foundation and began the long process of the collapse of America's public schools. Dewey's mistake, among many others, is that he believed that the schools should fulfill a social function as well as an academic one. His emphasis on the democratic ideals and functions of education gave impetus to a succession of innovations that dumbed down education, created in students the false impression that their self-esteem rests on anything other than competitive performance, and assigned equal weight to process and to content—if not greater weight to process.

Criticism of public school instruction, therefore, tends to center on pedagogical processes. It is not that the Christian Right necessarily objects to such innovations as collaborative learning, critical thinking, and problem solving. References to the usefulness of each of these techniques can be found in Christian Right educational literature. What determines their value is the context in which they are utilized. In a Christian context, they can be used to guide students toward a correct understanding of their world and an ability to function as a Christian in that world. In a secular humanist context, students are left without any absolute values and standards against which to judge their performance. This creates in them a sense of moral, cultural, and intellectual relativism in which their own needs, wants, and desires are more germane to them than are absolute standards. Any pedagogical assessment technique that moves away from a higher emphasis on content than process contributes to the students' loss of direction and their sense that "anything goes." For example, portfolios that contain samples of student work do not indicate how much understanding of truth the student has developed. Collaborative learning and peer counseling contribute to relaxed standards as students rely on each other rather than on absolute standards to assess their work.

Problem solving that admits the possibility of many alternative answers undermines the students' ability to master and properly apply truth standards to a given situation. Christian Right activists maintain that student assessments used in these processes are based on vague and unmeasurable standards that reflect unproven educational philosophies. Together, those new and innovative, but highly destructive, pedagogical and assessment techniques comprise Outcome-Based Education (OBE). The main failure of OBE, according to its critics, is that it shifts assessment away from content mastery to performance skill assessment.[65]

Such critiques also frame Christian Right objections to standardized testing, particularly when done by the government. According to movement critics, under the guise of "setting higher academic standards and developing appropriate assessments," the Clinton administration through Goals 2000 is attempting to substitute affective assessment for hard-core academic standards. In California, one legislator describes how the new standardized tests in that state "have changed and no longer are a guide to academic knowledge or achievement, but actually test students' attitudes and political correctness."[66] The same is true on the national level from the Christian Right perspective. The National Academy of Education, through the National Assessment of Education Process (NAEP), traditionally offered "the only nationally representative and ongoing assessment of American students' knowledge of academic subjects." That is changing as NAEP tests have been broadened to include assessment of students' affective abilities. A report of educational experts recommends that by 2015, NAEP reports should include assessment categories in "knowledge and skills, problem-solving and interpretation, and performance in groups. The panel also recommends administering the NAEP via computer."[67] The last point touches a raw nerve in Christian Right leaders, who particularly fear government intrusion into education. By putting all of this student data into computer banks, these activists fear that information about all aspects of the student's life and that of the student's family are being gathered by statist interests who will then use the data against the student and the student's family. Christian Right activists are not entirely against national testing of students. They seem willing to accept some form of national standards for assessment if those examinations focus only on academic subjects and are done on a competitive basis by private firms.

Another area of pedagogical concern for the Christian Right is reading, writing, and math instruction. Movement leaders claim that new emphases in these subjects also value process over content. Whole language is a useful example of the kind of attention the Christian Right directs at process-based pedagogy. Movement spokespersons oppose whole language to phonics, preferring the latter as the method of choice for teaching reading. Whole language approaches reading by allowing students to read and write using approximate, rather than precise, depictions of words. Its proponents believe that whole language better enables students to develop confidence and success as readers and writers because students are more concerned with meaning than spelling. By putting words in context, students can figure out the meaning of each word and spell it as it sounds to them. Christian Right authors point to a number of studies that purport to establish not only the inferiority of whole language, but its danger as well. Using these studies, activists argue that the failure of schools to produce students who are good readers and writers is the single greatest disaster of contemporary public education. Christian Right sources even attribute the steep increase in special education needs among America's students to whole language.[68]

Christian Right parents and activists strongly prefer phonics, which focuses on correct spelling and identifying words not from pictures, as is permitted in whole language, but from their actual appearance in written form. In other words, phonics requires students to sound out words from the way they appear and to write them using proper spelling. Putting aside the relative merits and weaknesses of the two approaches, the Christian Right preference for phonics relates to its theory of knowledge and of the transmission of knowledge. Facts are given to humans in propositional form, and humans have the responsibility for learning those facts. Words are given to students in a specific form, and students have the responsibility for learning that specific form and using it correctly. Here again, the responsibility of the teacher is to assess whether student performance is correct or incorrect. Either a word is spelled or identified correctly or it is not. Rather than to guess, as is permitted in whole language, students must learn by accurately mastering the material. The ambiguity associated with whole language is absent in phonics.

These examples of Christian Right concerns about educational pedagogy suggest how well they understand the correlation between the nature of knowledge and the way it is transmitted. Pedagogy is performance. Correct pedagogy is performance consistent with the order and structure of the world and the nature of the knowledge humans have about it. When schools permit teachers to assume roles and utilize processes that are inconsistent with the divinely ordained responsibilities of teachers, the schools have to be challenged. Although Christian Right critiques about content have received much more attention from the press,[69] pedagogical issues are of equal if not greater importance for the Christian Right. Movement leaders are aware that how teachers structure their classrooms determines in very large part the kinds of adults the schools will produce. When schools are in harmony with the behavioral standards of Christian parents and the divinely ordained structure of the family, the schools contribute to the development of responsible citizens. When schools utilize processes that contradict the behavioral standards of Christian parents, the schools undermine the students' proper orientation to the world. When the schools educate children of non-Christian parents in ways that contradict biblical principles, those children are lost because no one is providing them with the appropriate standards and values they need to live their lives as responsible adults.

In many ways, the divisions we have created among mythos, symbols, and ritual in our analysis of Christian Right criticism are artificial. The mythic, symbolic, and ritual presuppositions that shape its criticism apply to all three areas of controversy discussed. The divisions do, however, allow us to see how each of these three sets of presuppositions relates directly to specific criticism of public education. Although we have studied only those controversies that are the most widespread, the insights are transferable to other issues. I have not devoted extensive discussion to Outcome-Based Education for two reasons. In the first place, though OBE served as a lightning rod for the Christian Right in the mid-1990s, by the latter part of the decade it gave way to voucher issues, schools of choice, charter schools, religious freedom, and other concerns related to the overall structure of public education. In the second place, Christian Right criticism of OBE is derived from the specific curricular and pedagogical issues discussed here. For this reason, it would be redundant to consider OBE separately.

The larger issue is the future direction of the public schools. Utilizing presuppositional methods and strategies, Christian Right critics of public education have successfully raised their objections at the local, state, and national levels. Their particular mythos, symbols, and ritual preferences bear heavily on their assessment of the current status of public education and frame their vision of public education in the future. In order for schools to be "friendly" to Christian parents, Christian Right sources argue that each component of the educational process discussed in this chapter needs to be brought into conformity with biblical principles. This means that when confronted by Christian Right activists, local school districts must understand the full implications of Christian Right demands and must assess the consequences of such changes within the context of their own educational philosophy and the scholarly research that drives content and instruction.

8

Four Case Studies

Examining in some detail actual cases in which activists at the state and local level have applied the worldview and presuppositional strategy of the Christian Right movement will flesh out the foregoing theoretical discussions. The cases concern school districts in Adrian/Blissfield, Michigan; Vista, California; and Lake County, Florida; and a 1998 Colorado ballot initiative called Amendment 17. They are good illustrations for several reasons. They represent geographical diversity, they occurred in two different periods of time, and they illustrate the application of different aspects of the Christian Right worldview and presuppositional strategy. The first three cases date from the early 1990s. Each received national attention in educational circles. Immediately after Christian Right activists were successful in Vista and Lake County, national movement leaders called them exemplary representations of movement tactics and goals.

The first case comes from my hometown in Michigan and dates from 1991–92. It exemplifies an identifiably religious response to educational reforms promoted by the educational establishment early in the decade. In the Adrian/Blissfield case, local activists attacked the school improvement efforts of two school district boards, accusing them of trying to promote New Age religion and secular humanism in the classrooms. The criticism directed at the schools contained the overtly religious rhetoric and conspiratorial language that often characterized Christian Right protests in the early 1990s.

The initial success of their challenges reveals the degree to which the educational establishment and, in particular, the forces promoting reform, were totally unprepared to respond. Nationally known external consultants to the two school districts commented that they had never experienced anything like the opposition that appeared, seemingly out of nowhere. The organizational staffers consulting with the districts about the reform process, from the Institute for the Development of Educational

Activities (IDEA), were so struck by the intensity and nature of the charges that they sponsored the first national conference on the Christian Right relating to educational issues.

The next two controversies, Vista and Lake County, shared many similarities. Both centered on school board elections in which Christian Right majorities came to power. Both new board majority members had direct ties to movement organizations. Both played out in a six-year span between 1990, when the first Christian Right board member was elected, and 1996, when a mainstream majority was returned to the board. The two cases, however, had very different geographical and cultural settings, the cosmopolitan San Diego County, California, and the small towns of Central Florida, in the heart of the Bible belt. They provide good examples of the strategic, symbolic, and mythic dimensions of the Christian Right. In the Vista case, the most controversial elements were the stealth campaign strategy adopted by the Christian Right board candidates and the symbolic issues of creationism and sex education. In the Lake County controversy, the most provocative issue was rooted deeply in the Christian Right mythos. Here the board attempted to institute a pedagogical policy that required teachers to promote the superiority of American culture. The difference between the two cases is one of emphasis: sex education and creationism did become points of controversy in Lake County, and some elements of American cultural superiority appeared in Vista. In retrospect, it is clear that there was a great deal of commonality in the agendas of Christian Right school board members in the two locations, as there was in the responses of the two mainstream communities. Another side note: both the new Vista board and the new Lake County board dismissed the districts' attorneys and retained new ones with close ties to the Christian Right. Unlike the Adrian/Blissfield case, in which the central characteristic of the activists was ritual protest, in both Vista and Lake County the movement attempted to achieve its goals through the political process. The fact that the activists in both cases achieved political power by utilizing stealth tactics and limiting their appeal to a small segment of the electorate had a substantial impact on the subsequent response from the community. By advancing their agenda through proposed changes in district policy and curricula, the newly elected Christian Right board members inflamed enough members of both communities that the voters removed the activists from power as soon as they could.

The fourth case comes from the late 1990s and represents two important features of more recent Christian Right tactics at the state level. It demonstrates the way Christian Right strategists use past defeats and market research to advance their agenda and it illustrates the persistence of movement activists in the pursuit of their educational goals. In this case, the tactic preferred by the activists was the ballot initiative. More specifically, the leadership selected this approach when traditional legislative attempts to publicly fund religious schools failed. The 1998 ballot initiative, Amendment 17, stood on the shoulders of similar efforts that had failed in 1984, 1992, and 1996. After each of these failures, the activists redesigned their tactics, hoping to succeed the next time. This long-term strategy of incremental change, seeking victories where possible and learning from defeats when necessary, is characteristic of Christian Right legislative and judicial initiatives at the national and state levels. All four Colorado ballot campaigns were part of movement attempts to defund the public schools and to convert what would remain of public education into Christian worldview schools. In the 1998 effort, a conservative businessman without identifiable connections to the Christian Right helped head the drive. Thus, the Colorado case study also illustrates the high degree of strategic and ideological overlap between the Christian Right and more secular libertarian and free-market interests within conservative Republican politics.

Together, the four cases demonstrate some of the diversity of the tactics the Christian Right utilizes in executing its presuppositional strategy and advancing its goal of cultural transformation through a religiously grounded social movement. They also reflect the movement's change in strategy to a more local and state-level emphasis following the disappointment of the Reagan presidency. Behind each of the cases, the whisperings of Francis Schaeffer and Rousas John Rushdoony can be heard in the symbolic and mythic rhetoric that movement activists employ. The selection of these four cases does have some limitations, however. The choices restrict the range of issues for drawing explicit connections between the Christian Right and local controversies. The choices are meant to be representative of larger issues and may miss other issues or locations that provide insight into other important aspects of the Christian Right. In these cases, the focus is on the mythic, symbolic, and ritual expressions of the religious dimension of the movement. Overlying this discussion of the religious aspects of the Christian Right are the enormous financial resources, technical expertise, and political clout of the Christian Right. It remains for others to explore these institutional expressions.

New Age Religion: Adrian/Blissfield

The Christian Right's New Age/secular humanism tactic provided the backdrop for the educational reform controversy that erupted in Adrian and Blissfield, Michigan, school districts in 1991.[1] The drama began to unfold in 1991, when the Institute for the Development of Educational Activities (IDEA) invited the two districts to participate in a reform initiative called Communities for Developing Minds (CDM). The proposed project was in response to the 1990 passage by the Michigan legislature of Public Act 25, which mandated that each district in the state develop a school improvement plan. According to an information sheet distributed by the Adrian Public Schools, the purpose of the Adrian reform proposal was to "explore, consider, and reflect the best learning opportunities possible for students with broad school community involvement and input." The district described the future of the process in these terms: "Continue the exploration and consideration on ways to further help our Adrian kids learn with the help and input from the Adrian Community."[2] The focus of the process was the Three C's—cognition, collaboration, and communication. That is, the process was intended to develop collaboration between the schools and the community in order to increase communication. CDM would apply the best thinking strategies in order to come to a common understanding about the best way to educate our children.

IDEA offered to the district the coordinated services of their staff and some of the most respected educational authorities in the nation on higher order thinking, assessment, and curriculum design.[3] The two districts were to independently develop their own goals and decide precisely how the external resources would be utilized. In describing the process to Adrian and Blissfield schools, IDEA president John Bahner stated clearly that the hopes and goals would be defined by the local school communities within the limits set by the district committees and as approved by the boards of education. In January 1991, IDEA extended an invitation to both districts to develop CDM. Anticipating little opposition, the school boards in both districts voted to accept the IDEA invitation and become part of the CDM process.

Almost immediately, voices in the two communities raised concerns about the reform proposal. The critics formed two closely related groups. In Blissfield, they went by the name of Citizens for Quality Education (CQE). In Adrian, they called themselves Public Education Awareness

Forum (PEAF). PEAF representatives included a staff member of the local representative to the Michigan legislature, who was closely aligned with the Christian Right, several ministers from conservative evangelical churches, and the director of a local Christian family center. The center was built with substantial contributions from a major contributor to Christian Right organizations in Michigan and the nation.

By midsummer the opposition strategy was in full force. CQE packed school board meetings and demanded Blissfield's withdrawal from CDM. In addition to pursuing a similar strategy in Adrian, PEAF sponsored three public forums during midsummer and early fall. Using a presuppositional strategy, CQE and PEAF leaders seized upon the failure of the local districts to properly inform the citizenry of the reform initiative. Opposition materials and presentations intentionally provoked fear of IDEA and attempted to portray the elected school officials as dupes of a secular humanism conspiracy. The rhetoric used by these concerned citizens included frequent references to the anti-Christian, antifamily, and anti-American nature of IDEA, the National Education Association, Planned Parenthood, educational reformers Ted Sizer, Art Costa, and John Goodlad, and the Association for Supervision and Curriculum Development. Picking on educational packages that were not even included in the reform proposal, the critics equated values education with moral relativism and affective education with invasion of the students' privacy and violation of the sanctity of the family. They also condemned global education because it promoted one-world government, and multiculturalism because it destroyed patriotism.

PEAF held its first public forum in July. By the announced starting time, the meeting room at the local YMCA was packed to overflowing. The ground rules the moderator announced at the start of the program clearly suggested that PEAF intended to entertain no discussion of its charges against the district. Before the presentations began, the moderator announced that the speakers would address the audience in succession with no time allotted for questions or comments by the those in attendance. Citizens wanting further information about the dangers about to be launched on an unsuspecting community could find resource references on a table at the back of the room. The materials PEAF provided included an unpublished white paper against school reform entitled "Educational Restructuring of America—Education or Indoctrination," from which many of the speakers took their comments. Its author was Colorado activist and Littleton school board member Carol Belt.[4] Other materials included *The New Age Masquerade: The Hidden Agenda in Your Child's Classroom,* by Eric Buehrer; articles critical of the *Impressions* reading series published in *Citizen,* from James Dobson's Family Research Council; *Children at Risk: The Battle for the Hearts and Minds of Our Kids,* by James Dobson and Gary Bauer; and Pat Robertson's *The New World Order.*[5]

The charges made that night by the speakers linked almost every conceivable reform to New Age religion and a secular humanist one-world government conspiracy. A partial list of allegations included attacks on collaborative learning, imaging, higher order thinking, global education, site-based decision making, conflict management, and psychological counseling. Collaborative learning, for example, undermined individualism because it stressed "getting along with others" over competition. Site-based management and shared decision making contributed to the eradication of representative government because no one was charged with final responsibility. Conflict management built weakness in children and taught them to abandon their beliefs when necessary to get along with others. Educating students to live in a global world promoted globalism and communist-style one-world government. Higher order thinking encouraged moral relativism by teaching children to seek the best rather than the right answer. Finally, the report generated a causal link between known New Age religionists such as Jean Houston, globalists such as Robert Muller, educational theorists such as John Dewey and John Goodlad, and educational establishment organizations such as ASCD and IDEA.

The logic of the charges was simple, even if fallacious. Using guilt by association, the critics assumed that the endorsement of any educational reform process by ASCD or IDEA, or any similar organization, meant that the process being implemented in Adrian or Blissfield was part of a conscious strategy by New Agers to convert school children to the religion of those futurists. The conclusion drawn by PEAF and CQE representatives was that educational reform as contained in the CDM process is part of a globalist conspiracy with a political agenda to use the schools to indoctrinate school children with a secular humanist philosophy. Mastery learning and its related programs such as Outcome-Based Education were designed to dumb down the children to make them into compliant, manageable robots who would become part of a uniform, predictable, controlled citizenry. The picture painted by the activists was of two school boards duped by sinister international forces and being unwittingly led down a path that would result in the destruction of our children and our nation's way of life.

The groups continued the accusations made at the July meeting, a later meeting of the Adrian Ecumenical Fellowship, and two other public forums. During the July meeting of the fellowship, several ministers supportive of PEAF expressed concern about the reform proposal. A local Church of God minister accused the Adrian district of a "hidden agenda to promote New Age philosophy." A Salvation Army envoy said he had heard that "John Goodlad, who heads the IDEA Research Program, has written a New Age book and is a proponent of New Age religion."[6] In August, a newsletter published by the Christian Family Centre made the charges more explicitly:

> There is a substantial reason to believe that (educators associated with I.D.E.A. on the national level) align philosophically as secular humanists and/or globalists or as some may say, 'New Age.' John Goodlad is reported to be on the board of directors of Global Perspectives in Education is often referred to as 'Multicultural education.' Often an anti-Americanism theme is prevalent in global education.[7]

At the August PEAF-sponsored public meeting, Carol Belt was the featured speaker. She recommended that parents undermine the financial stability of the local school district in response to the district's reform initiative. She told them to keep their children home from school on the day that the district took the official student population count upon which the district's per-pupil funding rests. Another speaker employed Schaeffer's competing-worldviews model and associated the proposed reforms with New Age teachings. A third speaker claimed that another district had put her child in an altered state of consciousness using holistic teaching methods. None of the speakers made any explicit connection between their charges and the CDM proposal.[8] During the second community forum in September, Michigan Alliance for Families president Bettye Lewis charged that "IDEA and similar school improvement plans being implemented across the country are tools to educate children for a 'new social system' where they will be developed for use as resources of the federal government's choosing." Lewis also asserted that cooperative learning would "bring education down to its lowest common denominator. . . . I say cooperative learning is destroying the individualization of our children. . . . They say competition is bad, I say it's good. . . . Back to basics schooling is what we want." She then advocated home schooling and defeating school millages.[9] At both meetings, audience members were required to submit questions in writing. The PEAF moderator then screened the inquiries.

Through the summer and early fall, PEAF and CQE continued to turn school board meetings into acrimonious debates. Supporters of the groups wrote many letters to the editor claiming that the local news media were ignoring or distorting their complaints. In reality, the critics were "hanging" themselves. The more they detailed their objections, the more the citizens of Adrian, in particular, began to dismiss their charges. In Blissfield, CQE succeeded in convincing the board to withdraw from the IDEA project. Completely reversing a nearly unanimous earlier vote, the board simply did not have the stomach for the continuing controversy. In Adrian, the board stood fast. The tide began to turn in favor of the reform process when the local newspaper ran an editorial highly critical of the CDM opponents. The column decried the incivility of the critics and concluded:

> [Their] opposition has reached the point of unwarranted personal attacks on school officials, spreading rumors, spreading information that is untrue or taken out [of] context and attaching meanings that have no basis in fact. Through their own definitions of semantics, they have attached surrealistic meanings to certain words and phrases designed to play on the fears of many people, particularly those with narrowly defined educational backgrounds.[10]

At approximately the same time the editorial appeared, I wrote a series of four articles for the local paper using the same presuppositional strategy employed by the critics. In the series, I explored the meanings of the deep symbols they used and placed them in the theological context of the Christian Right. I also prepared and submitted to the two school boards a white paper that included much more detail and research on the same topics. The school leaders in Adrian also published several articles in the paper laying out the nature of IDEA's involvement and the objectives of the reform process. In combination, these efforts turned public opinion toward a more reasoned consideration of the board actions, and the controversy died down. In the spring of 1992, several Christian Right stealth candidates declared their candidacy for the Adrian school board, and two of the leaders of the opposition in Blissfield ran in Blissfield. In both elections, voters elected mainstream candidates to the boards. By the summer of 1992, the controversy was over and the opposition had disappeared below the radar screen.

Stealth Campaigns: Vista

The Vista, California, story is probably the best-known Christian Right school controversy. The drama started to unfold in 1990 with the election to the school board of Deidra Holliday. Holliday was part of a larger slate of Christian Right candidates for school board positions and minor municipal and county offices in San Diego County. These candidates eschewed the normal election process of voter forums and public appearances. Instead, they ran a campaign geared to a single segment of voters, those most likely to favor a "profamily" agenda. They identified their potential supporters through telephone surveys, church directory lists, and conservative Christian media in Southern California.[11] The candidates then solicited support through church networks by distributing voter guides at Sunday services and leafleting parking lots while worshipers were in church. The hopefuls managed to conceal their agenda from the general public by focusing only on their supporters and by providing background sheets for the press that were full of generalities, misrepresentative of qualifications, and similar in rhetoric, style, and grammar to other stealth contestants. The strategy worked. Voters elected sixty of the ninety stealth candidates to office in San Diego County. One school board member in La Mesa–Spring Valley learned of stealth opposition to the mainstream candidates the Sunday before the election when he found a profamily flyer on his car windshield in the parking lot after he left church.[12]

The political principle under which these stealth tactics worked was simple. School board and municipal elections tend to have light voter turnouts. By mobilizing a small block of voters around a particular slate of candidates, the contestants for office did not need the support of the larger public. The strategy was effective because the mainstream contestants did not know they faced any orchestrated ideological opposition. Two San Diego political consultants with strong conservative ties orchestrated the stealth campaign. The strategy served as a test for the Christian Coalition and other Christian Right groups such as Citizens for Excellence in Education, which wanted to extend their dominion principle into the public sector. The Christian Coalition's Ralph Reed bragged about the strategy's success to the national media, explaining, "We're trying to generate as large a voter turnout as possible among our constituency by communicating with them in a way that does not attract the fire of our opponents."[13] As noted previously, Reed later admitted, "Stealth was a big factor in San Diego's success. But that's just good strategy. It's like guerrilla warfare. If you reveal your location, all it does is allow your opponent to improve his artillery bearings. It's better to move quietly, with stealth, under cover of night."[14]

Once elected to school boards, the stealth candidates began to attack a shopping list of Christian Right educational targets. In Vista, Holliday continually disrupted the normal proceedings of the board with objections and critical attacks on the district's programs. Two years later, two more Christian Right candidates joined her on the board after a spirited campaign filled with charges and countercharges. The election of Joyce Lee, the wife of a conservative evangelical minister, and John Tyndall, an accountant at the Institute for Creation Research, gave the Christian Right a board majority.[15] For the next two years, Vista Unified School District board meetings became a central battleground for the culture wars. Two main issues provoked the greatest controversy. Debates over creationism and sex education in the classrooms continually split the board and the community. Other topics, such as opposition to school breakfast programs, recognition of the community's immigrant heritage, and efforts to find common ground between the two sides, also caused heated discussion. Perhaps the most unusual debate occurred over the content of a newly instituted course in comparative religion. The conservative board majority wanted to include secular humanism in the course content in order to establish its legitimacy as a religion. Moderates opposed it for the same reason.[16]

Because of Tyndall's association with the creationism institute, concerns quickly surfaced within the district regarding the board's intentions about the science curriculum. The public's fears were not quieted when board member Lee recommended that her critics visit the institute, saying a friend of hers went on their tour and was converted from atheism to Christianity.[17] In January 1993, two months after the election, the Christian Right majority attempted to reassure the community by declaring that they had no intention of infusing creationism into science courses. At the March board meeting, Tyndall recommended that the science textbook review committee include the book *Of Pandas and People: The Central Question of Biological Origins* to supplement the high school course offerings. The committee reviewed and recommended against the use of *Of Pandas and People*.[18]

In spite of the committee's recommendation, the board majority continued to push for a place for creationism in the curriculum. At the May meeting, two Christian Right board members proposed three new policies. Reading state mandates in an innovative way, the board declared that biblical creationism "shall be included" in history, social studies, and English classes. The second board proposal recommended that scientific evidence that challenged any theory of science should be presented in the classroom to "enhance scientific exploration and dialogue." The particular wording was meant to circumvent the issue of creationism, but according to the board majority, it expected creationist challenges to be included in that exploration and dialogue. The third proposal stated that "no theory of science shall be taught dogmatically, and no student shall be compelled to believe or accept any theory presented in the curriculum."[19] Modified versions of the second and third proposals eventually passed; a later recall election that removed the Christian Right majority made the first policy moot since the teachers had refused to implement the directive.

The second major confrontation between the community and the Christian Right board involved the board's challenge regarding the existing sex education class, called "Values and Choices." In March 1994, the elected majority replaced that course with an abstinence-only curriculum called "Sex Respect."[20] Anticipating the same type of legal challenges that surrounded the adoption of the materials in other districts in the nation, the board discontinued the services of its former attorney, who had written a legal opinion that recommended against inclusion of "Sex Respect,"[21] and retained David Llewellyn instead. Llewellyn, founder of the Western Center for Law and Religious Freedom, a Christian Right legal services organization, included the Institute for Creation Research on his list of clients. In its journal, the Center for Unplanned Pregnancy reported that Llewellyn had left the Western Center "to look for more effective ways to use his gifts to bring about Biblical Reform in government and culture." Llewellyn was also a columnist for the Coalition on Revival's "Christian Worldview Sphere Reports," where his assigned topic was "Law and Public Policy."[22] The curriculum the board adopted was for the seventh-grade class.

Another board action drew fire from the community in October 1994. Without seeking any public input, the board voted to change the district's mission statement to emphasize the American citizenship of its students. This action occurred several months after the board refused to approve a resolution expressing recognition for the contributions of Vista's immigrant families. The board substituted the phrase "contributing citizens of our nation" for "contributing members in a global society" in the mission statement,[23] reflecting the importance Christian Right leaders place on the American monomyth. According to that view, loyalties to a perceived past become more important than responsibilities to a shared present.

The four-year crisis came to a head in November 1994. Holliday did not seek a second term, and the voters recalled Lee and Tyndall by a 55–45 percent vote.[24] The election produced a moderate board with no Christian Right presence. During the controversy, five administrators had resigned, including a very highly respected superintendent. Because of the district's socioeconomic profile, the new board faced a number of serious budgetary and academic performance problems. The rocky path of the Vista board demonstrated that, though the stealth tactics worked in the short term, once the public became aware of the Christian Right agenda it rejected its initiatives.

The Vista school district was returned to the educational and social mainstream of San Diego County primarily through the efforts of several organizations that emerged to challenge the Christian Right. The Community for Responsible Education (CRE), founded by a former La Mesa–Spring Valley board member who was defeated by a stealth candidate, forced Christian Right board members to explain their agenda within the context of the larger framework of the movement. The stealth candidates thus were pressured to take responsibility for the movement's larger agenda. CRE also began to court the religious mainstream in order to counter the impression that the stealth candidates owned the religious constituency. Later, the organization worked to develop a non–Christian Right slate of candidates for the next election cycle. The Mainstream Voters Project (MVP) also came into existence to fight the Christian Right's tactics and agenda. MVP's purpose was to investigate the Christian Right and report its research to the general public. In addition, the group scrutinized the information and claims made by candidates to document their accuracy.

A third mainstream group, the Community Coalition Network (CCN), functioned as a political action committee, providing potential mainstream candidates with campaign services. CCN also circulated a document that asked candidates to accept a "Declaration of Principles," which pledged contestants for public office to acknowledge their agreement with a series of statements on church-state issues, to fully disclose their campaign positions, and to accurately list the organizations that endorsed them. In combination, the three groups helped inform mainstream voters and return the election process to democratic principles. From a religious standpoint, part of their success stemmed from their efforts to place the candidates and their agendas within the larger context of the Christian Right as a social movement.[25]

The American Monomyth: Lake County

In a number of important respects, the Lake County controversy mirrored that of Vista. The similarities began with the election in 1990 of a single Christian Right stealth candidate, Pat Hart. Like John Tyndall in Vista, Hart was a member of a Christian Right organization, Citizens for Excellence in Education. Once elected, Hart played a role similar to that of Deidra Holliday during her first two years on the Vista board. Both Hart and Holliday objected to matters that had been considered rather routine by previous boards. Their confrontational style disrupted board meetings and provoked intolerant responses from those attending the meetings as well as from the moderate majority members on the board. After two years in office, Hart and Holliday were each joined by two more Christian Right candidates. In Lake County, the second and third elected activists did not conduct stealth campaigns.

Once in office, the religious conservatives advanced similar agendas, though with different points of emphasis. Both groups attacked school meals programs, reviewed textbooks, hired new attorneys, and challenged curricular offerings. The most controversial common issues faced in the two districts were creationism, sex education, and multicultural education. The Vista board tended toward a greater emphasis on the first two issues, whereas the Lake County majority made national headlines on the third topic. Even though they controlled the boards in both locations, the Christian Right activists never had a major curricular impact outside of one or two issues, mostly because of community objections and because there were teachers who refused to compromise their academic and curricular standards. Yet, the pain and frustration they caused to the faculty, the administration, and the communities was incalculable. In both situations, the citizens of the districts rallied to defeat the new majority in subsequent elections.

The Lake County story began with the election of Pat Hart by twelve votes to the school board in 1990. Utilizing classic stealth tactics, Hart restricted her campaigning to appearances in conservative evangelical Christian churches and church circles.[26] Two years later, Claudia Ramsey, also a member of Citizens for Excellence in Education, and Judy Pearson were elected to the board. The connection of the three candidates to the Christian Right was so strong that Robert Simonds, president of CEE, commented at a conference in 1994 that "we now own that district." After the newly elected board members assumed their positions, the Christian Right majority demonstrated the type of leadership the movement envisioned for public education.

One of its first actions was to deny a request for a Head Start unit. Head Start officials merely requested the use of an existing facility at no cost to the district. The rationale provided by the new majority reflected the Christian Right symbolic understanding of the family. Mothers were to stay at home and provide for the needs of the children. In commenting on the board action, a local newspaper suggested that Hart had determined in her own mind that Head Start children were too young to be away from their mothers.[27] The Christian Right majority subsequently proposed deep cuts in the district's noninstructional personnel. The move was calculated to reduce administrative overhead and to decrease pupil-teacher ratio. They intended to accomplish this by moving administrative staff members into the classrooms. In one of the few instances in which the majority was divided, one new board member reversed her vote and the proposal was killed.[28]

In the months that followed, the Christian Right board placed the district in severe financial difficulty by cutting $3.5 million from the budget and declining another $1.2 in state-mandated millage reductions.[29] The triumvirate promoted these cost-cutting measures in order to reduce the financial burden to the taxpayers. But the actions also had the effect of putting severe pressures on teachers' salaries.

Curricular issues also dominated the policy recommendations of the new board. The first program they challenged was the existing sex education curriculum. They fought for implementation of "Sex Respect," the same abstinence-only curriculum that was involved in the Vista conflict.[30] The materials they recommended contained no information on pregnancy or disease prevention. Supporters of the existing sex education course attempted to convince the board that a state survey indicated that parents did not object to sex education that included information on prevention. The survey results were based on a telephone canvass of schools, in which administrators were asked for statistics on the number of parents who opted out of current sex education courses. Board president Pat Hart's response to the reference reflected one of the most common

Christian Right objections to opt-out provisions. She claimed that the results were invalid because students and their parents were under enormous peer pressure not to be different. Hart commented, "Calling the schools does not give you an accurate view of what parents would do if they had a choice. A lot of parents don't (opt their kids out) because they say, 'Don't do it, it'll embarrass me.'"[31] The Christian Right activists preferred "opt-in" provisions, in which the schools placed the burden on the parents and children who supported inclusion of information about sexuality in their instruction. Ironically, one of the teachers of the existing course who opposed any change in board policy was a Church of God minister. In a preliminary move, on a 3-1 vote, the district removed a sex education program for special needs students at two of the district's high schools. The resulting fight over the new course forced the postponement of its use in the other schools and programs. The broader implementation never occurred, because the board makeup changed as a result of new elections.[32] Before the Christian Right members were turned out of office, the board also proposed a policy directed at what they perceived to be New Age religious practices in the district. The proposed policy would prohibit teachers from utilizing relaxation exercises in classrooms and eliminate all programs designed to improve the students' self-esteem.[33]

The most controversial measure came after the proposed change in the sex education curriculum. In response to a new state law requiring schools to provide students with a program in multicultural education, the board attempted to counter the mandate with a curricular emphasis on American cultural superiority. The state law calling for multicultural education read, "Multicultural education is education that prepares students to live, learn, communicate and work to achieve common goals in a culturally diverse world by fostering understanding, appreciation and respect for people of other ethnic, gender, socioeconomic, language and cultural backgrounds."[34] The preamble of the bill contained a statement that excluded from school curricula any instruction regarding the inherent superiority of any culture. The major sponsor of the legislation in the Florida House Education Committee was Doug Jamerson, who, as state education commissioner, later played an important role in the Lake County controversy.[35]

In coming to its decision to act counter to the state mandate, the Christian Right board majority concluded that the multicultural directive raised respect for other cultures by denigrating America's heritage. To correct for what they felt was a bias against America, the board passed a policy that read, "[multicultural] instruction shall also include and instill in our students an appreciation of our American heritage and culture such as our republican form of government, capitalism, a free enterprise system, patriotism, strong family values, freedom of religion and other basic values that are superior to other foreign or historic cultures."[36] The last phrase, "superior to other foreign and historic cultures," created a furor in the community and drew national attention to the Lake County board. Some members of the community found the policy proposal to be racist, or at least insensitive to the minority populations that lived in the central Florida region. Hart, however, viewed the proposal as a proactive measure. "To me this is a proactive policy, not a reactive, to make sure we continue teaching our children the greatness of America." When asked to specify the values to which she was referring, Hart said:

> When we came, we were assimilated to the nation of America. And America was founded on the governmental principles that America was founded upon. I think our students need to be aware of that. They need to have the utmost knowledge and appreciation and understanding of our founding documents, our founding fathers, the principles of America and why America is great. We need to know that.[37]

The nature of Hart's comments clearly reflects the Christian Right's monomythic view of America at two points. The expectation is that immigrants will assimilate into the existing culture without disturbing it or significantly altering its composition. Furthermore, from the perspective of Christian Right activists such as Hart, the reference to the "principles of America and why America is great" suggests the movement's contention that these principles are biblical and that our greatness stems from our Christian cultural heritage.

The controversy escalated when Education Commissioner Jamerson wrote to the board asking them to rescind the policy because it was in violation of state law.[38] Hart and new board attorney Dick Langley rebuffed the commissioner. Langley commented, "That's his opinion. There are many other opinions out there. Jamerson's is no more weighty than the opinion of the woman in the supermarket. . . . We are the Lake County School Board. We are not subject to what Commissioner Jamerson thinks. I think it's all a bunch of hooey."[39]

Hooey or not, the board never implemented its new policy. Because of the nature of the policies advanced by Hart and the other board members, community members formed an organization in 1993 intended to bring the board back to a more moderate composition. Called People for Main-stream Values, the coalition included parents, educators, clergy, community members, and business leaders. The results of these efforts were similar to those in Vista. Hart chose not to run for reelection in 1994, the voters defeated three Christian Right candidates, and the board majority moved back toward the center. In 1996, when voters replaced Ramsey and Pearson, the Christian Right presence on the Lake County board evaporated.[40]

Adopted Liberalism: Colorado's Amendment 17

The final case study shifts our attention to ballot initiatives and state-level efforts by the Christian Right. Ballot initiatives are growing in popularity among Christian Right activists. Failing to achieve its goal of public funding for private, parochial, or sectarian schools through cultural conversion or state and federal legislatures, the movement is taking its case directly to the voters. Perhaps the best example of the use of ballot initiatives comes from the state of Colorado, where Christian Right activists tried once in 1984 and three times in the 1990s to change the existing funding mechanism for public education.

Christian Right Coloradans have taken a leadership role nationally in developing this tactic. In 1992, Colorado voters were the first in the nation to express their opinion on a pure voucher proposal (the 1984 voucher initiative never made it to the ballot). The measure provided for parents or guardians of every Colorado student to receive a voucher worth about twenty-one hundred dollars. Even though the proposal failed by a two-to-one margin, the measure's Christian Right proponents were undaunted. A similar effort in 1996 was tied up in the courts.[41] In 1998, the same activists garnered enough signatures to place a tuition tax credit amendment to the Colorado constitution on the ballot. That proposal also went down to defeat, but by a slightly smaller 60 percent of the vote.[42]

Initiative supporters changed their tactics from vouchers to tax credits in 1998 after conducting a survey that showed greater support in the general populace for the latter. In the 1998 version, parents and guardians would receive a tax credit of about twenty-five hundred dollars as tuition reimbursement for students choosing private, parochial, or sectarian education over the public schools. When asked to clarify the difference between the two alternatives, Steve Schuck, one of the 1998 measure sponsors, commented to a leader of the amendment opposition that no real difference existed between vouchers and tax credits.[43] After the amendment was defeated in the general election, Republican governor-elect Bill Owens, a supporter of Amendment 17, as the tuition tax credit initiative was called, indicated that efforts to publicly fund nonpublic schools should be dead for both the short and medium terms, given the election results. No sooner had Owens's words become public than talk began to circulate in conservative circles in Colorado that an outside organization had pledged about six hundred thousand dollars to move public support toward funding for nonpublic schools.[44]

Behind the 1992, 1996, and 1998 initiatives stood Tom Tancredo. A self-defined supporter of the Christian Right, Tancredo headed a think tank called the Independence Institute until he decided to run for the U.S. Congress in 1998.[45] Although the institute was one of Amendment 17's strongest supporters, Tancredo played a background role, dedicating most of his efforts to his own successful election campaign. He had long been an advocate for the Christian Right transformation of public education. Like other contemporary movement leaders such as Gary Bauer, Tancredo served in the Reagan Administration as the secretary of education's regional representative and was reappointed by President Bush. During his tenure, Tancredo slashed the regional education office's staff by 75 percent. A former public school teacher, he identified the teachers' union as one of his foremost targets.

Tancredo had been a leader in innovative tactics used by the Christian Right in opposing education in Colorado. In a Focus on the Family radio interview in 1995, Tancredo called for the abolishment of compulsory school attendance and worked for legislation toward that end in the Colorado legislature. He argued that the "people who are in school should be the people who want to be in school and when you have that kind of an arrangement, you find education occurring in that environment."[46] Tancredo wrote position papers for the Independence Institute condemning Outcome-Based Education and advocating school choice and parents' rights. He also compared America's public schools to those of the Soviet Union.[47]

The rhetorical strategy of the supporters of the 1998 Colorado ballot illustrated the way in which the Christian Right used the rights rhetoric of classic liberalism and democratic values such as equality and fairness to appeal to mainstream voters. Dubbed the Educational Opportunity Tax Credit, the measure was marketed to appear to benefit low-income students in poor neighborhoods. Coloradans for School Choice, the leading promoter of Amendment 17, distributed a brochure with pictures featuring minority children. The captions suggested that these students should not be stuck in bad schools and that all children deserved the same opportunities as "more fortunate families."[48] The brochure also prominently featured a highly provocative passage from *A Nation at Risk* that linked the current state of education in America with the effects of a war conducted by a foreign enemy on our soil.

The realities of the measure were quite different. The amendment did not include any reference to means-tested qualifications for the parents of public school children. It did include such a test for economically disadvantaged parents whose children already attended nonpublic schools. The measure gave first priority to children whose parents would decide in the future to transfer them from poor-performing school districts into private schools. The first priority also included parents of special needs children. The next priority was for parents of children who would leave the public schools from any district in the state, irrespective of the parents' financial condition or the quality of their local public schools. The third priority focused on low-income parents whose children were enrolled in private schools when the measure was enacted. The amendment also accorded relief to parents of any financial status whose children were already in private schools and to parents who would home school their children. Although the details were never worked out, the proposed amendment also called for tuition tax credits for parents who would leave their children in the public schools.

A mailing from Focus on the Family vice president Tom Minnery endorsed the measure, claiming that it would help all kids because it would not drain money from the public schools.[49] Minnery's claim was somewhat deceptive. The proposal mandated that state per-pupil expenditures would follow the children. Under this provision, schools would not lose any money per pupil, but they would lose a considerable amount, more than five thousand dollars, for every child who transferred out of the public schools. In effect, the measure redirected public funds to private schools at the same time it provided parents with incentives to take their children out of the public schools.

One concern the Christian Right has expressed about redirecting public funds to private and religious schools relates to the issue of accountability. Fearing government intrusion into religious freedom, Christian Right leaders framed the Colorado initiative to prevent the state from putting any restrictions on schools that received money from students who transferred from the public schools. Amendment 17 explicitly prohibited the government from placing any restrictions on private schools, either by holding them accountable or by restricting the religious requirements they might place on students and their families. Another provision disqualified any schools that promoted antisocial behavior. A white paper in support of Amendment 17, written by Tancredo, defined antisocial behavior. Schools "that discriminate on the basis of race or national origin, advocate illegal behavior, or teach hatred on the basis of race, national origin, religion, or gender" would be declared ineligible for voucher funds.[50] Presumably this provision was aimed at Afrocentric schools, since Tancredo has been a strong advocate of "dehyphenizing" American culture. By this Tancredo means ridding the culture of multiculturalism as expressed in ethnic American cultural voices.

According to Steve Sand, Denver chapter president of Americans United for the Separation of Church and State, even though Colorado voters defeated Amendment 17 by a substantial margin, the issue was not settled at the ballot box. Sand suggested that an organization known as the Greater Educational Opportunities Foundation (GEO) pledged a substantial amount of money to keep the issue in the minds of voters.[51] GEO is the brainchild of Indianapolis, Indiana, insurance magnate J. Patrick Rooney. Through the Golden Rule Insurance Company, Rooney created the Educational CHOICE Charitable Trust, which helps low-income Indianapolis children attend private schools by awarding them scholarships for up to half of their tuition costs.[52] Rooney's strategy started a national trend in which conservative philanthropists underwrite the cost of private school tuition. Through another organization, Children's Educational Opportunity Foundation, Wal-Mart heir John Walton, Jr., promotes similar philanthropic efforts.

Though reflecting the free-market philosophy of secular conservatives, the efforts of these charitable organizations to provide moneys for private, parochial, and sectarian schools are linked to Christian Right organizations with similar interests. For example, the Christian Alert Network (TCAN), a Texas-based Christian Right group, touts the connection between Walton's Children's Educational Opportunity Foundation and Exodus 2000, a Christian Right initiative to get Christian parents to remove their children from the public schools by the year 2000. TCAN describes Exodus 2000 as "a national movement to save our children from the universal socialistic/communistic re-indoctrination being forced upon them in the public school system." An Exodus 2000 promotional brochure clearly suggests that the project rests on dominionist presuppositions.[53] The TCAN Internet home page enthusiastically endorses both programs and notes that although the two initiatives are independent of each other, they can easily be used to complement each other.[54]

Given these features, the Colorado Amendment 17 illustrates three very important characteristics of the Christian Right's strategy to transform public education. The movement's appeal to rights and choice frames its agenda within mainstream American values. Amendment 17 also demonstrates the close connections between secular and religious conservatives in pursuit of their mutual goals of taking government out of American education. Finally, the Colorado ballot initiative models the Christian Right tactic of using the political and legal processes to advance its agenda.

These four case studies provide a good overview of the range of issues and strategies the Christian Right has employed during the 1990s to achieve its goal of the transformation of American education. The rhetoric appears to be more mainstream in the Colorado ballot measure than in the New Age charges in the Michigan case, but a quick survey of some of the organizational web sites cited here suggests the range of rhetoric that still defines the movement. For example, on the one hand, the Independence Institute's web pages display documents and arguments that do not outwardly appear to be connected to a religiously grounded social movement. The language and focus is geared directly to moderate middle Americans. But Tom Tancredo, the author of many of the institute's papers and the former director, describes himself as an activist in the Christian Right. On the other hand, a visit to the Christian Alert Network's web site throws the viewer into the midst of some of the most strident, explicitly religious rhetoric in the Christian Right. What we see here is the dual focus of the movement. It adopts mainstream rhetoric because it needs to convince mainstream Americans to support its agenda. At the same time, it uses the militant language characteristic of the Moral Majority at its strongest to build in constituents a greater sense of conflict so that the movement can grow. Yet, even with this diversity, both the Independence Institute and the Christian Alert Network are clear that the basis upon which American society should rest is that of biblical or Christian principles. This is what separates the Christian Right from the cultural mainstream it so wants to penetrate.

What is striking to me about the first three case studies (Adrian/Blissfield, Vista, and Lake County) is that all of them took place in very politically conservative regions. The people who developed local organizations to counter the movement initiatives were by no means liberals or secular humanists. One Lake County school board incumbent defeated by a Christian Right stealth candidate was a staunch conservative Republican who was very active in his church. Other school board members, such as the Episcopal priest in Vista, were strongly committed people of faith, to use Ralph Reed's expression. In such controversies, the record shows that it is these stalwarts of middle America from whom D. James Kennedy wants to take the culture back.

I am equally impressed by how persistent and dedicated the Christian Right is in achieving their cultural goals and how vulnerable they are to mainstream responses to their efforts. In Colorado, defeated, the movement rose again to fight the same fight using a different target. In the other three cases, the Christian Right activists seemed to fade below the radar screen again after their defeat. My sense is that they are there, ready to do battle for a Christian culture whenever the opportunity presents itself. In the meantime, the persistent criticism of public education takes its toll. The presuppositional strategy grinds like a millstone on coarse wheat, eventually wearing it down.

Mainstream Americans are not without resources to fight back, however. In all four cases, what eventually turned the public against the Christian Right was the ability of people at the local and state levels to turn the movement's presuppositional strategy on its head. By clearly and logically interpreting specific initiatives within the larger framework of the Christian Right worldview, mainstream organizations were able to identify precise points at which the movement diverges from the deeply and widely held democratic and pluralistic values of civility, tolerance, respect, and compromise.

9

A Concluding Assessment

When I first began to think about analyzing the Christian Right through the lenses of myth, ritual, and symbol, I felt confident that the strongest components of the Christian Right as a social movement were the mythos it advanced and the symbolic web it wove and that the weakest was the movement's ritual dimension. I have now completely reversed my opinion; I have concluded that ritual is by far the most powerful religious tool the Christian Right brings to its efforts to transform society. I have also concluded, paradoxically, that ritual is the point at which the movement is most immediately vulnerable.

That is not to say that the movement's mythos and symbolic web are not powerful tools. The Christian Right mythos contains themes that deeply resonate with the American religious consciousness. Many of its motifs provide people in a rapidly changing nation and world with a sense of meaning and identity that transcends mundane existence. Its mythos also gives many Americans a sense of place attached to higher meaning. Further, the mythic theme of a culture in moral decay confirms, for a large segment of the population, what they experience in their daily lives. The symbolic web also contains a great power of attraction for people. The Christian Right emphasis on family, traditional values, and moral principles seems to provide many Americans with an appropriate antidote to the circumstances of contemporary American culture. For example, moral values that emphasize personal responsibility are alluring to many people in a culture of entitlement. And the Ozzie and Harriet picture of home life tends to appeal to those who are caught in the tragedies of divorce, dysfunctional families, and abusive spouses and parents.

The mythos and symbolic web of the Christian Right begin to encounter resistance, however, when movement leaders insist that the mythos they construct and the interpretations they assign to their symbols are the only acceptable expressions—especially when the myths and symbols seem to be utilized in a univocal way for the support of a particular political, social, and economic ideology. Moreover, for a nation that has long been characterized by religious, racial, and ethnic diversity, the narrow parameters of the Christian Right run counter to our national experience. Nor is it true, as many in the Christian Right claim, that the larger culture is hostile to people of faith. Many Americans are quite willing to extend to conservative people of faith the same entry to cultural discourse they accord to other groups such as ethnic and racial minorities. They simply are not willing to grant to the Christian Right its claim of cultural and religious superiority. The resistance of the larger culture to the Christian Right's perception that Christianity has lost its favored place in the culture becomes the problem for Christians like D. James Kennedy.

The ritual dimension of the Christian Right as a social movement presents another set of strengths and weaknesses. My initial assessment of limited utility for it arose from my confusion. Beyond the limited environments where I thought it existed (e.g., political conventions, organizational rallies, and local chapter meetings), I did not know where to find it. Then I began to think of the Christian Right within the context of a religiously grounded social movement. I recalled Anthony F. C. Wallace's comment that meaning and significance arise from conflict and Lewis Coser's observation that groups use conflict to resolve crises of meaning. I realized that the ritual dimension of the Christian Right is located in the conflict or the culture war itself. The movement culture is built through the communitas or communal bonding generated in the fight against the larger culture. Suddenly, I became aware that the movement's very existence depends on the generation of conflict and that the conflict itself creates the necessary environment for ritual transformation of the participants. I also began to think of ritual transformation in terms of public school pedagogy. These two reflections suggested to me that not only is the conflict surrounding public education ritually transformative, but the reason why the Christian Right seeks to control the public schools is so that it can control the ritual process by which it prepares the students to live in a society dominated by a Christian cultural consensus.

Paradoxically, the Christian Right runs into difficulties in the ritual context when its efforts do generate the conflict it needs to exist and grow. My impression from years of observing the Christian Right in the context of public school controversies is that the same generation of conflict that the movement needs to achieve its goals tends to produce a mainstream backlash that is just as powerful, if not more powerful. For example, in all four cases presented in chapter 8, the initial successes of the

Christian Right collapsed into defeat because the results of the triumph provoked people to rise up against the agenda the movement advanced. When the mainstream challengers to the Christian Right either provided a counter mythos and symbolic web or exposed, at a fairly deep level, the vulnerabilities of the Christian Right myths and symbols, public support turned against the Christian Right. Of course, in each case the challenge was aided by a great deal of ritualizing, expressed as political organizing, on the part of the mainstream activists.

What the literature does not seem to tell us is in how many school districts the successes, generated in conflict, did not produce a backlash sufficient to undo Christian Right victories. My sense is that there are quite a few such instances, particularly in the more religiously conservative communities of the rural South and Midwest. We should suspect from the undocumented claims of Christian Right leaders like Robert Simonds and Elizabeth Ridenour that the number is not insubstantial. For example, in 1994, Robert Simonds claimed a figure of two thousand school boards controlled by religious conservatives, but he refused to provide a list to confirm his claim. In a similar vein, Elizabeth Ridenour claims that a large number of schools use the curriculum developed by the National Council on Bible Curriculum in the Public Schools, but again, she will not identify them. Since, however, the movement grows through conflict and not necessarily success, the Christian Right in many areas is like a phoenix, ready to arise from the ashes.

Before moving into a detailed discussion of the strengths and weaknesses of the religious tools the Christian Right brings to its campaign to transform public education, we must understand that any conclusions about the potential of the Christian Right have to be balanced against the fluid character of social movements. As instruments of social change, social movements themselves change over time. An illustration of the danger of attempting to predict the future may be found in Michael D'Antonio's premature announcement in 1989 regarding the disintegration of the Christian Right. In assessing the status of the movement at that point in time, he concluded, "With the demise of Robertson's campaign came the death of the Christian Right's political hopes. The born again movement soon ceased to be a significant religious or social force as well."[1] D'Antonio made the mistake of identifying the Christian Right as primarily a political movement tied to the fortunes of one activist leader. As D'Antonio's miscalculation shows us, predicting the fortunes of the Christian Right is a difficult task. This is a particular danger when, as in both D'Antonio's work and this current study, we focus on only one dimension of the movement.

Social Movements and Change

Social movements exhibit an enormous capacity for change. We should expect this because such movements have as one of their most important goals change—either in the individual or in the society. The tendency toward change characterizes the history of the Christian Right. The movement began as a reformative norm-oriented social movement in the 1920s in response to the growing influence of modernism in the culture. It remained a reformative norm-oriented movement through the 1970s, although the issues that defined the core agenda of the movement changed from one decade to the next.[2] Beginning in the 1980s, the movement began to change in character as well as in the issues that it emphasized. It metamorphosed into a transformative value-oriented movement grounded in identifiable theologies of culture and politics. At the time the Christian Right emerged as a transformative social movement, its leadership modified its rhetoric so that the movement's master protest frames corresponded more closely to the values and commitments of the larger culture.[3] Because of this demonstrated capacity to change, we should expect that the Christian Right will further evolve as a social movement in the future.

There are several areas where change might have a substantial effect on the Christian Right. Perhaps the most immediate area involves the tension within the Christian Right between movement purists and pragmatists. Though the purists, such as James Dobson and Pat Robertson, seem to have gained the upper hand in the late 1990s, their uncompromising stance might help them win the battle but later lose the war. Pragmatists, such as Ralph Reed and William Bennett, may recapture segments of the movement, particularly in light of the tensions between conservatives and moderates in the Republican Party. If the pragmatists recapture the movement, then the more dominionist elements of the Christian Right may recede and it may devolve back into a reformative norm-oriented movement.

A second area where we might look for change involves a cluster of issues related to geographical, cultural, stylistic, and generational factors. The Christian Right, as constructed in the late 1990s, exhibits a strong southern and western geographical and cultural bias. The southern influence is so strong within the movement, in terms of both its religious and its political influence, that the Christian Right could in some ways be characterized as the South rising again to regain a lost culture. Almost without exception, the current leadership of the Christian Right (and its fellow travelers in the leadership of the Republican Party) comes from the broad expanses of the Bible belt that stretch through the South from the shores of the Atlantic Ocean to the beaches of southern California. This influence has been so great that one of the biggest handicaps the movement has had to overcome is its image among the general public as a particular religious subculture, southern populist Fundamentalism. The Christian Right has been forced to energetically divorce itself from that image in order to project a national voice.[4] If the next generation of Christian Right leaders exhibits a wider geographical and cultural demeanor, that should have a substantial impact on both the style and the cultural expressions of the movement. In some ways, the incorporation of the Dutch Reformed tradition in the persons of Schaeffer and Rushdoony has already moved the Christian Right more out of the South and West and into middle America. Even so, in the popular mind, the movement is still identified with southern Fundamentalism.

A shift to a more diverse and cosmopolitan future leadership might also affect the monomythic character of the Christian Right's concept of culture and nationalism. Should that occur, however, the entire religious foundation of the movement would face a significant challenge. The very concept of American cultural superiority, for example, presumes a set of religious assumptions reflective of the values and mythos of only one segment of the American people. What makes the nation great, from the Christian Right perspective, is that it was conceived and born within a (Calvinist) Christian cultural consensus that accepted God's sovereignty over the nation and its people. Where the movement might cultivate greater diversity (and where it has begun to do so in the last decades of the twentieth century) is among persons of color and among Roman Catholics, Orthodox Jews, and Orthodox Christians who align their master protest frames with those of the Christian Right. The difficulty for these new recruits is that the mythos as presently constructed places all groups except white Protestants at a cultural disadvantage.

To the degree that people of color and non-Protestants have come into the movement, they have adjusted their protest frames to match those of the monomyth. This is one of the biggest problems the Christian Right faces in courting evangelical African Americans. That potential constituency is very much in line with biblical Christian and evangelical Protestant frames of reference, but the majority of the leadership of the African American religious community recognizes that the current ideological agenda of the Christian Right does not serve the best interests of African American people. The future ability of the Christian Right to effectively speak to this constituency is an important factor in the long-term success of the movement, and, recognizing that fact, the Christian Right has actively framed its rhetoric relating to educational initiatives to appeal to poor, inner-city African Americans trapped in failing schools. Colorado's Amendment 17 is a prime example of that strategy.

A third area where changes might occur in the Christian Right relates to the perceived effectiveness of the movement among its core constituents. As long as the Christian Right elite can achieve short-term objectives, the constituency will continue to accept their authority. Should the elite begin to fail, however, the adequacy of the entire canopy that defines the movement may be brought into question by dissatisfied activists at the grassroots level. The vulnerability of the movement to such challenges may have increased with the shift of the Christian Right center to the mythos and symbolic web derived from Schaeffer and Rushdoony, because the movement now rests on a set of presuppositions that are particular to one theological tradition, a radical form of Dutch Calvinism. The power of the movement to sustain that vision among the various religious traditions from which it draws its core membership is a key to the future success of the movement. One of the most significant developments within the movement in this regard is that James Dobson, born and raised in a strong Nazarene family, began attending a conservative Presbyterian church. In effect, Dobson has abandoned his own religious tradition because it has not been able to generate a set of protest frames that adequately express his ideological desire for a transformed America.

The problem for the movement is that its symbol engineers must construct the canopy in such a way that it speaks to constituents in religious traditions far removed from Calvinist theological presuppositions. Although no other religious constituency within the movement has yet offered a counter set of master protest frames, the possibility exists that in the future, one or more of these camps may rediscover the social component in their own doctrines and history. Should some within the holiness tradition, or any other constituent group, begin to construct an alternative set of effective protest frames, then the movement could either be pulled apart or forced to radically adapt its presuppositions. Thus, the perceived effectiveness of the Christian Right's leadership depends in part on whether the movement's elite can continue to successfully frame their worldview and agenda within a theological construct that is not native to most of the people that identify with the Christian Right at the grass roots.

Even if the movement is able to keep its deep symbols aligned with the various constituencies from which it draws its strength, it must also achieve at least limited success in transforming the culture in order to maintain the loyalty of its following. The leadership appears to be at a critical juncture in this regard. Given the enormous moral, emotional, and political capital the Christian Right has invested in the prolife issue, it has had only limited success in changing the larger culture in that area. The school wars therefore take on enormous significance.[5] If the leadership can demonstrate effectiveness in dismantling the present system of public education and produce, in its wake, a new social structure that allows Christian Right activists to achieve their educational goals, then the movement's elite will be able to point to a major success. This has not yet happened at the curricular or pedagogical level. With respect to structural changes in the institutions of public education, the Christian Right appears to be more successful. In particular, the leadership has achieved more than modest gains on the issue of schools of choice. Efforts at promoting parents' rights initiatives and public funding of religious schools as well as prayer and free religious expression in the schools have achieved more modest gains. In spite of all of these initiatives, though, the key to the Christian Right's success on the educational front is public funding of religious schools without government restrictions or accountability.

If the movement can achieve the goal of gaining public funds for sectarian schools, its chances of effecting the long-term transformation of the culture will improve significantly. Through such schools, Christian Right leaders stand a chance of influencing the ideational development of future generations because as the students mature and enter the public arena, they will take their frames of reference with them into the larger culture. The real power of such schools will be found in the way the mythos, symbols, and ritual processes that define the educational experience of students build a sense of shared identity among future generations of students. Through these processes, the movement culture should be strengthened and its impact in the larger society enhanced.

The Christian Right and Its Core Constituency

The Christian Right in its present incarnation—putting aside what it may look like in the future—gains its orientation and direction from the cultural theology of Schaeffer and the political theology of Rushdoony. To assess the degree to which the canopy that covers the movement might continue to hold and attract more participants from its core constituent groups, we return to a consideration of each of those groups, focusing, again, on their religious character and history. Pertinent to the topic of areas in which the movement might change in the future are the divisions that exist in each of these constituencies. A note of caution: the descriptions here presume a purity and independence for each tradition that exists only in an observer's mind. In reality, the lines between the subgroups is often far from clear. Further, in some cases the particular characteristics of these traditions have moved into the more mainstream denominations. Where they have, the likelihood for support for the Christian Right in the mainstream church will increase.

As a religious movement, Fundamentalism, the group that gave rise to the Christian Right in its earliest form, began in the last half of the nineteenth century as a negative response among conservative Christians to the growing influence of modernism in American Protestantism.[6] Fundamentalism and the Christian Right were born of the same religious impulse in the sense that Fundamentalism represented the religious challenge to modernism, whereas the early Christian Right expressed the cultural response. The symbolic roots of both movements grew from opposition to the publication of Charles Darwin's *Origin of the Species* in 1859. Darwin's book signaled what later fundamentalists identified as the most significant challenge to biblical authority up to that point in the history of American Christianity. His theory of evolution attacked conservative Protestantism at two important points. Besides challenging the literal interpretation of the first Genesis story of creation, it substituted scientific investigation for biblical revelation as the criterion by which truth claims are measured.

In subsequent years, biblical authority also came under attack from a quite different source, Higher Criticism. Beginning in German universities and then spreading to those in the United States, higher critics applied the secular methodologies of historical, literary, and cultural analysis to the Scriptures. As such secular forms of thought crept into mainstream churches, fundamentalists continued to withdraw and form their own churches and associations. When the new approach to knowledge moved into the public schools, the Christian Right was born as a reformative social movement. The first stirrings of the movement focused on keeping modernist ideas out of the science curricula in public schools. Fundamentalists attacked evolution in the courts, in the state legislatures, and through local school boards. A lack of willingness to compromise and a militant rhetoric characterized the movement during those battles. The undisputed leader of this protest against modernism was the populist leader William Jennings Bryan. When Bryan and Clarence Darrow confronted each other in the Scopes Trial in Dayton, Tennessee, in the summer of 1925, the event had lasting implications for both Fundamentalism and public education. The ridicule heaped on Bryan and Fundamentalism by Darrow and the northern press was a defeat from which Bryan never recovered; Fundamentalism took nearly a half-century thereafter to redefine its relationship to the larger culture.

Even well before the Scopes Trial, Fundamentalism began to divide into two camps. The first took the path of scholarly doctrinal defense of the faith against liberalism and modernism, revealing its commonality with the early Christian Right. It found its greatest expression in Princeton Theological Seminary under the leadership of Charles Hodge, Benjamin Warfield, and J. Gresham Machen. In this form, Fundamentalism continued to express a postmillennial vision of a redeemed Christian society in America. When liberals took control of the seminary in the 1920s, the remnant of the old Princeton Theology found a new home at Westminster Theological Seminary in Philadelphia. Here J. Gresham Machen and Cornelius Van Til instructed the future theologians of the Christian Right, Francis Schaeffer and Rousas John Rushdoony.

The other camp of fundamentalists took on a much more populist and premillennial form. Premillennialists held that Christians were still awaiting the Second Coming of Christ. When Christ returned at the end times, sinners would be punished and saints would be rewarded in heaven. Until then, humans could do nothing to redeem the world. Thus, efforts to transform society were fruitless. The most Christians could hope for was to keep the world from corrupting them. This view led populist fundamentalists to invest a great deal of energy in defining the points at which the evil of the world was most likely to impact them.

During the last decades of the nineteenth century, the dispensationalist teachings of John Nelson Darby also shaped the premillennialist wing of Fundamentalism. The core belief taught by Darby and other dispensationalists was that God had divided history into a series of ages, during each of which God "dispensed" a particular form of grace specific to that age. Combining a time line suggested in chapter 9 of the book of Daniel with the allegorical content of the book of Revelation, dispensationalists calculated the time of the promised Second Coming of Christ and concluded that the world was very near the end times. Popular premillennial dispensationalism became the dominant form of Fundamentalism in America, particularly in the South. Because of its premillennial flavor, this wing of the movement tended to be apolitical, preferring to wait for God to save the faithful and visit destruction on the sinners. A large segment of contemporary Fundamentalism continues to be resistant to the compromise in their beliefs that would be required if they became involved in a transformative social movement.

As premillennial fundamentalists moved into the economic mainstream of American culture in the third quarter of the twentieth century, however, their sense of responsibility for the larger culture reawakened. When Reagan operatives turned to the religious community for support for his presidential candidacy, fundamentalists were among the first to answer the call. Jerry Falwell formed the Moral Majority with Tim LaHaye as the head of its California chapter. Falwell and other fundamentalists did not escape criticism from the more strident premillennialist factions among southern fundamentalists. Nevertheless, the reemergence of the Christian Right in the 1980s owed a great deal to the leadership provided by populist fundamentalists.

The limitations the movement suffered under their leadership eventually required the Christian Right to go in a new direction. The most obvious problem was that the militant rhetoric of Falwell and other fundamentalists did not play well with the general public.[7] In addition, fundamentalists tended to be highly critical of other forms of conservative Protestantism. Fundamentalists and pentecostals, for example, feuded during much of the twentieth century. The final, and perhaps most important, limitation from the standpoint of a social movement was that Fundamentalism in its popular form lacked the necessary theological structure to take the movement from a norm-oriented reform movement into a value-oriented transformational social movement.

Characteristics peculiar to the holiness movement also present problems for the Christian Right.[8] From its beginnings in the first half of the nineteenth century, the holiness movement was not monolithic. Internal disputes reflected the multiple sources from which holiness perfectionism arose. Perhaps the most important theological point of dispute centered on the type of spiritual perfection Christians could expect to receive in this world, the degree to which they could reach the state of complete moral and spiritual perfection called "entire sanctification." Disagreements existed within holiness circles over the nature of that perfection. In one form, perfection referred to the individual's motivations and intent. As a result of the work of the Holy Spirit, the individual became free from voluntary transgressions against known laws of God. Sin was still possible. Perfection of this type did not extend to sinful acts derived from ignorance, error, infirmities, and temptations that led the individual to violate God's laws.[9] In a stronger version of perfectionism, entire or complete sanctification could be achieved by the individual in this world.[10] When sanctification was complete, the individual was no longer capable of sinning. Jim Bakker illustrated this belief. Even after his conviction for fraud, he was incapable of admitting his errors because he was convinced that he was beyond the capacity to sin. James Dobson's most substantial critic also reports that Dobson apparently reached the conclusion that he was entirely sanctified, beyond the capacity to sin.[11]

In the nineteenth century, segments of the holiness movement exhibited a rather strong social consciousness. Its people were involved in numerous social reforms, some related to improving the moral condition of society, others focused on assisting those who had material needs. These two emphases often came together in the form of rescue missions. Many holiness perfectionists were involved in the abolition movement; others took leadership roles in the numerous social reforms that characterized the last half of the nineteenth century. During these decades, however, holiness Christians increasingly found themselves in theological tension with mainstream Christians because of the holiness belief in the possibility of achieving moral and spiritual perfection. Mainstream Christian brothers and sisters increasingly viewed with disdain the cultivation of this higher life, and the tension eventually led to the separation of holiness Christians from the religious mainstream to form their own independent denominations. During the last years of the nineteenth century, many holiness Christians withdrew from participation in the social and cultural life of the nation as they were increasingly pushed to the culture's margins. In response, they generated their own movement culture in the form of a phalanx of schools, Bible colleges, summer camps, Bible conferences, and other activities that provided fellowship and legitimation.

During most of the twentieth century, holiness Protestants remained on the margins of the larger culture. In some holiness circles, education beyond that required by the state was seen as a threat to faith and was discouraged. In other circles, such as the one represented by James Dobson, education was valued even to the point where academic degrees provided legitimation to the faith. The relative position of holiness Christians to the larger culture began to change in the 1950s and 1960s, much as it happened with the fundamentalists. Holiness believers moved closer to the social and economic mainstream and began to feel they had a greater stake in the society. Dobson's growing political awareness and social involvement reflected, but did not lead, that trend. In moving deeper into the larger culture, many Christians within holiness circles recovered some of the social impulse that characterized the movement in its early decades.

To some degree, the perfectionist impulse within the holiness tradition, with its positive view of human nature, militates against the assumption that socially concerned holiness Protestants will naturally be drawn into the conservative political ideology of the Christian Right. Such persons are more likely to connect with the Christian Right on specific issues while remaining distant from the movement's larger dominionist agenda. The cultivation of the individual life of perfection leads others away from the social order and, by extension, away from the Christian Right. Nevertheless, for holiness Christians, the "home as a haven in a heartless world," remains the primary symbol of refuge and protection from the larger society. It is this powerful symbol that connects many holiness Christians with the Christian Right. Like popular Fundamentalism, however, the holiness tradition lacks a clearly articulated cultural or political theology. Therefore, entry into the movement forces many holiness Christians to draw on theological traditions with which they remain in tension.

Pentecostals also present problems for the Christian Right. Some of them are similar to those connected with the holiness movement, since pentecostalism grew out of that tradition in the early years of the twentieth century.[12] The exact origin of pentecostalism is a matter of some dispute, but scholars often cite two formative events. The first occurred at Charles F. Parham's Bethel Bible College in Topeka, Kansas, in 1900, when a student received the baptism of the Holy Spirit and began to speak in tongues. The second appeared in 1906, when a former African American apprentice of Parham's, William J. Seymour, sparked a series of revivals—continuing until 1929—at the Azusa Street Mission in Los Angeles. A small group involved in those revivals spoke in tongues. What the two occurences had in common was the ecstatic phenomenon of speaking in tongues. This became the distinguishing mark of the pentecostal movement.

A strong premillennialism characterized pentecostalism in its formative years. In those early decades, speaking in tongues had a different symbolic meaning than it took on later in the century. In its premillennial context, the gift of tongues was considered to be the means by which the Holy Spirit conveyed to humans the nearness of the end times. Certain that they were among those that God had chosen to save from the final conflagration, pentecostals were harsh in their condemnations of the culture. Pentecostalism began to change its character over the decades as its premillennial hope for the imminent return of Christ faded, and the symbolic meaning of the gift of tongues shifted to become the mark of a true Christian. Rather than continue to hope for a divinely transformed social order, in their disappointment many pentecostals turned inward to the subjective realization of the presence of God through the gifts of the Spirit.[13] For this reason, they share with dispensationalist fundamentalists a tendency to avoid political involvement.

As with other segments of conservative Protestantism, the gradual entry of pentecostals into the cultural mainstream during the last four decades of the twentieth century included a growing involvement in the political and social life of the nation. Premillennialism and ecstatic experience gradually gave way to a more positive view of the culture and a more restrained worship experience. Some of the largest megachurches in America, for example, are pentecostal. They feature theater-type seating and seem to cultivate a worship experience of warmth and praise rather than one of ecstatic utterances. In contrast, the sawdust trail of rural southern pentecostalism still expresses itself in a purer spiritual emotionalism. Because of their emphasis on experience rather than doctrine, pentecostals also did not develop the necessary cultural or political theology to sustain a social movement. Thus, the difficulties the Christian Right encounters in trying to garner support from pentecostals center around the need to politicize them and to generate for them a set of symbols or master protest frames that resonate with the pentecostal emphasis on spiritual experience. For pentecostals, the Christian Right needs to transform religious experience into political consciousness and will.

Born-again evangelicals present some of the same kinds of difficulties for the Christian Right as other groups do. Again, the specific challenges reflect the historical development of contemporary evangelicalism and the divisions within the evangelical camp. The born-again movement traces its roots to the dissatisfaction that arose in the 1930s in American Fundamentalism over dispensationalism's apocalyptic pessimism regarding the larger culture. Feeling that life was not as precarious as the dispensationalists suggested, evangelicals developed a more positive view of the world around them even while they continued to point out the sinfulness of the culture. The group that emerged as born-again evangelicals rejected the dispensationalist's insistence on the personal moral life at the cost of social involvement. They also expressed discomfort with the anti-intellectualism that characterized Fundamentalism's more populist and militant strains.

After World War II, these new evangelicals saw a unique opportunity to affirm a more positive view of society and, with the American victory, a chance to work toward the reestablishment of a Christian civilization.[14] In 1947, the neoevangelicals, as they were known, established Fuller Theological Seminary in Pasadena, California, to counter the more extreme dispensational tendencies within Fundamentalism. They remained steadfastly committed to biblical inerrancy and the militant defense of Christian doctrine, but their fight was more against militant Fundamentalism than modernism.[15] By the mid-1950s, Billy Graham emerged as their most important personality.

Although it is not easy to precisely describe born-again evangelicals, there are some characteristics that appear to be widely accepted. These include an experience of personal conversion, the inerrancy of the Scripture, and the expectation of a future apocalypse. Personal belief in the saving power of Jesus Christ is also central to the movement.[16] According to national surveys, about 40 percent of Americans identify themselves as born-again Christians. However, when the definition narrows to include a literal interpretation of the Bible and an effort to convert others to Christ, the proportion falls to about one-fifth to one-quarter of the population.[17]

While consistently theologically conservative, many born-again evangelicals, particularly African American evangelicals, are socially moderate or progressive. Evangelicals overwhelming supported the 1976 presidential candidacy of Jimmy Carter. Socially liberal evangelicals find expression in Jim Wallis and the Sojourner's attempts to recover the long tradition of constructive social activism within American evangelicalism. Even given this moderate-progressive strain within contemporary evangelicalism, most born-again evangelicals remain more politically and socially conservative than nonevangelical Protestants. Socially conservative born-again evangelicals who do identify with the Christian Right are just as likely to support the holiness work of James Dobson as the pentecostal ministry of Pat Robertson. Most, however, would not identify with the more militant fundamentalists like Jerry Falwell. Evangelicals are also most likely to be issue oriented in their support for the Christian Right and depart from the movement when its more strident theocultural agenda comes into view. They are quite supportive of improving the moral condition of society along lines compatible with Christian values, but they are less likely to force conformity to those values on other members of society or to demand that the Bible itself be used as the basis for social policy. For this reason, born-again evangelicals represent the most pivotal potential constituency for the Christian Right.

Roman Catholics are also a pivotal constituency for the Christian Right. As mentioned in chapter 5, on certain issues, such as abortion and the funding of private, religious, and parochial schools, socially conservative Catholics are likely to have common cause with the Christian Right. Phyllis Schlafly is the best example of this convergence. Nevertheless, there are some significant factors that limit Christian Right potential within the Catholic community. On the theological plain, the official Roman Catholic position on the Scriptures rejects a literal reading of the Bible but does affirm moral absolutes. On the historical front, Roman Catholics have long been the object of derision from conservative Protestants. This scorn comes at the level of both religious and ethnic identity. On the political level, Roman Catholics are among the most liberal segments of the American voting public. Because they reflect a working-class background, they are less likely to agree with the Christian Right on a host of economic issues from wages to unions. On the gender stage, divisions within the Roman Catholic church on the role and status of women have a direct relationship to the tendency of Catholics to identify with or reject the Christian Right deep symbol of the family. Finally, in the social realm, Roman Catholic political theology stands in stark contrast to the dominionist strains within the Christian Right. Despite all these reservations, on selected issues Catholics give strength to the Christian Right.

Reformed Christians constitute the final component of the movement's core. Support for the Christian Right is far from universal within this tradition even though, in many respects, it is theologically the closest. Significant voices such as George Marsden and Mark Noll suggest that the particular theologies that ground the movement are not characteristic of the Reformed tradition writ large. These differences are expressed in various ways. On the one hand, many in the Reformed tradition emphasize both doctrine and personal piety. They simply do not associate their faith with the kind and degree of political action the Christian Right entails. Others follow Abraham Kuyper's suggestion that a commitment to Christianity requires the application of biblical principles to all spheres of life, but they do not interpret it in dominionist terms. Kuyper himself seemed to advocate this approach.[18] In his view, the Christian worldview should guide Christian institutions and Christians should influence the public order. But Kuyper also recognized the value of religious pluralism in society and sought to respect it. Those who follow Kuyper in this respect attempt to shape their own religious institutions and influence the lives of their followers, but they do not believe that they should impose their worldview on the larger society.[19]

Within all of these traditions, there are elements of the Christian Right mythos and symbolic web that fit comfortably. That is why each group provides a significant constituency to the Christian Right. However, there are parts of the mythos and the symbolic web that stand in tension with each group. I have suggested the points of convergence and divergence, but up to this point I have ignored the relationship between these groups and the ritual dimension of the Christian Right. The connection here comes through most powerfully in the strong affective and moral components of religious life found in most of the traditions. When fundamentalist Tim LaHaye condemns the public schools for surrendering to the forces of secular humanism, fundamentalists begin taking up the sword of Christ. When Nazarene James Dobson warns his followers about the threats to the sanctity of the home, holiness Christians defend their moral boundaries. When pentecostal Pat Robertson identifies the Antichrist with the forces of public education, pentecostals prepare for the final conflagration. By tapping into these streams, the Christian Right's ritual generation of the rhetoric of an impending moral disaster and its provocation of conflict finds a compelling point of entry and a receptive audience. Under such rhetoric and in the midst of conflict, conservative Protestants on the margins of the movement may find themselves caught up in the power of the moment and become part of the movement, at least briefly. Whether these fellow travelers can be brought further into the movement depends on the degree to which local and state controversies can generate a movement culture in which the initial stirrings of support can be developed into normative and ideological bonds. Ritual, therefore, remains a powerful component of the religious resources the Christian Right brings to the culture wars.

Beyond the characteristics unique to each of these groups, perhaps the point at which support for the Christian Right pivots is in the attitudes of conservative Protestants toward connecting religion and the political order. Since the Christian Right worldview has such a strong positive view of this relationship, an examination of a typology that defines a number of different stances Protestant Christians can take on this issue may be of help. Although this typology was developed by Reformed Christians and relates specifically to that tradition, it applies as well to the wider subculture of theologically conservative Protestantism. In brief, two categories seem to describe those who do and do not identify with the Christian Right as a transformative social movement; *dominionism* and *principled pluralism*. Advocates of dominionism find common cause with the Christian Right, whereas principled pluralists do not.

Principled pluralists recognize and accept the religious and cultural pluralism of the nation. They confess that the world is not as it should be, but they do not believe that their faith should be normative for others in such a world. In one form of this position, *structural pluralists* argue that, although God established the various institutions of civic order, what qualifies persons to hold positions of authority within a given institution is not their religious faith but their competence at the tasks required of them in the fulfillment of their duties. As applied to public education, this means that what entitles a person to teach is her professional ability as an educator, not her religious faith. In another form, which sometimes overlaps with structural pluralism, *confessional pluralists* "confess" that Christians should be united into one church, but they accept the pluralistic nature of Christianity and the larger society, attributing such divisions among people to the existence of sin. Both forms of principled pluralism reject the idea that a particular faith or set of religious principles should be normative for all society.[20] Christians in these camps are not supportive of the Christian Right as a social movement even though they might be quite sympathetic to their analysis and criticisms of the social order.

Dominionists, however, do see Christianity as normative for the culture, but they do not always agree on what this implies. Some adopt a *Christian America* position, others a *theonomic* stance. Both are strongly represented in the Christian Right, although the Christian Americanists are far more numerous. Christian Americanists emphasize the Christian heritage of the United States even to the point of excluding any other major contributing influences. They further assert that their faith has a special legal status given to them by the nation's founders. The nation prospered, they argue, because a Christian consensus guided the country and because its political institutions were formed on the basis of biblical principles. That consensus has been lost to the forces of secularism and humanism, and as a nation, we have abandoned the biblical foundation that made America great. In order to restore the United States to its former glory, we need to recreate the Christian consensus and restore Christianity to its favored status. This means, in part, returning the nation to the biblical principles upon which its institutions are divinely intended to rest.[21]

Theonomists are much more specific about the particular character of a reconstructed American nation.[22] Agreeing with Christian Americanists about the need to exercise dominion over the nation, theonomists argue that literal Old Testament moral law ought to serve as the foundation for the country's legal system. They embrace democratic principles simply as the means by which biblical Christians can achieve dominion. Most theonomists believe that democracy itself is contrary to God's law. Civil laws, they continue, must correspond to biblical rules. Thus, anything that is immoral by biblical standards ought to be criminalized.[23] Rushdoony, a theonomist in this sense, argues that this includes the application of the death penalty for such offenses as adultery, homosexuality, and incorrigibility in children. Rushdoony's massive *Institutes of Biblical Law* explores in great detail the implications of the Ten Commandments literally applied for a reconstructed American society. When Christian Americanists carefully distance themselves from Rushdoony, it is because of the degree to which he embraces the theonomist position. Both Christian Americans and theonomists fit comfortably within the Christian Right, and all the movement's leaders can be found in one of these two categories. Again, what differentiates the pluralists from their dominionist counterparts is a rejection or acceptance of Schaeffer's theology of culture in combination with Rushdoony's political theology.

The Christian Right and the Larger Culture

What, then, are the Christian Right's prospects for success as a transformative social movement in the larger culture? The *consensus religion* of Americans is a key concept for this assessment, which continues to emphasize the religious dimension of the movement. Consensus religion means the common principles of the religions followed by the vast majority of Americans. These tenets stand at the center of the culture and have a profound influence on the character of the culture.[24] Since the founding of the colonies, the dominant source of consensus religion has been Protestantism. The influence of Protestantism in the shaping of our national consciousness has been so strong that some scholars believe it defines the parameters of the public life of the nation.[25]

Although Catholics, Jews, Native Americans, African traditionalists, Muslims, Orthodox Christians, Bahais, Shintoists, Hindus, Buddhists, New Agers, Pagans, and secularists may object to this emphasis on Protestantism, it is absolutely essential in assessing the adequacy of the Christian Right's mythos, symbolic web, and ritual processes. My assumption is that the points at which non-Protestants differ from the Christian Right will be far more obvious (and thus have less need to be articulated here) than the points at which the movement touches the heart and soul of the majority of Americans who are Protestants. Furthermore, since the national consciousness has been so strongly shaped by Protestantism, it is through an examination of that tradition that we can best assess the degree to which the Christian Right is likely to succeed or fail. The fact is that unless the Christian Right can penetrate consensus religion, it is doomed to fail as a religiously grounded transformative social movement.

We start with an observation that is central to our assessment of the Christian Right's prospects. From its colonial beginnings, America has always been religiously diverse. In addition to the numerous Native American cultures that existed in what became the colonies, the European emigrants brought to America's shores a number of fairly distinct religious traditions. There were Puritan Congregationalists, Baptists, Quakers, Anglicans, Roman Catholics, Moravians, Dutch and German Calvinists, Lutherans, Presbyterians, and Deists. During the colonial period, the consensus religion had a strong Calvinist flavor. In the eighteenth and nineteenth centuries, Methodists, Christians (Disciples of Christ), Latter-day Saints, Christian Scientists, Amish, Mennonites, Brethren, Shakers, Unitarians, Universalists, southern and eastern European Catholics and Jews, Buddhists, and Hindus joined the mix. If we add to these groups the various religious expressions that emerge from African American and Hispanic cultural traditions, it should be clear that the chief characteristic of American religion is its history of diversity growing ever more diverse. Set against the Christian Right's monomythic view of America, that diversity provides fairly compelling evidence that the foundations upon which that myth rests are historically inaccurate.

The Christian Right monomyth is not that simple, however. Its argument rests at the level of consensus religion, not at the level of the actual diversity of religious groups present in America. As it relates to consensus religion, the myth is somewhat more supportable, but only for a particular period of time. From the beginning of English colonization, the American religious consensus was strongly informed by Calvinism. The principles that defined that consensus are remarkably similar to those that define the contemporary Christian Right. A religious elite claimed a superior source of religious knowledge and authority and sought to shape society in accordance with their beliefs. But that consensus changed profoundly during the years between 1780 and 1830.

During those decades, the character of American consensus religion shifted dramatically away from the old republican worldview of a nation run by an aristocratic elite.[26] Calvinists, who embodied that elite, came under fierce attack from a new democratic form of Christianity that emphasized religious freedom, individual conscience, and the equality of all people. Some of their strongest criticism focused on the Calvinists' zeal for cultural dominance. This new democratic form of religion, represented by Methodists, Christians (Disciples of Christ), and Baptists, fought its own culture war against the Calvinist desire to conform society to its theological, ideological, and social standards. As Nathan Hatch describes it, "these Methodists, Christians, and Baptists were obsessed with Calvinist designs for social control."[27] The new populist, egalitarian form of religion that found its strength in the common person was so tolerant of diversity that in the years immediately following Jefferson's election in 1800, "it became anachronistic to speak of [religious] dissent in America."[28]

The new religious consensus differed profoundly from the old Calvinist culture in several important ways. It denied that any group of persons was of a separate class able to decide religious issues for any other group of persons. It further associated virtue with the ordinary person by taking actions at their face value rather than judging them by the religious standards of an elite. Finally, it rejected tradition and the past as a fount of wisdom.[29] The religious model that seemed most appropriate to this age was "that the first should be last, and that the chief should not lord it over others but become a servant of all."[30] Based on these religious principles, as well as similar ones derived from Baptists and Deists, the idea of religious liberty and freedom from religious coercion by the government or any single sectarian group was so much a part of the American consciousness that it became woven into the Constitution. By the time the Constitution was ratified, religious liberty was a reality legally, as well as theologically.[31]

When the French aristocrat Alexis de Tocqueville visited America in 1831, this new religious consensus was well in place. Thus, any interpretation of Tocqueville's observations about the role and significance of religion in American must be placed in this context rather than the context of the earlier Calvinist consensus. In his writing, Tocqueville emphasized the critical importance religion plays in a democratic society. Though in other ages the elite might have had the time and financial resources to pursue truth through reason, for the common person in American society this was not possible. Religion, therefore, fulfilled the practical function of restraining the individual impulse toward self-interest, redirecting human action to the common good. It was that utilitarian dimension of religion rather than a commitment to the superiority of a particular set of religious doctrines that Tocqueville found so impressive in America.[32]

The utilitarian emphasis on religion also found its way into the center of the common school movement that began about the same time as Tocqueville's visit. As one of the chief proponents of the common school movement, Horace Mann railed against the sectarian character of education in his day. Rather than to remove religion from the schools, Mann sought to incorporate it but in a generalized, albeit Protestant, form. Far from being a social radical, Mann viewed the schools as the chief means by which all segments of society could assimilate the values of the dominant Protestant consensus. The fact that he defined that consensus in broader terms than Calvinist orthodoxy led Calvinists to brand him an enemy of religion.[33] Mann's idea that the dominant cultural values of the American people should be transmitted through the schools via religion remained a central tenet of American education well into the twentieth century. For Mann, the importance of religion was to advance and inculcate moral values in school children. The end that inclusion of religion should serve was the promotion of the common good. Although Mann's insistence on a generalized rather than a sectarian form of Protestantism in the public schools was reflective of the principle of religious pluralism, his concept of the purpose of the public schools was still tied to the old Calvinist republicanism of the colonial period.[34] The translation of the moral utility of public education into a more egalitarian, democratic framework was left to John Dewey.[35]

From the Puritans forward, the principle of religious liberty has been a central feature of America's consensus religion, even if it did not always extend to religious tolerance for diversity in colonial New England. Tolerance for diversity did become a key element in consensus religion during the national period, when the consensus shifted to a more democratic foundation. Already mentioned are these important components of the consensus: a tendency toward anti-intellectualism, a search to simplify, and an inclination to define social problems in moral terms. In combination, these dispositions often characterize public school controversies. Thus, the Christian Right is reflective of some of the habits of the American heart, to use Robert Bellah's phrase. The Christian Right also finds support for its generation of conflict through incendiary populist rhetoric in the tradition of revivalism in American religion. Exhortation by charismatic figures to improve oneself and society morally and religiously was not only characteristic of the great preachers of the Great Awakenings in American history; it is also characteristic of the leadership of the contemporary Christian Right. The Christian Right embodies a number of key features of consensus American religion as it has developed historically, and in that sense it does represent the American mainstream.

Yet, alongside these tendencies rests another set of principles that contribute to the sometimes contradictory pattern of American consensus religion. Through the Enlightenment tradition, Americans came to value the power of reason even when placed in the hands of the common person. As Americans, we trust reason and believe that through it humans can learn to live with each other and in harmony with the divine creation. Reason may be seen as a contributing tool that has allowed us as a people to transcend the sectarian divisions that threaten to pull us apart. It is central to many of the strategies that well-meaning educators and citizens have brought to the table when confronted with local controversies over education. Faith in reason as a central part of public discourse can be found in segments of all the religious traditions.

Perhaps the best example of American consensus religion is found in modified religionists. Modified religionists see little or no distinction between the secular and the religious worlds. In particular, the symbol of secular humanism destroying religion in American culture does not fit into their frame of reference. Therefore, they simply do not experience the same incongruity that drives Christian Right leaders to condemn existing social institutions. Modified religionists who are public school teachers, for example, do not typically experience the same crisis of faith as Christian Right activists do when they have responsibility for teaching biology, sex education, and history lessons. Another characteristic of modified religionists is that they feel relatively at home in the larger culture.[36] At times, this leads to a complacency: they do not take seriously the very legitimate concerns and protests of others. At the same time, they are not likely to want to transform the social institutions and the presuppositions upon which they rest. In fact, their degree of comfort with the social order extends to the presuppositional level. A third feature of consensus religion as expressed in the lives of modified religionists is their respect for religion and its role in the development of the American nation. They hold dear cultural traditions that bind them to biblical principles such as those expressed in the Ten Commandments and the teachings of Jesus. They do not, however, hold themselves to a literal obedience to the laws of the Bible, and they understand the need for reinterpreting those teachings when appropriate to the historical and theological evidence.[37] Finally, modified religionists are inclusive of others, open to new ideas, tolerant of a diversity of persons and traditions. Those ideals are not always practiced by mainstream Americans, but when they are, those who call them to account on such issues stand a good chance of receiving a positive hearing.[38] Nevertheless, on these basic principles, the mythos and symbolic web of American consensus religion stands in stark contrast to that of the Christian Right.

In a curious way, one of the greatest strengths of the Christian Right is the degree to which its mythos, symbolic web, and ritual processes are reflective of American religion, both historically and in its contemporary expression. The Christian Right testifies to the enduring vitality of religion among the American people. It expresses the nation's attraction for populist leaders who appeal to the values and concerns of the common people. Jerry Falwell, Pat Robertson, and James Dobson in this sense continue the long tradition of democratic populism. Not only in its rhetoric but also in its goals, the Christian Right is a clear expression of the democratic impulse in American religion. The problem the Christian Right faces is that it represents the losing side of that tradition. Its theology and cultural vision stand on the side of the Calvinist elite who sought to control the culture. Thus, it stands outside the values that inform the democratic impulse in American Protestantism. It is democratic in style, not in substance.

We arrive at the question of the movement's future prospects again. That the Christian Right embodies many of the stylistic elements of the populist tradition in American religion places it in good stead for the future. That its grounding presuppositions run counter to that tradition bodes ill for the movement. The answer will depend on whether mainstream Americans are able to articulate a counter mythos and symbolic web that bring the more democratic character of consensus American religion to the arena of public discourse. It also depends on whether the financial and organizational resources of the Christian Right are able to sustain it as it uses conflict to generate a movement culture among its followers and to increase that number. When the Christian Right's presuppositionalism is turned on its head, as it was in the four case studies, and when the mainstream is willing and able to bring its considerable resources to the defense of democracy and the public system of American education, the Christian Right does not prosper.

Notes

NOTES TO THE INTRODUCTION

1. Tom Curry, "An Exodus from the Public Schools? Call for 5 Million Students to Quit Public Schools by Year 2000" (MSNBC, 1997), web site, www.msnbc.com/news/124752.asp.

2. Doug McAdam and David A. Snow, "Introduction—Social Movements: Conceptual and Theoretical Issues," in *Social Movements: Readings on Their Emergence, Mobilization, and Dynamics*, ed. Doug McAdam and David A. Snow (Los Angeles: Roxbury, 1997), xviii.

3. Anthony F. C. Wallace, *Religion: An Anthropological View* (New York: Random House, 1966), 36, 38, 39.

4. Neil Smelser draws a distinction between "value-oriented" and "norm-oriented" social movements. Norm-oriented movements seek specific, limited changes within the social system, particularly in relation to who has access to what in the society. Value-oriented movements seek more fundamental change. They attempt to alter the basic values and institutional foundation upon which the society rests. See Neil Smelser, *Theory of Collective Behavior* (New York: Free Press of Glencoe, 1962).

5. For a discussion of this approach to revitalization movements, see Melissa A. Pflüg, *Ritual and Myth in Odawa Revitalization: Reclaiming a Sovereign Place* (Norman: University of Oklahoma Press, 1998), 239–43.

6. For a discussion of transformative social movements, see David Aberle, "The Prophet Dance and Reactions to White Contact," *Southwest Journal of Anthropology* 15, no. 1 (1959): 74–83.

7. This is a term often used by Christian Right writers to describe the larger religious constituency from which the movement draws most of its core constituency. We will see later that further divisions exist within that group.

8. For a discussion of these modifications, see Ronald L. Numbers, *The Creationists: The Evolution of Scientific Creationism* (Berkeley: University of California Press, 1992), 3–101.

9. Bridgebuilders is run by Wayne Jacobsen, a fundamentalist minister. His group consults with public school districts to reduce conflicts between conservative Christian parents and the schools. See the Bridgebuilders web page at www.lifestream.org.

10. I borrow this term from Fred Clarkson, "Wildmon Kingdom," *Mother Jones,* November–December 1990, 11. The term is particularly descriptive of the Christian Right because of the way it fuses specific theological and political ideologies together.

11. Evangelical Protestants are distinguished by their belief in the full authority of the Scriptures, the necessity of a conversion experience as a means to salvation, and the necessity of evangelism. See Louise J. Lorentzen, "Evangelical Life Style Concerns Expressed in Political Action," in *Religion North American Style,* ed. Patrick H. McNamara, 2d ed. (Belmont, Calif.: Wadsworth, 1984), 230.

12. Two themes seemed to dominate this early phase. Politically active Christian fundamentalists did experience some success in counteracting the encroachment of modernism in southern public schools. The Scopes Trial in Dayton, Tennessee, is the archetypal example of these skirmishes. Even when the Christian activists did succeed in getting several states to pass legislation mandating creationism, the courts eventually reversed many of these victories. In later decades, fervent opposition to communism dominated the attention of fundamentalist Christian activists. Even though the spirit of their crusade worked its way into national politics, culminating with Sen. Joseph McCarthy's hearings, the religious organizations that carried this torch never achieved national prominence. For a discussion of the modernist issue, see George M. Marsden, *Fundamentalism and American Culture* (New York: Oxford University Press, 1980). For a discussion of the anticommunist crusade, see Clyde Wilcox, *God's Warriors: The Christian Right in Twentieth-Century America* (Baltimore: Johns Hopkins University Press, 1992).

13. Pentecostals/charismatics emphasize spiritual gifts such as "speaking in tongues" as the mark of the Christian life. Holiness Christians emphasize spiritual and moral perfection through a baptism of the Holy Spirit known as "entire sanctification." Reformed Christians trace their theological orientation to the writings of the French/Swiss reformer John Calvin and to John Knox in England and Scotland. Born-again evangelicals stress a explicit conversion experience in which believers accept Jesus Christ as their personal savior. These distinctions will be developed in fuller detail in a later chapter.

14. For a history of the Christian Right, see Wilcox, *God's Warriors;* and William Martin, *With God on Our Side: The Rise of the Religious Right in America* (New York: Broadway Books, 1996). For a detailed examination of the organizational, political, and technological maturation of the Christian Right, see Matthew C. Moen, *The Transformation of the Christian Right* (Tuscaloosa: University of Alabama Press, 1992).

15. See, for example, Mark J. Rozell and Clyde Wilcox, eds, *God at the Grass Roots, 1996: The Christian Right in the 1996 Elections* (Lanham, Md.: Rowman and Littlefield, 1997); John C. Green, ed., *Religion and the Culture Wars: Dispatches from the Front* (Lanham, Md.: Rowman and Littlefield, 1996); Bruce Nesmith, *The New Republican Coalition: The Reagan Campaigns and White Evangelicals,* series X, American

University Studies, vol. 41 (New York: Peter Lang, 1994); Robert Booth Fowler and Allen D. Hertzke, *Religion and Politics in America: Faith, Culture, and Strategic Choices* (Boulder: Westview Press, 1995); and Justin Watson, *The Christian Coalition: Dreams of Restoration, Demands for Recognition* (New York: St. Martin's Press, 1997).

16. Throughout this work I will use the phrase *culture war* to characterize the social mobilization of the Christian Right. Although scholars provide varying interpretations of the movement, I employ *culture war* because the military metaphor appears more frequently than other terms in the literature of Christian Right organizations. For a discussion of alternative perspectives, see Fowler and Hertzke, *Religion and Politics,* 236–51. For criticism of the culture war metaphor, see Robert D. Woodberry and Christian Smith, "Fundamentalism et al.: Conservative Protestants in America," *Annual Reviews of Sociology* 24 (1998): 42–44.

17. For a discussion of the rhetoric and moral concerns of the Christian Right, see James Davison Hunter, *Culture Wars: The Struggle to Define America* (New York: Basic Books, 1991); Michael Lienesch, *Redeeming America: Piety and Politics in the New Christian Right* (Chapel Hill: University of North Carolina Press, 1993); and Warren A. Nord, *Religion and American Education: Rethinking a National Dilemma* (Chapel Hill: The University of North Carolina Press, 1995).

18. See, for example, Jaroslav Pelikan, "Fundamentalism and/or Orthodoxy? Toward an Understanding of the Fundamentalist Phenomenon," in *The Fundamentalist Phenomenon,* ed. Norman J. Cohen (Grand Rapids, Mich.: Eerdmans, 1990), 3–21; Erling Jorstad, *The New Christian Right, 1981–1988* (Lewiston, N.Y.: Edward Mellon Press, 1987); and Lloyd Averill, *Religious Right, Religious Wrong: A Critique of the Fundamentalist Phenomenon* (New York: Pilgrim Press, 1989).

19. Catherine A. Lugg, *For God and Country: Conservatism and American School Policy* (New York: Peter Lang, 1996), 87.

20. Moen, *Transformation,* 16–17.

21. Pat Robertson is an exception to this scenario. Instead of being used by the Republican Party to further its political agenda, Robertson used the Republican Party to facilitate his political ambitions. Robertson's immense power as a televangelist puts him in a separate class from the other Christian Right leaders courted by the Republicans.

22. Woodberry and Smith acknowledge this problem and seek to solve it in "Fundamentalism et al."

23. For a discussion of the social dimensions of the Christian Right, see Hunter, *Culture Wars,* and Lienesch, *Redeeming America.*

24. For a comparison between the Christian Right and historic evangelical Protestantism, see Gabriel Fackre, *The Religious Right and Christian Faith* (Grand Rapids, Mich.: Eerdmans, 1982); Jorstad, *The New Christian Right;* Walter H. Capps, *The New Religious Right: Piety, Patriotism, and Politics* (Columbia: University of South Carolina Press, 1990); Averill, *Religious Right;* and Pelikan, "Fundamentalism."

25. Robert Conover, comments on C-Span's *Washington Journal,* October 28, 1998.

26. Gerardus van der Leeuw, *Religion in Essence and Manifestation: A Study in Phenomenology,* trans. J. E. Turner (New York: Harper and Row, 1963), 1:23–28.

27. Peter Berger and Thomas Luckmann, *The Social Construction of Reality: A Treatise in the Sociology of Knowledge* (New York: Anchor Books, 1966), 73–76.

28. Capps, *The New Religious Right.*

29. See Pflüg, *Ritual and Myth in Odawa Revitalization.*

30. See Jonathan Z. Smith, "The Bare Facts of Ritual," in *Imagining Religion: From Babylon to Jonestown,* ed. Jonathan Z. Smith (Chicago: University of Chicago Press, 1982), 53–65. For a general discussion of the role of crisis and conflict in social movements, see Lewis Coser, *The Functions of Social Conflict* (New York: Free Press, 1956); and Kenelm Burridge, *New Heaven, New Earth: A Study of Millenarian Activities* (New York: Schocken Books, 1969).

31. Mel and Norma Gabler have been active in providing Christian Right activists with such an analysis of public school textbooks since they first gained national attention in the 1961 textbook battle in Kanawha County, Illinois. Since 1975, their Educational Research Analysts has become the primary national clearinghouse for Christian Right assessments of textbook content. See Carol Flake, *Redemptorama: Culture, Politics, and the New Evangelicalism* (Garden City, N.Y.: Anchor Press, Doubleday, 1984), 39–40; and Roy Eleutherios Grimm, "'Community Impact Evangelism' and Pluralism in Public Education," Ph.D. diss., University of Colorado, 1991, 109. See also Nord, *Religion,* 138–59 for a detailed discussion of the issue.

32. See Nord, *Religion,* 199–235.

33. This practice appears to be fairly widespread. In my conversations with educators throughout the country, when I have raised this issue, they have concurred that it has happened in their districts more than a few times.

34. For a detailed analysis of this strategy, see David C. Berliner and Bruce J. Biddle, *The Manufactured Crisis: Myths, Fraud, and the Attack on America's Public Schools* (Reading, Mass.: Addison-Wesley, 1995); Lugg, *For God and Country.*

NOTES TO CHAPTER 1

1. Gerardus van der Leeuw, *Religion in Essence and Manifestation: A Study in Phenomenology,* trans. J. E. Turner (New York: Harper and Row, 1963), 1:157.

2. "Tao Te Ching," trans. and comp. Wing-tsit Chan, in *A Source Book in Chinese Philosophy* (Princeton, N.J.: Princeton University Press, 1963), 139. I have modified the text from "Tao" to "Dao" to conform to the presently accepted canons of the Pinyin system.

3. See Mircea Eliade, *The Sacred and the Profane* (New York: Harcourt Brace Jovanovich, 1957).

4. Most Hindus and many Mahayana Buddhists would disagree with this phrasing. For Hindus, *atman* exists at our very center, not outside us. For certain Buddhists, the Buddha nature is in us as our essential self. In both cases, however, the quality of *atman,* or our Buddha nature, is something that transcends our ordinary awareness. In this sense, it transcends our normal apprehension of the world.

5. For a detailed discussion of the problem of evil, see Paul Ricouer, *The Symbolism of Evil,* trans. Emerson Buchanan (Boston: Beacon Press, 1967).

6. See Julia Mitchell Corbett, *Religion in America*, 3d ed. (Upper Saddle River, N.J.: Prentice-Hall, 1997), 20.

7. Leeuw, *Religion,* 28.

8. James C. Dobson and Gary L. Bauer, *Children at Risk: The Battle for the Hearts and Minds of Our Kids* (Dallas: Word, 1990), 183.

9. Alan Watts, "Psychedelics and Religious Experience," *California Law Review* 56, no. 1 (1968): 74–85, web site, www.druglibrary.org/schaffer/lsd/watts.htm.

10. Peter Berger and Thomas Luckmann, *The Social Construction of Reality: A Treatise in the Sociology of Knowledge* (New York: Anchor Books, 1966), 67–68.

11. Robert Redfield, cited in A. Irving Hallowell, "Ojibwa Ontology, Behavior, and World View," in *Teachings from the American Earth,* ed. Dennis Tedlock and Barbara Tedlock (1975; reprint, New York: Liveright, 1992), 142.

12. For a discussion of these questions, see Roger Schmidt, *Exploring Religion* (Belmont, Calif.: Wadsworth, 1980), 29–36.

13. Jacqueline Suthern Hirst, "Hinduism," in Holm and Bowker, *Myth and History,* 69.

14. Ibid., 69.

15. See Berger and Luckmann, *Social Construction,* 124; and Ninian Smart, *Worldviews: Crosscultural Explorations of Human Beliefs,* 2d ed. (Englewood Cliffs, N.J.: Prentice-Hall, 1995), 2.

16. Peter Berger, *The Sacred Canopy: Elements of a Sociological Theory of Religion* (Garden City, N.Y.: Doubleday, 1967), 27.

17. Ibid.

18. Lawrence S. Cunningham, John Kelsay, R. Maurice Barineau, and Heather Jo McVoy, *The Sacred Quest: An Invitation to the Study of Religion* (New York: Macmillan, 1991), 46.

19. For a discussion of the issues involved in the question of the source of moral values, see ibid., 163–66.

20. Bill Moyers, "God and Politics: On Earth as It Is in Heaven," produced by Gregg Pratt and Jan Falstad (Public Affairs Television, 1987).

21. See Arnold van Gennep, *The Rites of Passage* (London: Routledge and Kegan Paul, 1960; originally published in 1908); and Victor Turner, *The Ritual Process* (London: Routledge, 1969). Van Gennep and sociologist Emile Durkheim were interested in the social construction of ritual. Turner emphasizes the possibility of creativity,

which ritual creates. In this sense he uses van Gennep as a critique of Durkheim by transforming ritual into a critique of the status quo.

22. See Jonathan Z. Smith, "The Bare Facts of Ritual," in *Imagining Religion: From Babylon to Jonestown,* ed. Jonathan Z. Smith (Chicago: University of Chicago Press, 1982), 53–65; and Jonathan Z. Smith, *To Take Place: Toward Theory in Ritual* (Chicago: University of Chicago Press, 1987).

23. Leeuw, *Religion,* 192.

24. Clifford Geertz, *Islam Observed* (New Haven, Conn.: Yale University Press, 1968), 116.

25. Ibid., 122.

26. Smith, "Bare Facts," 63, emphasis deleted from the original. See also Smith, *To Take Place,* 74–96.

27. For a discussion of these three phases, see Gennep, *The Rites of Passage;* and Turner, *The Ritual Process.*

28. Victor Turner, *The Forest of Symbols* (Ithaca, N.Y.: Cornell University Press, 1967), 30.

29. Victor Turner, *The Anthropology of Performance* (New York: PAJ, 1986), 44.

30. Robert L. Simonds, *A Guide to the Public Schools: For Christian Parents and Teachers, and Especially for Pastors* (Costa Mesa, Calif.: NACE/CEE, 1993), 12.

31. Colleen McDannell provides an insightful discussion of the application of this point to Christian home schooling. See Colleen McDannell, "Creating the Christian Home: Home Schooling in Contemporary America," in *American Sacred Space,* eds. David Chidester and Edward T. Linenthal (Bloomington: Indiana University Press, 1995), 187–219.

32. Clifford Geertz, *The Interpretation of Cultures* (New York: Basic Books, 1973), 46.

33. Kathi Hudson, *Reinventing America's Schools: A Practical Guide to Components of Restructuring and Non-Traditional Education,* rev. ed. (Costa Mesa, Calif.: NACE/CEE, 1993), 1:5–6.

34. Ricouer, *Symbolism,* 15.

35. George E. Tinker, *Missionary Conquest: The Gospel and Native American Cultural Genocide* (Minneapolis: Fortress Press, 1993), 113–14.

36. Edward Farley, *Deep Symbols: Their Postmodern Effacement and Reclamation* (Valley Forge, Pa.: Trinity Press International, 1996), 1.

37. Tom F. Driver, *The Magic of Ritual: Our Need for Liberating Rites That Transform Our Lives and Our Communities* (New York: HarperSanFrancisco, 1991), 24.

38. George Gallup, Jr., and Jim Castelli, *The People's Religion: American Faith in the 90's* (New York: Macmillan, 1989), 6.

39. Ibid., 5.

40. "Latest Religious Preferences," *Emerging Trends* 19, no. 3 (March 1997): 3.

41. See J. Gordon Melton, ed., *The Encyclopedia of American Religions: A Com-*

prehensive Study of the Major Religious Groups in the United States and Canada, 3 vols. (Tarrytown, N.Y.: Triumph Books, 1991).

42. "Redeeming right" suggests the transformative dimension of the religious impulse within conservative Christianity in American culture. Religionists in this camp define transformation both in individual and cultural terms. For a description of the redemptive dimension of the Christian Right, see Justin Watson, *The Christian Coalition: Dreams of Restoration, Demands for Recognition* (New York: St. Martin's Press, 1997).

43. In the context of American culture in the 1990s, my categories correspond roughly to H. Richard Niebuhr's "Christ of culture," "Christ in tension with culture," and "Christ against culture." See H. Richard Niebuhr, *Christ and Culture* (New York: Harper and Row, 1951).

44. Center for National Policy, "Squaretable Discussion on 'The Diminishing Divide: American Churches, American Politics'" (Washington, D.C., 1997), web site, www.access.digex.net/cnp/relchat4.html.

45. This rejection is not complete. Redeeming right religionists both adapt and adopt parts of modern culture while rejecting other elements on the basis of a fundamental incompatibility with biblical faith. For a discussion of the antimodernist character of conservative Protestantism in America, see Bruce B. Lawrence, *Defenders of God: The Fundamentalist Revolt against the Modern Age* (1989; reprint, Columbia: University of South Carolina Press, 1995); and George M. Marsden, *Fundamentalism and American Culture* (New York: Oxford University Press, 1980). For a discussion of the counter position, which argues that redeeming right religionists blend Christian and secular ideas, see McDannell, "Creating the Christian Home"; and Belinda Bollar Wagner, *God's Schools: Choice and Compromise in American Society* (New Brunswick, N.J.: Rutgers University Press, 1990).

46. Part of the difficulty in determining precise statistics is that the numbers change significantly according to how questions about religious beliefs are worded. See, for example, Warren A. Nord, *Religion and American Education: Rethinking a National Dilemma* (Chapel Hill: University of North Carolina Press, 1995), 57; Corbett, *Religion,* 19–20; Robert Wuthnow, *The Restructuring of American Religion: Society and Faith since World War II* (Princeton, N.J.: Princeton University Press, 1988), 165; and Garry Wills, *Under God: Religion and American Politics* (New York: Touchstone, 1990), 388.

47. See James Davison Hunter, *Evangelicalism: The Coming Generation* (Chicago: University of Chicago Press, 1987); and Mark A. Shibley, *Resurgent Evangelicalism in the United States: Mapping Cultural Change since 1970* (Columbia: University of South Carolina Press, 1996).

48. See Hunter, *Evangelicalism,* 19–75.

49. "Latest Religious Preferences," 3.

50. Berger and Luckmann, *Social Construction,* 25.

NOTES TO CHAPTER 2

1. For a discussion of the role Reagan played in advancing the Christian Right as a political force, see Matthew C. Moen, *The Christian Right and Congress* (Tuscaloosa: University of Alabama Press, 1989), 50–56.

2. Sara Diamond, *Spiritual Warfare: The Politics of the Christian Right* (Boston: South End Press, 1989), 66.

3. See Peter Berger, *The Sacred Canopy: Elements of a Sociological Theory of Religion* (Garden City, N.Y.: Doubleday, 1967).

4. Jonathan Z. Smith, "A Pearl of Great Price and a Cargo of Yams," in *Imagining Religion: From Babylon to Jonestown,* ed. Jonathan Z. Smith (Chicago: University of Chicago Press, 1982), 101.

5. Ibid., 100–101.

6. See Lewis Coser, *The Functions of Social Conflict* (New York: Free Press, 1956); David Aberle, "The Prophet Dance and Reactions to White Contact," *Southwest Journal of Anthropology* 15, no. 1 (1959): 74–83; and Kenelm Burridge, *New Heaven, New Earth: A Study of Millenarian Activities* (New York: Schocken Books, 1969).

7. I have borrowed this term from Robert Jewett and John Lawrence, who use it in another context. See *The American Monomyth* (Garden City, N.Y.: Anchor/Doubleday, 1977).

8. Cited in "The Christian Coalition," *Washington Spectator,* 15 October 1994, 3.

9. Rus Walton, *One Nation under God* (Nashville, Tenn.: Thomas Nelson, 1987), 24.

10. Cited in Robert Wuthnow, *The Restructuring of American Religion: Society and Faith since World War II* (Princeton, N.J.: Princeton University Press, 1988), 246.

11. Tim LaHaye, *The Battle for the Mind* (Old Tappan, N.J.: Revell, 1980), 26.

12. For example, see Rousas John Rushdoony, *The Messianic Character of American Education* (1963; reprint, Nutley, N.J.: Craig Press, 1972), 2, 18, 31; Tim LaHaye, *Faith of Our Founding Fathers: A Comprehensive Study of America's Christian Foundations* (1987; reprint, Green Forest, Ark.: Master Books, 1994), 26; and Blair Adams, *Who Owns the Children? Public Compulsion, Private Responsibility, and the Dilemma of Ultimate Responsibility,* 5th ed. (Waco, Tex.: Truth Forum, 1991; originally published in 1983), 122.

13. See Rushdoony, *Messianic Character,* 96–97, 145–60; and LaHaye, *Battle for the Mind,* 37.

14. Gerald Bracey and David Berliner and David Biddle dispute the report's conclusions. See David C. Berliner and Bruce J. Biddle, *The Manufactured Crisis: Myths, Fraud, and the Attack on America's Public Schools* (Reading, Mass.: Addison-Wesley, 1995); Gerald Bracey, "Why Can't They Be Like We Were?" *Phi Delta Kappan,* October 1991, 104–17; Gerald Bracey, "The Second Bracey Report on the Condition of Public Education," *Phi Delta Kappan,* October 1992, 104–17;

Gerald Bracey, "The Third Bracey Report on the Condition of Public Education," *Phi Delta Kappan,* October 1993, 104–17; Gerald Bracey, "The Fourth Bracey Report on the Condition of Public Education," *Phi Delta Kappan,* October 1994, 114–27.

15. Pat Robertson, "Is America Headed for Judgment?" television broadcast (Christian Broadcasting Network), web site, www.cbn.org/pat/pat-judgment.asp.

16. Pat Robertson, "Pat's Perspective: Violence in Schools," television broadcast (Christian Broadcasting Network, 1998), web site, www.cbn.org/news/stories/980527c.asp?h1=pat&h2=archives.

17. Michael Farris, "Living Room or Classroom? A Look at the Home School Movement," television broadcast (Christian Broadcasting Network, 1998), web site, www.cbn.org/news/stories/980902.asp.

18. "The 'Dumbing Down' of American Education," television broadcast (Christian Broadcasting Network, 1998), web site, www.cbn.org/news/stories/980515.asp.

19. See Pat Robertson, *The New World Order* (Dallas: Word, 1991).

20. See, for example, Pat Robertson, *The New Millennium* (Dallas: Word, 1990); Robertson, *New World Order;* and Pat Robertson, *The Turning Tide: The Fall of Liberalism and the Rise of Common Sense* (Dallas: Word, 1993).

21. Julie Ingersoll drew this point to my attention. See "Train Up a Child: A Study of Evangelical Views on Education," master's thesis, George Washington University, 1990, 28–29.

22. Cited in James Davison Hunter, *Culture Wars: The Struggle to Define America* (New York: Basic Books, 1991), 204.

23. Cited in ibid., 202.

24. The shift was not entirely voluntary for Robertson. Robertson and the Freedom Council were forced to abandon their efforts because the Internal Revenue Service ruled that the Freedom Council's activities violated the provisions governing its tax status.

25. Cited in Skipp Porteous, "Christian Coalition Update," *Free Inquiry* 12, no. 2 (spring 1992): 16.

26. Cited in David Hill, "Christian Soldier," *Teacher Magazine,* October–November 1992, 20.

27. Cited in Lawrence I. Barrett, "Fighting for God and the Right Wing," *Time,* 13 September 1993, 59–60.

28. Ralph Reed, Jr., *Politically Incorrect* (Dallas: Word, 1994).

29. Duane M. Oldfield, *The Right and the Righteous: The Christian Right Confronts the Republican Party* (Lanham, Md.: Rowman and Littlefield, 1996), 226.

30. Conservative commentator Michael Medved positions Reed "on the far left of the Christian Coalition." Cited in Jeremy Lott, "Why the Religious Right Will Win" (Intellectual Capital, 1998), web site, www.intellectualcapital.com/issues/98/0924/iccon.asp.

31. "Money, Membership Woes Drive Christian Coalition's Agenda" (Washington, D.C.: People for the American Way, 1998), E-mail press release, presslst@ pfaw.org.

32. "Christian Coalition Names New President and Executive Director: A New Era Dawns with New Leaders Who Link the Reagan Revolution with the Rising Influence of Active People of Faith" (Chesapeake, Va.: Christian Coalition, 1997), web site, www.cc.org/publications/ccnews/ccnews97.html#tate. Don Hodel resigned as president of the Christian Coalition in February 1999, for reasons that are not clear. The *Washington Times* and James Dobson report that it was over a disagreement with Pat Robertson over whether the Christian Coalition should forge ahead with a more purist approach (Hodel) or a more pragmatic approach (Robertson). For a comparative discussion of this issue, see Lawrence Morahan, "Update—Hodel Resignation not Related to Clinton Trial, Christian Coalition Says" (Conservative News Service, 1999), web site, www .conservativenews.net/InDepth/archive/199902/IND19990210g.html; and Jeff Johnson, "Controversy at Christian Coalition" (Colorado Springs, Colo.: Family News in Focus), web site, www.family.org/cforum/fnif/news/a0004748.html. A search for information on the Hodel resignation on the Christian Coalition website on 30 March 1999 was not successful.

33. Mark J. Rozell and Clyde Wilcox, "Conclusion: The Christian Right in Campaign '96," in *God at the Grass Roots, 1996: The Christian Right in the 1996 Elections,* ed. Mark J. Rozell and Clyde Wilcox (Lanham, Md.: Rowman and Littlefield, 1997), 264.

34. Peter Steinfels, "Why Psychologist without a Pulpit Is Called Religious Right's New Star," *New York Times,* 5 June 1990.

35. Cited in Matthew C. Moen, *The Transformation of the Christian Right* (Tuscaloosa: University of Alabama Press, 1992), 62.

36. Gil Alexander-Moegerle, *James Dobson's War on America* (Amherst, N.Y.: Prometheus Books, 1997), 14–15.

37. See Focus on the Family web page at www.fotf.org/welcome/aboutfof/ A0000090.html.

38. Alexander-Moegerle, *Dobson's War,* 14–15.

39. For example, a search of the indexes of recent representative writings on the Christian Right reveals a strong bias toward Robertson. Fowler and Hertzke have 4 references for Dobson and 11 for Robertson. Robert Booth Fowler and Allen D. Hertzke, *Religion and Politics in America: Faith, Culture, and Strategic Choices* (Boulder: Westview Press, 1995). Wilcox has 2 for Dobson and 36 for Robertson. Clyde Wilcox, *Onward Christian Soldiers? The Religious Right in American Politics* (Boulder: Westview Press, 1996). Moen has 8 for Dobson (who is incorrectly identified as a "fundamentalist minister") and 33 for Robertson. Moen, *Transformation;* Lienesch has 3 for Dobson and 74 for Robertson. Michael Lienesch, *Re-*

deeming America: Piety and Politics in the New Christian Right (Chapel Hill: University of North Carolina Press, 1993).

40. Alexander-Moegerle, *Dobson's War,* 12.

41. James C. Dobson and Gary L. Bauer, *Children at Risk: The Battle for the Hearts and Minds of Our Kids* (Dallas: Word, 1990), 19.

42. Ibid., 19–20.

43. Ibid., 37.

44. Ibid.

45. James C. Dobson, *Focus on the Family Letter,* May 1994, 6.

46. James C. Dobson, "Dr. Dobson's Study," *Focus on the Family Newsletter,* April 1998, web site, www.family.org/docstudy/newsletters/a0001274.html.

47. Dobson, *Focus on the Family Letter,* 6.

48. Francis Beckwith, "Is Public Education Really Neutral?" *Teachers in Focus,* October 1998, web site, www.family.org/cforum/teachersmag/features/a0002814.html.

49. Dobson, *Focus on the Family Letter,* 6.

50. Rosalie Beck and David W. Hendon, "Notes on Church State Affairs," *Journal of Church and State* 36, no. 2 (spring 1994): 443.

51. Dobson and Bauer, *Children at Risk,* 16.

52. James C. Dobson, "Dr. Dobson Answers Your Questions," *Focus on the Family,* February 1994, 7.

53. Cited in John Whitehead, *The Rights of Religious Persons in Public Education,* rev. ed. (Wheaton, Ill.: Crossway Books, 1994), 31.

54. Stephen S. Gottlieb, "The Right to Read: Censorship in the School Library," in *ERIC Digest* (Bloomington, Ind.: ERIC Clearinghouse on Reading and Communication Skills, 1990).

55. James C. Dobson, *Citizen* 6, no. 7 (July 1992): 2.

56. The National Association of Christian Educators and Citizens for Excellence in Education are technically separate organizations, although the lines between the two are not always clear in organizational publications. NACE focuses on teachers. In the early years, Simonds evidently hoped that it would become an alternative to the National Education Association for conservative Christian teachers. CEE's focus is on parents and concerned citizens; it encourages the formation of local chapters. Since most of the controversies involving Simonds's organization were spawned by CEE materials and chapters, I will refer to it without linking it to NACE.

57. Robert L. Simonds, *Communicating a Christian World View in the Classroom* (Costa Mesa, Calif.: National Association of Christian Educators, 1983), i.

58. Cited in Roy Eleutherios Grimm, "'Community Impact Evangelism' and Pluralism in Public Education," Ph.D. diss., University of Colorado, 1991, 145.

59. Ibid.

60. Ibid.

61. Ibid., 214.

62. Robert L. Simonds, "Newsletter," in *President's Report* (Costa Mesa, Calif.: NACE/CEE, 1994), 3.

63. Robert L. Simonds, *President's Report,* July 1994, 3. "Real" thinking skills here refers to teaching students to identify and apply the internal logic of a closed worldview, the Christian worldview, to the content of all the courses offered. It does not include what progressive educational reformers mean by "higher order thinking," tolerance for diverse ideas, or acceptance of ambiguity.

64. Telephone conversation with Bonnie Dana, assistant superintendent of DeForest, Wisconsin, public school, 15 May 1996. Dana was doing research on the Spady-Simonds project and gained this information from a telephone conversation with Simonds.

65. Robert L. Simonds, "Read This Letter in Its Entirety," 1998, web site, www.nace-cee.org/strategy.html.

66. Ibid.

67. Ibid.

68. Ibid.

NOTES TO CHAPTER 3

1. James C. Dobson, *Citizen* 6, no. 7 (July 1992), 2.

2. Ibid.

3. The terminology here is specific. *Biblical Christians* refers to Christians within the larger evangelical community who hold to an inerrant and literal interpretation of the Scriptures and who insist on the primacy of doctrine and belief in defining true Christians. The larger evangelical community includes other Protestants with differing emphases in their definitions of true Christians.

4. Higher Criticism emphasized the methods of modern literary, historical, and philosophic investigations of the Bible.

5. W. Andrew Hoffecker, "Princeton Theology," in *Dictionary of Christianity in America,* ed. Daniel Reid, Robert D. Linder, Bruce L. Shelley, and Harry S. Stout (Downers Grove, Ill.: InterVarsity Press, 1990), 941–42.

6. See Julie Ingersoll for a further discussion of this connection. "Train Up a Child: A Study of Evangelical Views on Education," master's thesis, George Washington University, 1990, 30–31.

7. See Jaroslav Pelikan, "Fundamentalism and/or Orthodoxy? Toward an Understanding of the Fundamentalist Phenomenon," in *The Fundamentalist Phenomenon,* ed. Norman J. Cohen (Grand Rapids, Mich.: Eerdmans, 1990), 3–21; James Barr, *Fundamentalism* (London: SCM Press, 1977); George M. Marsden, *Understanding Fundamentalism and Evangelicalism* (Grand Rapids, Mich.: Eerdmans, 1991); Niels C. Nielsen, Jr., *Fundamentalism, Mythos, and World Religions* (Albany: State University of New

York Press, 1993); and Lloyd Averill, *Religious Right, Religious Wrong: A Critique of the Fundamentalist Phenomenon* (New York: Pilgrim Press, 1989).

8. Barr, *Fundamentalism,* 93.

9. Ibid., 55–72.

10. Howard Simon, "Federal Court Issues Order in Lee County Bible History Case," press release of the American Civil Liberties Union of Florida (Washington, D.C.: American Civil Liberties Union, 1998), web site, www.aclu.org/news/n012098d.html.

11. Jay Grimstead, "A Manifesto for the Christian Church," in *The Christian World View Documents: Applying Biblical Principles to Every Sphere of Life and Thought,* ed. Jay Grimstead (Sunnyvale, Calif.: Coalition on Revival, 1990), xi.

12. "S.I.E.C.U.S's Prescription for Herpes?" in *News Flash* (Washington, D.C.: Concerned Women for America, 1997), web site, www.cwfa.org/archive/newsflash/news_herpes1297.html.

13. Grimstead, "A Manifesto," xi.

14. The fact that "112 national theologians and leaders working with 500 experts in those 17 different fields" contributed to the COR documents demonstrates the degree to which the those documents represent a wide and highly representative sample of Christian Right intellectuals and knowledge workers. The past leadership of COR includes such Christian Right leaders as John Whitehead, Michael Farris, Randall Terry, Francis Schaeffer's son Franky, Don Wildmon, Beverly LaHaye, Robert Dugan, Tim LaHaye, and D. James Kennedy. Frederick Clarkson, *Eternal Hostility: The Struggle between Theocracy and Democracy* (Monroe, Maine: Common Courage Press, 1997), 97–98.

15. Richard Lappert and Robert Simonds, "The Christian World View of Education," in Grimstead, *Christian World View Documents,* doc. 5, pp. 5, 6, 10.

16. David Barton, "Food for Thought: A Correct Biblical Response Is Essential," *Wallbuilders Report,* spring 1996, web site, www.christiananswers.net/wall/wbrspg96.html.

17. Tim Stafford, "His Father's Son," *Christianity Today,* March 1998, 17.

18. This is a random selection. I merely looked up the first entry with a single scriptural reference in the section on "The Nature and the Role of the Teacher." See Lappert and Simonds, "Christian World View," doc. 5, p. 11.

19. Cited in Clarkson, *Eternal Hostility,* 95.

20. Gil Alexander-Moegerle, *James Dobson's War on America* (Amherst, N.Y.: Prometheus Books, 1997), 134.

21. Lappert and Simonds, "Christian World View," doc. 5, p. 7.

22. Roy Eleutherios Grimm, "'Community Impact Evangelism' and Pluralism in Public Education," Ph.D. diss., University of Colorado, 1991, 214.

23. George M. Marsden, "Everyone One's Own Interpreter? The Bible, Science, and Authority in Mid-Nineteenth Century America," in Hatch and Noll, *The Bible in America,* 83.

24. This precise situation was described to me by a high school science teacher in Adrian, Michigan, who had come under scrutiny by a parent active in the Christian Right.

25. John Corrigan, "The Enlightenment," in Encyclopedia of the American Religious Experience: Studies of Traditions and Movements, ed. Charles H. Lippy and Peter W. Williams (New York: Scribner's, 1988), 2:1095.

26. A. A. Baker, The Successful Christian School (Pensacola, Fla.: A Beka Book, 1979), 45–46.

27. See, for example, Rousas John Rushdoony, The Messianic Character of American Education (1963; reprint, Nutley, N.J.: Craig Press, 1972).

28. Personal communication with Dr. Larry Wilson, superintendent, Blissfield Public Schools, September 1992.

29. Marsden, Understanding, 119.

30. Francis A. Schaeffer, Escape from Reason (Downers Grove, Ill.: Inter-Varsity Press, 1968), 88–89.

31. Cornelius Van Til, The Defense of the Faith (Philadelphia: Presbyterian and Reformed, 1976), 37.

32. Cited in Paul F. Parsons, Inside America's Christian Schools (Macon, Ga.: Mercer University Press, 1987), 80.

33. Averill, Religious Right, 9.

34. Marsden, "Everyone," 83.

35. Gordon J. Spykman, "The Principled Pluralist Position," in Smith, God and Politics, 78–99.

36. Mark A. Noll, The Scandal of the Evangelical Mind (Grand Rapids, Mich.: Eerdmans, 1994), 12.

37. Ibid., 14.

38. Ibid.

39. The Diminishing Divide: American Churches, American Politics (Philadelphia: Pew Research Center for the People and the Press, 1997), 57, web site, www .people-press.org/relgrpt.htm.

40. Barr, Fundamentalism, 72.

41. Ronald L. Numbers, The Creationists: The Evolution of Scientific Creationism (Berkeley: University of California Press, 1992).

42. Barr, Fundamentalism, 56, 93.

43. Ibid., 55.

44. George Gallup, Jr., and Jim Castelli, The People's Religion: American Faith in the 90's (New York: Macmillan, 1989), 60–61. In 1989, Gallup reported that approximately 31 percent of Americans believed the Bible was "the actual word of God and is to be taken literally, word for word." That figure has consistently declined over the past forty years. Yet among conservative evangelicals it is still one of the defining characteristics (60–61). See also James Davison Hunter, Evangelicalism: The Coming Generation (Chicago: University of Chicago Press, 1987).

45. See Matthew C. Moen, *The Transformation of the Christian Right* (Tuscaloosa: University of Alabama Press, 1992).

NOTES TO CHAPTER 4

1. Alan Elsner, "Christian Right Could Lose Clout after U.S. Elections," *Yahoo! News Politics Headlines,* 5 November 1998, web site, www.dailynews.yahoo .com/headlines/pl/story.html?s=v/nm/19981105/pl/christians_1.html.

2. "Coalition Exit Poll Reveals Pro-Family Voters Can't Be Taken for Granted," *Christian Coalition,* posted 4 November 1998 (Chesapeake, Va.), web site, www.cc .org/publications/ccnews/ccnews98.html#elresults.

3. Nancy Coleman, "Every Candidate for Top Three GOP Posts Scored 100 Percent on Latest Christian Coalition Scorecard" (Washington, D.C.: People for the American Way, 1998), web site, www.pfaw.org/news//show.cgi?/article= 911335327; "Dennis Hastert, New Speaker for the House of Representatives" (Washington, D.C.: People for the American Way, 1999), electronic newsletter.

4. Harry Stout suggests this concept in the context of his examination of the role of the Bible in the public life of Colonial New England. "Word and Order in Colonial New England," in Hatch and Noll, *The Bible in America,* 19–38.

5. Ibid., 26, 34.

6. Sara Diamond, *Roads to Dominion: Right-Wing Movements and Political Power in the United States* (New York: Guilford Press, 1995), 138.

7. Jay Grimstead, gen. ed., *The Christian World View Documents: Applying Biblical Principles to Every Sphere of Life and Thought* (Sunnyvale, Calif.: Coalition on Revival, 1986), xii.

8. Peter Heslam, *Creating a Christian Worldview: Abraham Kuyper's Lectures on Calvinism* (Grand Rapids, Mich.: Eerdmans, 1998), 97.

9. Harro W. Van Brummelen, *Telling The Next Generation: Educational Development in North American Calvinist Christian Schools* (New York: University Press of America, 1986), 281.

10. George M. Marsden, *Understanding Fundamentalism and Evangelicalism* (Grand Rapids, Mich.: Eerdmans, 1991), 123.

11. Ibid., 108, 123.

12. Harro W. Van Brummelen, *Telling the Next Generation,* 3–4.

13. Gregory John Maffet, "The Educational Thought of Cornelius Van Til: An Analysis of the Ideological Foundations of His Christian Philosophy of Education," Ph.D. diss., University of Akron, 1984, 31.

14. Ibid., 140–41.

15. Cited in ibid., 141.

16. Maffet, "The Educational Thought," 139.

17. David Hall, "Abraham Kuyper: An Influential and Overlooked Political Theorist," *Covenant Syndicate,* 28 May 1998, web site, www.capo.org/opeds/dh528.htm.

18. These observations are drawn from extended conversations in 1998 with Mark Eckle, chaplain of the Lenawee Christian School, Adrian, Michigan. Mr. Eckle is a nationally known proponent of the Kuyperian approach to Christian education.

19. "Who Is Francis Schaeffer?" (Briarcliff Manor, N.Y.: Francis A. Schaeffer Foundation), web site, www.qns.com/parkhurst/fasfound.htm.

20. Michael S. Hamilton, "The Dissatisfaction of Francis Schaeffer, Part 1," *Christianity Today*, 3 March 1997, 22, web site, www.christianity.net/ct/7T322a.html.

21. See Francis A. Schaeffer, *Escape from Reason* (Downers Grove, Ill.: Inter-Varsity Press, 1968); and Francis A. Schaeffer, *The God Who Is There* (Downers Grove, Ill.: Inter-Varsity Press, 1968).

22. Francis A. Schaeffer, *The Great Evangelical Disaster* (Westchester, Ill.: Crossway Books, 1984), 23.

23. Francis A. Schaeffer, "A Christian Manifesto," keynote address (Fort Lauderdale, Fla., 1982), web site, www.toolcity.net/pfl/francis.html.

24. This is not to say that all people who honor Schaeffer's contributions belong to the Christian Right. Many evangelical Christians have been influenced by his presuppositional method while not heeding his call to activism. Most of those who have heeded his call, however, would fall into the Christian Right category. See Hamilton, "The Dissatisfaction."

25. Francis A. Schaeffer, *How Should We Then Live? The Rise and Decline of Western Thought and Culture* (Westchester, Ill.: Crossway Books, 1976), 32.

26. Ibid., 43.

27. Ibid., 40.

28. Ibid., 80.

29. Ibid., 81–82.

30. Ibid., 134.

31. Ibid., 110.

32. Clifford Geertz, *The Interpretation of Cultures* (New York: Basic Books, 1973), 5.

33. Edward Farley, *Deep Symbols: Their Postmodern Effacement and Reclamation* (Valley Forge, Pa.: Trinity Press International, 1996), 1.

34. Rushdoony is a controversial figure within the Christian Right. Many thinkers and activists who take seriously the more controversial aspects of Rushdoony's thought do not fall within the mainstream of the contemporary Christian Right. This would include such people as the Rev. Pete Peters and others who advocate the imposition of literal Old Testament law as the legal foundation of the society. However, Rushdoony's ideas regarding the nature of the state and its proper organization are widely held in the movement's mainstream. Here we will concentrate on the less controversial aspects of Rushdoony's writings.

35. Rousas John Rushdoony, *The Messianic Character of American Education* (1963; reprint, Nutley, N.J.: Craig Press, 1972), 219.

36. Ibid., 220.

37. Ibid., 339.

38. Ibid., 23.

39. Ibid., 220.

40. Ibid.

41. Ibid., 222.

42. Ibid., 222–23.

43. Baird Tipson, "Calvinist Heritage," in *Encyclopedia of the American Religious Experience: Studies of Traditions and Movements,* ed. Charles H. Lippy and Peter W. Williams (New York: Scribner's, 1988), 1:454.

44. Rousas John Rushdoony, *The Institutes of Biblical Law* (Nutley, N.J.: Craig Press, 1973), 749.

45. Ibid., 742.

46. Ibid.

47. Ibid., 764.

48. Robert L. Simonds, *How to Elect Christians to Public Office* (Costa Mesa, Calif.: NACE/CEE, 1985), 4.

49. Cited in Lloyd Averill, *Religious Right, Religious Wrong: A Critique of the Fundamentalist Phenomenon* (New York: Pilgrim Press, 1989), 97.

50. Rushdoony, *Institutes,* 164.

51. For example, see Tim LaHaye and Beverly LaHaye, *The Act of Marriage: The Beauty of Sexual Love* (Grand Rapids, Mich.: Zondervan, 1976); Tim LaHaye, *How to Be Happy though Married* (Wheaton, Ill.: Tyndale House, 1968); and Beverly La-Haye, *The Restless Woman* (Grand Rapids, Mich.: Zondervan, 1984).

52. Phyllis Schlafly, *The Power of the Christian Woman* (Cincinnati, Ohio: Standard, 1981), 103.

53. For example, see James C. Dobson, *Love Must Be Tough* (Waco, Tex.: Word, 1983), 159, 164.

54. Maffet, "The Educational Thought," 209.

55. See James C. Dobson, *Parenting Isn't for Cowards* (Waco, Tex.: Word, 1987), 106, 107; and James C. Dobson, *Dare to Discipline* (Wheaton, Ill.: Tyndale House, 1973).

NOTES TO CHAPTER 5

1. D. James Kennedy and the Coral Ridge Presbyterian Church are affiliated with the Presbyterian Church in America. That denomination, begun in 1973 (present name adopted in 1974) formed from a coalition of conservative Presbyterians who opposed some of the theological and social policies of the mainstream Presbyterian Church (U.S.A.).

2. George Gallup, Jr., and Jim Castelli, *The People's Religion: American Faith in the 90's* (New York: Macmillan, 1989), 6, 5.

3. "Latest Religious Preferences," *Emerging Trends* 19, no. 3 (March 1997): 3.

4. For a discussion of this sophistication and the role it has played in transforming the Christian Right into a major political force, see Matthew C. Moen, *The Transformation of the Christian Right* (Tuscaloosa: University of Alabama Press, 1992).

5. Michael Lienesch refers to politically active biblical Christians as a social movement based on beliefs and inspired by values. *Redeeming America: Piety and Politics in the New Christian Right* (Chapel Hill: University of North Carolina Press, 1993), 20.

6. David Aberle and Omer Stewart refer to such phenomena as nativistic social movements. See *Navaho and Ute Peyotism: A Chronology and Distributional Study* (Boulder: University of Colorado Press, 1957). In a subsequent work, Aberle distinguishes between those nativistic movements that seek personal change and those that seek supraindividual change. The reference here is to the former kind. "The Prophet Dance and Reactions to White Contact," *Southwest Journal of Anthropology* 15, no. 1 (1959): 74–83.

7. Melissa A. Pflüg, *Ritual and Myth in Odawa Revitalization: Reclaiming a Sovereign Place* (Norman: University of Oklahoma Press, 1998), 239. Neil Smelser distinguishes these two types of movements on the basis of the breadth of their focus and the specificity of their issues. "Norm-oriented" social movements seek limited but specific changes in the social system, whereas "value-oriented" social movements seek broad-based fundamental change in the society. See *Theory of Collective Behavior* (New York: Free Press of Glencoe, 1962).

8. For a discussion of the role of conflict in social movements, see Anthony F. C. Wallace, *Religion: An Anthropological View* (New York: Random House, 1966).

9. For a discussion of the way social movements use conflict in a positive manner, see Lewis Coser, *The Functions of Social Conflict* (New York: Free Press, 1956); Jonathan Z. Smith, "A Pearl of Great Price and a Cargo of Yams," in *Imagining Religion: From Babylon to Jonestown*, ed. Jonathan Z. Smith (Chicago: University of Chicago Press, 1982), 94–95, 99–101; and Pflüg, *Ritual and Myth in Odawa Revitalization*, 239–45.

10. Kenelm Burridge, *New Heaven, New Earth: A Study of Millenarian Activities* (New York: Schocken Books, 1969).

11. Pflüg, *Ritual and Myth in Odawa Revitalization*, 241.

12. Doug McAdam and David A. Snow, "Introduction—Social Movements: Conceptual and Theoretical Issues," in *Social Movements: Readings on Their Emergence, Mobilization, and Dynamics*, ed. Doug McAdam and David A. Snow (Los Angeles: Roxbury, 1997), xxviii.

13. James Davison Hunter, *Culture Wars: The Struggle to Define America* (New York: Basic Books, 1991), 60.

14. Peter Heslam, *Creating a Christian Worldview: Abraham Kuyper's Lectures on Calvinism* (Grand Rapids, Mich.: Eerdmans, 1998), 5–8.

15. See the Center for the Advancement of Paleo Orthodoxy web page at www.capo.org.

16. These include Michael Bauman at Hillsdale (Michigan) College; Joel Belz, editor of the influential *World* magazine; George Grant, considered to be one of the leading economic theorists in the Christian Right; Doug Bandow, a senior fellow at the CATO Institute; and a number of professors and deans at theological seminaries. Of note for educational issues is the listing of Francis J. Beckwith as a periodic contributor to CAPO publications. Beckwith is cited frequently in Christian Right publications on educational issues. He was one of the designers of the New Age criticism of educational reform during the early 1990s.

17. Jay Grimstead, "A Manifesto for the Christian Church," in *The Christian World View Documents: Applying Biblical Principles to Every Sphere of Life and Thought,* ed. Jay Grimstead (Sunnyvale, Calif.: Coalition on Revival, 1990), xvi.

18. Here is a partial list of the contributors and steering committee members with their affiliations as of 1990: Richard Bliss and Duane Gish (Institute for Creation Research), Colonel Donner (Christian Action Network), Robert Dugan (National Association of Evangelicals), Michael Farris (Home School Legal Defense Association), Marshall Foster (Mayflower Institute), Dee Jepsen (Board of Regents, Regent University), Roy Jones (Republican Senatorial Committee), D. James Kennedy (Coral Ridge Ministries), Paul Kienel (Association of Christian Schools, International), Tim LaHaye (American Coalition for Traditional Values), Ted McAteer (Religious Roundtable), Josh McDowell (Josh McDowell Ministries), Gary North (Institute for Christian Economics), Edith Schaeffer (widow of Francis Schaeffer), Robert Simons (National Association of Christian Educators), Jack Van Impe (Jack Van Impe Ministries), Rus Walton (Plymouth Rock Foundation), Donald Wildmon (American Family Association), Peter Marshall (author), Joseph Morecraft (Chalcedon Presbyterian Church), and Bob Thoburn (Fairfax Christian School). Grimstead, "A Manifesto," xvi–xxi.

19. See the Alliance for Revival and Reformation Internet homepage at www.repent.org.

20. The Council for National Policy should not be confused with the more mainstream Center for National Policy.

21. Sara Diamond, *Spiritual Warfare: The Politics of the Christian Right* (Boston: South End Press, 1989), 106–7.

22. Roy Eleutherios Grimm, "'Community Impact Evangelism' and Pluralism in Public Education," Ph.D. diss., University of Colorado, 1991, 134.

23. Frederick Clarkson, *Eternal Hostility: The Struggle between Theocracy and Democracy* (Monroe, Maine: Common Courage Press, 1997), 195.

24. In addition to those already mentioned, the membership list includes Gary Bauer (Family Research Council), John Whitehead (Rutherford Institute), Michael Farris (Home School Legal Defense Association), D. James Kennedy (Coral Ridge Presbyterian Church), Beverly LaHaye (Concerned Women for

America), Ralph Reed (late of the Christian Coalition), Bill Bright (Campus Crusade for Christ), Home School Legal Defense Association, Alan Keyes (1996 Republican candidate for president and radio talk-show host), Donald Wildmon (American Family Association), Henry Morris (Institute for Creation Research), Rep. Louis "Woody" Jenkins, Sen. Jesse Helms, Jeff Coors (ACX Technologies, Adolph Coors Co.), Morton C. Blackwell (International Policy Forum), Reed E. Larson (National Right to Work Committee), Rich DeVos, Sr. (cofounder of Amway Corporation), Oliver North (U.S.M.C. Ret. and the Freedom Alliance), Paul Weyrich (Free Congress Foundation), Larry Pratt (Gun Owners of America), Ronald S. Godwin (Washington Times Corp.).

25. Diamond, *Spiritual Warfare,* 57.

26. "Council for National Policy Unofficial Home Page" (Great Barrington, Mass.: Institute for First Amendment Studies, 1998), web site, www.berkshire.net/ifas/cnp/index.html.

27. Ibid.

28. Ibid.

29. Ibid.

30. Robert Wuthnow, *The Restructuring of American Religion: Society and Faith since World War II* (Princeton, N.J.: Princeton University Press, 1988), 101, 130.

31. Leigh S. Schaffer, "The Word of God and Recipe Knowledge: The Road to Dogmatism in Religion,'" *High School Journal,* February–March 1985, 205–10.

32. Ibid., 206.

33. Ralph Reed, Jr., "Statement by Ralph Reed, Jr. concerning His Resignation from the Christian Coalition," Christian Coalition press release, 23 April 1997. Cited in Justin Watson, *The Christian Coalition: Dreams of Restoration, Demands for Recognition* (New York: St. Martin's Press, 1997), 54.

34. The membership figure provided by the Christian Coalition may be significantly overestimated. Each Coalition member receives a subscription to the organization's monthly magazine *The Christian American.* According to figures listed therein, the circulation of the magazine is considerably lower than the Coalition's estimated membership. See Watson, *The Christian Coalition,* 205–6, n. 39.

35. "Pat's Empire," *Freedom Writer,* September 1998, 3.

36. Joseph L. Conn, "God, Guns and the GOP," *Church and State* 51, no. 10 (November 1998): 7, 8.

37. See Regent University web home page at www.regent.edu. The Christian Right emphasis of the university is seen in the faculty profiles. For example, three of the faculty in the Robertson School of Government show very strong Christian Right ties. Kay James is a former employee of the Family Research Council, Joseph Kickasola has strong Christian Reconstructionist ties, and Alan Snyder is the founder of the Foundation for Biblical Government, an educational foundation devoted to the restoration of biblical principles in government.

38. "James Dobson's CNP Address" (Great Barrington, Mass.: Institute for First Amendment Studies, 1998), web site, www.ifas.org/cnp/index.html.

39. "Teachers Should Fight School 'Secularism,' Dobson Magazine Urges," *Church and State* 51, no. 10 (November 1998): 18.

40. Libby Quaid, "Ashcroft Won't Run for President," *Yahoo! Daily News,* 5 January 1999, web site, dailynews.yahoo.com/headlines/ap/elections/story.html?s=v/ap/19990105/el/Ashcroft_2000_1.html.

41. Bauer first joined the department in 1982 as deputy undersecretary for planning, budget and evaluation; he represented the department on the White House Cabinet Council for Human Resources, was chairman of the Working Group on School Discipline (1984), and in 1995 was appointed undersecretary of the U.S. Department of Education.

42. NACE/CEE web page at www.nace-cee.org/bob.html.

43. NACE/CEE web page at www.nace-cee.org/enspr97.html.

44. A tally of the *Phyllis Schlafly Report* for the past three years shows that about one-third of the articles focused on education.

45. Eagle Forum web page, www.eagleforum.org/misc/descript.html.

46. The Eagle Forum's Internet web home page at www.eagleforum.org, emphasis in original.

47. See the legal brief filed by the American Civil Liberties Union, "In the United States District Court Middle District of Florida, Fort Myers Division," at www.aclufl.org/leecompl.htm.

48. Ingersoll also makes this observation about the critical importance of conflict in Christian Right strategy. See Julie Ingersoll, "Train Up a Child: A Study of Evangelical Views on Education," master's thesis, George Washington University, 1990, 117.

49. Although Mormons tend to be socially conservative, they do not fit well into the Christian Right due both to certain theological doctrines unique to the Mormons and to a historical experience that makes them cautious about combining the power of religion and government. For a discussion of these points, see Frederick Mark Gedicks, "*No Man's Land": The Place of Latter-Day Saints in the Culture War,* monograph (Bloomington: Poynter Center for the Study of Ethics and American Institutions, Indiana University, 1999).

50. The term *mainline* refers to those denominations that have comprised the culturally dominant faiths since the founding of the nation. They include Congregationalists, Episcopalians, Baptists, Methodists, Presbyterians, Lutherans, and Disciples of Christ. Cited in Wade Roof Clark and William McKinney, *American Mainline Religion: Its Changing Shape and Future* (New Brunswick, N.J.: Rutgers University Press, 1987), 6.

51. George M. Marsden, "Fundamentalism," in *Encyclopedia of the American Religious Experience: Studies of Traditions and Movements,* ed. Charles H. Lippy and Peter W. Williams (New York: Scribner's, 1988), 2:954.

52. These three sources are the Wesleyan tradition, the Keswick Movement, and Oberlin Perfectionism.

53. See Rolf Zettersten, *Dr. Dobson: Turning Hearts toward Home—the Life and Principles of America's Family Advocate* (Dallas: Word, 1989).

54. Grant Wacker, "Pentecostalism," in *Encyclopedia of the American Religious Experience: Studies of Traditions and Movements,* ed. Charles H. Lippy and Peter W. Williams (New York: Scribner's, 1988), 2:934.

55. Corwin E. Smidt and James M. Penning, "Michigan: Veering to the Left?" in Rozell and Wilcox, *God at the Grass Roots,* 127.

56. Mary Jo Weaver and R. Scott Appleby, eds, *Being Right: Conservative Catholics in America* (Bloomington: Indiana University Press, 1995), 1–3.

57. See the Pew Center web page at www.people-press.org/oct96typ.htm.

58. "Queen's: God and Society in North America, 1996" (Pew Charitable Trust), web site, www.arda.tm/archive.QUEEN'S.html. The numbers here are for respondents from the United States.

NOTES TO CHAPTER 6

1. Fritz Detwiler, "Let's Be Fair about This: Democratic Pluralism and the Christian Right," conference presentation videotape (Dayton, Ohio: Institute for the Development of Educational Activities, 1993).

2. David C. Berliner and Bruce J. Biddle, *The Manufactured Crisis: Myths, Fraud, and the Attack on America's Public Schools* (Reading, Mass.: Addison-Wesley, 1995), 129–72.

3. Garry Wills, *Under God: Religion and American Politics* (New York: Touchstone, 1990), 322.

4. Ibid., 321.

5. See Francis A. Schaeffer, *A Christian Manifesto* (Westchester, Illinois: Crossway Books, 1981), 101; and John Whitehead, *The Second American Revolution* (Westchester, Ill.: Crossway Books, 1982), 28.

6. Schaeffer, *A Christian Manifesto,* 101.

7. Ibid., 99.

8. Ibid., 54.

9. Ibid., 93.

10. Ibid., 106.

11. Ralph Reed, Jr., *Politically Incorrect* (Dallas: Word, 1994), 24.

12. William Martin, *With God on Our Side: The Rise of the Religious Right in America* (New York: Broadway Books, 1996), 224.

13. For an overview of the ideological context of Ronald Reagan and his Administration's educational policy, see Catherine A. Lugg, *For God and Country: Conservatism and American School Policy* (New York: Peter Lang, 1996), 1–8; and

Matthew C. Moen, *The Christian Right and Congress* (Tuscaloosa: University of Alabama Press, 1989), 50–56. Lugg pictures Reagan as less involved in promoting the Christian Right agenda than does Moen.

14. For an extended discussion of the centrality of the democratic principle to American conceptions of public education, see Amy Gutman, *Democratic Education* (Princeton, N.J.: Princeton University Press, 1987), 48–70.

15. David Berliner and Bruce Biddle categorize Edwin Meese as a "Far Right" rather than a "Religious Right" conservative. However, William Martin believes that Meese was far closer to the Christian Right, particularly on issues of abortion and education, than other Reagan advisers. Meese, Martin suggests, led the "values" faction within the Administration. See Berliner and Biddle, *The Manufactured Crisis,* 135; and Martin, *With God on Our Side,* 223, 224.

16. Matthew C. Moen, *The Transformation of the Christian Right* (Tuscaloosa: University of Alabama Press, 1992), 61.

17. Berliner and Biddle, *The Manufactured Crisis,* 3.

18. The National Commission on Excellence in Education, *A Nation at Risk: The Imperative for Educational Reform* (Washington, D.C.: Government Printing Office, 1983), 5.

19. Lugg, *For God and Country,* 135.

20. Ronald Reagan, "Weekly Compilation of Presidential Documents," 2 May 1983, vol. 9, no. 17, p. 593, National Archives and Records Administration, Washington, D.C.

21. Lugg, *For God and Country,* 136.

22. Erling Jorstad, *The New Christian Right, 1981–1988* (Lewiston, N.Y.: Edward Mellon Press, 1987), 217–18.

23. Cited in James Davison Hunter, *Culture Wars: The Struggle to Define America* (New York: Basic Books, 1991), 203.

24. Jorstad, *The New Christian Right,* 217–18.

25. Cited in Skipp Porteous, "The New Religious Right—Phase Three: Christianizing America," *Freedom Writer,* May–June 1991, 1.

26. Cal Thomas, "Religious Expression Is a Free Speech Issue," *Detroit Free Press,* 15 June 1993, A9.

27. *Lamb's Chapel v. Center Moriches School District,* 508 U.S. 384, 113 S.Ct. 2141 (1993).

28. *Jones v. Clear Creek Indep. Sch. Dist.,* 977 F.2d 963 (5th Cir. 1992), cert. denied, 508 U.S. 967 113 S.Ct. 2950 (1993).

29. Thomas, "Religious Expression."

30. *Family Research Council Washington Watch,* July–August, 1991, 3

31. For a discussion of this tactic, see Fritz Detwiler, "'A Place at the Table': An Analysis of the Christian Right Anti-OBE Campaign and Its Impact on Public Education," *Religion and Education* 23, no. 2 (fall 1996): 56–64.

32. Kathi Hudson, *Reinventing America's Schools: A Practical Guide to Components of Restructuring and Non-Traditional Education*, rev. ed. (Costa Mesa, Calif.: NACE/CEE, 1993), 1:9.

33. Ibid., 5.

34. Ibid., 16–17.

35. Ibid., 28.

36. Ralph Reed, Jr., and Robert L. Simonds, "The Agenda of the Religious Right," *School Administrator* 50, no. 9 (October 1993): 16–20, 22.

37. Robert L. Simonds, "A Plea for the Children," *Educational Leadership* 51, no. 4 (December–January 1993–1994): 12–15.

38. In a telephone conversation in 1994, William Spady admitted to me that his motivation for seeking accommodation was to give Simonds a platform to air his grievances so that Spady could get on with his consulting business.

39. Comments by Robert Simonds in a breakout session at D. James Kennedy's Reclaiming America Conference, January 1994, Fort Lauderdale, Fla.

40. Personal conversation with non–Christian Right parents regarding educational reforms criticized by Christian Right parents. Romeo, Michigan, November 1992.

41. "Report on Citizens for Excellence in Education," information sheet (People for the American Way, Washington, D.C.).

42. Robert L. Simonds, "Newsletter," in *President's Report* (Costa Mesa, Calif.: NACE/CEE, 1994), 3.

43. Quoted in Lily Eng, "A Cry against Education Reform," *The Seattle Times*, 23 March 1993.

44. Telephone conversation with Bonnie Dana, an educational administrator doing research on OBE opposition, 15 May 1996. Dana was given this information by Robert Simonds in a telephone conversation. The telephone number Luksik distributed for contacting her was the NACE/CEE number.

45. For a further description of this argument, see Julie Ingersoll, "Train Up a Child: A Study of Evangelical Views on Education," master's thesis, George Washington University, 1990, 24.

46. Eric Buehrer, *The New Age Masquerade: The Hidden Agenda in Your Child's Classroom* (Brentwood, Tenn.: Woglemuth and Hyatt, 1990).

47. Pat Robertson, *The New World Order* (Dallas: Word, 1991).

48. The November 1993 issue of *Focus on the Family* magazine recommends a pamphlet titled *A Gift for Teacher*, published by Eric Buehrer's Gateways to Better Education group in Lake Forest, California. Steve Green, counsel for Americans United for the Separation of Church and State, concluded after reading the booklet that it leads teachers to violate the law. Cited in "Notes on Church-State Affairs," *Journal of Church and State* 36, no. 2 (spring 1994): 443.

49. Personal communication with an Adrian, Michigan, high school science teacher, March 1992.

50. Robert L. Simonds, "Special Insert to President's Report," *President's Report*, July 1992 (Costa Mesa, Calif.: NACE/CEE, 1992).

51. James A. Barnes, "Parent Power," *National Journal*, 12 December 1993, 1400.

52. Phyllis Schlafly, "Ten Objections to OBE," *Phyllis Schlafly Report*, May 1993, 2.

53. James C. Dobson, *Focus on the Family Letter*, May 1994, 3.

54. Robert L. Simonds, *President's Report*, July 1992, 2 (Costa Mesa, Calif.: NACE/CEE, 1992).

55. Cited in Michael Lienesch, *Redeeming America: Piety and Politics in the New Christian Right* (Chapel Hill: University of North Carolina Press, 1993), 167.

56. Cited in Wills, *Under God*, 394 n.

57. The case studies of Vista, California, and Lake County, Florida, described in chapter 8, illustrate this response.

58. J. R. Wynsma, "Educational Reform: The HELP Scholarships Amendment of 1997," *Neopolitique*, December 1997, web site, www.neopolitique.org/articles/dec97-help.html.

59. "Fathers, do not provoke your children to anger, but bring them up in the discipline and instruction of the Lord" (Eph. 6:4, RSV).

60. Wynsma, "Educational Reform."

61. Rousas John Rushdoony is not the only source for such linkages. These same associations appear in the conspiratorial theories of the John Birch Society, an organization with secular purposes. The singular importance of Rushdoony here is related to our focus on the religious dimensions of the movement.

62. For illustrations of this linkage see the Internet homepages of Focus on the Family, the Christian Coalition, NACE/CEE, the Eagle Forum, and Concerned Women for America. Tim LaHaye popularized this idea in *The Battle for the Public Schools: Humanism's Threat to Our Children* (Old Tappan, N.J.: Revell, 1983).

63. Wynsma, "Educational Reform."

64. Moen, *Transformation*, 89–118.

65. Wynsma, "Educational Reform."

66. Ibid.

67. Linell E. Cady, *Religion, Theology, and American Public Life*, SUNY Series in Religious Studies (Albany: State University of New York Press, 1993), 19.

68. Walter H. Capps, *The New Religious Right: Piety, Patriotism, and Politics* (Columbia: University of South Carolina Press, 1990), 9.

69. Cited in ibid.

70. Chris Freund and Candice J. Zouhary, "A Reasonable Budget Target: Government Schools, Part I," *NeoPolitique*, March 1996, web site, www.neopolitique.org/articles/education.html.

71. Randall J. Hekman, executive director of the Michigan Family Forum, personal conversation, Adrian, Michigan, 8 December 1994.

72. Wynsma, "Educational Reform."

73. Section 4 (D) (ii) reads, "Receipt of funds under this title is not conditioned with requirements or regulations that preclude the use of such funds for sectarian educational purposes or require removal of religious art, icons, scripture, or other symbols." See Frank Riggs, *Helping Empower Low-Income Parents (HELP) Scholarships Amendments of 1997,* House res. 2746 (Washington, D.C.: U.S. House of Representatives, 1997), web site, www.thomas.loc.gov/cgi-bin/query/D?c105:./temp/~c105LeC95P:e3980.

74. Section 6505 reads, "(a) NOT SCHOOL AID.—Subject to subsection (b), funds used under this title to establish a voluntary government and private parental choice program shall be considered assistance to the student and shall not be considered as assistance to any school that chooses to participate in such program." Riggs, *Helping Empower.*

75. Section 6505 (b) reads, "NO FEDERAL CONTROL—The Secretary is not permitted to exercise any direction, supervision, or control over curricula, program of instruction, administration, or personnel of any school that chooses to participate in a voluntary government and private choice program established under 6309(b)(9)." Riggs, *Helping Empower.*

NOTES TO CHAPTER 7

1. Cited on a Summit Ministries web page, www.christiananswers.net/summit/leadrshp.

2. Bill Jack distributed copies of *Issues and Answers* at his breakout session at the 1994 Reclaiming America Conference, Fort Lauderdale, Florida. The major focus of the session was to present the resources Jack uses in his seminars to help students frame all issues within the context of two competing and mutually exclusive worldviews—God-centered and man-centered. *Issues and Answers* is available through the Caleb Campaign, P.O. Box 174, Cary, IL 60013.

3. "DNA and Neanderthals," Newsflash (Washington, D.C.: Concerned Women for America, 1997), web site, www.cwfa.org/archive/newsflash/news_dna0797.html.

4. Linda Page, "The Potential Effects on Education Curricula and Policy of Homosexual 'Marriage,'" briefing on Capitol Hill regarding the Defense of Marriage Act, At the Podium (Washington, D.C.: Family Research Council, 1996), web site, www.frc.org/frc/podium/pd96g7hs.html.

5. Phyllis Schlafly, *Phyllis Schlafly Report,* May 1993.

6. David Barton, *America's Godly Heritage* (1990; reissued, Aledo, Tex.: Wall-Builders, 1992), videotape.

7. "A Right Wing and a Prayer: The Religious Right in Your Public Schools," executive summary (Washington, D.C.: People for the American Way, 1997), web site, www.pfaw.org/wing/rwpb.html.

8. "Help Restore Christian Holidays to the Public Schools," *Christian Ameri-*

can, November–December 1997, web site, www.cc.org/publications/ca/1197/holidays.html. Emphasis added.

9. Glen Chambers and Gene Fisher, *United States History for Christian Schools* (Greenville, S.C.: Bob Jones University Press, 1984), 11.

10. Ibid., 86.

11. Cited in Michael Lienesch, *Redeeming America: Piety and Politics in the New Christian Right* (Chapel Hill: University of North Carolina Press, 1993), 141.

12. Tim LaHaye, *The Battle for the Mind* (Old Tappan, N.J.: Revell, 1980), 37.

13. "Mission Statement" (Alton, Ill.: Eagle Forum), web site, www.eagleforum.org/misc/descript.html.

14. Phyllis Schlafly, "Bilingualism Is the Wrong Way to Go" (Alton, Ill.: Eagle Forum, 1995), web site, www.eagleforum.org/column/dec95/col12-14.html.

15. Kathi Hudson, *Reinventing America's Schools: A Practical Guide to Components of Restructuring and Non-Traditional Education,* rev. ed. (Costa Mesa, Calif.: NACE/CEE, 1993), 1:66.

16. Robert L. Simonds, *President's Report,* July 1992, 2 (Costa Mesa, Calif.: NACE/CEE, 1992).

17. Hudson, *Reinventing,* 1:77.

18. Tim LaHaye, *Faith of Our Founding Fathers: A Comprehensive Study of America's Christian Foundations* (1987; reprint, Green Forest, Ark.: Master Books, 1994), 5.

19. Gary L. Bauer, "National History Standards: Clintonites Miss the Moon," perspective papers (Washington, D.C.: Family Research Council), web site, www.frc.org/frc/perspective/pv95c2ed.html.

20. "Who Will Teach the Children? A Battle between Federal and Local Control," Policy Papers (Washington, D.C.: Concerned Women for America), web site, www.cwfa.org/policypapers/pp_educate.html.

21. Bauer, "National History Standards."

22. Jennifer A. Marshall and Eric Unsworth, "Freeing America's Schools: The Case against the U.S. Education Department," Family Policy Documents (Washington, D.C.: Family Research Council, 1995), web site, www.frc.org/frc/fampol/fp95ded.html.

23. "Who Will Teach the Children?"

24. The case is *Abingdon v. Schempp,* 374 U.S. 203, 215 (1963) at 225. Cited in George C. Bedell, Leo Sandon, Jr., and Charles T. Wellborn, *Religion in America,* 2d ed. (New York: Macmillan, 1982), 82–83.

25. "Can Public Schools Teach Bible Curriculum?" *Maranatha Christian Journal,* 13 February 1998, top news headlines, web site, www.mcjonline.com/news/news2355.htm.

26. Ibid.

27. Michael J. Gerson, "Public Schools Teach Bible as History. What Role Is There for Jesus and Jeroboam?" *U.S. News and World Report,* 1998, web site, www.usnews.com/usnews/issue/980112/12bibl.htm.

28. Stephen L. Carter, *The Culture of Disbelief: How American Law and Politics Trivialize Religious Devotion* (New York: Basic Books, 1993), 87.

29. Cited in James Davison Hunter, *Culture Wars: The Struggle to Define America* (New York: Basic Books, 1991), 109–10.

30. Robert Wuthnow, *The Restructuring of American Religion: Society and Faith since World War II* (Princeton, N.J.: Princeton University Press, 1988), 257.

31. Hunter, *Culture Wars,* 71.

32. "Education Briefs," Education Reporter (Alton, Ill.: Eagle Forum, 1997), web site, www.eagleforum.org/educate/1997/apr97/briefs.html.

33. Jennifer A. Marshall, "Illegitimacy: Compassion's Offspring," Perspective Papers (Washington, D.C.: Family Research Council), web site, www.frc.org/frc/perspective/pv95c4wl.html.

34. See, for example, Tim LaHaye, *Sex Education Is for the Family* (Grand Rapids, Mich.: Zondervan, 1985), 29; and James C. Dobson and Gary L. Bauer, *Children at Risk: The Battle for the Hearts and Minds of Our Kids* (Dallas: Word, 1990), 32.

35. See Phyllis Schlafly, "NEA Convention Delegates Gather to Gloat" (Alton, Ill.: Eagle Forum, 1997), web site, www.eagleforum.org/column/1997/july97/97-07-23.html; and "Parents Unable to Teach Children," *Defense of the Family News Flash,* December 1997 (Washington, D.C.: Concerned Women for America, 1997), web site, www.cfa.org/archive/newsflash/news_homoedu1297.html.

36. Robert H. Knight, "School Days, Sex Daze," Perspective Papers (Washington, D.C.: Family Research Council), web site, www.frc.org/frc/perspective/pv95i8hs.html.

37. "Kinsey, Sex, and Lies," Policy Papers (Washington, D.C.: Concerned Women for America), web site, www.cwfa.org/policypapers/pp_kinsey.html.

38. "Planned Parenthood Devises New Strategy to Boost Birth-Control Sales," Education Reporter (Alton, Ill.: Eagle Forum, 1997), web site, www.eagleforum.org/educate/1997/feb97/er_feb97.html.

39. Knight, "School Days."

40. "New Welfare Law Backs Chastity," newsflash (Washington, D.C.: Concerned Women for America, 1997), web site, www.cwfa.org/archive/newsflash/news_siecus0697.html.

41. "Sex Education: What Works?" In Focus (Washington, D.C.: Family Research Council, 1995), web site, www.frc.org/infocus/if95k2ab.html.

42. "Idaho Education Department Adopts 'Abstinence-Only' Role," Education Reporter (Alton, Ill.: Eagle Forum, 1997), web site, www.eagleforum.org/educate/1997/jan97/er_jan97.html.

43. LaHaye, *Sex Education,* 16.

44. Onalee McGraw and Margaret Whitehead, *Foundations for Family Life Education* (Arlington, Va.: Educational Guidance Institute, 1991), 19–24.

45. Gary L. Bauer, "National Education Summit," Straight Talk (Washington, D.C.: Family Research Council), web site, www.frc.org/frc/net/st96d3.html.

46. Page, "The Potential Effects."

47. "Clinton Urges School Diversity Training," Education Reporter (Alton, Ill.: Eagle Forum, 1998), web site, www.eagleforum.org/educate/1998/jan98/values.html.

48. Ibid.

49. Cited in Robert L. Maginnis, "Federal Drug War Ignoring Great Ally: Faith-Based Treatment," Insight (Washington, D.C.: Family Research Council), web site, www.frc.org/frc/insight/is96gldr.html.

50. "Writer Dares to Expose D.A.R.E," Education Reporter (Alton, Ill.: Eagle Forum, 1997), web site, www.eagleforum.org/educate/1997/mar97/er_mar97.html.

51. William R. Mattox, Jr., "Education Debate Needs to Focus on the Family," Perspective Papers (Washington, D.C.: Family Research Council), web site, www.frc.org/frc/perspective/pv95j3ed.html.

52. Phyllis Schlafly, "Is the Government Planning Your Child's Career?" (Alton, Ill.: Eagle Forum, 1995), web site, www.eagleforum.org/column/col-10-5.html.

53. Robert Holland, "Focus: What's Wrong with School-to-Work?" address to conference on Capitol Hill, Education Reporter (Alton, Ill.: Eagle Forum, 1997), web site, www.eagleforum.org/educate/1997/may97/holland.html.

54. Holland, "Focus."

55. The American Community Renewal Act of 1997, S. 432.IS, and HR. 1031.IH. For the Senate version, see the legislative web site at thomas.loc.gov/cgi-bin/query/D?c105:9:./temp/~c105aN4k2b:. For the House bill, see thomas.loc.gov/cgi-bin/query/D?c105:10:./temp/~c105aN4k2b:.

56. Cited in Paul F. Parsons, *Inside America's Christian Schools* (Macon, Ga.: Mercer University Press, 1987), 82.

57. George M. Marsden, *Understanding Fundamentalism and Evangelicalism* (Grand Rapids, Mich.: Eerdmans, 1991), 137, 138.

58. In *Epperson,* the Supreme Court ruled that Arkansas could not prohibit the teaching of evolution in its public schools because the purpose of the law was to advance a sectarian religious belief. In *McLean,* a district court judge ruled that "balance" was not required in Arkansas schools because creationists could not present any scientific arguments.

59. Bill Jack, workshop on evolution, Reclaiming America Conference, Fort Lauderdale, Fla., January 1994. Jack also holds training sessions for Christian public school students and their parents during Christmas vacations in Denver, Colorado, to teach them more strategies for defeating evolution and promoting creationism in the public schools.

60. Jennifer A. Marshall and Kristina Twitty, "Confusing the Call for Professionalism: The National Board for Professional Teaching Standards," Insight (Washington, D.C.: Family Research Council), web site, www.frc.org/frc/insight/is97h2ed.html.

61. Liberals also accept the idea of the necessary correspondence between pedagogy and presuppositional values. See, for example, Amy Gutman, *Democratic*

Education (Princeton, N.J.: Princeton University Press, 1987); and Theodore Lewis Becker and Richard A. Couto, eds, *Teaching Democracy and Being Democratic* (Westport, Conn.: Praeger, 1996).

62. Fritz Hinrichs, "Classical Education," adapted from a speech given at the 1995 Homeschool Curriculum fair in San Diego, At the Podium (Washington, D.C.: Family Research Council), web site, www.frc.org/frc/podium/pd95i2ed.html.

63. Ibid.

64. Ibid.

65. For a discussion of Outcome-Based Education as an umbrella for Christian Right objections to public education, see Fritz Detwiler, "'A Place at the Table': An Analysis of the Christian Right Anti-OBE Campaign and Its Impact on Public Education," *Religion and Education* 23, no. 2 (fall 1996): 56–64.

66. Representative Henry Hyde (R-IL), chairman, House Judiciary Committee, hosted an education conference entitled "What Goals 2000 Means to the States" on February 12 on Capitol Hill. "Conference Explains Problems with Goals 2000 and School-to-Work," Education Reporter (Alton, Ill.: Eagle Forum, 1997), web site, www.eagleforum.org/educate/1997/mar97/er_mar97.html.

67. "NAEP Targeted for Change," Education Reporter (Alton, Ill.: Eagle Forum, 1997), web site, www.eagleforum.org/educate/1997/may97/naep.html.

68. Phyllis Schlafly, "The New Crisis in California" Column (Alton, Ill.: Eagle Forum, 1995), web site, www.eagleforum.org/colum/col-9-28.html.

69. In my research on local controversies, the overwhelming majority of press reports focus on content issues rather than pedagogy. I will illustrate this emphasis in the case studies on Vista, California, and Lake County, Florida (see chapter 8).

NOTES TO CHAPTER 8

1. For a fuller discussion of this controversy, see Fritz Detwiler, "A Tale of Two Districts: A Case Study in Democratic Responses to Public Education," *Educational Leadership* 51, no. 4 (December–January 1993–1994): 24–28.

2. "Adrian Public Schools Community Information Sheet" (Adrian, Mich.: Adrian Public Schools, n.d.).

3. The external staff to be provided through IDEA included independent consultants Art Costa, Marian Leibowitz, and Bena Kallick, and IDEA staff members John Bahner, Jon Paden, Steve Thompson, and Fred Morton.

4. I attended the meeting and picked up one of the few copies of the Belt report available to the public.

5. Eric Buehrer, *The New Age Masquerade: The Hidden Agenda in Your Child's Classroom* (Brentwood, Tenn.: Woglemuth and Hyatt, 1990); James C. Dobson and Gary L. Bauer, *Children at Risk: The Battle for the Hearts and Minds of Our Kids* (Dallas: Word, 1990); Pat Robertson, *The New World Order* (Dallas: Word, 1991).

6. "School Officials Meet with Ministers," *Adrian (Michigan) Daily Telegram,* 1 July 1991, 1.

7. *Centre Views,* August 1991, 2.

8. "Big Crowd Packs Dawson to Discuss School Plan," *Adrian (Michigan) Daily Telegram,* 20 August 1991, 1.

9. "IDEA Opponents Hear from Analyst," *Adrian (Michigan) Daily Telegram,* 16 September 1991, 1.

10. "Developing an IDEA to Improve Education," editorial, *Adrian (Michigan) Daily Telegram,* 7 August 1991.

11. Matthew Freeman, *The San Diego Model: A Community Battles the Religious Right* (Washington, D.C.: People for the American Way, 1993), 17.

12. Ibid.

13. *San Diego Union,* 29 September 1991, cited in Freeman, *The San Diego Model,* 18.

14. *Los Angeles Times,* 22 March 1992, cited in Freeman, *The San Diego Model,* 18.

15. Lisa Petrillo, "Religious Right's Biggest Victory Here Short-Lived," *San Diego Union Tribune,* 4 August 1996, A19.

16. Ibid.

17. "Religious Right Takes School Board," *Freedom Writer,* November–December 1992, web site, www.ifas.org/fw/9211/vista.html.

18. See Ernesto Portillo, Jr., "Vista Controversy Brews over Recommended Text Called Veiled Creationism," *San Diego Union Tribune,* 9 March 1993, B1, 2, 3; Ernesto Portillo, Jr., "Vista School Panel Rejects Text Pushing Intelligent Design of Life," *San Diego Union Tribune,* 5 May 1993, B3, A1; Lisa Petrillo, "Vista OKs 'Biblical Creation' in Schools," *San Diego Union Tribune,* 13 August 1993, A1, B3.

19. Ernesto Portillo, Jr., "2 Vista School Trustees Reignite Creationism Debate," *San Diego Union Tribune,* 21 May 1993, B1, 2.

20. Ernesto Portillo, Jr., and Lisa Petrillo, "Vista Adopts Sex Respect in Heated Board Meeting," *San Diego Union Tribune,* 18 March 1994, A1.

21. Kathy Frasca, "Sex and a Single School Board: Radical Right Experiments in California," *Front Lines Research* 1, no. 1 (June 1994), web site, www.plannedparenthood.org/Library/opposition/Vol1Num1/art4vol1num1.htm.

22. "Religious Right Update: COR Influence on Vista Board?" *Freedom Writer,* June 1994, web site, www.ifas.org/fw/9406/update.html.

23. Ernesto Portillo, Jr., "Vista School Board Alters District Mission Statement," *San Diego Union Tribune,* 7 October 1994, B1, B3.

24. "Election 1994: San Diego County School Election Results," *San Diego Union Tribune,* 9 November 1994, B5.

25. For a description of these organizations, see Freeman, *The San Diego Model,* 27–41.

26. Mary Smith Fletcher and Frances Ann Meador, *Saving Our Schools from the Religious Right: The Lake County, Florida, Story* (Lake County, Fla.: [Lake County Educational Foundation], 1995), 3.

27. Ibid., 6.

28. Ibid., 7–8.

29. Ibid., 9–10.

30. T. M. Mader, "Lake Schools Prepare Sex-Education Battle," *Leesburg, Florida Daily Commercial,* 5 June 1994, A3.

31. T. M. Mader, "Do Parents Object to Sex Ed?" *Leesburg, Florida Daily Commercial,* 21 November 1993, A3.

32. Fletcher and Meador, *Saving Our Schools,* 11–12.

33. Ibid., 13.

34. Phil Long, "Is U.S. Culture Best? County That Says Yes Faces Lawsuit," *Miami Herald,* 25 May 1994, 1A.

35. "Lake County Board Snubs Jamerson, Won't Rethink Policy on American Culture," *Miami Herald,* 30 July 1994, 5B.

36. Long, "Is U.S. Culture Best?"

37. T. M. Mader, "'Lake Leader' Who Wouldn't Like Policy?" *Leesburg, Florida Daily Commercial,* 3 April 1994, A1.

38. "State Education Chief: Change County's America-First Rule," *Miami Herald,* 16 July 1994, 2B.

39. "Lake County Board."

40. Fletcher and Meador, *Saving Our Schools,* 3.

41. Mark Walsh, "Proposed Tax Credit Drawing Support in Colorado," *Educational Week,* 21 October 1998, web site, www.edweek.org/ew/vol-18/08colo.htm.

42. "Protecting Public Schools," editorial, *Denver Post,* 8 November 1998, web site, www.denverpost.com/opinion/edit1108b.htm.

43. Steve Sand, telephone conversation, 30 December 1998.

44. Ibid.

45. "Election '98: Tom Tancredo," *Inside Denver,* web site, www.insidedenver.com/extra/campaign/sixth/tancredo.html.

46. Cited at web page qrd.rdrop.com/qrd/education/1995/two.new.rrr.tactics.

47. Tom Tancredo, "Education Vouchers: America Can't Afford to Wait," *Issue Papers* (Denver: Independence Institute), web site, www.I21.org/SuptDocs/IssuPprs/IPvouch.htm.

48. Campaign flyer distributed by Coloradans for School Choice, Parker, Colorado.

49. Tom Minnery, Focus on the Family letter addressed to "Colorado Friends," October 1998.

50. Tom Tancredo, "The Educational Opportunity Tax Credit: A White Paper Prepared for Colorado Editors, Publishers, and Reporters" (Parker, Colo.: Coloradans for School Choice, 1998), unpublished paper.

51. Steve Sand, telephone conversation, 30 December 1998.

52. See the Heritage Foundation, web page www.heritage.org/schools/indiana .html.

53. E. Ray Moore, Jr., *Exodus 2000* (Columbia, S.C.: Exodus 2000), promotional pamphlet. The brochure lists the organization's web site as www.exodus2000.org.

54. Curt Tomlin, "'Let My Children Go': Exodus 2000 Project," *Christian Alerts* A50 (1998) (Killeen, Tex.: Christian Alert Network, 1998), web site, www .vvm.com/~ctomlin/a50.htm.

NOTES TO CHAPTER 9

1. Michael D'Antonio, *Fall from Grace: The Failed Crusade of the Christian Right* (Boston: South End Press, 1989), 239.

2. For a history of the Christian Right that describes this capacity for change, see Clyde Wilcox, *God's Warriors: The Christian Right in Twentieth-Century America* (Baltimore: Johns Hopkins University Press, 1992); and Matthew C. Moen, *The Transformation of the Christian Right* (Tuscaloosa: University of Alabama Press, 1992).

3. For a discussion of master protest frames, see David A. Snow and Robert D. Benford, "Master Frames and Cycles of Protest," in *Frontiers in Social Movement Theory,* ed. A. D. Morris and C. McClurg-Mueller (New Haven, Conn.: Yale University Press, 1992), 133–55.

4. Mark Shibley's observations about the transformation of evangelicalism in the United States during the last quarter of the twentieth century are important here. Shibley concludes that the southern evangelical culture expanded into other regions of the country, most notably the Midwest. However, in the process, that culture was modified and liberalized by the regional cultures to which it spread. See Mark A. Shibley, *Resurgent Evangelicalism in the United States: Mapping Cultural Change since 1970* (Columbia: University of South Carolina Press, 1996).

5. I borrow the phrase "school wars" from the title of a book by Barbara Gaddy, T. William Hall and Robert Marzano. See *School Wars: Resolving Our Conflicts over Religion and Values* (San Francisco: Jossey-Bass, 1996).

6. For an overview of American Fundamentalism, see George M. Marsden, "Fundamentalism," in *Encyclopedia of the American Religious Experience: Studies of Traditions and Movements,* ed. Charles H. Lippy and Peter W. Williams (New York: Scribner's, 1988), 2:947–62.

7. For an example of this rhetoric, see Jerry Falwell, *Listen, America!* (New York: Bantam Books, 1980).

8. For an overview of the American holiness movement, see Jean Miller Schmidt, "Holiness and Perfection," in *Encyclopedia of the American Religious Experience: Studies of Traditions and Movements,* ed. Charles H. Lippy and Peter W. Williams (New York: Scribner's, 1988), 2:813–29.

9. Ibid., 813.

10. Ibid., 815.

11. Gil Alexander-Moegerle, *James Dobson's War on America* (Amherst, N.Y.: Prometheus Books, 1997), 98.

12. For an overview discussion of American pentecostalism, see Grant Wacker, "Pentecostalism," in *Encyclopedia of the American Religious Experience: Studies of Traditions and Movements,* ed. Charles H. Lippy and Peter W. Williams (New York: Scribner's, 1988), 2:933–45.

13. Robert Mapes Anderson, *Vision of the Disinherited: The Making of American Pentecostalism* (New York: Oxford University Press, 1979), 84, 90, 97.

14. George M. Marsden, *Understanding Fundamentalism and Evangelicalism* (Grand Rapids, Mich.: Eerdmans, 1991), 72.

15. George M. Marsden, "Unity and Diversity in the Evangelical Resurgence," in *Altered Landscapes—Christianity in America, 1935–1985,* ed. David W. Lotz et. al (Grand Rapids, Mich.: Eerdmans, 1989), 69.

16. Randall Balmer, *Mine Eyes Have Seen the Glory: A Journey into the Evangelical Subculture in America* (New York: Oxford University Press, 1993), 278.

17. See George Gallup, Jr., and Jim Castelli, *The People's Religion: American Faith in the 90's* (New York: Macmillan, 1989), 13; and "Queen's: God and Society in North America, 1996" (Pew Charitable Trust), web site, www.arda.tm/archive.QUEEN'S.html.

18. Peter Heslam, *Creating a Christian Worldview: Abraham Kuyper's Lectures on Calvinism* (Grand Rapids, Mich.: Eerdmans, 1998), 2, 6.

19. James D. Bratt, *Abraham Kuyper: A Centennial Reader* (Grand Rapids, Mich.: Eerdmans, 1998), 16.

20. Gary Scott Smith, ed., *God and Politics: Four Views on the Reformation of Civil Government,* with a foreword by John H. White (Phillipsburg, N.J.: Presbyterian and Reformed, 1989), 75–76.

21. Ibid., 123–25.

22. This meaning of the term follows the typology set forth in a symposium entitled "Consultation on the Biblical Role of Civic Government" at Geneva (Pennsylvania) College in 1987. Inside the "theonomist" school, the term takes on specific meaning. In this more technical sense, Rousas John Rushdoony is more correctly a Christian reconstructionist than a theonomist. For a discussion of these distinctions, see "Christian Reconstruction" (Interfaith Alliance), web site, www.religioustolerance.org/reconst.htm.

23. For a full discussion of the theonomist position see Smith, *God and Politics,* 17–53.

24. Julia Mitchell Corbett, *Religion in America,* 3d ed. (Upper Saddle River, N.J.: Prentice-Hall, 1997), 29.

25. See, for example, Catherine L. Albanese, *America: Religions and Religion,* 2d ed. (Belmont, Calif.: Wadsworth, 1992), 396–431.

26. Nathan O. Hatch, *The Democratization of American Christianity* (New Haven, Conn.: Yale University Press, 1989), 6.

27. Ibid., 174.

28. Ibid., 7.

29. Ibid., 9–11.

30. Ibid., 45.

31. Albanese, *America,* 402–3.

32. Alexis de Tocqueville, *Democracy in America,* edited and abridged by Richard D. Heffner (New York: Mentor Books, 1956), 150–56.

33. Robert E. Potter, *The Stream of American Education* (New York: American Book, 1967), 225.

34. Robert L. Church, *Education in the United States* (New York: Free Press, 1976), 70.

35. See John Dewey, *A Common Faith* (New Haven, Conn.: Yale University Press, 1934); and John Dewey, *Democracy in Education* (New York: Macmillan Paperbacks, 1961). I will leave the discussion of the relationship between democracy and public education to others. My concluding thoughts are restricted to the central principles of consensus religion as it presently exists.

36. Corbett, *Religion,* 30.

37. Robert N. Bellah, ed., *Habits of the Heart: Individualism and Commitment in American Life* (Berkeley: University of California Press, 1985), 237.

38. Corbett, *Religion,* 30–31.

Bibliography

Abanes, Richard. *American Militias: Rebellion, Racism, and Religion.* With a foreword by Roy Innis. Downers Grove, Ill.: InterVarsity Press, 1996.

Aberle, David. "The Prophet Dance and Reactions to White Contact." *Southwest Journal of Anthropology* 15, no. 1 (1959): 74–83.

Aberle, David, and Omer Stewart. *Navaho and Ute Peyotism: A Chronology and Distributional Study.* Boulder: University of Colorado Press, 1957.

Adams, Blair. *Who Owns the Children? Public Compulsion, Private Responsibility, and the Dilemma of Ultimate Responsibility.* 5th ed. Waco, Tex.: Truth Forum, 1991. Originally published in 1983.

"Adrian Ecumenical Fellowship Meets." *Adrian (Michigan) Daily Telegram,* 12 July 1991, A1.

"Adrian Public Schools Community Information Sheet." Adrian, Mich.: Adrian Public Schools, n.d.

Affective Education. Special Rept. no. 18. Costa Mesa, Calif.: CEE, n.d.

Ahlstrom, Sydney. *A Religious History of the American People.* New Haven, Conn.: Yale University Press, 1972.

"Alan Sears." Fort Lauderdale, Fla.: Reclaiming America, 1998. Web site: www .reclaimamerica.org/html/as.htm.

Albanese, Catherine L. *America: Religions and Religion.* 2d ed. Belmont, Calif.: Wadsworth, 1992.

Alexander-Moegerle, Gil. *James Dobson's War on America.* Amherst, N.Y.: Prometheus Books, 1997.

"Alliance Defense Fund." *Right Wing Watch,* 6 June 1997. Washington, D.C.: People for the American Way. Web site: www.pfaw.org/rww/rw060697.htm.

"Alliance Defense Fund." *Right Wing Watch,* 21 March 1997. Washington, D.C.: People for the American Way. Web site: www.pfaw.org/rww/rw032197.

Ammerman, Nancy. *Bible Believers: Fundamentalists in the Modern World.* New Brunswick, N.J.: Rutgers University Press, 1987.

———. "The Fundamentalist Worldview: Ideology and Social Structure in an Independent Fundamental Church." Ph.D. diss., Yale University, 1983.

Anderson, Robert Mapes. *Vision of the Disinherited: The Making of American Pentecostalism.* New York: Oxford University Press, 1979.

Averill, Lloyd. *Religious Right, Religious Wrong: A Critique of the Fundamentalist Phenomenon.* New York: Pilgrim Press, 1989.

Bahnsen, Greg L. "False Antithesis: A Critique of the Notion of Antithesis in Francis Schaeffer's Apologetic." *Antithesis* 1, no. 3 (May–June 1990). Web site: www .wavefront.com/Contra_M/antithesis/v1n3/ant_v1n3_schaeffer.html.

Bainton, Roland H. *The Reformation of the Sixteenth Century.* Boston: Beacon Press, 1952.

Baker, A. A. *The Successful Christian School.* Pensacola, Fla.: A Beka Book, 1979.

Balmer, Randall. *Mine Eyes Have Seen the Glory: A Journey into the Evangelical Subculture in America.* New York: Oxford University Press, 1993.

Barkun, Michael. *Religion and the Racist Right.* Chapel Hill: University of North Carolina Press, 1994.

Barnes, James A. "Parent Power." *National Journal,* 12 December 1993.

Barr, James. *Beyond Fundamentalism: Biblical Foundations for Evangelical Christianity.* Philadelphia: Westminster Press, 1984.

————. *Fundamentalism.* London: SCM Press, 1977.

Barrett, Lawrence I. "Fighting for God and the Right Wing." *Time,* 13 September 1993, 59–60.

Barton, David. *America's Godly Heritage.* 1990. Reissued, Aledo, Tex.: WallBuilders, 1992. Videotape.

————. "Food for Thought: A Correct Biblical Response Is Essential." *Wallbuilders Report,* spring 1996. Web site: www.christiananswers.net/wall/wbrspg96.html.

Bauer, Gary L. "National Education Summit." Straight Talk. Washington, D.C.: Family Research Council. Web site: www.frc.org/frc/net/st96d3.html.

————. "National History Standards: Clintonites Miss the Moon." Perspective Papers. Washington, D.C.: Family Research Council. Web site: www.frc.org/frc/perspective/pv95c2ed.html.

Beck, Rosalie, and David W. Hendon. "Notes on Church-State Affairs." *Journal of Church and State* 36, no. 2 (spring 1994): 417–50.

Becker, Theodore Lewis, and Richard A. Couto, eds. *Teaching Democracy and Being Democratic.* Westport, Conn.: Praeger, 1996.

Beckwith, Francis. "Is Public Education Really Neutral?" *Teachers in Focus,* October 1998. Web site: www.family.org/cforum/teachersmag/features/a0002814.html.

Bedell, George C., Leo Sandon, Jr., and Charles T. Wellborn. *Religion in America.* 2d ed. New York: Macmillan, 1982.

Bellah, Robert N. *The Broken Covenant: American Civil Religion in a Time of Trial.* New York: Seabury Press, 1975.

Bellah, Robert N., ed. *Habits of the Heart: Individualism and Commitment in American Life.* Berkeley: University of California Press, 1985.

Bellant, Russ. *The Religious Right in Michigan Politics.* Silver Spring, Md.: Americans for Religious Liberty, 1966.

Belt, Carol. "Belt Report Part I, Part II: Education or Indoctrination, Direction 2000 Connection, Littleton Public Schools Analysis." White paper, 1993.

Benen, Steve. "Educational Opportunity or Educational Scam?" *Church and State* 51, no. 9 (October 1998): 11–12.

———. "Evolving Debate." *Church and State* 51, no. 9 (October 1998): 13–16.

———. "Rocky Mountain High." *Church and State* 51, no. 11 (December 1998): 7–8.

Bennett, William J., ed. and commentator. *The Book of Virtues: A Treasury of Great Moral Stories.* New York: Simon and Shuster, 1993.

Berger, Peter. *The Sacred Canopy: Elements of a Sociological Theory of Religion.* Garden City, N.Y.: Doubleday, 1967.

Berger, Peter, and Thomas Luckmann. *The Social Construction of Reality: A Treatise in the Sociology of Knowledge.* New York: Anchor Books, 1966.

Berlet, Chip, ed. *Eyes Right: Challenging the Right-Wing Backlash.* Boston: South End Press, 1995.

Berliner, David C., and Bruce J. Biddle. *The Manufactured Crisis: Myths, Fraud, and the Attack on America's Public Schools.* Reading, Mass.: Addison-Wesley, 1995.

"Big Crowd Packs Dawson to Discuss School Plan." *Adrian (Michigan) Daily Telegram,* 20 August 1991, 1.

Blue Mountain Working Group. "A Call to Defend Democracy and Pluralism." In Berlet, *Eyes Right,* 316–26.

Boston, Rob. "The Public School Bashers." *Church and State* 51, no. 9 (October 1998): 4–8.

———. *Why the Religious Right Is Wrong about Separation of Church and State.* Prometheus Books, 1993.

Bracey, Gerald. "The Fourth Bracey Report on the Condition of Public Education." *Phi Delta Kappan,* October 1994, 114–27.

———. "The Second Bracey Report on the Condition of Public Education." *Phi Delta Kappan,* October 1992, 104–17.

———. "The Third Bracey Report on the Condition of Public Education." *Phi Delta Kappan,* October 1993, 104–17.

———. "Why Can't They Be Like We Were?" *Phi Delta Kappan,* October 1991, 104–17.

Bratt, James D. *Abraham Kuyper: A Centennial Reader.* Grand Rapids, Mich.: Eerdmans, 1998.

Brown, Harold O. J. *The Reconstruction of the Republic.* New Rochelle, N.Y.: Arlington House. 1977.

Brummelen, Harro W. Van. *Telling the Next Generation: Educational Development in North American Calvinist Christian Schools.* New York: University Press of America, 1986.

Bryant, Anita. *The Anita Bryant Story: The Survival of Our Nation's Families and the Threat of Militant Homosexuality.* Old Tappan, N.J.: Revell, 1977.

Buehrer, Eric. *The New Age Masquerade: The Hidden Agenda in Your Child's Classroom.* Brentwood, Tenn.: Woglemuth and Hyatt, 1990.

Burridge, Kenelm. *New Heaven, New Earth: A Study of Millenarian Activities.* New York: Schocken Books, 1969.

Burson, Scott R., and Jerry L. Walls. *C.S. Lewis and Francis Schaeffer: Lessons for a New Century from the Most Influential Apologists of Our Time.* Downers Grove, Ill.: InterVarsity Press, 1998.

Butler, Jonathan. "Adventism and the American Experience." In *The Rise of Adventism: A Commentary on the Social and Religious Ferment of Mid-Nineteenth Century America,* ed. Edwin Scott Gaustad, 173–206. New York: Harper and Row, 1974.

Cady, Linell E. *Religion, Theology, and American Public Life.* SUNY Series in Religious Studies. Albany: State University of New York Press, 1993.

———. *Religion, Theology, and American Public Life.* Albany, N.Y.: State University of New York Press, 1993.

"Can Public Schools Teach Bible Curriculum?" *Maranatha Christian Journal,* 13 February 1998. Top News Headlines. Web site: www.mcjonline.com/news/news2355.htm.

Cannon, Dale. *Six Ways of Being Religious: A Framework for Comparative Studies of Religion.* Belmont, Calif.: Wadsworth, 1996.

Cantor, David. *The Religious Right: The Assault on Tolerance and Pluralism in America.* New York: Anti-Defamation League, 1994.

Capps, Walter H. *The New Religious Right: Piety, Patriotism, and Politics.* Columbia: University of South Carolina Press, 1990.

Carter, Stephen L. *The Culture of Disbelief: How American Law and Politics Trivialize Religious Devotion.* New York: Basic Books, 1993.

Center for National Policy. "Squaretable Discussion on 'The Diminishing Divide: American Churches, American Politics.'" Washington, D.C., 1997. Web site: www.access.digex.net/cnp/relchat4.html.

Center Views, August 1991, 2.

"Chalcedon." Vallecito, Calif.: Chalcedon. Web site: www.chalcedon.edu/announce/ann_1195.html.

Chambers, Glen, and Gene Fisher. *United States History for Christian Schools.* Greenville, S.C.: Bob Jones University Press, 1984.

Cherry, Conrad, ed. *God's New Israel: Religious Interpretations of American Destiny.* Englewood Cliffs, N.J.: Prentice-Hall, 1971.

"Christian Coalition Names New President and Executive Director: A New Era Dawns with New Leaders Who Link the Reagan Revolution with the Rising Influence of Active People of Faith." Chesapeake, Va.: Christian Coalition, 1997. Web site: www.cc.org/publications/ccnews/ccnews97.html#tate.

"Christian Coalition School Board Majority Loses Control in Lee County, Fla." *Church and State* 51, no. 9 (October 1998): 3.

"Christian Reconstruction." Interfaith Alliance. Web site: www.religioustolerance .org/reconst.htm.

Church, Robert L. *Education in the United States.* New York: Free Press, 1976.

Cimino, Richard P., ed & publ. *Religion Watch* 5, no. 4.

Clarkson, Fred. *Eternal Hostility: The Struggle between Theocracy and Democracy.* Monroe, Maine: Common Courage Press, 1997.

———. "Wildmon Kingdom." *Mother Jones,* November–December 1990, 11.

Clebsch, William A. *American Religious Thought: A History.* Chicago: University of Chicago Press, 1973.

———. *From Sacred to Profane America: The Role of Religion in American History.* New York: Harper and Row, 1968.

"Clinton Urges School Diversity Training." Education Reporter. Alton, Ill.: Eagle Forum, 1998. Web site: www.eagleforum.org/educate/1998/jan98/values.html.

"Coalition Exit Poll Reveals Pro-Family Voters Can't Be Taken for Granted." *Christian Coalition,* posted 4 November 1998. Chesapeake, Va. Web site: www.cc.org/ publications/ccnews/ccnews98.html#elresults.

Coleman, Nancy. "Every Candidate for Top Three GOP Posts Scored 100 Percent on Latest Christian Coalition Scorecard." Washington, D.C.: People for the American Way, 1998. Web site: www.pfaw.org/news//show.cgi?/article= 911335327.

Collins, Randall, and Michael Makowsky. *The Discovery of Society.* 4th ed. New York: Random House, 1989.

"Conference Explains Problems with Goals 2000 and School-to-Work." Education Reporter. Alton, Ill.: Eagle Forum, 1997. Web site: www.eagleforum.org/ educate/1997/mar97/er_mar97.html.

Conn, Joseph L. "God, Guns and the GOP." *Church and State* 51, no. 10 (November 1998): 4–8.

Cooper, James. F., Jr. "Half-Way Covenant." In *Dictionary of Christianity in America,* ed. Daniel G. Reid, Robert D. Linder, Bruce L. Shelly, and Harry S. Stout, 505–6. Downers Grove, Ill.: InterVarsity Press, 1990.

Corbett, Julia Mitchell. *Religion in America.* 3d ed. Upper Saddle River, N.J.: Prentice-Hall, 1997.

Corrigan, John. "The Enlightenment." In *Encyclopedia of the American Religious Experience: Studies of Traditions and Movements,* ed. Charles H. Lippy and Peter W. Williams, 2:1089–102. New York: Scribner's, 1988.

Coser, Lewis. *The Functions of Social Conflict.* New York: Free Press, 1956.

"Council for National Policy Unofficial Home Page." Great Barrington, Mass.: Institute for First Amendment Studies, 1998. Web site: www.berkshire.net/ifas/ cnp/index.html.

Cunningham, Lawrence S., John Kelsay, R. Maurice Barineau, and Heather Jo McVoy. *The Sacred Quest: An Invitation to the Study of Religion.* New York: Macmillan, 1991.

Curry, Tom. "An Exodus from the Public Schools? Call for 5 Million Students to Quit Public Schools by Year 2000." MSNBC, 1997. Web site: www.msnbc.com/news/124752.asp.

D'Antonio, Michael. *Fall from Grace: The Failed Crusade of the Christian Right.* Boston: South End Press, 1989.

D'Arcy, Eric. *Human Acts: An Essay in Their Moral Evolution.* Oxford: Oxford University Press, 1963.

Davies, Douglas. "Christianity." In Holm and Bowker, *Myth and History,* 40–68. London: Pinter Publishers, 1994.

————. "Introduction: Raising the Issues." In *Rites of Passage,* ed. Jean Holm and John Bowker. London: Pinter, 1994.

Davis, Charles. *Temptations of Religion.* New York: Harper and Row, 1973.

Dawson, Cole P. "Ingersoll, Robert Green (1833–1899)." In *Dictionary of Christianity in America,* ed. Daniel G. Reid, Robert D. Linder, Bruce L. Shelley, and Harry S. Stout, 575–76. Downers Grove, Ill.: InterVarsity Press, 1990.

"Dennis Hastert, New Speaker for the House of Representatives." Washington, D.C.: People for the American Way, 1999. Electronic newsletter.

Dennis, Lane, ed. *Francis A. Schaeffer: Portraits of the Man and His Work.* Westchester, Ill.: Crossway, 1986.

Detwiler, Fritz. "Let's Be Fair about This: Democratic Pluralism and the Christian Right." Dayton, Ohio: Institute for the Development of Educational Activities, 1993. Videotape.

————. "'A Place at the Table': An Analysis of the Christian Right Anti-OBE Campaign and Its Impact on Public Education." *Religion and Education* 23, no. 2 (fall 1996): 56–64.

————. "A Response to P.E.A.F.: The Language of the Christian Right." Adrian, Mich., 1991. Unpublished paper.

————. "A Tale of Two Districts: A Case Study in Democratic Responses to Public Education." *Educational Leadership* 51, no. 4 (December–January 1993–1994): 24–28.

"Developing an IDEA to Improve Education." Editorial. *Adrian (Michigan) Daily Telegram,* 7 August 1991.

Dewey, John. *A Common Faith.* New Haven, Conn.: Yale University Press, 1934.

————. *Democracy in Education.* New York: Macmillan Paperbacks, 1961.

Diamond, Sara. *Roads to Dominion: Right-Wing Movements and Political Power in the United States.* New York: Guilford Press, 1995.

————. *Spiritual Warfare: The Politics of the Christian Right.* Boston: South End Press, 1989.

Dierenfield, Richard B. *Religion in American Public Schools.* Washington, D.C.: Public Affairs Press, 1962.

The Diminishing Divide: American Churches, American Politics. Philadelphia: Pew Re-

search Center for the People and the Press, 1997. Web site: www.people-press
.org/relgrpt.htm.

"DNA and Neanderthals." Newsflash. Washington, D.C.: Concerned Women for
America, 1997. Web site: www.cwfa.org/archive/newsflash/news_dna0797.html.

"Dobson Meets with Third Party Extremist in Colorado Springs." *Church and
State* 48, no. 8 (September 1995): 184.

Dobson, James C. *Citizen* 6, no. 7 (July 1992): 2.

———. *Dare to Discipline*. Wheaton, Ill.: Tyndale House, 1973.

———. "Dr. Dobson Answers Your Questions." *Focus on the Family,* February
1994, 7.

———. "Dr. Dobson's Study." *Focus on the Family Newsletter,* April 1998. Web site:
www.family.org/docstudy/newsletters/a0001274.html.

———. *Focus on the Family Letter,* May 1994.

———. *Love Must Be Tough*. Waco, Tex.: Word, 1983.

———. *Parenting Isn't for Cowards*. Waco, Tex.: Word, 1987.

Dobson, James C., and Gary L. Bauer. *Children at Risk: The Battle for the Hearts and
Minds of Our Kids*. Dallas: Word, 1990.

Dolan, Jay. *The American Catholic Experience*. Garden City, N.Y.: Image Books,
1987.

Driver, Tom F. *The Magic of Ritual: Our Need for Liberating Rites That Transform Our
Lives and Our Communities*. New York: HarperSanFrancisco, 1991.

"The 'Dumbing Down' of American Education." Television broadcast. Christian
Broadcasting Network, 1998. Web site: www.cbn.org/news/stories/980515.asp.

Educational Restructuring. Costa Mesa, Calif.: CEE, n.d.

"Education Briefs." Education Reporter. Alton, Ill.: Eagle Forum, 1997. Web site:
www.eagleforum.org/educate/1997/apr97/briefs.html.

Elam, Stanley, Lowell C. Rose, and Alec M. Gallup. "The 25th Annual Phi Delta
Kappa/Gallup Poll of the Public's Attitudes toward the Public Schools." *Phi
Delta Kappan,* October 1993, 137–52.

"Election 1994: San Diego County School Election Results." *San Diego Union Tribune,* 9 November 1994, B5.

"Election '98: Tom Tancredo." *Inside Denver.* Web site: insidedenver.com/extra/
campaign/sixth/tancredo.html.

Eliade, Mircea. *Patterns in Comparative Religion*. Trans. Rosemary Sheed. Cleveland:
World, 1968.

———. *The Sacred and the Profane*. New York: Harcourt Brace Jovanovich, 1957.

Ellis, John Tracy. *American Catholicism*. Rev. ed. Chicago History of Civilization series. Chicago: University of Chicago Press, 1956.

Elsner, Alan. "Christian Right Could Lose Clout after U.S. Elections." *Yahoo! News
Politics Headlines,* 5 November 1998. Web site: www.dailynews.yahoo.com/
headlines/pl/story.html?s=v/nm/19981105/pl/christians_1.html.

Eng, Lily. "A Cry against Educational Reform." *Seattle Times,* 23 March 1993.

Fackre, Gabriel. *The Religious Right and Christian Faith.* Grand Rapids, Mich.: Eerdmans, 1982.

Falwell, Jerry. *Listen, America!* New York: Bantam Books, 1980.

————. *Strength for the Journey.* New York: Simon and Schuster, 1987.

Farley, Edward. *Deep Symbols: Their Postmodern Effacement and Reclamation.* Valley Forge, Pa.: Trinity Press International, 1996.

Farris, Michael. "Living Room or Classroom? A Look at the Home School Movement." Television broadcast. Christian Broadcasting Network, 1998. Web site: www.cbn.org/news/stories/980902.asp.

Finke, Roger, and Rodney Stark. *The Churching of America, 1776–1990: Winners and Losers in Our Religious Economy.* New Brunswick, N.J.: Rutgers University Press, 1992.

Fitzgerald, Francis. *America Revised.* New York: Vintage Books, 1980.

Flake, Carol. *Redemptorama: Culture, Politics, and the New Evangelicalism.* Garden City, N.Y.: Anchor Press, Doubleday, 1984.

Fletcher, Mary Smith, and Frances Ann Meador. *Saving Our Schools from the Religious Right: The Lake County, Florida, Story.* Lake County, Fla.: [Lake County Educational Foundation], 1995.

Fowler, Robert Booth. *A New Engagement: Evangelical Political Thought, 1966–1976.* Grand Rapids, Mich.: Eerdmans, 1982.

————. *Unconventional Partners: Religion and Liberal Culture in the United States.* Grand Rapids, Mich.: Eerdmans, 1989.

Fowler, Robert Booth, and Allen D. Hertzke. *Religion and Politics in America: Faith, Culture, and Strategic Choices.* Boulder: Westview Press, 1995.

Franklin, Ben A., ed. "The Christian Coalition." Newsletter. *Washington Spectator,* 15 October 1994.

Frasca, Kathy. "Sex and a Single School Board: Radical Right Experiments in California." *Front Lines Research* 1, no. 1 (June 1994).

Freeman, Matthew. *The San Diego Model: A Community Battles the Religious Right.* Washington, D.C.: People for the American Way, 1993.

Freund, Chris, and Candice J. Zouhary. "A Reasonable Budget Target: Government Schools, Part I." *NeoPolitique,* March 1996. Web site: www.neopolitique.org/articles/education.html.

Furst, Peter T. "To Find Our Life: Peyote among the Huichol Indians of Mexico." In *Flesh of the Gods: The Ritual Use of Hallucinogens,* ed. Peter T. Furst, 136–84. Prospect Heights, Ill.: Waveland Press, 1972.

Gaddy, Barbara, T. William Hall, and Robert J. Marzano. *School Wars: Resolving Our Conflicts over Religion and Values.* San Francisco: Jossey-Bass, 1996.

Gallup, George, Jr., and Jim Castelli. *The People's Religion: American Faith in the 90's.* New York: Macmillan, 1989.

Garfinkel, Harold. *Studies in Ethnomethodology.* Englewood Cliffs, N.J.: Prentice-Hall, 1967.

Gaustad, Edwin Scott. *Dissent in American Religion.* Chicago: University of Chicago Press, 1973.

Gedicks, Frederick Mark. *"No Man's Land": The Place of Latter-Day Saints in the Culture War.* Monograph. Bloomington: Poynter Center for the Study of Ethics and American Institutions, Indiana University, 1999.

Geertz, Clifford. *The Interpretation of Cultures.* New York: Basic Books, 1973.

————. *Islam Observed.* New Haven, Conn.: Yale University Press, 1968.

————. "Religion as a Culture System." In Geertz, *Interpretation of Cultures,* 100–108.

Gennep, Arnold van. *The Rites of Passage.* London: Routledge and Kegan Paul, 1960. Originally published in 1908.

Gergen, Kenneth J. *The Saturated Self: Dilemmas of Identity in Contemporary Life.* [New York]: Basic Books, 1991.

Gerson, Michael J. "Public Schools Teach Bible as History. What Role Is There for Jesus and Jeroboam?" *U.S. News and World Report,* 1998. Web site: www.usnews.com/usnews/issue/980112/12bibl.htm.

Giroux, Henry A. *Schooling and the Struggle for Public Life: Critical Pedagogy in the Modern Age.* American Culture series. Minneapolis: University of Minnesota Press, 1988.

"God and Society in North America, 1996." Pew Charitable Trust. Web site: www.arda.tm/archive.QUEEN'S.html.

Goffman, Erving. *The Presentation of the Self in Everyday Life.* New York: Doubleday Anchor Books, 1959.

Goodlad, John. *A Place Called School.* New York: McGraw-Hill, 1984.

"GOP Governors Tout School Voucher 'Battle Plan.'" *Church and State* 51, no. 9 (October 1998): 3.

Gore, Liz. "R. J. Rushdoony Turns 80." *Freedom Writer,* July 1996. Web site: www.ifas.org/fw/9607/rushdoony.html.

Gottlieb, Stephen S. "The Right to Read: Censorship in the School Library." In *ERIC Digest.* Bloomington, Ind.: ERIC Clearinghouse on Reading and Communication Skills, 1990.

Grant, George. *Bringing in the Sheaves: Transforming Poverty into Productivity.* Rev. and exp. ed. Brentwood, Tenn.: Wolgemuth and Hyatt, 1988.

Green, John C. "The Christian Right and the 1996 Elections: An Overview." In Rozell and Wilcox, *God at the Grass Roots,* 1–14.

Green, John C., ed. *Religion and the Culture Wars: Dispatches from the Front.* Lanham, Md.: Rowman and Littlefield, 1996.

Grimm, Roy Eleutherios. "'Community Impact Evangelism' and Pluralism in Public Education." Ph.D. diss., University of Colorado, 1991.

Grimstead, Jay, gen. ed. *The Christian World View Documents: Applying Biblical Principles to Every Sphere of Life and Thought*. Sunnyvale, Calif.: Coalition on Revival, 1986.

———. "A Manifesto for the Christian Church." In Grimstead, *The Christian World View Documents*.

"Group Urges 'Biblical Tests of Character' for Candidates." *Freedom Writer*, March–April 1998, 1.

Guth, James L. "The Politics of the Christian Right." In Green, *Religion and the Culture Wars*, 7–29.

Guth, James L., and Oran P. Smith. "South Carolina Christian Right: Just Part of the Family Now?" In Rozell and Wilcox, *God at the Grass Roots*, 15–31.

Gutman, Amy. *Democratic Education*. Princeton, N.J.: Princeton University Press, 1987.

Hadden, Jeffrey K. "Televangelism and the New Christian Right." In *Religion and Religiosity in America*, ed. Jeffrey K. Hadden and Theodore E. Long, 114–27. Studies in Honor of Joseph H. Fichter series. New York: Crossroad, 1983.

Hall, David. "Abraham Kuyper: An Influential and Overlooked Political Theorist." *Covenant Syndicate*, 28 May 1998. Web site: www.capo.org/opeds/dh528.htm.

Hallowell, A. Irving. "Ojibwa Ontology, Behavior, and World View." In *Teachings from the American Earth*, ed. Dennis Tedlock and Barbara Tedlock, 141–78. 1975. Reprint, New York: Liveright, 1992.

Hamilton, Michael S. "The Dissatisfaction of Francis Schaeffer, Part 1." *Christianity Today*, 3 March 1997, 22. Web site: www.christianity.net/ct/7T322a.html.

Handy, Robert T. *A Christian America: Protestant Hopes and Historical Realities*. 2d ed. New York: Oxford University Press, 1984.

Harrell, David E. *Pat Robertson: A Personal, Religious, and Political Portrait*. San Francisco: Harper and Row, 1988.

Hatch, Nathan O. *The Democratization of American Christianity*. New Haven, Conn.: Yale University Press, 1989.

Hatch, Nathan O., and Mark A. Noll, eds. *The Bible in America: Essays in Cultural History*. New York: Oxford University Press, 1982.

"Help Restore Christian Holidays to the Public Schools." *Christian American*, November–December 1997. Web site: www.cc.org/publications/ca/1197/holidays.html.

Herberg, Will. *Protestant, Catholic, Jew: An Essay in American Religious Sociology*. Garden City, N.Y.: Doubleday, 1955.

Herron, Mark. "Conservative Firewall Stops Ballot Meltdown." *Christian American* 8, no. 1 (1997): 24.

Hertzke, Allen. *Representing God in Washington*. Knoxville: University of Tennessee Press, 1988.

Heslam, Peter. *Creating a Christian Worldview: Abraham Kuyper's Lectures on Calvinism*. Grand Rapids, Mich.: Eerdmans, 1998.

Hill, David. "Christian Soldier." *Teacher Magazine,* October–November 1992, 18–22.

Hill, Samuel S., and Dennis E. Owen. *The New Religious Political Right in America.* Nashville, Tenn.: Abingdon Press, 1982.

Hinrichs, Fritz. "Classical Education." Adapted from a speech given at the 1995 Homeschool Curriculum fair in San Diego. At the Podium. Washington, D.C.: Family Research Council. Web site: www.frc.org/frc/podium/pd95i2ed.html.

Hirst, Jacqueline Suthern. "Hinduism." In Holm and Bowker, *Myth and History,* 69–96.

Hoffecker, W. Andrew. "Princeton Theology." In *Dictionary of Christianity in America,* ed. Daniel Reid, Robert D. Linder, Bruce L. Shelley, and Harry S. Stout, 941–42. Downers Grove, Ill.: InterVarsity Press, 1990.

Holland, Robert. "Focus: What's Wrong with School-to-Work?" Address to conference on Capitol Hill. Education Reporter. Alton, Ill.: Eagle Forum, 1997. Web site: www.eagleforum.org/educate/1997/may97/holland.html.

Holm, Jean, and John Bowker, eds. *Myth and History.* London: Pinter Publishers, 1994.

Hook, Sidney. *Education for Modern Man: A New Perspective.* New York: Humanities Press, 1973.

Hornbeck, Mark. "Multiculturalism in the Hands of the GOP." *Detroit News,* 20 November 1994, 1A, 8A.

Hudson, Kathi. "Focus on the Clinton Administration: Richard W. Riley, Secretary of Education." *Education Newsline,* July–August 1993, 4.

———. "Goals 2000: A Federal Power Grab." *Education Newsline,* July–August 1993, 3–4.

———. "Newsflash." *Education Newsline,* July–August 1993, 2.

———. "Newsflash." *Education Newsline,* January–February 1994, 2.

———. *Reinventing America's Schools: A Practical Guide to Components of Restructuring and Non-Traditional Education.* Vol. 1. Rev. ed. Costa Mesa, Calif.: NACE/CEE, 1992, 1993.

———. *Reinventing America's Schools: A Practical Guide to Components of Restructuring and Non-Traditional Education.* Vols. 2–3. Costa Mesa, Calif.: NACE/CEE, 1992.

———. "Self-Esteem: The Chicken or the Egg?" *Education Newsline,* January–February 1994, 3.

———. "The State of Reform." *Education Newsline,* March–April 1994, 1, 4.

———. "Students Prayerfully Consider Their Rights." *Education Newsline,* January–February 1994, 3.

Hunnex, Milton D. *Philosophies and Philosophers.* San Francisco: Chandler, 1961.

Hunter, James Davison. *Conservative Religion and the Quandary of Modernity.* New Brunswick, N.J.: Rutgers University Press, 1983.

———. *Culture Wars: The Struggle to Define America.* New York: Basic Books, 1991.

Hunter, James Davison. *Evangelicalism: The Coming Generation*. Chicago: University of Chicago Press, 1987.

Hutchison, William R. *The Modernist Impulse in American Protestantism*. Cambridge, Mass.: Harvard University Press.

"Idaho Education Department Adopts 'Abstinence-Only' Role." *Education Reporter*. Alton, Ill.: Eagle Forum, 1997. Web site: www.eagleforum.org/educate/1997/jan97/er_jan97.html.

"IDEA Opponents Hear from Analyst." *Adrian (Michigan) Daily Telegram*, 16 September 1991, 1.

Ingersoll, Julie. "Train Up a Child: A Study of Evangelical Views on Education." Master's thesis, George Washington University, 1990.

"James Dobson's CNP Address." Great Barrington, Mass.: Institute for First Amendment Studies, 1998. Web site: www.ifas.org/cnp/index.html.

James, William. *The Varieties of Religious Experience*. New York: Modern Library, 1902.

Jewett, Robert, and John Shelton Lawrence. *The American Monomyth*. Garden City, N.Y.: Anchor/Doubleday, 1977.

Johnson, Jeff. "Controversy at Christian Coalition." Colorado Springs, Colo.: Family News in Focus. Web site: www.family.org/cforum/fnif/news/a0004748.html.

Jorstad, Erling. *Holding Fast/Pressing on: Religion in America in the 1980s*. New York: Praeger, 1990.

———. *The New Christian Right, 1981–1988*. Lewiston, N.Y.: Edward Mellon Press, 1987.

———. *The Politics of Doomsday*. Nashville, Tenn.: Abingdon Press, 1970.

Kellstedt, Lyman A., John C. Green, James L. Guth, and Corwin E. Smidt. "The Puzzle of Evangelical Protestantism: Core, Periphery, and Political Behavior." In Green, *Religion and the Culture Wars*, 240–66.

Kelly, George A. *The Battle for the American Church*. Garden City, N.Y.: Image Books, 1981.

Kertzer, David I. *Rituals, Politics, and Power*. New Haven, Conn.: Yale University Press, 1988.

Kessler, Sanford. *Tocqueville's Civil Religion: American Christianity and the Prospects for Freedom*. Albany: State University of New York Press, 1994.

"Kinsey, Sex, and Lies." Policy Papers. Washington, D.C.: Concerned Women for America. Web site: www.cwfa.org/policypapers/pp_kinsey.html.

Klemm, David E. *The Hermeneutical Theory of Paul Ricoeur: A Constructive Analysis*. Lewisburg, Pa.: Bucknell University Press, 1983.

Knight, Robert H. "School Days, Sex Daze." Perspective Papers. Washington, D.C.: Family Research Council. Web site: www.frc.org/frc/perspective/pv95i8hs.html.

LaHaye, Beverly. *The Restless Woman*. Grand Rapids, Mich.: Zondervan, 1984.

LaHaye, Tim. *The Battle for the Family*. Old Tappan, N.J.: Revell, 1982.

———. *The Battle for the Mind*. Old Tappan, N.J.: Revell, 1980.

————. *The Battle for the Public Schools: Humanism's Threat to Our Children.* Old Tappan, N.J.: Revell Company, 1983.

————. *The Bible's Influence on American History.* San Diego, Calif.: Master Books, 1976.

————. *Faith of Our Founding Fathers: A Comprehensive Study of America's Christian Foundations.* 1987. Reprint, Green Forest, Ark.: Master Books, 1994.

————. *How to Be Happy though Married.* Wheaton, Ill.: Tyndale House, 1968.

————. *The Race of the 21st Century.* Nashville, Tenn.: Thomas Nelson, 1986.

————. *Sex Education Is for the Family.* Grand Rapids, Mich.: Zondervan, 1985.

————. *Understanding the Male Temperament.* Old Tappan, N.J.: Revell, 1977.

LaHaye, Tim, and Beverly LaHaye. *The Act of Marriage: The Beauty of Sexual Love.* Grand Rapids, Mich.: Zondervan, 1976.

"Lake County Board Snubs Jamerson, Won't Rethink Policy on American Culture." *Miami Herald,* 30 July 1994, 5B.

Lappert, Richard, and Robert Simonds. "The Christian World View of Education." In Grimstead, *Christian World View Documents,* doc. 5, pp. 1–16.

"Latest Religious Preferences." *Emerging Trends* 19, no. 3 (March 1997): 3.

Lawrence, Bruce B. *Defenders of God: The Fundamentalist Revolt against the Modern Age.* 1989. Reprint, Columbia: University of South Carolina Press, 1995.

Leeuw, Gerardus van der. *Religion in Essence and Manifestation: A Study in Phenomenology.* Trans. J. E. Turner. Vol. 1. New York: Harper and Row, 1963.

————. *Religion in Essence and Manifestation: A Study in Phenomenology.* Trans. J. E. Turner. Vol. 2. Gloucester, Massachusetts: Peter Smith, 1967.

Lienesch, Michael. *Redeeming America: Piety and Politics in the New Christian Right.* Chapel Hill: University of North Carolina Press, 1993.

Lindberg, Stanley, ed. *The Annotated McGuffey.* New York: Van Nordstrand Reinhold, 1976.

Long, Phil. "Is U.S. Culture Best? County That Says Yes Faces Lawsuit." *Miami Herald,* 25 May 1994, 1A.

Lott, Jeremy. "Why the Religious Right Will Win." Intellectual Capital, 1998. Web site: www.intellectualcapital.com/issues/98/0924/iccon.asp.

Luckmann, Thomas. *The Invisible Religion: The Problem of Religion in Modern Society.* New York: Macmillan, 1967.

Lugg, Catherine A. *For God and Country: Conservatism and American School Policy.* New York: Peter Lang, 1996.

Mader, T. M. "Do Parents Object to Sex Ed?" *Leesburg (Florida) Daily Commercial,* 21 November 1993, A3.

————. "'Lake Leader' Who Wouldn't Like Policy?" *Leesburg (Florida) Daily Commercial,* 3 April 1994, A1.

————. "Lake Schools Prepare Sex-Education Battle." *Leesburg (Florida) Daily Commercial,* 5 June 1994, A3.

Maffet, Gregory John. "The Educational Thought of Cornelius Van Til: An Analysis of the Ideological Foundations of His Christian Philosophy of Education." Ed.D. diss., University of Akron, 1984.

Maginnis, Robert L. "Federal Drug War Ignoring Great Ally: Faith-Based Treatment." Insight. Washington, D.C.: Family Research Council. Web site: www.frc .org/frc/insight/is96gldr.html.

Marsden, George M. "Afterword: Religion, Politics, and the Search for an American Consensus." In *Religion and American Politics: From the Colonial Period to the 1980s,* ed. Mark A. Noll, 380–89. New York: Oxford University Press, 1990.

———. "Everyone One's Own Interpreter? The Bible, Science, and Authority in Mid-Nineteenth Century America." In Hatch and Noll, *The Bible in America:,* 79–100.

———. "Fundamentalism." In *Encyclopedia of the American Religious Experience: Studies of Traditions and Movements,* ed. Charles H. Lippy and Peter W. Williams, 2:947–62. New York: Scribner's, 1988.

———. *Fundamentalism and American Culture.* New York: Oxford University Press, 1980.

———. "Religious Professors Are the Last Taboo." *Wall Street Journal,* 22 December 1993, A10.

———. *The Soul of the American University.* New York: Oxford University Press, 1994.

———. *Understanding Fundamentalism and Evangelicalism.* Grand Rapids, Mich.: Eerdmans, 1991.

———. "Unity and Diversity in the Evangelical Resurgence." In *Altered Landscapes—Christianity in America, 1935–1985,* ed. David W. Lotz, Donald W. Shriver, Jr., and John F. Wilson, 61–76. Grand Rapids, Mich.: Eerdmans, 1989.

Marshall, Jennifer A. "Illegitimacy: Compassion's Offspring." Perspective Papers. Washington, D.C.: Family Research Council. Web site: www.frc.org/frc/ perspective/pv95c4wl.html.

Marshall, Jennifer A., and Kristina Twitty. "Confusing the Call for Professionalism: National Board for Professional Teaching Standards." Insight. Washington, D.C.: Family Research Council. Web site: www.frc.org/frc/insight/is97h2ed.html.

Marshall, Jennifer A., and Eric Unsworth. "Freeing America's Schools: The Case against the U.S. Education Department." Family Policy Documents. Washington, D.C.: Family Research Council, 1995. Web site: www.frc.org/frc/fampol/ fp95ded.html.

Martin, William. *With God on Our Side: The Rise of the Religious Right in America.* New York: Broadway Books, 1996.

Marty, Martin E. *Religion and Republic: The American Circumstance.* Boston: Beacon Press, 1987.

———. "The Twentieth Century: Protestants and Others." In *Religion & American Politics: From the Colonial Period to the 1980s,* ed. Mark A. Noll, 322–36. New York: Oxford University Press, 1990.

Mattox, William R., Jr. "Education Debate Needs to Focus on the Family." Perspective Papers. Washington, D.C.: Family Research Council. Web site: www .frc.org/frc/perspective/pv95j3ed.html.

May, Henry F. *The Enlightenment in America.* New York: Oxford University Press, 1976.

May, Rollo. "The Significance of Symbols." In *Symbolism in Religion and Literature,* ed. Rollo May, 11–49. New York: George Braziller, 1960.

McAdam, Doug, and David A. Snow. "Introduction—Social Movements: Conceptual and Theoretical Issues." In *Social Movements: Readings on Their Emergence, Mobilization, and Dynamics,* ed. Doug McAdam and David A. Snow. Los Angeles: Roxbury, 1997.

McCarthy, Rockne M., James Skillen, and William Harper. *Disestablishment a Second Time: Genuine Pluralism for America's Schools.* Grand Rapids, Mich.: Christian University Press, 1982.

McDannell, Colleen. "Creating the Christian Home: Home Schooling in Contemporary America." In *American Sacred Space,* ed. David Chidester and Edward T. Linenthal, 187–219. Bloomington: Indiana University Press, 1995.

Melton, J. Gordon, ed. *The Encyclopedia of American Religions: A Comprehensive Study of the Major Religious Groups in the United States and Canada.* 3 vols. Tarrytown, N.Y.: Triumph Books, 1991.

Menendez, Albert J. *Visions of Reality: What Fundamentalist Schools Teach.* Buffalo, N.Y.: Prometheus Books, 1993.

Miller, Lori-Anne, and Oralandar Brand-Williams. "New Curriculum Plan Triggers an Uproar." *Detroit News,* 18 November 1994, 1A, 10A.

Miller, Perry. *Errand into the Wilderness.* 2d ed. New York: Harper and Row, 1964.

Mills, C. Wright. *The Power Elite.* New York: Oxford University Press, 1956.

"The Ministry of Chalcedon." Vallecito, Calif.: Chalcedon. Web site: www.chalcedon .edu/chalcedon_info.html.

Minnery, Tom. "The Fritz and Frosty Show." *Citizen* 7, no. 9 (20 September 1993): 5.

"Mission Statement." Alton, Ill.: Eagle Forum. Web site: www.eagleforum.org/ misc/descript.html.

Moen, Matthew C. *The Christian Right and Congress.* Tuscaloosa: University of Alabama Press, 1989.

———. *The Transformation of the Christian Right.* Tuscaloosa: University of Alabama Press, 1992.

"Money, Membership Woes Drive Christian Coalition's Agenda." Washington, D.C.: People for the American Way, 1998. E-mail press release, presslst@ pfaw.org.

Montgomery, Peter. "Nationwide Poll Shows Concern for Values, Rejection of Religious Right Agenda." *People for the American Way News* 1, no. 1 (fall 1994): 1–2.

Moorhead, James H. "Theological Interpretations and Critiques of American Society and Culture." In *Encyclopedia of the American Religious Experience: Studies of Traditions and Movements*, ed. Charles H. Lippy and Peter W. Williams, 1:101–15. New York: Scribner's, 1988.

Morahan, Lawrence. "Update—Hodel Resignation Not Related to Clinton Trial, Christian Coalition Says." Conservative News Service, 1999. Web site: www.conservativenews.net/InDepth/archive/199902/IND19990210g.html.

Morrow, Lance. "The Real Points of Light: Its Charter Fading, Its Goals Diverging, the Nation Needs to Redefine What Leadership Means." *Time*, 5 December 1994, 76–77.

Mouw, Richard J. "The Bible in Twentieth-Century Protestantism: A Preliminary Taxonomy." In Hatch and Noll, *The Bible in America*, 139–62.

Moyers, Bill. "God and Politics: On Earth as It Is in Heaven." Produced by Gregg Pratt and Jan Falstad. Public Affairs Television, 1987.

"NAEP Targeted for Change." Education Reporter. Alton, Ill.: Eagle Forum, 1997. Web site: www.eagleforum.org/educate/1997/may97/naep.html.

National Commission on Excellence in Education. *A Nation at Risk: The Imperative for Educational Reform*. Washington, D.C.: Government Printing Office, 1983.

Nesmith, Bruce. *The New Republican Coalition: The Reagan Campaigns and White Evangelicals*. Vol. 41 of Series X, American University Studies. New York: Peter Lang, 1994.

Neuhaus, Richard John. *The Naked Public Square: Religion and Democracy in America*. Grand Rapids, Mich.: Eerdmans, 1984.

"New Welfare Law Backs Chastity." Newsflash. Washington, D.C.: Concerned Women for America, 1997. Web site: www.cwfa.org/archive/newsflash/news_siecus0697.html.

Niebuhr, H. Richard. *Christ and Culture*. New York: Harper and Row, 1951.

———. *The Social Sources of Denominationalism*. 1929. Reprint, New York: New American Library, 1975.

Nielsen, Niels C., Jr. *Fundamentalism, Mythos, and World Religions*. Albany: State University of New York Press, 1993.

Noll, Mark. *One Nation under God? Christian Faith and Political Action in America*. San Francisco: Harper, 1988.

———. *The Scandal of the Evangelical Mind*. Grand Rapids, Mich.: Eerdmans, 1994.

Noll, Mark, Nathan Hatch, and George Marsden, eds. *The Search for Christian America*. Westchester, Ill.: Crossway Books, 1983.

Nord, Warren A. *Religion and American Education: Rethinking a National Dilemma*. Chapel Hill: University of North Carolina Press, 1995.

Numbers, Ronald L. *The Creationists: The Evolution of Scientific Creationism*. Berkeley: University of California Press, 1992.

Oldfield, Duane M. *The Right and the Righteous: The Christian Right Confronts the Republican Party.* Lanham, Md.: Rowman and Littlefield, 1996.

Ottinger, Larry. "People for Litigation Focuses on School Prayer Issues: Major Victory in Mississippi." *People for the American Way News* 1, no. 1 (fall 1994): 5.

Otto, Rudolph. *The Idea of the Holy.* New York: Oxford University Press, 1958.

Outcome-Based Education. Costa Mesa, Calif.: CEE, n.d.

Page, Linda. "The Potential Effects on Education Curricula and Policy of Homosexual 'Marriage.'" Briefing on Capitol Hill regarding the Defense of Marriage Act. At the Podium. Washington, D.C.: Family Research Council, 1996. Web site: www.frc.org/frc/podium/pd96g7hs.html.

"Parents Unable to Teach Children." *Defense of the Family News Flash,* December 1997. Washington, D.C.: Concerned Women for America. Web site: www.cfa .org/archive/newsflash/news_homoedu1297.html.

Parsons, Paul F. *Inside America's Christian Schools.* Macon, Ga.: Mercer University Press, 1987.

"Pat's Empire." *Freedom Writer,* September 1998, 3.

Pelikan, Jaroslav. "Fundamentalism and/or Orthodoxy? Toward an Understanding of the Fundamentalist Phenomenon." In *The Fundamentalist Phenomenon,* ed. Norman J. Cohen, 3–21. Grand Rapids, Mich.: Eerdmans, 1990.

People for the American Way. *Attacks on the Freedom to Learn: 1990–91 Report.* Washington, D.C.: People for the American Way, 1991.

———. "Citizens for Excellence in Education." Washington, D.C.: People for the American Way, n.d.

———. "The Religious Right and School Boards 1992 and 1993." Executive summary. Washington, D.C.: People for the American Way, n.d.

Peshkin, Alan. *God's Choice: The Total World of a Fundamentalist Christian School.* Chicago: University of Chicago Press, 1986.

Petrillo, Lisa. "Religious Right's Biggest Victory Here Short-Lived." *San Diego Union Tribune,* 4 August 1996, A19.

———. "Vista OKs 'Biblical Creation' in Schools." *San Diego Union Tribune,* 13 August 1993, A1, B3.

Pfeffer, Leo. *Church, State, and Freedom.* Rev. ed. Boston: Beacon Press, 1967. Originally published in 1953.

Pflüg, Melissa A. *Ritual and Myth in Odawa Revitalization: Reclaiming a Sovereign Place.* Norman: University of Oklahoma Press, 1998.

Piepenburg, Erik. "Elections '94." *People for the American Way News* 1, no. 1 (fall 1994): 5.

"Planned Parenthood Devises New Strategy to Boost Birth-Control Sales." *Education Reporter.* Alton, Ill.: Eagle Forum, 1997. Web site: www.eagleforum.org/educate/1997/feb97/er_feb97.html.

Porteous, Skipp. "Christian Coalition Update." *Free Inquiry* 12, no. 2 (Spring 1992): 16–17.

Porteous, Skipp. "The New Religious Right—Phase Three: Christianizing America." *Freedom Writer,* May–June 1991, 1.

Portillo, Ernesto, Jr. "2 Vista School Trustees Reignite Creationism Debate." *San Diego Union Tribune,* 21 May 1993, B1, 2.

———. "Vista Controversy Brews over Recommended Text Called Veiled Creationism." *San Diego Union Tribune,* 9 March 1993, B1, 2, 3.

———. "Vista School Board Alters District Mission Statement." *San Diego Union Tribune,* 7 October 1994, B1, B3.

———. "Vista School Panel Rejects Text Pushing Intelligent Design of Life." *San Diego Union Tribune,* 5 May 1993, B3, A1.

Portillo, Ernesto, Jr., and Lisa Petrillo. "Vista Adopts Sex Respect in Heated Board Meeting." *San Diego Union Tribune,* 18 March 1994, A1.

Potter, Robert E. *The Stream of American Education.* New York: American Book, 1967.

"Profile: Chalcedon." *Freedom Writer,* January 1995. Web site: www.ifas.org/fw/9501/chalcedon.html.

"Protecting Public Schools." Editorial. *Denver Post,* 8 November 1998. Web site: www.denverpost.com/opinion/edit1108b.htm.

Quaid, Libby. "Ashcroft Won't Run for President." *Yahoo! Daily News,* 5 January 1999. Web site: www.dailynews.yahoo.com/headlines/ap/elections/story.html?s=v/ap/19990105/el/Ashcroft_2000_1.html.

"Queen's: God and Society in North America 1996." Pew Charitable Trust, 1996. Web site: www.arda.tm/archive/QUEEN'S.html.

Reagan, Ronald. "Weekly Compilation of Presidential Documents." 2 May 1983, vol. 19, no. 17, pp. 592–94. National Archives and Records Administration, Washington, D.C.

Reed, Ralph, Jr. *Active Faith.* New York: Free Press, 1996.

———. *Politically Incorrect.* Dallas: Word, 1994.

———. "We Stand at a Crossroads." *Newsweek,* 13 May 1996, 28–29.

Reed, Ralph, Jr., and Robert L. Simonds. "The Agenda of the Religious Right." *School Administrator* 50, no. 9 (October 1993): 16–20, 22.

Reid, Daniel G., Robert D. Linder, Bruce L. Shelly, and Harry S. Stout. "Calvinism." In *Dictionary of Christianity in America,* ed. Daniel G. Reid, Robert D. Linder, Bruce L. Shelly, and Harry S. Stout, 211–12. Downers Grove, Ill.: InterVarsity Press, 1990.

"The Religious Right on the Issues: 'With God on Our Side.'" *People for the American Way News* 1, no. 1 (fall 1994): 6, 8.

"Religious Right Takes School Board." *Freedom Writer,* November–December 1992. Web site: www.ifas.org/fw/9211/vista.html.

"Religious Right Update: COR Influence on Vista Board?" *Freedom Writer,* June 1994. Web site: www.ifas.org/fw/9406/update.html.

"Report on Citizens for Excellence in Education." Information sheet. People for the American Way, Washington, D.C.

Ribuffo, Leo P. "Liberals and That Old Time Religion." *Nation,* 29 November 1980, 570–73.

Ricouer, Paul. *The Symbolism of Evil.* Trans. Emerson Buchanan. Boston: Beacon Press, 1967.

Riggs, Frank. *Helping Empower Low-Income Parents (HELP) Scholarships Amendments of 1997.* House res. 2746. Washington, D.C.: U.S. House of Representatives, 1997. Web site: thomas.loc.gov/cgi-bin/query/D?c105:./temp/~c105LeC95P:e3980.

"A Right Wing and a Prayer: The Religious Right in Your Public Schools." Executive summary. Washington, D.C.: People for the American Way, 1997. Web site: www.pfaw.org/wing/rwpb.html.

Risinger, C. Frederic. "Teaching about Religion in the Social Studies." Bloomington, Indiana: Eric Clearinghouse for Social Studies/Social Science Education, 1988. ERIC Digest.

Robertson, Pat. *America's Date with Destiny.* Nashville, Tenn.: Thomas Nelson, 1986.

———. "Is America Headed for Judgment?" Television broadcast. Christian Broadcasting Network. Web site: www.cbn.org/pat/pat-judgment.asp.

———. *The New Millennium.* Dallas: Word, 1990.

———. *The New World Order.* Dallas: Word, 1991.

———. "Pat's Perspective: Violence in Schools." Television broadcast. Christian Broadcasting Network, 1998. Web site: www.cbn.org/news/stories/980527c.asp?h1=pat&h2=archives.

———. *The Secret Kingdom: A Promise of Hope and Freedom in a World of Turmoil.* Nashville, Tenn.: Thomas Nelson, 1982.

———. *The Turning Tide: The Fall of Liberalism and the Rise of Common Sense.* Dallas: Word, 1993.

———. "Welcome." Chesapeake, Va.: The Christian Coalition. Web site: www.cc.org/publications/ca/welcome/welcome1.html.

Rose, Susan D. *Keeping Them Out of the Hands of Satan: Evangelical Schooling in America.* New York: Routledge, 1988.

Ross, Ralph. *Symbols and Civilization: Science, Morals, Religion, Art.* New York: Harcourt, Brace and World, 1957.

Rozell, Mark J., and Clyde Wilcox. "Conclusion: The Christian Right in Campaign '96." In Rozell and Wilcox, *God at the Grass Roots,* 255–69.

———. *God at the Grass Roots, 1996: The Christian Right in the 1996 Elections.* Lanham, Md.: Rowman and Littlefield, 1997.

Ruegsegger, Ronald, ed. *Reflections on Francis Schaeffer.* Grand Rapids, Mich.: Zondervan, 1986.

Rushdoony, Rousas John. *By What Standard? An Analysis of the Philosophy of Cornelius Van Til.* Fairfax, Va.: Thoburn Press, 1974.

Rushdoony, Rousas John. *The Foundations of Social Order: Studies in the Creeds and Councils of the Early Church.* N.p.: Presbyterian and Reformed, 1968.

―――. *The Institutes of Biblical Law.* Nutley, N.J.: Craig Press, 1973.

―――. *The Messianic Character of American Education.* 1963. Reprint, Nutley, N.J.: Craig Press, 1972.

―――. *Systematic Theology.* Vallecito, Calif.: Ross House Books, 1994. Web site: www.chalcedon.edu/article3.html.

―――. *This Independent Republic: Studies in the Nature and Meaning of American History.* Nutley, N.J.: Craig Press, 1964.

Russell, Ron, and Mark Hornbeck. "School Deregulation Plan Criticized." *Detroit News,* 22 January 1995, 1B, 5B.

Sandeen, Ernest. *The Roots of Fundamentalism.* Chicago: University of Chicago Press, 1970.

Sandlin, Andrew. "Recapturing the Vision of Christian Reconstructionism." Vallecito, Calif.: Chalcedon Foundation. Web site: www.chalcedon.ed/article_as_26.html.

Schaeffer, Francis A. *A Christian Manifesto.* Westchester, Ill.: Crossway Books, 1981.

―――. "A Christian Manifesto." Keynote address. Fort Lauderdale, Fla., 1982. Web site: www.toolcity.net/pfl/francis.html.

―――. *Escape from Reason.* Downers Grove, Ill.: Inter-Varsity Press, 1968.

―――. *The God Who Is There.* Downers Grove, Ill.: Inter-Varsity Press, 1968.

―――. *The Great Evangelical Disaster.* Westchester, Ill.: Crossway Books, 1984.

―――. *How Should We Then Live? The Rise and Decline of Western Thought and Culture.* Westchester, Ill.: Crossway Books, 1976.

―――. *Who Is for Peace?* Nashville, Tenn.: Thomas Nelson, 1983.

Schaffer, Leigh S. "The Word of God and Recipe Knowledge: The Road to Dogmatism in Religion.'" *High School Journal,* February–March 1985, 205–10.

Schlafly, Phyllis. "Bilingualism Is the Wrong Way to Go." Alton, Ill.: Eagle Forum, 1995. Web site: www.eagleforum.org/column/dec95/col12-14.html.

―――. "Is the Government Planning Your Child's Career?" Alton, Ill.: Eagle Forum, 1995. Web site: www.eagleforum.org/column/col-10-5.html.

―――. "NEA Convention Delegates Gather to Gloat." Alton, Ill.: Eagle Forum, 1997. Web site: www.eagleforum.org/column/1997/july97/97-07-23.html.

―――. "The New Crisis in California." Alton, Ill.: Eagle Forum, 1995. Web site: www.eagleforum.org/colum/col-9-28.html.

―――. *Phyllis Schlafly Report,* May 1993.

―――. *The Power of the Christian Woman.* Cincinnati: Standard, 1981.

―――. "Ten Objections to OBE." *Phyllis Schlafly Report,* May 1993, 1–4.

Schmidt, Jean Miller. "Holiness and Perfection." In *Encyclopedia of the American Religious Experience: Studies of Traditions and Movements,* ed. Charles H. Lippy and Peter W. Williams, 2:813–29. New York: Scribner's, 1988.

Schmidt, Roger. *Exploring Religion.* Belmont, Calif.: Wadsworth, 1980.

"School Officials Meet with Ministers." *Adrian (Michigan) Daily Telegram,* 1 July 1991, 1.

"Sex Education: What Works?" In Focus. Washington, D.C.: Family Research Council, 1995. Web site: www.frc.org/infocus/if95k2ab.html.

Shaw, John. "The Committee for Biblical Principles in Government." *Chalcedon Report,* November 1997. Vallecito, Calif.: Chalcedon. Web site: www.chalcedon.edu/report/97nov/Shaw_Committee.html.

Shibley, Mark A. *Resurgent Evangelicalism in the United States: Mapping Cultural Change since 1970.* Columbia: University of South Carolina Press, 1996.

"S.I.E.C.U.S's Prescription for Herpes?" In *News Flash.* Washington, D.C.: Concerned Women for America, 1997. Web site: www.cwfa.org/archive/newsflash/news_herpes1297.html.

Simon, Howard. "Federal Court Issues Order in Lee County Bible History Case." Washington, D.C.: American Civil Liberties Union, 1998. Web site: www.aclu.org/news/n012098d.html.

Simonds, Robert L. "A Brief History of the National Association of Christian Educators and Citizens for Excellence in Education." Information sheet, n.d.

———. *Communicating a Christian World View in the Classroom.* Costa Mesa, Calif.: National Association of Christian Educators, 1983.

———. *Communicating a Christian World View in the Classroom: A Manual.* Costa Mesa, Calif.: National Association of Christian Educators, 1983.

———. *A Guide to the Public Schools: For Christian Parents and Teachers, and Especially for Pastors.* Costa Mesa, Calif.: NACE/CEE, 1993.

———. *How to Elect Christians to Public Office.* Costa Mesa, Calif.: NACE/CEE, 1985.

———. "Newsletter." In *President's Report.* Costa Mesa, Calif.: NACE/CEE, 1994.

———. "A Plea for the Children." *Educational Leadership* 51, no. 4 (December–January 1993–1994): 12–15.

———. "President's Report." Newsletter. *President's Report,* December 1994. Costa Mesa, Calif.: NACE/CEE.

———. *President's Report,* June 1992–July 1994. Costa Mesa, Calif.: NACE/CEE.

———. "Read This Letter in Its Entirety," 1998. Web site: www.nace-cee.org/strategy.html.

———. "Special Insert to President's Report." *President's Report,* July 1992. Costa Mesa, Calif.: NACE/CEE.

Skillen, James W. *The Scattered Voice: Christians at Odds in the Public Square.* Grand Rapids, Mich.: Zondervan, 1990.

Smart, Ninian. *Worldviews: Crosscultural Explorations of Human Beliefs.* 2d ed. Englewood Cliffs, N.J.: Prentice-Hall, 1995.

Smelser, Neil. *Theory of Collective Behavior.* New York: Free Press of Glencoe, 1962.

Smidt, Corwin E., and James M. Penning. "Michigan: Veering to the Left?" In Rozell and Wilcox, *God at the Grass Roots,* 115–34.

Smith, Gary Scott, ed. *God and Politics: Four Views on the Reformation of Civil Government.* With a foreword by John H. White. Phillipsburg, N.J.: Presbyterian and Reformed, 1989.

Smith, Jonathan Z. "The Bare Facts of Ritual." In *Imagining Religion: From Babylon to Jonestown,* ed. Jonathan Z. Smith, 53–65. Chicago: University of Chicago Press, 1982.

———. *Map Is Not Territory: Studies in the History of Religions.* Leiden: E. J. Brill, 1978.

———. "A Pearl of Great Price and a Cargo of Yams." In *Imagining Religion: From Babylon to Jonestown,* ed. Jonathan Z. Smith, 90–101. Chicago: University of Chicago Press, 1982.

———. *To Take Place: Toward Theory in Ritual.* Chicago: University of Chicago Press, 1987.

Snow, David A., and Robert D. Benford. "Master Frames and Cycles of Protest." In *Frontiers in Social Movement Theory,* ed. A. D. Morris and C. McClurg-Mueller, 133–55. New Haven, Conn.: Yale University Press, 1992.

Snow, David A., E. Burke Rochford, Jr., Steven K. Worden, and Robert D. Benford. "Frame Alignment Process, Micromobilization, and Movement Participation." *American Sociological Review* 51, no. 4 (1986): 464–81.

Spykman, Gordon J. "The Principled Pluralist Position." In Smith, *God and Politics,* 78–99.

Stafford, Tim. "His Father's Son." *Christianity Today,* March 1998, 17.

Stark, Rodney, and Charles Y. Glock. *American Piety: The Nature of Religious Commitment.* Berkeley: University of California Press, 1968.

"State Education Chief: Change County's America-First Rule." *Miami Herald,* 16 July 1994, 2B.

Steinfels, Peter. "Why Psychologist without a Pulpit Is Called Religious Right's New Star." *New York Times,* 5 June 1990.

Stepp, Laura Sessions. "The Empire Built on Family & Faith: Psychologist James C. Dobson, Bringing His Evangelical Focus to Politics." *Washington Post,* 8 August 1990, C1.

———. "Falwell Says Moral Majority to Be Dissolved." *Washington Post,* 12 June 1989, A11.

Stout, Harry S. "Word and Order in Colonial New England." In Hatch and Noll, *The Bible in America,* 19–38.

Stout, Jeffrey. *Ethics of Babel: The Language of Morals and Their Discontents.* Boston: Beacon Press, 1988.

Streiker, Lowell D. *The Gospel Time-Bomb: Ultrafundamentalism and the Future of America.* Buffalo, N.Y.: Prometheus Books, 1984.

Streng, Frederick J. *Understanding Religious Life.* 3d ed. Religious Life of Man series. Belmont, Calif.: Wadsworth, 1985.

Swomley, John M. "The Religious Right Wants America." *National Newsletter of the A.C.L.U.,* no. 380 (spring 1994).

Tancredo, Tom. "The Educational Opportunity Tax Credit: A White Paper Prepared for Colorado Editors, Publishers, and Reporters." Parker, Colo.: Coloradans for School Choice, 1998. Unpublished paper.

———. "Education Vouchers: America Can't Afford to Wait." *Issue Papers.* Denver: Independence Institute. Web site: www.I21.org/SuptDocs/IssuPprs/IPvouch.htm.

"Tao Te Ching." Trans. and comp. Wing-tsit Chan. In *A Source Book in Chinese Philosophy,* chap. 1. Princeton, N.J.: Princeton University Press, 1963.

"Teachers Should Fight School 'Secularism,' Dobson Magazine Urges." *Church and State* 51, no. 10 (November 1998): 18.

"10 Years Ago: Abortion Clinic Bombings." *Freedom Writer,* January 1985. Web site: www.ifas.org/fw/9503/10years.html.

Thomas, Cal. "Religious Expression Is a Free Speech Issue." *Detroit Free Press,* 15 June 1993, A9.

Tillich, Paul. *Dynamics of Faith.* New York: Harper and Row, 1957.

———. *Systematic Theology: Reason and Revelation, Being and God.* Vol. 1. Chicago: University of Chicago Press, 1951.

———. *Theology of Culture.* Ed. Robert C. Kimball. London: Oxford University Press, 1959.

Tinker, George E. *Missionary Conquest: The Gospel and Native American Cultural Genocide.* Minneapolis: Fortress Press, 1993.

Tipson, Baird. "Calvinist Heritage." In *Encyclopedia of the American Religious Experience: Studies of Traditions and Movements,* ed. Charles H. Lippy and Peter W. Williams, 1:451–66. New York: Scribner's, 1988.

Tocqueville, Alexis de. *Democracy in America.* Edited and abridged by Richard D. Heffner. New York: Mentor Books, 1956.

Tomlin, Curt. "'Let My Children Go': Exodus 2000 Project." *Christian Alerts* A50 (1998). Killeen, Tex.: Christian Alert Network. Web site: www.vvm.com/~ctomlin/a50.htm.

Turner, Victor. *The Anthropology of Performance.* New York: PAJ, 1986.

———. *The Forest of Symbols.* Ithaca, N.Y.: Cornell University Press, 1967.

———. *The Ritual Process.* London: Routledge, 1969.

Tyack, David, and Elizabeth Hansot. *Managers of Virtue: Public School Leadership in America.* New York: Basic Books, 1982.

Van Til, Cornelius. *The Defense of the Faith.* Philadelphia: Presbyterian and Reformed, 1976.

"Voter Typology." Philadelphia: Pew Research Center for the People and the Press, 1996. Web site: www.people-press.org/oct96typ.htm.

Wacker, Grant. "Pentecostalism." In *Encyclopedia of the American Religious Experience: Studies of Traditions and Movements,* ed. Charles H. Lippy, and Peter W. Williams, 2:933–45. New York: Scribner's, 1988.

Wagner, Belinda Bollar. *God's Schools: Choice and Compromise in American Society.* New Brunswick, N.J.: Rutgers University Press, 1990.

Wallace, Anthony F. C. *Religion: An Anthropological View.* New York: Random House, 1966.

Walsh, Mark. "Proposed Tax Credit Drawing Support in Colorado." *Educational Week,* 21 October 1998. Web site: www.edweek.org/ew/vol-18/08colo.htm.

Walton, Rus. *One Nation under God.* Nashville, Tenn.: Thomas Nelson, 1987.

Watson, Justin. *The Christian Coalition: Dreams of Restoration, Demands for Recognition.* New York: St. Martin's Press, 1997.

Watt, David Harrington. "The Private Hopes of American Fundamentalists and Evangelicals, 1925–1975." *Religion and American Culture* 1, no. 2 (summer 1991): 155–75.

Watts, Alan. "Psychedelics and Religious Experience." *California Law Review* 56, no. 1 (1968): 74–85. Web site: www.druglibrary.org/schaffer/lsd/watts.htm.

Weaver, Mary Jo, and R. Scott Appleby, eds. *Being Right: Conservative Catholics in America.* Bloomington: Indiana University Press, 1995.

Weber, Timothy P. *Living in the Shadow of the Second Coming: American Premillennialism, 1875–1982.* Enlarged ed. Grand Rapids, Mich.: Academie Books, 1983.

———. "Millenarian Movements." In *Dictionary of Christianity in America,* ed. Daniel G. Reid, Robert D. Linder, Bruce L. Shelly, and Harry S. Stout, 738–39. Downers Grove, Ill.: InterVarsity Press, 1990.

Westerhoff, John. *McGuffey and His Readers.* Nashville, Tenn.: Abingdon Press, 1978.

Whitehead, John. *An American Dream.* Westchester, Ill.: Crossway Books, 1987.

———. *The End of Man.* Westchester, Ill.: Crossway Books, 1986.

———. *The Rights of Religious Persons in Public Education.* Rev. ed. Wheaton, Ill.: Crossway Books, 1994.

———. *The Second American Revolution.* Westchester, Ill.: Crossway Books, 1982.

———. *The Separate Illusion.* Milford, Mich.: Mott Media, 1977.

———. *The Stealing of America.* Westchester, Ill.: Crossway Books, 1983.

"Who Is Francis Schaeffer?" Briarcliff Manor, N.Y.: Francis A. Schaeffer Foundation. Web site: www.qns.com/parkhurst/fasfound.htm.

"Who Will Teach the Children? A Battle between Federal and Local Control." Policy Papers. Washington, D.C.: Concerned Women for America. Web site: www.cwfa.org/policypapers/pp_educate.html.

Wilcox, Clyde. *God's Warriors: The Christian Right in Twentieth-Century America.* Baltimore: Johns Hopkins University Press, 1992.

———. *Onward Christian Soldiers? The Religious Right in American Politics.* Boulder, Colo.: Westview Press, 1996.

Williams, Peter W. *America's Religions: Traditions and Cultures.* New York: Macmillan, 1990.

Wills, Garry. *Under God: Religion and American Politics.* New York: Touchstone, 1990.

Wilson, Charles Reagan. *Baptized in Blood.* Athens: University of Georgia Press, 1980.

Winthrop, John. "A Model of Christian Charity." In *The Annals of America,* ed. Mortimer J. Adler, vol. I, 109–15. Chicago: Encyclopedia Britannica, 1976.

Winton, Ben. "Dobson Declares War on GOP! Disclosure Comes Out at Secret CNP Meeting in Phoenix." Great Barrington, Mass.: Institute for First Amendment Studies, 1998. Press release. Web site: www.berkshire.net/ifas/press/dobson.html.

Wood, James E., Jr. "Religious Fundamentalism and the New Right." In *Church and State in American History,* ed. John F. Wilson and Donald L. Drakeman, 2d ed., 246–50. Boston: Beacon Press, 1987.

"Writer Dares to Expose D.A.R.E." Education Reporter. Alton, Ill.: Eagle Forum, 1997. Web site: www.eagleforum.org/educate/1997/mar97/er_mar97.html.

Wuthnow, Robert. *Christianity and Civil Society: The Contemporary Debate.* Rockwell Lecture Series. Valley Forge, Pa.: Trinity Press International, 1996.

———. *The Restructuring of American Religion: Society and Faith since World War II.* Princeton, N.J.: Princeton University Press, 1988.

Wynsma, J. R. "Educational Reform: The HELP Scholarships Amendment of 1997." *Neopolitique,* December 1997. Web site: www.neopolitique.org/articles/dec97-help.html.

Yinger, J. Milton. *Religion, Society, and the Individual: An Introduction to the Sociology of Religion.* New York: Macmillan, 1957.

Zettersten, Rolf. Dr. *Dobson: Turning Hearts toward Home—the Life and Principles of America's Family Advocate.* Dallas: Word, 1989.

Index

About the Author

Fritz Detwiler is professor of philosophy and religion at Adrian College, where he specializes in religion and culture. Since 1991 he has researched issues related to the Christian Right and public education. In 1995 he began a consulting firm, Education Reform Resources, to aid educators at the local, state, and national levels in their understanding of the Christian Right. He lives in Adrian, Michigan, with his wife, who is a public school teacher, and three children.